Race, Law, and American Society

Some recent titles from the Criminology
and Justice Studies series:

Series Editor: Shaun L. Gabbidon

Community Policing in America
Jeremy M. Wilson

Surveillance and Society
Torin Monahan

Forthcoming titles in the Criminology
and Justice Studies series:

Criminological Perspectives on Race and Crime
Shaun L. Gabbidon

*Criminal Justice Theory: Explaining the Nature and Behavior of Criminal
Justice*
David E. Duffee and Edward R. Maguire

White Collar Crime
Michael Benson

Race, Law, and American Society

1607 to Present

Gloria J. Browne-Marshall

Foreword by Derrick Bell

Routledge
Taylor & Francis Group
New York   London

Routledge is an imprint of the
Taylor & Francis Group, an informa business

Routledge
Taylor & Francis Group
270 Madison Avenue
New York, NY 10016

Routledge
Taylor & Francis Group
2 Park Square
Milton Park, Abingdon
Oxon OX14 4RN

© 2007 by Taylor & Francis Group, LLC
Routledge is an imprint of Taylor & Francis Group, an Informa business

Printed in the United States of America on acid-free paper
10 9 8 7 6 5 4

International Standard Book Number-10: 0-415-95294-8 (Softcover) 0-415-95293-X (Hardcover)
International Standard Book Number-13: 978-0-415-95294-1 (Softcover) 978-0-415-95293-4 (Hardcover)

Library of Congress Cataloging-in-Publication Data

Browne-Marshall, Gloria J.
  Race, law, and American society : 1607 to present / by Gloria J. Browne-Marshall.
    p. cm. -- (Criminology and justice studies)
  Includes bibliographical references and index.
  ISBN 0-415-95293-X (hb) -- ISBN 0-415-95294-8 (pb) 1. Race discrimination--Law
  and legislation--United States--Cases. 2. African Americans--Civil rights--Cases.
  3. African Americans--Legal status, laws, etc.--Cases. 4. United States--Race
  relations. I. Title.

  KF4755.B76 2007
  342.7308'73--dc22   2006023277

Visit the Taylor & Francis Web site at
http://www.taylorandfrancis.com

and the Routledge Web site at
http://www.routledge-ny.com

Dedicated to Harriet Tubman (1822–1913) and all courageous women and men in the fight for racial justice.

Contents

Acknowledgments

This book was a dream held close to my heart for ten years. I am quite grateful to my family, friends, and colleagues who, in ways large and small, assisted in bringing this book to fruition. I wish to thank the editors at Routledge for their support of this project. My brilliant friend, Philip Aka, provided invaluable expertise, scholarly advice, and spiritual support. I am an appreciative beneficiary of the scholarship and trailblazing spirit of John Hope Franklin and Derrick Bell. I wish to thank David Levering Lewis for that encouraging conversation many years ago. Thank you John Edgar Wideman for your thoughtful advice. My colleagues at John Jay College of Criminal Justice have given a wealth of support, especially Zelma Henriques, Delores Jones-Brown, Christopher Morse, Dara Byrne, Maki Haberfeld, Dorothy Schultz, Vincent Del Castillo, Adina Schwartz, Michael Liddie, Eugene O'Donnell, Robert Panzarella, jon-christian suggs, Kwando Kinshasa, Nilsa Santiago, Andrew Karmen, Larry Sullivan, and Blanche Wiesen Cook.

I would like to express my deep gratitude to research assistants Amilcar Herbert, Misha Lars, Ozen Kinik, Lynda Hu, and to the many John Jay College students who gave of their time, especially Virginia Gonzales, Anthony Illiano, and Sandra Watson. I wish to thank my colleagues in the American Bar Association's Individual

Rights and Responsibility Section and the National Bar Association for their support. I am grateful to the CUNY Fellowship Program and the input of Joanne Pierre-Louis, Karen Miller, Prudence Cumberbatch, Aviva Zelzer-Zubida, Jennifer Kyle, CarolAnn Daniel, and Stephen Steinberg. I also wish to thank Jacqueline Pica and Christina Czechowicz for their technical assistance. I appreciate the assistance given by the library staff at John Jay College of Criminal Justice, the Seward Park Branch of the New York Public Library, the Schomberg Center for Research in Black Culture, New York University, and the Library of Congress.

I am a legacy of the many generations who fought for freedom. God is good.

Foreword

"I love to tell the story" is the opening line of an old hymn, but the lyric fits as well the often told racial history of this country. And like religion, the story has been told again and again because so many people do not hear it or, having heard, do not choose to believe or learn from it.

We need the new Browne-Marshall book because American history, as generally taught in most public school classrooms and more than a few college courses, is aimed at emphasizing the positive while eliminating the negative. This, of course, is accomplished through a long practiced selective memory that has ignored the degradation and exploitation of law-enforced black slavery and segregation—a practice that seems to justify this passing-over without much mention of the degradation and exploitation of a large percentage of the white population as well.

Not long ago, I was visiting a class where a law student was reporting on a paper he had written about the history of Italian Americans. He admitted that he was shocked to learn of the discrimination, humiliation, and outright hostility that Italians faced when they came to this country in substantial numbers in the first two decades of the twentieth century—and this student was Italian American. He explained that he did not remember his grandparents, who had immigrated here in the 1930s, and his parents never talked to him about any anti-Italian experiences they had suffered. What they likely told him is that they and their parents worked their way up from the bottom and got ahead in the world through hard work and, perhaps, through reliance on their faith in God. What they almost certainly did not tell him is that Italians, Irish, and other European immigrants gained a foothold in this country in part by identifying with White Americans (initially they were not deemed White) and not identifying with Blacks, with whom, except for color, they shared so much economic and political disadvantage.

European immigrants adapted quickly to the racial segregation laws and policies widely enforced during that era. Their acceptance provided a shared feeling of superiority to Blacks, a psychic insulation given their exploitation by the mine and factory owners for whom they toiled long hours under brutal conditions for subsistence wages. Many of these immigrants were far more recent arrivals than the Blacks they shunned. Policies of racial segregation simultaneously subordinated Blacks while providing Whites with a comforting sense of their position in society.

Racism's stabilizing force was not limited to poorer Whites. Even for wealthier Whites, their identities were unstable because they intrinsically depended upon an "other." White racist antipathy belied the extent to which White people desperately needed—and, I fear, still need—Blacks in a subordinate status in order to sustain the myriad fictions of White racial integrity.

Ideologically, then, the statement "I am not Black" has functioned as a kind of border...a psychic demarcation that allows "American" to be quickly (perhaps even thoughtlessly) distinguished from "not American."[1] America has been able to define itself as a White country by marking Blacks as that which does not constitute it. The law has served to rationalize racial boundaries with fictions that, in fact, conceal exploitation and marginalization actions that do not observe the color line.

Consider how legal fictions adapted by the Court in *Plessy v. Ferguson* in 1896 and *Lochner v. New York* in 1905, served to disadvantage both groups. In *Lochner*,[2] the fiction was that employer and worker were each equally free to bargain on an employment contract. In *Plessy*, the fiction was that separate but equal actually provided equality of treatment. Both decisions protected existing property arrangements at the expense of powerless groups: exploited workers in *Lochner* and degraded Blacks in *Plessy.* Wage and race oppression were mutually reinforcing. Whites applauded, even insisting on the subordination of Blacks as a self-distracting mechanism for a system that transformed them into wage slaves.

Browne-Marshall's book joins so much of what is usually deemed White history by offering an otherwise hard-to-recognize view of that history. It reveals that the price of racial dominance is ignorance of those who are subordinated and the costs of that subordination. This is the point one of my constitutional law students, William Van Esveld, made as he commented on the value he gained from the course he had taken:

> My sense is that, today, there are virtually no White middle-class people who would ever think of themselves as racist. At least for my generation of Northern, middle-class Whites, racism has taken on a new form: It is an ugly, disavowed reflex, seldom a matter of conscious belief; we repress it when it is brought before our eyes; we reject and deny the evidence that it lives on in us. If confronted, I would deny (out of fear or shame or my liberal self-image) that I have ever been racist. Yet I have to admit that I think of racism far differently after this class, because I now have a better appreciation of how enormously important race is for people who lack the luxury of a false "ignorance" of race which I have, in retrospect, enjoyed. Racism is at least in part—in large part—in the eye of the beholder, and at some point, White claims of "I didn't intend my actions to be understood as hurtful, therefore you shouldn't feel hurt" are simply irrelevant.
>
> Not to belabor the point, but the racial education I received...was all the more important for being linked to the Constitution. As law students we are encouraged to embody the role of "America's" legislators, a role we may grow too comfortable in, too easily. A class that troubles and complicates one's self-image as being somehow "innocent" of race and racism is all the more valuable in the law-school environment.

The student's statement is a most welcome indication that, while the effort to teach what most Americans do not want to learn is a mostly frustrating endeavor, there is some reason to believe that beyond the inherent value of offering truth for truth's sake, a few may gain the perspective on race in our lives and theirs that we are trying to convey.

Thus, Gloria Browne-Marshall's compelling addition to the literature will tell an old story to new readers, some of whom will accept rather than reject and, one hopes, act on the long available but little utilized learning it contains. I hope educators at every level are attracted to this book as a teaching tool.

Derrick Bell
Visiting Professor
New York University Law School and University of Pittsburgh Law School

Back row, from left: Jeremiah Bradshaw, cousin; Cora Bradshaw, cousin; Ralph Bradshaw, great-great-uncle; and Stella Bradshaw, cousin.

Front row, from left: Levi Bradshaw, grandfather; George Bradshaw, great-grandfather; Hugh Nelson, great-uncle; Sarah Melissa, cousin.

Preface

The destinies of the two races, in this country, are indissolubly linked together, and the interests of both require that the common government of all shall not permit the seeds of race hate to be planted under the sanction of law.

Plessy v. Ferguson **(1896) (Harlan, J., dissenting)**

Despite the obstacles to equality under law, Blacks in America have set a determined path to make the words of the U.S. Constitution a reality for themselves and others. This book is designed as a tool to better understand the role of race in American society through the prism of legal cases brought by and against Blacks. The analysis will include American colonial laws, state statutes, and landmark Supreme Court cases of the nineteenth, twentieth, and twenty-first centuries. In examining these laws and cases, the reader will discern the great impact racism has had on American society as well as the effect our society has had on the legal system with regard to race. However, these cases are more than plaintiffs, defendants, victims, and perpetrators. These cases evidence the human struggle for freedom at its greatest and lowest points.

I wrote this book to pay homage to those who struggled for the rights that I and others enjoy or take for granted. I imagine an enslaved woman in the cotton field who kept the protest alive in her heart, hoping that someone who looked like her would one day live free. The meaning of freedom has evolved with each generation of Blacks in America. A primary part of that evolution took place and still takes place in the courts. This book follows the legal fight against that designated "place" of my ancestors and other Blacks as beasts of burden outside of the human family and well beyond constitutional protections to that of persons recognized by law as full citizens. That fight was against an insidious socioracial hierarchy made malignant by the force of law. Their battle and that of other people of color was Herculean because racism was supported by the rule of law and perpetrated by constitutional mandate.

I have witnessed the destruction caused by racism and I live with its residue. Racism kills the body, mind, and spirit.[1] Pressing against oppression is one method of healing. I write this knowing that in the not too distant past, forgetting one's place, for Blacks, could result in a midnight raid by marauding Whites and death by lynching as a message to the entire Black community to stay in their "place." Blacks were forced to feign ignorance and self-deprecation in order to survive. To display ambition or independence threatened a White self-serving social, economic, and political order predicated on greed and racism. Strong, intelligent, independent Blacks (or minorities, generally) created insecurity among the majority society and were, therefore, kept under the watchful eye of the criminal justice system. Today, the label of "uppity" or arrogant Black could mean termination of employment, racial epithets, and, less frequently, physical harm by marauding members of law enforcement. These consequences, to me, are all remnants of slavery and "Jim Crow" racial segregation.

I see the remnants of slavery and Jim Crow discrimination on a daily basis. I see it in the disproportionate number of incarcerated Blacks, racially isolated schools and housing, and disenfranchised Black voters. A caste system such as it exists in the United States is difficult to remove, especially when its continued existence benefits members of the majority society. This caste system was developed in the colonial period, codified by state legislatures, and made law of the land by the

Supreme Court. It has evolved with the country. Blacks and a small group of Whites opposed this system through a number of strategies: legislation, grassroots organizing, protest, law, politics, and religion. The most successful strategies overlapped. I do *not* believe that the courts can legislate a person's heart. However, love and freedom are not the same things.

Historically, social change, involving, for example, labor unions, immigrant rights, and gender equality, was forced upon this democracy. These cases represent the centuries-long forced movement for racial equality in America. As in any movement, the human sacrifice was monumental. Whether a legal action was brought based on strategy or circumstance, it represented an intense commitment of human capital. To use the courts to oppose oppression is to demand formal recognition as an aggrieved human being with rights who expects the protection of law. That concept took more than three centuries to manifest for Blacks. Unfortunately, fundamental fairness continues to depend as much on American society as it does on the American legal system.

In this book I chose to focus on U.S. Supreme Court decisions for three reasons. First, as the court of last resort in this country, its decisions are the law of the land affecting all of American society. Second, the effort and resources required to gain review by the Supreme Court demonstrate the dedication of aggrieved parties and reveal their sacrifice and courage.[2] Third, decisions of this court are American history. Societal issues gave rise to conflicts, the outcomes of which have consequences well beyond the parties or issues involved.

The Supreme Court moves in fits and starts, by activists, Congress, and societal upheaval. In conjunction with legislation and activism from many different communities with diverse philosophies, the Court has played a role in moving America toward racial justice in certain cases and maintaining racism in many others. When I read the opinions of the Supreme Court I see racial justice through the eyes of this country's most powerful legal figures. I have tried to present the language of the Court as often as practicable. Whether the justices' words are cruel or sympathetic, reading them brings a human perspective to their rulings. One realizes that these justices are human beings influenced not only by legal precedent but also by their social backgrounds, concerns for the country, and ideological views. Examining the Court's decisions over a span of many centuries reveals the great victories in racial justice, missed opportunities, and abject failures. The ensuing chapters represent an intersection of law and American life. Given the hundreds of cases involving racism decided by the U.S. Supreme Court, only a relatively small number of cases and controversies are examined here. That said, the strength of this book lies in the breadth of the cases, the accessibility of the language, and the combination of rarely read Supreme Court cases with the more familiar decisions. I believe these lesser known U.S. Supreme Court cases provide a wealth of information on and a needed lens into American history and society. In upholding a discriminatory status quo, the Supreme Court played an important role in maintaining America's racial hierarchy—its skewed rule of law.

In the face of difficult odds, my ancestors threw off their shackles and fought against a centuries-old, government-enforced caste system only to have the law undermine their political, economic, and social advancement. In 1889, my forebearers traveled from Kentucky to Kansas as homesteaders in search of opportunity and freedom from racial oppression. We have been blessed to know victory slightly more than defeat. But, as with any Black family we, too, bear the embedded wounds inflicted by racism and grapple constantly with the vestiges of *Plessy*. I understand that the rights and privileges enjoyed today are all part of an arduous journey started long ago. I am in a position to write this book because they refused to accept a position at the bottom of the American caste system. At minimum, my obligation is to maintain that tradition.

I began the story of this journey of race, law, and American society in 1607. Despite the passage of time and all of the hard-fought battles, remnants of slavery and court-enforced racial segregation remain. Greed and xenophobia placed Blacks in chattel slavery. Tradition and greed maintain systemic racism. The fight to uproot vestiges of slavery requires knowledge of the depth of the problem, desire to create change, and vigilance. Each generation is presented with the problem of racism. I hope this book acts as a catalyst for any potential advocate for racial justice who fears that racism is too entrenched for change or an inspiration for those with battle fatigue. Progress will ebb and flow. However, far too many fought against overwhelming odds with too few assurances of success for me to be defeated—change is always possible.

Racism is a beast of human creation and it is long past time we sent it away.

Gloria J. Browne-Marshall

Timeline of Selected Cases and Events

The Court was created to sit in troubled times as well as in peaceful days.

Bell v. Maryland **(1964)**

1607   Jamestown colony founded.

1619   Twenty Blacks arrive by Dutch ship to Jamestown, Virginia;
        some Blacks had arrived even earlier. Virginia's House of
        Burgesses, America's first legislative body, holds its first
        meeting.

1620   The *Mayflower* lands.

1712   Slave revolt in New York City.

1739   Slave revolt in South Carolina.

1741   Slaves accused of conspiracy in New York City are tortured
        and murdered.

1772   *Somerset v. Steuart*. British High Court decides slavery issue.

1776   Delaration of Independence. America's Revolutionary War
        begins.

1783   *Commonwealth v. Jennison*. Massachusetts outlaws slavery.

1789   U.S. Constitution ratified. Art. III creates U.S. Supreme
        Court. Art. IV contains the Fugitive Slave Act.

1808   Importation of slaves illegal.

1829   *Appeal to the Colored Citizens of the World* published by David Walker.

1831   Nat Turner leads slave rebellion.

1836   *Rachael, a woman of color, v. Walker.* Slave taken to live in free territory is free.

1836   Cherokee are forced to walk from Georgia to Oklahoma, known as the Trail of Tears, by the federal government under the Indian Removal Act.

1841   *U.S. v. Libellants and Claimants of The Amistad.* Supreme Court rules Cinque and others aboard *The Amistad* are not property.

1842   *Prigg v. Pennsylvania.* Fugitive Slave Act upheld.

1849   *Boston v. Roberts.* Blacks challenge racially segregated schools.

1850   Fugitive Slave Act. More restrictive slave provisions further divide the nation.

1854   *People v. Hall.* Court upholds California statute prohibiting Chinese and Blacks from testifying against any White person, reversing Hall's conviction for the murder of Ling Sing.

1857   *Dred Scott v. Sandford.* Court denies Blacks U.S. citizenship.

1858   *Bailey v. Poindexter.* Virginia court decides Blacks lack free will to make choices of any kind.

1861   The Civil War begins.

1863   President Lincoln delivers Emancipation Proclamation speech freeing slaves in the South.

1863   Poor Whites in New York City murder Blacks during riots against the National Conscription Act.

1863   Bureau of Colored Troops is created.

1865   Civil War ends.

1865   Thirteenth Amendment abolishes slavery, except as punishment for a crime.

1865   President Lincoln is assassinated.

1866   Reconstruction era begins.

1866   Civil Rights Act of 1866 passed.

1866   Ku Klux Klan founded.

1868   Fourteenth Amendment gives Blacks full citizenship, equal protection, due process, privileges and immunities.

1870   Fifteenth Amendment grants Black males suffrage.

1870   U.S. Congress enacts Civil Rights Act (Enforcement Act of 1870) to protect the rights of Blacks.

1871   Whites attack Chinese in Los Angeles race riot.

1872   *Slaughterhouse* cases. Restrictions on application of Thirteenth and Fourteenth Amendments.

1872   *Blyew v. U.S.* Black witness prohibited from testifying against Whites who murdered her family.

1873   Nearly 300 Blacks are murdered during the Colfax Massacre following a contested election in Colfax, Louisiana.

1875   *United States v. Cruikshank.* White defendants convicted in the Colfax Massacre released. Enforcement Act of 1870 does not apply to private acts of racism.

1876   *U.S v. Reese.* Court rules Civil Rights Act of 1870 cannot punish judges of election who exclude Black voters. Convictions of judges overturned.

1880   *Strauder v. W. Va.* Criminal jury restricted to Whites violates Constitution.

1883   *Civil Rights Cases.* Court limits application of Civil Rights Act to federal cases.

1883   *Pace v. Alabama.* Interracial couple can receive harsher punishment under law than Whites.

1884   Blacks attacked in Cincinnati, Ohio, race riot.

1886   *Yick Wo v. Hopkins.* Court rules racial bias in enforcement of statute violates rights of Chinese.

1889   Ida B. Wells-Barnett organizes Anti-Lynching Bureau.

1896   *Plessy v. Ferguson.* Court rules states can legally separate the races in social situations.

1898   Spanish-American War begins.

1898   Wilmington, North Carolina, race riot takes place.

1900   First Pan-African Conference is held.

1900   Race riots in New York and New Orleans occur.

1905   Niagara, Canada, is site of interracial strategy meeting led by W. E. B. DuBois to plan challenge to *Plessy v. Ferguson.*

1906   During the Brownsville Incident, Black soldiers of 25th Infantry Regiment defend themselves against White mobs. The soldiers are later dishonorably discharged.

1908   *Berea College v. Kentucky.* Court rules private college violated state law by educating Black and White students.

1909   *U.S. v. Shipp.* Black suspect is lynched in defiance of Supreme Court order.

1909   NAACP is founded.

1910   After Black boxer Jack Johnson defeats Jim Jeffries, Whites attack Blacks across America.

1914   Marcus Garvey founds the Universal Negro Improvement and Conservation Association and African Communities League.

1915   *Myers v. Anderson.* "Grandfather" voting clause is struck down.

1917   World War I begins.

1917   Race riots erupt in East St. Louis, Illinois; Philadelphia and Chester, Pennsylvania; and Houston, Texas, as Whites retaliate against Black progress. Black servicemen are the primary targets.

1917   *Buchanan v. Warley.* State's racial zoning violates Constitution.

1919   The Red Summer. Whites attack Blacks during twenty-six race riots across America.

1919   NAACP publishes *Thirty Years of Lynching in the United States: 1889–1918.*

1920   Nineteenth Amendment grants women the right to vote.

1921   Tulsa, Oklahoma, race riot occurs. Whites destroy wealthy Black community after false rumor of a White woman being raped.

1922   U.S. Senate defeats antilynching legislation passed by House of Representatives.

1923   Whites attack Blacks in Rosewood, Florida.

1925   *Garvey v. United States.* Marcus Garvey loses appeal of mail fraud conviction and is deported.

1927   *Gong Lum v. Rice.* States may treat Asians comparably to Blacks.

1927   *Nixon v. Herndon.* States cannot hold "White-only" primary elections.

1928   Marcus Garvey presents *Petition of the Negro Race* to the League of Nations.

1929   U.S. stock market crashes. Great Depression begins.

1932   Racially motivated murder of Joe Kahahawai in Honolulu, Hawaii.

1932   *Powell v. Alabama.* State's failure to provide counsel in death penalty case violated rights of "Scottsboro Boys."

1934   Wagner–Constigan Anti-Lynching Bill defeated in Senate.

1941   Pearl Harbor is attacked by Empire of Japan.

1941   United States enters World War II.

1943   Race riots in Detroit, Harlem, and Los Angeles as Whites retaliate against Blacks in competition for jobs.

1944   *Smith v. Allwright.* Statute allowing political party to exclude Blacks from voting in primary violates constitution.

1944   *Korematsu v. U.S.* Internment of Japanese Americans is sanctioned.

1945   *Screws v. U.S.* Conviction of White police officers who murdered a Black suspect in custody is overturned.

1945   World War II ends.

1945   Cold War begins.

1948   *Shelley v. Kraemer.* State courts are prohibited from enforcing racially restrictive covenants of private homeowners.

1948   President Harry S. Truman signs Executive Order 9981 desegregating U.S. military.

1948   The United Nations prohibits all forms of slavery.

1950   Korean War begins.

1951   *We Charge Genocide* petition is presented to the United Nations protesting the lynching and murder of Blacks.

1954   *Brown v. Board of Education of Topeka.* Court rules racial segregation in public schools is inherently unequal.

1955   Fourteen-year-old Emmett Till murdered by lynch mob in Mississippi for talking back to a White woman.

1955   *Lucy v. Adams.* Autherine Lucy and Polly Anne Myers desegregate the University of Alabama.

1955   *Brown v. Board of Education of Topeka II.* Court rules school districts to desegregate "with all deliberate speed."

1955   Rosa Parks refuses to give her seat to a White passenger as required by law.

1955   Montgomery bus boycott begins.

1957   Ghana gains independence from United Kingdom.

1957   Nine Black high school students desegregate Central High School in Little Rock, Arkansas. Governor Orval Faubus retaliates by closing public schools.

1958   *NAACP v. Alabama.* Civil rights organizations are not required to provide membership lists to states.

1958   *Kent v. Dulles.* Federal government cannot prevent international travel of Paul Robeson.

1960   Students at North Carolina A & T College begin sit-in protests of segregated businesses.

1960   Student Non-Violent Coordinating Committee (SNCC) is started at Shaw University.

1960   *Gomillion v. Lightfoot.* Gerrymandering of voting districts to exclude Blacks violates Constitution.

1961   *Mapp v. Ohio.* Exclusionary rule prohibiting evidence obtained through an unreasonable police search applies to states.

1961   Freedom Riders challenge segregation in interstate transportation. Many are beatened and jailed.

1962   U.S. enters Vietnam War.

1962   Cesar Chavez and Dolores Huerta form the National Farmworkers Association, a precursor to the United Farmworkers Association.

1963   Alabama Governor George Wallace declares "segregation today, segregation tomorrow, segregation forever."

1963   *Watson v. Memphis.* Racial segregation of public parks and recreational facilities violates Constitution.

1963   March on Washington, D.C. for Jobs and Freedom.

1963   President John F. Kennedy is assassinated in Dallas, Texas.

1964   Twenty-fourth Amendment abolishes poll taxes in national elections.

1964   *Anderson v. Martin.* States cannot require race of candidate on voting ballot.

1964   Voting-rights workers James Chaney, Michael Schwerner, and Andrew Goodman are murdered in Philadelphia, Mississippi.

1964   Fannie Lou Hamer gives speech at televised Democratic National Convention critical of Mississippi's exclusion of Blacks from the Democratic Party.

1964   *Katzenbach v. McClung.* Privately owned restaurant cannot segregate if engaged in interstate commerce.

1964   *New York Times v. Sullivan.* Politicians must prove criticism by Black protesters and newspaper was motivated by actual malice.

1964   U.S. Congress enacts the Civil Rights Act prohibiting discrimination based on race, color, creed, sex, and national origin.

1964   Martin Luther King, Jr., is awarded the Nobel Peace Prize.

1964   *Hamilton v. Alabama.* Contempt of court conviction against Black witness ill-treated by judge is overturned.

1964   *Hamm v. Rock Hill.* Conviction for sit-in protests at segregated stores is overturned.

1965   Malcolm X (aka El-Hajj Malik El-Shabazz) is assassinated in New York City.

1965   *Cox v. Louisiana.* Student civil-rights protest did not violate state laws.

1965   Blacks attacked by White police on the Edmund Pettus Bridge in Selma, Alabama; second march proceeds peacefully.

1965   Voting Rights Act is passed.

1965   Watts riots take place in California. Police brutality sparks eruption of Black community frustrated by unemployment and lack of progress in civil rights.

1965   President Lydon B. Johnson signs Executive Order 11246 establishing affirmative action.

1966   Black Panther Party is founded.

1966   *Bond v. Floyd.* Court upholds Black state legislator's right to protest Vietnam War.

1967   Riots occur in Detroit and Newark.

1967   *Loving v. Virginia.* State cannot restrict marriage based on race.

1968   *Lee v. Washington.* State cannot segregate inmates by race.

1968   Martin Luther King, Jr., is assassinated in Memphis, Tennessee.

1968   Riots erupt in Black communities nationwide following assassination of Martin Luther King, Jr.

1968   U.S. Congress enacts Fair Housing Act.

1968   *Green v. County School Board.* Court strikes down freedom-of-choice desegregation plan.

1968   *Terry v. Ohio.* Court rules police can stop and frisk person who has not committed a crime, based on reasonable suspicion.

1970   *Adickes v. Kress.* Court rules state law cannot prohibit peaceful protest at segregated lunch counters.

1971   *Palmer v. Thompson.* Court rules municipality cannot exclude Blacks from public pools.

1971   *Swann v. Charlotte–Mecklenberg Board of Education.* Court upholds busing of students for desegregation purposes.

1971   *Clay aka Ali v. U.S.* Court upholds Muhammad Ali's, former heavyweight boxing champion, conscientious objector status.

1974   *Richardson v. Ramirez.* Court overturns a California ruling that favored ex-felon rehabilitation.

1975   Vietnam War ends.

1976   *Hills v. Gautreaux.* Court finds government-sanctioned racial discrimination exists in Chicago's public-housing assignments.

1978   *University of California Regents v. Bakke.* Court rules in favor of White plaintiff who alleged affirmative action is reverse discrimination.

1980   Miami erupts in riots following police shooting of unarmed Black man.

1980   *Mobile v. Bolden.* Court overturns successful challenge by Blacks in vote dilution case.

1986   *Batson v. Kentucky.* Court rules prosecutors cannot employ preemptory strikes based on race to eliminate potential Black jurors.

1987   *McCleskey v. Kemp.* Court requires proof of purposeful discrimination in administration of death penalty.

1990   Iraq War I begins.

1992   Los Angeles riot erupts in aftermath of Rodney King verdict acquitting White police officers of brutality despite video of the beating.

1992   *Hopwood v. University of Texas Law School.* White student brings successful reverse discrimination action.

1995   *Jenkins v. Missouri.* Court rules city's desegregation plan cannot include suburbs.

1996   *U.S. v. Armstrong.* Court rules prosecutor is not required to submit requested documents that could demonstrate racial profiling in arrest and prosecution of drug cases.

1998   James Byrd lynched in Texas.

1999   *Chicago v. Morales.* Court rules city's racial profiling law is unconstitutional.

2000   Governor of Illinois enacts moratorium suspending state's death penalty following exoneration of several death-row inmates.

2000   *Bush v. Gore.* Court rules Florida's recount of votes in presidential election violates Bush's constitutional rights.

2002   *Grutter v. Bollinger and University of Michigan Law School.* Court rules race can be a factor in law school admissions.

2002   *Gratz v. Bollinger and University of Michigan.* Court rules college affirmative action plan unconstitutional.

2003   Iraq War II begins.

2004   *Pigford v. Veneman.* Black farmers challenge decades of race discrimination by U.S. Department of Agriculture.

2005   *Johnson v. California.* Inmate challenges intentional racial segregation of inmates in state's correctional facilities.

2005   U.S. Senate apologizes for failing to pass antilynching laws.

2005   Hurricane Katrina deluges Gulf Coast causing numerous deaths and catastrophic property damage. Thousands of Blacks in New Orleans are left stranded by local, state, and national governments.

2006   *Parents Involved in Comm. Schs. v. Seattle Sch. Dist. No. 1* and *Meredith v. Jefferson.* White parents challenge admissions policy that seeks racial and ethnic diversity in public schools.

2006   *In Re: African-American Slave Descendants Litigation.* U.S. Appellate Court held that fraud claims may be brought against corporations misrepresenting past ties to slavery.

Introduction

> Racial ostracism...extended to churches and schools, to housing and jobs, to eating and drinking. Whether by law or by custom, that ostracism eventually extended to virtually all forms of public transportation, to sports and recreation, to hospitals, orphanages, prisons, and asylums, and ultimately to funeral homes, morgues, and cemeteries.
>
> *Garner v. Louisiana* (1961)

This book stands for several propositions on race and the law. First, Blacks in America have courageously fought a centuries-old battle for equal rights under law against unfathomable legal obstacles. Second, Blacks played an active role in every legal victory. Third, vestiges or remnants of slavery and post-*Plessy* racial discrimination remain in American society. The cases and controversies presented here speak to the determination of a people intent on being free. Each incremental step toward full citizenship was a hard-fought struggle against societal racism codified into law. The law was utilized to maintain racial differences and remove non-Whites from economic, political, and social competition. Laws were enacted to create slavery, deprive Blacks and other people of color of their basic human rights, and maintain a socioracial hierarchy based on a White power structure. For centuries,

Blacks and their advocates of goodwill have utilized every available method to challenge a socioracial hierarchy that would relegate those of African descent to the lowest tier of American society. The challenge has been nearly four hundred years long. Too often scholars begin the determined journey for racial justice with *Brown v. Board of Education of Topeka* in 1954 or *Plessy v. Ferguson* in 1896. In fact, Blacks began their battle against racial discrimination before the arrival of the Mayflower. Their strategies have not always included nonviolence. Court cases can hardly describe the blood, sweat, and tears that stain the road to justice. However, the facts and decisions of the courts will inform the reader about the obstacles to freedom and the tireless efforts needed to overcome those obstacles. It is an ongoing quest. Freedom for Blacks in America, and other people of color, began as a fight for physical liberty, continued as a struggle for constitutional protections, and remains a battle against forces that would relegate them to a perpetual underclass. Thus, each chapter ends with the present-day vestiges or remnants of slavery and segregation that continue to infest American society.

The Chapters

This book was written for anyone with a desire to know more about race and the law in America. It can provide an introduction or a supplement to those with prior knowledge in this area of scholarship. This book is designed as a tool to better understand the role of race in the United States through the prism of legal cases brought by and against Blacks. The analysis will include American colonial laws, landmark Supreme Court cases from the nineteenth, twentieth, and twenty-first centuries and political controversies involving race from slavery to the present.

Scholars and laypersons alike have debated why Blacks and other people of color were selected as America's labor class. Theories run the gamut from political,[1] economic,[2] religious,[3] historical,[4] genetic,[5] and social control.[6] This book accepts that a combination of these factors contributed to the enslavement of Africans in America. Laws were enacted to maintain a permanent labor class comprised primarily of persons of African descent. Until the last quarter century, America's highest court perpetuated enslavement and postslavery discrimination. It is against this backdrop that Blacks waged their legal battles.

This book is organized by topic area: education, property rights, civil liberties, voting rights, the military, criminal justice, and internationalism. Each topic presents an aspect of American life with which the reader can identify. Few things in law or life are mutually exclusive, so the areas overlap in certain places. Cases and controversies relevant to each topic area are examined. The cases reflect the obstacles that Blacks, seeking to extricate themselves from the caste to which they had been unfairly relegated based on their race, have had to overcome to live as free persons. Historical context is provided to assist the reader in better understanding the interconnection between law and society. However, the vast expanse of time and a desire for this book to remain accessible to readers must limit an examination of all the historical events, courageous participants, and legal consequences that make up the progression of racial justice from the inception of this country to the twenty-first century. The legal analysis is limited to U.S. Supreme Court cases. Although issues of discrimination involving other people of color are examined, the primary focus is that of Blacks in America. For in most cases, the treatment of Blacks has tested the validity of American ideals and constitutional protections. Each chapter provides a sweep of time, legal challenge, and change ending with the vestiges or remnants of slavery and racial segregation that remain among us.

Overview of Race and the Law in America. This initial chapter examines the colonial laws enacted to reduce human beings to slaves or property without human rights. The U.S. Constitution includes several references to slavery. The development of America from colony to nation-state coincides with the legal oppression of Africans in America. This chapter examines *Dred Scott v. Sandford* (1857) and *Plessy v. Ferguson* (1896).[7] These two cases have had far-reaching influence on American society and are, accordingly, referenced throughout the book.

Race and the Struggle for Education in American Schools. This chapter demonstrates that obtaining an education for Black children has been an ongoing struggle nearly from the arrival of Blacks in the

American colonies. Education represented a level of physical and intellectual freedom. From the earliest cases, filed in the midst of slavery, Blacks fought for access to educational opportunities. After slavery, segregation and poor facilities undermined the quest of Blacks for equal education. Gained primarily through Court action, desegregation and more equitable school funding brought progress in racial justice in many other aspects of American life. The legal and social obstacles constructed to prevent Blacks from receiving educational opportunities are explored as well. "Reverse discrimination" is placed in context.

Property Rights and Ownership. The battle of Blacks to freely choose where they wish to live is explored in this chapter. As slaves, Blacks had little choice in their living space. Even free Blacks were prevented from purchasing property in certain areas. After slavery ended, the promise of forty acres and a mule was made but never kept. Blacks challenged government-enforced laws restricting them to neighborhoods zoned by race, as well as racial restrictions in deeds and leases prohibiting Blacks from purchasing White-owned homes. Desegregation of public spaces and accommodations is examined. Court cases in this chapter evidence the ongoing battle against racism in housing, which restricts access to public housing, farm loans, and home mortgages. This chapter also examines legal challenges brought to integrate public places such as parks, swimming pools, buses, and hotels. Public accommodations are places open to the public. However, Blacks were prevented from coming into public contact with Whites. These cases illustrate how separation of the races in public accommodations was maintained well after legal segregation was ruled unconstitutional.

Civil Liberties and Racial Justice. The civil liberties chapter examines how Blacks gained civil liberties and then used those rights to fight for full citizenship. Each exercise of civil liberty was met with governmental and social reprisal. However, Blacks protested oppression through sit-ins, demonstrations, and acts of civil disobedience. Cases illustrate how Blacks challenged laws that restricted their right to free association and marriage.

Voting Rights and Restrictions. This chapter examines how Blacks obtained voting privileges and the threats to that power. The passage of the Fifteenth Amendment removed racial obstacles thus providing Black men the right to vote. That vote was instrumental in electing Blacks to state offices and to the U.S. Congress. However, Blacks had to challenge grandfather clauses, poll taxes, literacy tests, and gerrymandering in order to exercise their right to vote. U.S. Supreme Court decisions, a constitutional amendment, and the Voting Rights Act were required to reopen America's elections to Black voters. The continued disenfranchisement of Black voters is examined.

Race and the Military. The military chapter examines more than three centuries in which Blacks served honorably in the military while battling racism. Enslaved Blacks fought on behalf of this country without a guarantee of freedom. Black soldiers have faced controversies involving salaries, working conditions, courts martial, and promotions. Returning from World Wars I and II, Black soldiers had faced lynching and oppression. The chapter also examines discrimination against the Japanese during World War II as well as the conflicts wrought by the Vietnam War within the Black community.

Race, Crime, and Injustice. The disparity in the administration of justice that began during slavery and continued well after slavery was abolished is examined in this chapter. Enslaved Blacks were not protected by law and were systematically denied access to the courts as witnesses, jurors, and victims. Slavery was abolished except as punishment for a crime. Thus, the criminal justice system became a tool for continued oppression of Blacks. Lynching, an American phenomenon, and its underlying myths are addressed. "Black Codes"—criminal laws created after slavery was abolished—ensured control over Blacks through incarceration. Unscrupulous labor contracts, chain gangs, and convict lease programs reduced Black citizens to involuntary servitude. Police brutality, racial profiling, and the death penalty are examined.

Race and Internationalism. This chapter explores how Blacks escaped to other countries, emigrated, and traveled abroad to gain international allies against slavery and oppression. For two centuries, Blacks have accessed the international arena in their struggle for justice. After slavery, Blacks took the issue of lynching to the international community. They sought access to the United Nations to protest the lynching and murder of Black Americans with impunity. The American civil rights struggle influenced world events. International treaties on minority rights and the elimination of race discrimination are also examined.

In examining these cases and the selected events, the reader will discern the great impact the demand for racial justice has had on American society as well as the manner in which this country has responded to those who would challenge its racial hierarchy. *Race, Law, and American Society: 1607 to Present* establishes the connection between slavery, "Jim Crow" segregation, and the pressing socioracial concerns of present-day America.

1

OVERVIEW OF RACE AND THE LAW IN AMERICA

Slavery was not born of racism, racism was the consequence of slavery.[1]

America began as a small commercial enterprise founded by British interests. King James I of England chartered the Virginia Company of London as a commercial and political enterprise. Earlier in 1590, the fledgling Roanoke colony disappeared under mysterious circumstances. To survive and become profitable in producing the goods England needed, the new American colony of Jamestown would require a more substantial number of people, commerce, and a rule of law.[2] King James appointed a royal council to oversee it.[3] When the Jamestown, Virginia, colony was formed in 1607, slavery existed but England was not a major player in the Atlantic slave trade.[4] However, that changed after twenty Africans, male and female, were introduced to Jamestown in 1619.[5] Coincidently, 1619 was the same year the Virginia House of Burgesses, America's first legislative body, held its first meeting. The Europeans of Jamestown did not consider all Africans slaves.[6] In fact, Matthieu Da Costa, an African explorer, translated for French and Dutch fur traders during the late sixteenth and early seventeenth centuries. However, Europeans in Jamestown had little interaction with Africans. Thus, Africans had no previously established place in custom or law. They were simply outsiders. The colony's social order placed Native Americans and White servants on the lowest tiers of legal protection. White free servants, indentured Whites, and White captives who had accompanied the families were expected to meet the pressing need for labor.[7]

Prior to 1619, distinctions were among European peoples and based primarily on class, religion, and intra-European ethnic divisions.[8] A year later, in 1620, the *Mayflower* landed in what would become Massachusetts establishing English prominence in the new world. After several failed attempts, in 1624, the Dutch East India Company founded New Amsterdam. To survive, all of these colonies needed to build a sustainable infrastructure of labor, laws, and largesse. The Crown and corporations supplied the largesse. Africans and White servants accompanied the Dutch to provide labor. Each colony was maintained based on the laws of the ruling country. When New Amsterdam fell to the English in 1664 and became New York, the more restrictive English common law and custom replaced that of the Dutch. England's laws and customs would come to dictate the treatment of Africans in nearly all of the American colonies.

Africans were brought by ship across the Atlantic from Africa to the Caribbean islands and then into the Americas.[9] No other group, race, or ethnicity was designated nonhuman by law and treated as cargo. Travel from Africa across the Atlantic, known as the "Middle Passage," would span three to four months.[10] Nearly 40 percent of those human beings chained onboard died from disease, mutiny, and suicide.[11] The English abolitionist and politician William Wilberforce stated that "never can so much misery be found condensed into so small a space as in a slave ship" crossing the Middle Passage.[12] The lives lost during the Atlantic crossing do not include the millions who died during slave raids in Africa, the wars associated with those raids, or the walk from the Africa's interior to its coast.[13]

As catastrophic as any prior slave trade was to humanity, the Middle Passage sets American slavery apart.[14] The transatlantic slave trade commercialized human beings.[15] That character of slavery had not existed on the African continent.[16] Africans captured in battle on that continent were maintained as servants. Europeans transformed an African domestic institution into an international commercial trade in which people were stripped of their names, religion, identities, nationality, and legal status as human beings.[17] The western slave trade became a global enterprise involving tens of millions of Africans and tens of thousands of Europeans over a period of ten generations.[18] In its wake, an American empire was created and African empires were destroyed.[19]

By 1672, the king of England commissioned the charter of the Royal Africa Company to "set to sea such as many ships, pinnaces and barks as shall be thought fitting...for the buying, selling, bartering and exchanging of, for or with any gold, silver, Negroes, Slaves, goods, wares and manufactures..." The Royal Africa Company sought gold and silver but was obsessed with the capture of Africans.[20] Slavery soon permeated the social, political, economic, and legal fabric of the New World.[21] Initially, Africans in the New World colonies were not chattel; upon the termination of their indenture, they could purchase property and earn a living.[22] However, they were precluded from attaining a legal status equal to that of White nonservants.[23]

Scholars write of the various levels of American slavery. Whatever their status, no free scholar would willingly submit to the deprivation of human rights and liberty of an enslaved person.[24] Being a slave was a unique horror.[25] Slave owners in the Virginia colony protected their rights with race-based legislation.[26] As profits increased, legal protections for Africans decreased.[27] Enslaving Africans was considered a better investment than using servants.[28] By the 1630s, the Virginia Council enacted restrictions on the rights of free and enslaved Africans.[29] Indians were also enslaved in several of the colonies.[30] In contrast, White indentured servants served as uncompensated laborers to the colony for a predetermined time and then released.[31] However, unlike the Irish or Scottish indentured servant, the African's time of servitude continued in perpetuity.[32]

Greed justified replacing White servants with African slaves. The American colonists depended on tobacco crops. For instance, when Africans were assigned to farm the crops, the profit increased because colonists did not pay for the labor. Laws were quickly enacted to move the judicial process out of the reach of Africans and at the same time prevent armed retaliation. In 1639, statutes were enacted by the Virginia Council specifically prohibiting Blacks from arming themselves. By as early as 1660, Africans in Virginia were relegated by statute to the lowest human status.[33] Comprehensive slave codes restricting the freedoms of Africans were enacted between 1680 and 1682 in direct correlation with the colonists' desire for the higher profits created from free labor.[34] England had an exceptionally profitable investment in Virginia's tobacco crops farmed with African labor.

It was not the custom of all Whites to own human beings for profit. From the onset of slavery in the American colonies, abolitionists such as Lucretia Mott were fervently against it.[35] Quakers, and later Calvinists, denounced the owning of human beings.[36] Initially, Africans who converted to Christianity were allowed greater freedoms. However, laws were quickly enacted to prevent Christian conversion from breaking the chains of slavery.

The Bible was quoted as well by slave owners to support slavery. Africans were reputed to bear the mark of Cain (Genesis 4:10-15). Blacks, depicted as children of Ham, were considered cursed by Noah to be servants of servants (Genesis 9:25). A statute enacted by South Carolina provides insight into the nexus between laws, racism, and the colonies' economic dependence on slave-based labor:

> WHEREAS, the plantations and estates of this Province cannot be well and sufficiently managed and brought into use, without the labor and service of Negroes and other slaves; and forasmuch as the said Negroes and other slaves brought unto the people of this Province for that purpose, are of barbarous, wild, savage natures, and as such...renders them wholly unqualified to be governed by the laws, customs, and practices of this Province....[37]

In placing Blacks outside the protection of law and civil society, statutes such as this one with its references to "savage natures," served to exclude Africans from the family of man and provided a basis for enslavement.[38] Thus, the law created a socioracial hierarchy that placed Blacks beneath Whites in all aspects of life.[39] Maintaining that racial hierarchy required the continued creation of discriminatory laws.[40]

Ironically, the colonists were depriving Africans of their humanity while denouncing King George as an inhumane tyrant.[41] The Declaration of Independence, a document replete with claims of suffering under King George, was written in the presence of Africans living as chattel.[42] John Jay, an abolitionist who would later become the first chief justice of the U.S. Supreme Court, readily admitted that a slaveholder's prayers of freedom from the British were impious.[43] In the northern colonies, the economic necessity of slavery was challenged because slave labor undermined the value of White labor leading to gradual emancipation laws. Blacks received free and semislave status in New York, Vermont, Pennsylvania, and Massachusetts primarily to bolster the economic condition of Whites.

Slavery in the Constitution

The colonists freed themselves from England but left the African in America in chains. Following America's victory over England, slavery was the center of controversy at the Continental Congress. The Revolutionary War was fought in the name of freedom and the preamble of the U.S. Constitution speaks of "securing liberty to ourselves and our posterity" as the basis for establishing this country.[44] However, when the Constitution was ratified in 1789, the Framers refused to abolish the institution of slavery or accept that enslaved persons were, in fact, people. The Constitution refers to slaves as persons. However, enslaved Africans were only referred to as persons in the Constitution as a compromise to certain "sensitive" Framers of the Constitution.[45] In *Smith v. Turner*, the Supreme Court made clear that references to importation of persons pertain only to slaves and not White immigrants.[46] The Framers debated including "slave" as opposed to "person" in the Constitution. The U.S. Supreme Court clarified that importation of "persons" meant "slaves." "[T]he word 'persons' is used, not to embrace others as well as slaves, but slaves alone....The word slave [in the Constitution] was avoided, from a sensitive feeling; but clearly no others were intended."[47]

England turned from the slave trade as profits dwindled. However, the United States refused to end its direct participation in the declining slave trade. Instead, a constitutional compromise provided that, in 1808, America would cease importing slaves into the country. From that year until slavery was abolished in 1865, a $10 tax was levied on each slave brought into the United States. Article I, Section 9, of the U.S. Constitution states:

> The migration or importation of such persons as any of the states now existing shall think proper to admit, shall not be prohibited by the Congress prior to the year one thousand eight hundred and eight, but a tax or duty may be imposed on such importation, not exceeding ten dollars for each person.[48]

The $10 tax was imposed only if the slave traffickers were apprehended, tried, and convicted of the offense. This provision did not end slavery in 1808—just the importation of slaves.

The institution of slavery would continue until the Thirteenth Amendment was ratified. The Framers' intent to continue slavery is evidenced in the fugitive slave clause within the U.S. Constitution. Article IV of the Constitution mandates the return of any escaped slaves:[49]

> No Person held to Service or Labour in one State, under the Laws thereof, escaping into another, shall in Consequence of any Law or Regulation therein, be discharged from such Service or Labour, but shall be delivered up on Claim of the Party to whom such Service or Labour may be due.[50]

This provision of the Constitution was enforced through state laws, federal legislation, and the U.S. Supreme Court. Under Article 1 of the Constitution, Africans in America were counted as three-fifths of a person. That provision allowed southern states to include slaves for the purpose of calculating representatives to the U.S. Congress:[51]

> Representative and direct Taxes shall be apportioned among the several States which may be included within this Union, according to their respective Numbers, which shall be determined by adding to the whole Number of free Person, including those bound to Service for a Term of Years, and excluding Indians not taxed, three fifths of all other Persons.[52]

In states such as South Carolina, Blacks outnumbered Whites, thus increasing the political power of politicians in slave states without providing any representation to those responsible for that status.

By 1836, Africans had provided two hundred years of slave labor to the United States. Their legal rights were subject to the whim of Whites.[53] Forbidden to defend themselves or their loved ones, Blacks were in a constant battle against the rule of law.

Blacks as Nonpersons: *Dred Scott v. Sandford*

In 1857, the case of *Dred Scott v. Sandford* captured worldwide attention when the U.S. Supreme Court decided the "place" of Blacks was permenantly outside of American society. Dred Scott brought suit for assault after John Sandford beat Scott and his wife and daughter.[54] A free person could bring assault charges but, in contrast, Scott and his family, as slaves, had to submit to physical punishment at the hands of any White person, especially the slaveholder. The country was in the midst of a debate over legislating free and slave states. Under the Missouri Compromise, each territory receiving statehood entered the Union designated as a slave state or free state. Dred Scott was an enslaved Black man who had been taken into a free territory. He was later sold and taken back to a slave state.

Scott argued that he was free by virtue of having resided in a free territory. He based his claim to freedom on the change of status that attached to residing in a free state. He brought his case in Missouri. In 1836, the Missouri court ruled that a slave is made free once he or she is brought into territory northwest of the Ohio River, where slavery had been outlawed by the Ordinance of 1787.[55] Prior to this, in *Rachael, woman of color, v. Walker,* a military man forfeited ownership of his slave, Rachael, when he took her with him to the Northwest Territory.[56] Rachael won her freedom based on the controversial Missouri Compromise. Based on this case, Scott's argument should have been firmly placed. However, the Missouri Compromise had become an unsettled issue of law and politics. In the *Dred Scott* case, the trial judge ruled in favor of Scott. However, Sandford appealed. The appellate court favored Sandford. Scott appealed. After many years of appeals, *Dred Scott v. Sandford* was heard by the U.S. Supreme Court.[57]

Justice Roger B. Taney, an advocate of original intent and slavery, wrote the opinion on behalf of the Court.[58] The Court ruled that Scott was not a citizen and therefore could not bring an action in any U.S. court. The ruling then denied a state's right to give freedom to a slave without the slave owner's expressed permission. Although it was not before the Court, the Missouri Compromise, an act of the U.S. Congress, was ruled unconstitutional. Prior to the decision in *Dred Scott,* the Supreme Court had not reversed an act of Congress since *Marbury v. Madison.*[59] The Court also decided that Africans in America could never be considered citizens, stating that only the federal government could confer citizenship.

> As relates to these States, it is too plain for argument, that they [Blacks] have never been regarded as a part of the people or citizens of the State, nor supposed to possess any political rights which the dominant race might not withhold or grant at their pleasure.[60]

Blacks, deemed neither United States citizens or people, existed to merely better the lives of Whites. Dred Scott was prohibited from physically defending himself during an assault and from bringing any legal action on behalf of himself or his family.[61] The Court, relying on the pivotal documents of American freedom, supported this proposition as follows:

> We have the language of the Declaration of Independence and of the Articles of Confederation, in addition to the plain words of the Constitution itself; we have the legislation of the different States, before, about the time, and since, the Constitution was adopted; we have the legislation of Congress, from the time of its adoption to a recent period; and we have the constant and uniform action of the Executive Department, all concurring together, and leading to the same result. And if anything in relation to the construction of the Constitution can be regarded as settled, it is that which we now give to the word "citizen" and the word "people."[62]

The Court then claimed a Black man had no rights that a White man needs to respect.[63] It would take a civil war, Congress, and three constitutional amendments to address the damage created by the Court's decision in *Dred Scott*.

From 1861 to 1865, America fought a civil war over the economic future of the United States and states's rights. The Civil War, a conflict between political as well as economic philosophies, divided the country by region and position on the slave issue. The North, experiencing the throes of the Industrial Revolution, sought to expand an economy based on factory labor.[64] On the other hand, the South, an agrarian economy, depended heavily on enslaved Africans to work the fields.[65] In the midst of this, President Lincoln made clear that if he could save the Union and maintain slavery he would do so.[66] He could not. The South created its own nation—the United States of the Confederacy—led by President Jefferson Davis.

Blacks fought in the Civil War for their physical freedom and the American ideal of freedom. When President Lincoln's Emancipation Proclamation freed the enslaved Africans residing in slave states those Blacks fought for the North; their participation in the war greatly influenced the outcome. In 1865, the Thirteenth Amendment to the U.S. Constitution abolished slavery and vested

Congress with the power to pass all laws necessary and proper for abolishing all badges and incidents of slavery in the United States.[67] Following the war, the Freedmen's Bureau, officially known as the Bureau of Refugees, Freedmen and Abandoned Land, was created by an act of Congress in 1865 to assist in the transition from slavery to freedom.[68] The concept of a Freedmen's Bureau was met with great political resistance from Lincoln's successor, President Andrew Johnson, who vetoed the Reconstruction Acts.[69] Congress overrode Johnson's veto. However, the bureau would remain a volatile measure vulnerable to political pressures from the South. The Freedmen's Bureau assisted millions of poor Whites and formerly enslaved Blacks to gain an education and housing. The freedmen legislation was initially intended to assist former slaves only. However, Whites were included in the legislation as a compromise to avoid total defeat of the measure. The success of the Freedmen's Bureau was undermined by politics, limited staff, and scarcity of funds.[70] Despite these obstacles, hundreds of thousands of Blacks used the bureau as a stepping stone into life as a free person. Great strides were made toward franchising Blacks. In response, White Southerners, who had been staunch Republicans, renounced allegiance to a party responsible for abolishing slavery, registering instead as Democrats.

The Civil Rights Act of 1866 bestowed citizenship rights on African Americans deprived them by the *Dred Scott* decision.[71] The act provided formerly enslaved as well as free Blacks with the right to enforce contracts, sue in courts of law, possess and dispose of real property, enjoy equal protection of the laws, and to be subject to equal punishment under law.[72] Blacks were free. The Civil Rights Act stated that "all citizens of the United States shall have the same right, in every state and territory, as is enjoyed by white citizens thereof to inherit, purchase, lease, sell, hold and convey real and personal property."[73]

In 1868, Congress ratified the Fourteenth Amendment, granting citizenship at birth to all persons.[74] The amendment was needed to ensure that states recognized the rights of Blacks:

> All persons born or naturalized in the United States, and subject to the jurisdiction thereof, are citizens of the United States and of the State

wherein they reside. No State shall make or enforce any law which shall abridge the privileges or immunities of citizens of the United States; nor shall any State deprive any person of life, liberty, or property, without due process of law; nor deny to any person within its jurisdiction the equal protection of the laws.[75]

Congress then passed the Civil Rights Act of 1870. That act provided that "all persons within the jurisdiction of the United States shall have the same right in every state and territory to make and enforce contracts."[76] Soon after African-American men were granted the right to vote in 1870 the political climate changed.[77]

Reprisal came swiftly on the heels of freedom. The Civil Rights Act of 1871, also known as the Ku Klux Klan Act, was enacted in response to the widespread terrorism by Southern Whites seeking revenge against Blacks and Northern Whites. The act made it unlawful to "conspire...or go in disguise upon the public highway or upon the premises of another for the purpose...of depriving any person...of the equal protection of the laws, or...privileges or immunities" and allowed civil damage awards against law enforcement officers who failed to enforce the provisions of the act.[78] The passage of the Civil Rights Act of 1875 aimed to: (1) provide equal enjoyment of inns and other public accommodations; (2) impose civil damages if such discrimination were to occur; and (3) establish the right of Blacks to serve as jurors in court cases.[79]

President Ulysses S. Grant, a Union general in the Civil War, was succeeded by Rutherford B. Hayes in 1876 amid racial violence. In a compromise to appease Southerners, President Hayes withdrew federal troops stationed in the South. With the withdrawal of military protection, Blacks were subject to pervasive racial violence and acts of political vengence. Blacks challenged discrimination under the Civil Rights Act of 1875. But courts in the South refused to enforce the laws. In 1883, the Supreme Court decided the *Civil Rights Cases*, five cases brought by Blacks alleging violation of the civil rights statute.[80] In those cases, Black patrons were denied service equal to Whites, at a hotel, in a railroad car in Tennessee, at a San Francisco theater, and an opera house in New York. Upon appeal to the U.S. Supreme Court, the cases were consolidated.[81] The Court found against all of the Black plaintiffs, ruling that civil rights legislation did not protect Blacks from private discrimination.[82] The theater, opera house, and hotel were private enterprises. The Court held that civil rights acts only addressed discrimination by the state government. Similarly, the equal-protection clause of the Fourteenth Amendment applied only to state misconduct. Private race discrimination by individuals was beyond the responsibility of the federal government to legislate. Unless the state was involved in misconduct, there was nothing the federal courts could do to protect Blacks from discrimination.

With each hard-earned advance, laws were enacted to restrict their progress or narrowly interpreted to limit intended protections. Despite the failure of the courts and Constitution to protect them, African Americans ascended from the lowest rung on the socioracial hierarchy. Blacks continued to seek education, property, military service, public office, employment, and a rightful place as full citizens in American society.

The Dark Ages of Civil Rights:
Plessy v. Ferguson

In Louisiana, Homer Plessy refused to accept legalized segregation. The Separate Car Act of 1890, a newly enacted state statute, segregated the seating on the intrastate railroad train by race. Based on this act, Blacks were relegated to the soot-filled front cars of the local railroad. Homer Plessy joined with others to draft a strategy to defeat the law. *Plessy v. Ferguson* placed the issue of state-imposed segregation before the U.S. Supreme Court.[83]

Plessy, a Black man who claimed to be seven-eighths White, sat in the segregated Whites-only section of the train. Under the law, a conductor had to remove any interloper or risk jail and a fine. The conductor asked Plessy to move to the Negro-only car. When he refused, Plessy was arrested and convicted of violating the Separate Car Act. He appealed the decision, arguing that the act violated his Thirteenth and Fourteenth Amendment rights, and placed a badge of inferiority on Blacks. U.S. Supreme Court Justice Henry Billings Brown delivered the now infamous opinion in which Plessy's claims of discrimination were soundly defeated.[84]

The Court dismissed Plessy's argument that a badge of inferiority would be placed on Blacks segregated from the general population, stating: "If one race be inferior to the other socially, the Constitution of the United States cannot put them upon the same plane."[85] Every aspect of American life was affected by this ruling. The state was given the power to legislate social interaction between the races.

The *Plessy v. Ferguson* opinion instituted the "separate but equal" doctrine, which imposed on the country an Americanized version of apartheid. In hypocritical rhetoric, the Court states:

> A statute which implies merely a legal distinction between the white and colored races—a distinction which is founded in the color of the two races and which must always exist so long as white men are distinguished from the other race by color—has no tendency to destroy the legal equality of the two races... The object of the [Fourteenth Amendment] was undoubtedly to enforce the absolute equality of the two races before the law, but in the nature of things it could not have been intended to abolish distinctions based upon color, or to enforce social, as distinguished from political equality, or a commingling of the two races upon terms unsatisfactory to either.[86]

Justice John Marshall Harlan's dissent confirms that there has always been a relatively small number of Whites willing to withstand social ostracism, threats, and assault to do what is just.[87] Additionally, the opinion in *Dred Scott* was not a unanimous one.[88] Justice Harlan spoke directly to the racial hierarchy sanctioned by the *Plessy* majority. He stated, "In view of the Constitution, in the eye of the law, there is in this country no superior, dominant, ruling class of citizens. There is no caste here. Our Constitution is color-blind, and neither knows nor tolerates classes among citizens."[89]

Justice Harlan continued with a prescient statement: "In my opinion, the judgment this day rendered will, in time, prove to be quite as pernicious as the decision made by this tribunal in the Dred Scott case."[90] This one case, *Plessy v. Ferguson,* ushered in a doctrine of segregation condoned by this country's highest Court that would lead to nearly a century of legalized racial oppression: *de jure* segregation. *Plessy v. Ferguson* heralded the "Dark Ages" of civil rights.[91] For the next fifty years following this decision, the Supreme Court would do little to uphold the intent of the Civil Rights Act.[92]

Challenging an Oppressive Rule of Law

Whether by law or by custom racial ostracism extended to virtually every aspect of American life—from public transportation, schools, and housing to sports and recreation, to hospitals, orphanages, prisons, and cemeteries.[93] In response, Blacks formed clubs and associations intent on challenging legalized subordination.[94] W. E. B. DuBois, the prominent intellectual and most vocal member of the NAACP, set his sights on combating racial oppression fostered by *Plessy*.[95] In 1909, the National Association for the Advancement of Colored People (NAACP) was formed to construct a strategy to address the social and economic conditions under which Blacks in America toiled.[96] The NAACP was created as an interracial phalanx with which Blacks could challenge America's racial restrictions.[97]

Charles Hamilton Houston, a Black Harvard Law School graduate and dean of Howard Law School, became the architect of the civil rights legal strategy. The racist treatment he received in the U.S. military motivated him to defeat segregation. Under Houston's strategy a state would have to either admit Black applicants or build a separate school. He trained a team of NAACP lawyers and local attorneys in the South to argue appellate cases. Houston viewed lawyers as social engineers.[98] Each case formed an incremental but progressive foundation of Supreme Court jurisprudence, leading eventually to desegregation.[99] Houston trained Black law students, such as Thurgood Marshall, to be civil rights specialists.

Houston, Marshall, and hundreds of others mounted a decades-long effort to steer the power of the Supreme Court toward racial justice. They dedicated themselves to the reversal of *Plessy* and racial disfranchisement. Decades of activism before the courts and within the Black communities culminated with the *Brown v. Board of Education of Topeka* decision. It was a legal victory with symbolic and emotional underpinnings for Blacks as well as Whites.[100] The significance of the *Brown* decision, as with *Plessy*, reverberated within every aspect of American society. For those invested in the well established socioracial hierarchy of subordinate Black status, the *Brown* decision was a declaration of war. The brutality captured on national television was never as frightening as the reality of rampant terrorism in towns and rural areas across the country. Uninvestigated acts of barbarism, lynchings, and beatings of Blacks remain the secret of many Southern towns.

Facing assault and possibly death, Blacks stood their ground against racial oppression. Protests (both nonviolent and violent) were mounted in the South and North. Black leaders became spokespeople for the morality as well as the constitutionality of racial justice in America. The Civil Rights Act of 1964, Voting Rights Act of 1965, and Fair Housing Act secured better governmental protections against racial discrimination as well as discrimination against women and ethnic minorities.[101] A tradition of racial separation and oppression continued even after *de jure* (legal) segregation ended. Nuanced or blatant, discrimination against Blacks continued to challenge the ideals of American freedom, democracy, and the intention of a rule of law.

Debates rage as to whether the U.S. Supreme Court should participate in social engineering. Article III of the Constitution established a supreme court. Unlike the executive and legislative branches, the Supreme Court was given scant direction. Thus, its powers have evolved with time. Comprising only nine members nominated by the president, the Supreme Court's decisions are shown to be influenced as much by its composition and political dictates as by the parameters of precedent. Thurgood Marshall became the first Black justice of the U.S. Supreme Court in 1967. At the time of his nomination, Blacks had been an integral part of American society for nearly three hundred fifty years. President Lyndon Johnson said of Marshall's nomination: "[I]t was the right thing to do, the right time to do it, the right man and right place." Yet, there appears to be little chance of the Court gaining another Black member intent on racial justice. In the latter part of the twentieth century, the struggle for civil rights was upended by reverse discrimination lawsuits brought by Whites opposed to affirmative action. Without acknowledging the manner in which the racial hierarchy disfranchised Blacks for centuries, White plaintiffs and the courts have denounced affirmative action for Blacks and other minorities as unfairly disadvantaging Whites.

Present-Day Vestiges of Slavery and "Jim Crow"

As a result of slavery and the *Plessy v. Ferguson* decision, generations of Blacks in America have been scarred and American society has experienced untold damage the result of which extend well beyond its borders. Empire building provided little time or incentive to consider future social, political, or economic consequences. America has wrestled with racism from the time of its inception. Too often her resolve to confront this insidious problem waned once faced with political expediencies, self-interest, and greed. Yet, Blacks have little choice but to persevere. With each legal challenge to discrimination, whether due to racially discriminatory laws or the effect of racially neutral laws, there remains the risk of failure and loss of ground. The lesson of *Plessy* remains inescapable: Supreme Court rulings on race will reverberate for generations to come. However, the resolve of the disenfranchised to gain justice from America cannot wane.

The opposition in the struggle for racial justice is great. Those who continue to believe in the subordination of Blacks are present examples of *Plessy*'s intransigence. Their strategy may be summarized by the crude statement of a Klansman in *Brandenburg v. Ohio* (1969), a free-speech case. He says, "N-gg-r [*sic*] will have to fight for every inch he gets from now on."[102] The present-day disparities in education, housing, voting rights, and criminal justice speak volumes about injustice, vestiges from *Plessy*, and the remnants of slavery. An examination of the role race has played in America's past places current issues of affirmative action, "reverse discrimination," busing, integration, housing segregation, redistricting, urban blight, and capital punishment in context.

Following this legal journey from the colonial period to the present reveals a country still living with the vestiges of slavery and post-slavery race discrimination and unwilling to accept how those past unconscionable acts of racism continue to undermine the ideals of justice. The following cases and controversies evidence the remarkable determination of Blacks and other racial minorities in America who have engaged in a centuries-long battle to make real the promise of justice set forth in the U.S. Constitution and that tangible known to many as the American dream.

2

RACE AND THE STRUGGLE FOR EDUCATION IN AMERICAN SCHOOLS

Merely striking off the fetters of the slave, without removing the incidents and consequences of slavery, would hardly have been a boon to the colored race.[1]

Blyew v. United States (1871)

The [Mississippi] Constitution divided the educable children into those of the pure white or Caucasian race, on the one hand, and the brown, yellow and black races, on the other.[2]

Gong Lum v. Rice (1927)

Black parents have waged a centuries-long legal battle to gain a proper education for their children. Yet, today, most Black children receive their education in segregated and underfunded public schools. This chapter examines the legal obstacles faced by Black parents from slavery to the present day. The enslaved African in America was deemed chattel or moveable property without need of formal education. The societal arguments were twofold. Blacks were believed to be "uneducable."[3] Yet, Whites feared that an enslaved person who learned to read would be rendered unfit for slave labor.[4] Learning to read and write were deemed dangerous enough to be criminalized. In Georgia, the financial penalty when Whites taught a slave to read was 50 percent higher than for willfully castrating or cutting off the limb of a slave.[5]

The Early Fight for Education:
Roberts v. Boston

Although slavery was abolished in Massachusetts as early as 1781, racism persisted.[6] Black children in Boston were excluded from public school education. Prince Hall, a Black Mason, led the first recorded campaign by free Black parents to gain access to public schools.[7] In 1787, Hall presented a petition to the Massachusetts Legislature requesting that the City of Boston provide an education for the children of Black taxpayers.[8] In it he and other free Black parents argued that they paid taxes that supported the public schools. Therefore, their children should have the benefit of those schools. Hall stated that:

> ...as by woeful experience we now feel the want of a common education. We, therefore, must fear for our rising offspring to see them in ignorance in a land of gospel light...and for not other reason can be given this they are black...[9]

Although Hall's petition was denied, Black children were eventually admitted into Boston's public schools with few restrictions.

However, once admitted, Black children were treated so poorly by White teachers and White classmates that Black parents requested a separate school for their children. The physical and emotional discrimination against Black children led to the creation in 1798 of the Smith School, a private school for Blacks. At that time, Black parents could choose between the ill-treatment of Boston's public schools or a private school. Soon thereafter the City of Boston enacted legislation to require racially separate schools, precluding Black children from attending any school other than one designated for Blacks. Blacks petitioned the legislature "that schools for colored children might be abolished" as early as 1846.[10] In response, the primary school committee of Boston passed a resolution stating "the regular attendance of all such children...is not only legal and just, but is adapted to promote the education of that class of our population."[11]

In 1850, Benjamin F. Roberts filed suit on behalf of his daughter, Sarah. *Roberts v. Boston* is the earliest reported education case brought by Blacks in America.[12] Roberts argued that separate schools violated the rights of Black children.[13] The Massachusetts court disagreed, ruling that:

Conceding, therefore, in the fullest manner, that colored persons, the descendants of Africans, are entitled by law in this Commonwealth to equal rights, constitutional, political, civil and social, the question then arises whether the regulation in question which provides separate schools for colored children is a violation of any of their rights.[14]

Roberts also argued that separate schools perpetuated caste distinction. To this argument the court responded that "this prejudice, if it exists, is not created by law, and probably cannot be changed by law."[15]

The Black community in Boston was divided on the issue of segregated schools. There was considerable disagreement within the Black community as to whether attending schools with hostile Whites was the most beneficial environment for Black children.[16] Black civic leaders in favor of desegregated education continued to seek relief in the Massachusetts legislature.[17] In 1855, the legislature repealed public school admission requirements based on race as well as color and religion. Unfortunately, the *Roberts v. Boston* decision, sustaining racial separation, would form the cornerstone of future court decisions legally segregating children in public schools.

Reconstruction and the Quest for Education: The Freedmen's Bureau

A relative handful of Africans in America were college graduates during slavery. These include Fannie M. Jackson Coppin, who in 1836 graduated from Oberlin College in Ohio, and Edward Jones, who graduated from Amherst College in 1826.[18] Northern states allowed varying degrees of liberty. However, any education for Africans in America was subject to the whim of Whites. Colleges, created for free Blacks by White missionaries, among those Lincoln University and Wilberforce University founded in 1854 and 1855, respectively, educated the Black elite.[19] The Civil War brought the issue of legal rights, educational opportunity, and civil liberties of Blacks to the fore. When the Thirteenth Amendment to the U.S. Constitution abolished slavery in 1865, Blacks had the freedom to seek an education.[20] In 1868, under the Fourteenth Amendment, Africans in America were granted due-process rights and equal protection of the laws, as well as privileges and immunities of U.S. citizenship as a birthright allowing them access to public education.[21] With the ratification of these amendments and the Civil Rights Act of 1866, millions of formerly enslaved and manumitted Africans were free to seek an education in earnest without the constant fear of reprisal by Whites.

Blacks understood the necessity of education. Despite confronting issues of postslavery homelessness and oppression, these Blacks hungered for education.[22] Thousands of teachers arrived from the North determined to provide an education.[23] By 1870, there were nearly two hundred fifty thousand Blacks attending over four thousand schools across the South.[24] Churches established schools. Hundreds of organizations were created in the 1800s by Blacks to fund educational initiatives, lobby political forces, protect Black children, and remove obstacles to progress.[25] Elementary and high schools, trade schools, and colleges were created to teach the millions of newly freed Black people who had been denied formal education.[26] Hampton Institute (1868), Howard University (1867), Philander Smith College (1877), and St. Augustine's University (1867) were among the many colleges founded during Reconstruction to teach African Americans.[27]

From 1880 to 1910, illiteracy among Blacks in the South decreased from 70 percent to 33 percent.[28] The short-lived Freedmen's Bureau was established to oversee the process.[29] The Freedmen's Bureau, formerly known as the Bureau of Refugees, Freedmen and Abandoned Land, was created by an act of Congress in 1865.[30] The bureau was established despite political hostility and the opposition of President Andrew Johnson.[31] Although initially intended to assist former slaves only, the bill would have been defeated without the inclusion of Whites. The success of the Freedmen's Bureau was undermined by politics, limited staff, and a scarcity of funds. In actuality, there was relatively little money or motivation on the part of American society because educating Blacks represented a change in social status and a challenge to the established socioracial hierarchy.[32] A North Carolina newspaper warned "Education has but one tendency: to give higher hopes and aspirations"; "we want the negro to remain here, just about as he is—with mighty little change."[33]

Initially, a public education for Black children equal to that of White children was not universally opposed. In 1868, the constitution of South Carolina provided for a system of universal education with both races educated in the same school.[34] General Oliver Otis Howard, commissioner of the Freedmen's Bureau, lobbied Congress for additional funds to educate children former slaves. However, support for Black education was short-lived. W. E. B. DuBois wrote of the opposition to educating Blacks:

> [T]he South believed an educated Negro to be a dangerous Negro. And the South was not wholly wrong; for education among all kinds of men always has had, and always will have, an element of danger and revolution, of dissatisfaction and discontent. Nevertheless, men strive to know. It was some inkling of this paradox, even in the unquiet days of the Bureau, that allayed an opposition to human training, which still to-day lies smoldering, but not flaming. Fisk, Atlanta, Howard, and Hampton were founded in these days, and nearly $6,000,000 was expended in five years for educational work, $750,000 of which came from the freedmen themselves.[35]

Howard was dismissed from the Freedmen's Bureau by President Andrew Johnson. Reconstruction ended. Southerners of the former Confederacy received presidential pardons from President Johnson. The bureau was left in shambles by 1870.[36] Federal troops were withdrawn from the South, placing Blacks in positions of physical and economic vulnerability.

The withdrawal of federal troops left Blacks vulnerable to retribution by Southerners enraged by the loss of the war and drastic economic circumstances. "Black Codes" were enacted under which homeless or jobless Blacks were arrested for trespass and vagrancy.[37] Constitutional protections and civil rights statutes became meaningless as Whites forced free Blacks into shareholding and political disfranchisement reminiscent of slavery. Laws restricting segregating Blacks from Whites were enacted around the country, particularly in the South.[38] Laws such as these effectively relegated Blacks to a subordinated status of second-class citizen. Racially segregated education became the practice in the North as well as the South. In 1883, a Brooklyn, New York, court considered the question of racial segregation in education in the case of *King v. Gallagher*.[39] That court ruled that a Black child could not attend the school of her choice when a school designated for Blacks was made available.[40]

Similar state court decisions consistently quashed efforts by Black parents to overturn laws segregating public schools. In *State ex rel. Garnes v. McCann*, the Ohio Supreme Court had to decide whether a statute segregating school children by race violated their equal-protection rights.[41] That court relied on *Roberts v. Boston* in its support of segregated public schools.[42] As in *Roberts*, the school board was given broad discretion to decide the needs and wants of the district.[43] State courts across the country, presented with the viability of race laws, upheld education statutes racially segregating students. These decisions were among a wave of hundreds of segregation laws enacted in response to the emancipation of Blacks.

A Separate and Unequal Education: *Plessy v. Ferguson*

Blacks in Louisiana refused to accept a newly enacted statute segregating the seating on the local train. It was the challenge to the Separate Car Act relegating Blacks to the soot-filled front car of the local railroad that was at issue in *Plessy v. Ferguson*.[44]

Plessy argued that the act violated his Thirteenth and Fourteenth Amendment rights and that a badge of inferiority would be placed on Blacks forcibly segregated away from the general population. Plessy's claims were roundly rejected.[45] The Court relied on previous state court decisions upholding racial segregation, placing particular emphasis on *Roberts v. Boston*[46] and *People v. Gallagher*.[47] The *Plessy* decision provided the states with the power to regulate social interaction between the races instituting "separate but equal" with special regard to education.[48] The Court states:

> [The] *establishment of separate schools for white and colored children...*has been [deemed] a valid exercise of the legislative power even by courts of States where the political rights of the colored race have been longest and most earnestly enforced.[49] (author's emphasis)

Dismissing Plessy's argument that a badge of inferiority would be placed on Blacks segregated away from the general population, the Court continues:

Laws permitting, and even requiring, their separation in places where they are liable to be brought into contact do not necessarily imply the inferiority of either race to the other, and have been generally, if not universally, recognized as within the competency of the state legislatures in the exercise of their police power.[50]

Justice John Halan's dissent provides early insight into the path America could have taken had she the fortitude:

The white race deems itself to be the dominant race in this country. And so it [is], in prestige, in achievements, in *education*, in wealth, and in power. So, I doubt not, it will continue to be for all time, if it remains true to its great heritage, and holds fast to the principles of constitutional liberty. But in view of the constitution, in the eye of the law, there is in this country no superior, dominant, ruling class of citizens.[51] (author's emphasis)

Soon after the *Plessy* decision, the U.S. Supreme Court was presented with the case of *Cumming v. Richmond County Board of Education* (1899).[52] In *Cumming*, Black parents raised the same question at issue in *Roberts v. Boston*: why pay taxes for schools their children cannot attend? The high schools in this Georgia county were restricted to White students. Black parents were forced to pay tuition for a private Black high school as well as taxes that supported the public high school for Whites. A Georgia statute required tax dollars from all residents to support free public schools. But, "separate schools shall be provided for the white and colored races."[53] The Richmond County School Board had converted the only Black high school into a primary school on the grounds that Blacks needed only "the rudiments of education."[54] The U.S. Supreme Court denied the equal-protection claims of Black parents in Richmond. The Court determined that the interest and convenience of the White majority did not require a high school for Blacks. Furthermore, as in *Roberts*, the state could decide how it would distribute its funds.[55]

In 1908, the Supreme Court upheld the conviction and sentence of several White administrators of Berea College who chose to operate a racially integrated college. In *Berea College v. Kentucky*, the U.S. Supreme Court entrenched racial segregation in education.[56] Berea

College, a private college, was established to promote the cause of Christ and provide an education to all persons. However, a Kentucky statute made it "unlawful to operate any college, school or institution where persons of the white or negro races are both received as pupils for instruction."[57] Violators would be arrested and fined $1,000 and fined another $100 per day of continued offense. In affirming the convictions of Berea College administrators, the Supreme Court swept away the ability of Whites to choose to cross the color line without suffering criminal as well as societal penalties.

In 1909, the National Association for the Advancement of Colored People (NAACP) was formed to construct a strategy to address the conditions under which Blacks endured in America.[58] The NAACP began as the Conference on the Status of the Negro with two divergent conceptions of itself: "the first, as primarily a white organization dedicated to African-American uplift through well-financed suasion; the second, as an interracial phalanx challenging the mainstream public to accept ever-greater civil and social rights for the nation's historic minority."[59] The NAACP was formed from the Niagara Movement, comprised of Black and politically powerful Whites.[60] W. E. B. DuBois, the prominent intellectual and most vocal member of the NAACP, arose as its formidable leader.[61]

Under the *Plessy* doctrine, school children were treated as either Black or White. In 1927, Martha Lum, a Chinese student, was classified as colored and denied admission to a Whites-only Mississippi public school.[62] Her father, Gong Lum, brought legal action, alleging that forcing Martha to attend the school for Blacks violated her equal-protection rights under the Fourteenth Amendment. She lost in the Mississippi state courts and appealed to the U.S. Supreme Court. The U.S. Supreme Court affirmed her exclusion. William Howard Taft, chief justice and former president of the United States, wrote the opinion for the majority:

> [This] case reduces itself to the question whether a state can be said to afford to a child of Chinese ancestry born in this country, and a citizen of the United States, equal protection of the laws by giving her the opportunity of a common school education in a school which receives only colored children of the brown, yellow or black races.[63]

The Court left the placement in racial categories to the discretion of each state.[64] As in *Roberts v. Boston* and *Cumming v. Richmond County*, the logistics of separating the races in public schools was an exercise of state legislative powers.[65] However, by this logic, if the state segregated its public school students by race, then it was responsible for building dual facilities. It was a double-edged sword, and a successful legal strategy would be based squarely on the financial burden building and maintaining a dual system would cause state governments.

Building the Case:
State of Missouri Ex Rel. Gaines v. Canada and Sipuel v. Oklahoma

In Missouri, Lloyd Gaines graduated from Lincoln University, the designated Black college. Gaines wished to attend law school at the racially restricted University of Missouri-Columbia.[66] He was denied admission due to his race. A Missouri statute afforded him the opportunity to attend a school out of state if facilities could not be provided within the state of Missouri. Gaines challenged the decision in *State of Missouri Ex Rel. Gaines v. Canada* (1938).[67] He argued that "separate but equal" meant either admitting him into the University of Missouri or building a Black law school at Lincoln University financed by the state of Missouri. Government officials offered promises of a law school for Blacks.

In 1938, the Supreme Court decided Gaines should be admitted to the University of Missouri School of Law until such a school was built at Lincoln University.[68] Missouri chose to admit one Black student into its law school rather than build an entire facility that would develop Black lawyers. In his dissent, Justice McReynolds condemned the Court's decision to integrate the law school. He states that "to break down the settled practice concerning separate schools [would]...damnify both races."[69] McReynolds notwithstanding, the decision was a major victory for civil rights advocates, equal education, and the Black community.

Gaines was a legal weapon against the separate but equal doctrine. Under the leadership of Charles Hamilton Houston, a legal strategy was implemented that consisted of laying an incremental foundation of Supreme Court jurisprudence that would lead unequivocally to an end to racial segregation.[70] Houston described the work of lawyers as that of "social engineers or leeches."[71] Their primary target would be education. Most states practicing segregation in higher education lacked a separate Black graduate school, medical school, or law school; this failure became the impetus for court challenges on behalf of those Black applicants.[72] By 1947, cases challenging segregation were pending in Oklahoma, Texas, Louisiana, and South Carolina.[73]

The success of *Gaines* led to victory in *Sipuel v. Board of Regents* (1948).[74] Ada Lois Sipuel was deemed qualified for law school by the trial court.[75] However, she was denied admission to Oklahoma's law school because of her color.[76] Without a state law school for Blacks in Oklahoma, the Supreme Court ruled that Sipuel must be admitted to the University of Oklahoma. She was offered a roped off area of the capitol building with separate teachers and classes and only permitted to use the library at the state capitol. Both Sipuel and Gaines were treated poorly once admitted. However, the *Sipuel* and *Gaines* cases established Supreme Court precedent for admitting Blacks into graduate school programs.

In *McLaurin v. Oklahoma* (1950), George W. McLaurin, a Black applicant, was admitted to graduate school at the University of Oklahoma. As in the case of Ada Sipuel, McLaurin was segregated from the other students in the classroom and forced to sit at a special table in the library and cafeteria.[77] The Supreme Court ruled against the state university, finding that such an isolated environment prevented McLaurin from gaining full educational benefits in violation of his equal-protection rights.[78] In an effort to circumvent Court-mandated desegregation, state legislatures quickly created professional schools especially for Black students. However, in *Sweatt v. Painter* (1950), a makeshift law school for Blacks created by the state of Texas was deemed unequal in its resources, staff, and facilities, leading to the integration of the University of Texas Law School by Herman Marion Sweatt.[79]

Considered by many to be the home of the Confederacy, Alabama and its segregation laws were dealt another blow when the Supreme Court decided the state could not prevent Autherine Lucy and Polly Anne Myers, Black college applicants, from attending the all-White flagship college, University of Alabama. In 1952, Lucy and Myers were denied admission to the university based on their race. The Supreme Court decided *Brown v. Board of Education* in 1954. Despite the Court's decision, William Adams, dean of admissions at the University of Alabama, refused to admit Lucy and Myers. Attorneys from the NAACP represented the women in their appeal to the U.S. Supreme Court. In *Lucy v. Adams*, 350 U.S. 1 (1955), the Court ruled that the university must admit the women. The victories in *Sweatt, Gaines, McLaurin, Lucy,* and other cases cleared the path for the Court to decide *Brown v. Board of Education of Topeka*, striking a fatal blow to segregated education in public schools.

A Blow to Segregation:
Brown v. Board of Education of Topeka

In 1954, the U.S. Supreme Court handed down *Brown v. Board of Education of Topeka.*[80] *Brown*, a class-action, was consolidated with cases filed on behalf of Black children in Delaware, Virginia, and South Carolina relegated to schools segregated.[81] The cases were premised on slightly different facts. But, the common legal question was the validity of separate public schools for Black and White children.[82]

The all-White public school was within a few blocks of the home of Linda Brown, the plaintiff in *Brown v. Board*. She was a Black public school student forced to attend the all-Black school located across dangerous railroad tracks miles from her home. The Kansas Supreme Court denied the claims of *Brown*, upholding *Plessy*. Leading a team of civil rights attorneys, Thurgood Marshall, of the NAACP, appealed the case to the U.S. Supreme Court. The NAACP focused on Justice Harlan's dissent in *Plessy* to form the basis for its legal arguments against segregation.[83] Social scientists led by Black psychologists Drs. Kenneth and Mamie Clark presented studies that demonstrated the invidious emotional scars ("badge of inferiority") left on Black children attending segregated schools.[84]

The *Brown* opinion was, by some accounts, a politically driven decision.[85] The country was in the midst of the Cold War with the Soviet Union and international criticism surrounding the treatment of Blacks in America was of growing concern to the State Department.[86] President Harry Truman signed Executive Order 9981 desegregating the military in 1948.[87] Chief Justice Earl Warren, former governor of California, ascended to the Court in 1953 as a nominee of President Eisenhower.[88] Although Chief Justice Warren was himself resolutely against racial segregation, the Constitution, as interpreted by the Court in prior decisions, supported de jure segregation.[89] The *Brown* case, having originated in the Midwest, offered the Court an opportunity to overturn *Plessy* without directly implicating the South.

Given the high stakes, Chief Justice Warren needed to draft the legal argument in a manner that would result in unanimity on the Court due to the social and political obstacles awaiting the decision.[90] The Supreme Court wrestled with the breadth of the Fourteenth Amendment and the legislatures' intent at the time of its ratification.[91] The Court's decision turned on the ignorance of Justice Brown and his colleagues in the majority—specifically, ignorance regarding the psychological effects of racial segregation.[92] Using the psychological evidence presented by the NAACP, the Court assumed that if Justice Brown and the *Plessy* majority had been aware of the emotional damage caused by separating Black children, that Court would have ruled differently. In 1896, the Court refused to accept that racial segregation would place a badge of inferiority on Blacks. In 1954, the Court decided that racial segregation in public schools violated the Fourteenth Amendment. Segregation is declared inherently unequal in public schools.

Brown v. Board became a social, political, legal, and spiritual symbol of concerted Black efforts for full citizenship. The *Brown* decision is attributed with the commencement of a twentieth century civil rights movement. After *Brown*, Blacks organized regionally or nationally to strategically challenge legal segregation in every aspect of American life.

A Prior Legacy in Kansas:
Williams v. City of Parsons

Brown stemmed from a strong legacy of school cases in the state of Kansas. Within a year of the abolition of slavery, Kansas enacted a statute giving local boards of education the power to choose to racially segregate schools. Most major school districts were not segregated until the *Plessy* decision. In 1881, Leslie Tinnon, a Black student, sued the city of Ottawa, Kansas, to permit him to attend a racially integrated high school.[93] The Ottawa administrators had recently decided "colored children…be place[d] in the frame school house and a teacher of their own color be employed to instruct them; [this would] remedy the evil complained of."[94] The Kansas Supreme Court ruled in favor of the plaintiff. The ruling had little to do with justice for Tinnon, turning instead on whether a small, second-class city such as Ottawa could racially segregate children. Based on Kansas common law, only first-class or large cities such as Topeka could segregate their students. Nonetheless, it was a victory.

In 1903, the Kansas Supreme Court decided *Reynolds v. Topeka.*[95] The suit involved William Reynolds, who sued because he was denied admission into a school for Whites only. Quoting from Brooklyn's *King v. Gallagher* case, in which the Black child was denied access to the Whites-only school, the Kansas Supreme Court asked the rhetorical question:

> [C]onceding, therefore, the fullest manner, that colored persons, the descendants of Africans, are entitled…to equal rights, constitutional and political, civil and social, the question then arises, whether the regulation in question, which provided separate schools for colored children, is a violation of any of these rights….[96]

The response, at that time, was a resounding no. Topeka could segregate its schools without violating the Constitution. The Kansas state court then taunted Black parents, bragging that their failure to appeal segregation in public education to the U.S. Supreme Court "disclose[d] a remarkable consensus of opinion…as to the [negative] result of such an appeal."[97]

Then, in *Williams v. Board of Education of the City of Parsons*, decided in 1908, the Kansas Supreme Court found in favor of Black students challenging the school district's segregation policy.[98] The Court found inequality based on travel distance as opposed to race. The children were forced to walk to a school designated for Blacks located across thirteen train tracks over which one hundred trains of the Texas Railway Company passed daily. Then, they crossed another eight tracks over which the St. Louis and San Francesco Railroad Company ran its trains. In *Thurman Watts v. Coffeyville* (1924),[99] a Black student was denied admission to the high school due to lack of space. The school board claimed if one Black were admitted to the White school, all of them might want to attend, causing future space problems in the building. The Kansas Supreme Court agreed.[100]

Post-Brown Battles:
Brown v. Board of Education of Topeka II
and *Green v. New Kent County School Board*

Unfortunately, Linda Brown and other Black school children in the initial *Brown v. Board I* case would have to wait for integrated schools.[101] In 1955, the NAACP argued *Brown v. Board of Education of Topeka II*. In that case, the NAACP called for immediate integration of public schools. Instead, the U.S. Supreme Court ruled that the school districts would develop their own plans for implementing desegregation monitored by the local federal courts.[102] School districts were under a mandate to desegregate their schools "with all deliberate speed."[103] This theoretical timeline meant little to school boards where racism was embedded in the culture and politics. If *Brown I* was a declaration of war on White-centered American life, then *Brown II* offered a reprieve from any immediate change in the *status quo*. For Blacks, the *Brown II* decision undermined *Brown I* and turned desegregation efforts into an exercise in futility impacting generations of Black school children.

The ruling in *Brown II* was a legal disappointment.[104] Once again, the Court had sought a compromise on the backs of Black people.[105] *Brown II* provided a list of criteria that the U.S. District Courts were to follow in making a determination that school districts were complying in "good faith" with the Court's order.[106] However, without a specific time-frame for implementation, state governments, school boards, and White parents vigorously resisted any plan that would result in real desegregation.[107] In response to *Brown*, state legislatures across the South enacted at least forty-two segregationist laws.[108] In *Southern Manifesto*, segregationists set forth resistance to *Brown*, which they considered an unconstitutional violation of states' rights.[109] The drafters of the *Southern Manifesto* advocated only "lawful means" should be used to reverse it; however, terrorism and violence remained tactics as well.[110]

After inciting White parents, the Little Rock school district used the volatile situation as a pretext for abandoning desegregation of its schools. In 1957, in the case of *Cooper v. Aaron*, the Supreme Court upheld desegregation of the Little Rock, Arkansas, public schools, in spite of threats of violence.[111] The school district refused, arguing that desegregation was dangerous and any efforts to do so would certainly lead to loss of life.[112] When school opened, few White students enrolled in schools with a majority of Black students and Blacks who attempted to enroll in White public schools were assaulted and threatened.[113] When civil rights leader Fred Shuttlesworth attempted to enroll his daughter in an all-White public school, he was brutally beaten by a White mob.[114] Arkansas Governor Orval Faubus called forth the state's National Guard to *prevent* Black children from enrolling in White public schools.[115]

When he discovered that the Black students were secretly enrolled anyway, Faubus allowed an angry White mob to surround the school.[116] President Dwight Eisenhower, former Army general, reluctantly sent in the 101st Airborne paratroopers to restore order. The military had to provide a daily escort to protect Black children attending Central High School in Little Rock.[117] President Eisenhower stated that the enforcement of *Brown* "should not be allowed to create hardship or injustice [for Whites]."[118] There is little evidence that the Black children and adults injured while attempting to attend a desegregated school were ever financially compensated by state or local governments.

Resistance

School boards resisted desegregation at every turn. The Prince Edward County School Board in Virginia decided to close its public schools and contribute financial support to the private, segregated White schools in the county.[119] Upon receiving the Court's edict to desegregate, the school board refused to appropriate money to finance public schools, rationalizing:

The School Board of this county is confronted with a court decree which requires the admission of white and colored children to all the schools of the county without regard to race or color. Knowing the people of this county as we do, we know that it is not possible to operate the schools of this county within the terms of that principle and, at the same time, maintain an atmosphere conducive to the educational benefit of our people.[120]

Other school districts attempted to twist Justice Harlan's dissent in *Plessy* against the plaintiffs by producing an alleged "color-blind" school assignment plan.[121] These so-called desegregation plans tried but failed to allow White students to voluntarily attend the school of their choice.

Although states resisted desegregation, there were certain victories. Within months of the *Brown I* decision, challenges against segregated colleges in Florida and Louisiana were decided in favor of the Black plaintiffs.[122] After a decade of protest and litigation, a Philadelphia private K–12 school restricted to "White male orphans" was desegregated. In that case, deceased steel magnate Stephen Girard provided in his will that only White orphans could receive an education at Girard College. However, the will stated that the trustees of the school must be appointed by the City of Philadelphia. In *Commonwealth of Pennsylvania v. Board of Directors of City Trusts*, the Supreme Court held that the trustees under the will of Girard, appointed by the City of Philadelphia, could not discriminate against Black male orphans.[123] The court reasoned that the will created a trust account from Girard's private fortune, however, the Fourteenth Amendment applied to the operation of the trust by the City of Philadelphia. Public control was evident in that the trustees of the Girard Trust were publicly appointed trustees in complete control of the operation of a privately endowed trust.[124] The desegregation of Girard College served notice as to the breadth of creativity required by the Court to meet the recalcitrance of White school leaders.

School districts attempted to produce an alleged "color-blind" school assignment plan.[125] The color-blind plan was defeated because the Court began to appreciate that with "the background of segregation," such a "limit on remedies would render illusory the promise of *Brown*."[126] Such color-blind plans included offers to White students to voluntarily attend the school of their choice. Of course, they did not choose to attend schools in which the majority of students was Black.

In *McDaniel v. Barresi* (1971), the U.S. Supreme Court held that voluntary desegregation plans are tantamount to maintaining a segregated system.[127] In *Monroe v. Board of Commissioners* (1968), White students were assigned to Black schools and then allowed to transfer.[128] That plan failed. The Supreme Court was presented with the depth of racial bigotry wrought by *Plessy*. Given the history and background of segregation, tepid remedies would render illusory the promise of *Brown*.[129] In *Green v. New Kent County School Board* (1968), the Supreme Court directed school districts to develop affirmative plans to desegregate their schools and evenly distribute the district's resources.[130] The previous dual school systems—one Black, one White—had to be replaced with a unitary, single school system with equal facilities and resources.[131] Transportation, extracurricular activities, faculty and staff salaries, buildings, and the like should bear no evidence of racial distinction.[132]

Busing

After several years of court battles, busing was implemented as a means of desegregating schools. In *Swann v. Charlotte–Mecklenburg*, decided in 1971, the Supreme Court upheld the Charlotte–Mecklenburg, North Carolina, school board's busing policy as a legitimate method for integrating public schools.[133] The Court had demanded a busing plan that "promises realistically to work, and promises realistically to work now."[134] However, busing for integration purposes was a controversial short-lived success. The tactics of evasion practiced by the school districts would continue for decades as lawyers and Black parents were enmeshed in time-consuming and resource-draining litigation.[135] Black communities bore the brunt of busing efforts.

Black public schools built during segregation were demolished. Black students were then bused to the formerly all-White schools. In order to attend those schools, Black students rose early and returned home late.[136] "White flight" proliferated. White parents removed their children from public schools to newly created private Christian academies.[137] Black children were denied admission to these private schools. In *Runyon v. McCrary* (1976), the Supreme Court found that Virginia's racially discriminatory admission to private schools violated a federal civil rights statute.[138] Millions of White parents moved to the suburbs. Legal remedies were sought that would reach suburban schools. However, in *Jenkins v. Missouri* (1995), the Court decided that suburban school districts had not violated the rights of Black urban school children.[139] Therefore, any attempts by city school districts to fashion an interdistrict school assignment plan reaching into the suburbs were unconstitutional.[140]

Desegregation orders were necessary to integrate schools in the North as well as in the South. Schools in California were separated by race and categories—Indian children or children of Chinese, Japanese, or Mongolian parents; Latinos were not permitted to attend schools with White students.[141] Latinos have been subject to segregation and isolation based on poverty and language.[142] Until 1947, the California Education Code provided:

§ 8003. *Schools for Indian children, and children of Chinese, Japanese, or Mongolian parentage: Establishment.* The governing board of any school district may establish separate schools for Indian children, excepting children of Indians who are wards of the United States Government and children of all other Indians who are descendants of the original American Indians of the United States, and for children of Chinese, Japanese, or Mongolian parentage.

§ 8004. *Same: Admission of children into other schools.* When separate schools are established for Indian children or children of Chinese, Japanese, or Mongolian parentage, the Indian children or children of Chinese, Japanese, or Mongolian parentage shall not be admitted into any other school.[143]

However, post-*Brown* busing for desegregation purposes was resisted.[144]

In *Gomperts v. Chase* (1971), the San Mateo, California, school board was unceremoniously voted out after it submitted a viable busing plan. Another school board replaced it, which then approved a voluntary student assignment plan similar to the ineffective plans initiated in the South.[145] Parents of Black and Latino students requested an injunction to stop the new plan.[146] They argued:

California's Bayshore Freeway effectively isolated the Blacks and resulted in a separate and predominantly Black high school.

State planning groups fashioned and built the Black community around that school.

Realtors licensed by the state kept "White property" White and "Black property" Black.

Banks chartered by the state shaped the policies that handicapped Blacks in financing homes other than in Black ghettoes.

Residential segregation, fostered by state-enforced restrictive covenants, resulted in segregated schools.[147]

The Court sympathized with the plaintiffs.

The Court observed that public schools for Blacks and Latinos were "subnormal" and unequal to those of White students.[148] However, the injunction was denied because there was not enough time available to develop a workable plan before the start of school. In another California case, *Guey Heung Lee* (1971), the Court stated that it was apparent that the force of segregation remained even after the statute providing for the establishment of separate schools had been repealed.[149] The San Francisco School Board continued to draw school assignment districts meticulously along racial lines.[150] More urgent measures were needed to remove segregation from the public schools root and branch.

Yet, after the state's highest court developed a busing remedy for de facto (by tradition) segregation in Los Angeles public schools, California voters amended the state's constitution, thus nullifying the court's ruling. Mary Ellen Crawford, the lead plaintiff in this case action, appealed to the Supreme Court, arguing that the state's referendum, Proposition I, was a violation of the Fourteenth Amendment. Proposition I was crafted as if the major concern was "enhancing the ability of parents to participate in the educational process, preserving harmony and tranquility in this state and its public schools, preventing the waste of scarce fuel, resources, and protecting the environment."

Poorer Schools:
San Antonio School District v. Rodriguez

Public schools in low-income communities evidence generations of discrimination and the lack of investment in children of color. A legal strategy to equalize financing of public schools was rebuffed by the U.S. Supreme Court. In 1973, the Supreme Court was presented with a Texas school district's appeal of a finding that schools financed by property taxes favored the wealthy while leaving poor neighborhoods with struggling schools and less than adequate educational opportunities. In *San Antonio v. Rodriguez*, the district court found in favor of the Latino student plaintiffs who had been disadvantaged by underfunded schools.[151] That court found that wealth was a suspect class and education was a fundamental right. However, on appeal, the U.S. Supreme Court, led by Chief Justice Warren Burger, reversed the decision.[152] In an opinion authored by Justice Louis Powell, a public school education was not deemed a fundamental right guaranteed under the U.S. Constitution, economic status did not rise to the level of analysis under the strict scrutiny standard, and therefore, the state's property tax system used for funding schools did not violate the equal protection clause of the Constitution.[153]

In *Crawford v. Board of Education of Los Angeles*, 458 U.S. 527 (1982), Justice Powell, on behalf of the Court, wrote that the state must have the power to decide how to best use its resources; racial segregation was not mandated by state law.[154] The Court sustained Proposition I as a nonracial exercise of the voter's political will. Unsure whether future desegregation efforts might become reality, White residents of Los Angeles fled to the suburbs.

White Flight

In similar fashion, public schools in cities across the country were attended mainly by minorities.[155] White parents opposed to busing and desegregation left the cities in "White flight." White havens were created in suburbs that precluded Blacks[156] (see Chapter 3). Racial integration became one of a number of reasons to abandon public schools for private ones.[157] Between 1968 and 1980, White student enrollment declined in all major city schools.[158] For example, Atlanta's White student enrollment dropped from 62 percent in 1962 to 12 percent in 1975.[159]

CITY	% DECLINE IN WHITE STUDENTS
New York City	45.7
Los Angeles	63.4
Chicago	62.1
Philadelphia	41.2
Detroit	77.8
Houston	62.8
Baltimore	58.0
Memphis	54.6
San Diego	37.9
Washington, D.C.	59.9
Milwaukee	58.2
New Orleans	71.0
Cleveland	66.3
Atlanta	85.7
Boston	63.3
Denver	58.7

De facto (by tradition) segregation replaced de jure (legal) segregation in America's schools as school districts in the North and South refused to comply with court orders to integrate.[160] In the South, federal courts upheld the rights of the Ku Klux Klan to hold regular meetings in a Baton Rouge, Louisiana, public school.[161]

For many urban school districts in the North, busing for desegregation within the city is no longer practicable given the small number of White students.[162] Urban school boards and the courts focused extraordinary resources on coaxing White students from the suburbs or private schools into public city schools.[163] At city schools, underachievement resulted from overcrowded classrooms, limited resources, and inequitable funding levels.[164] Black and Latino students have become more racially segregated.[165] The urban middle-class tax base is dwindling. Too many schools for children of color are now in communities of poverty, "associated with low parental involvement, lack of resources, less experienced and [less] credentialed teachers with high teacher turnover—all of which combine to exacerbate educational inequality for Black students."[166] For decades, desegregation efforts, specifically busing, overshadowed the education of Black students.

In 2002, President George W. Bush signed the No Child Left Behind Act. This legislation, intended to raise the academic standards of all children in public education, directed especially at those children in "failing" schools.[167] Unfortunately, there is relatively little federal funding for states to reach the problems and fully implement the program. The New York State Appellate Court made clear where children in schools in the New York City public school system with a majority of minorities enrolled fell within the socioracial hierarchy. In *Campaign for Fiscal Equity, Inc. v. State of New York* (2002), that court ruled New York State need only provide an eighth-grade education to meet the state's mandate of an adequate education.[168] That court explained that "the skills required to enable a person to obtain employment, vote and serve on a jury are imparted between grades 8 and 9…"[169] The presumption is that Black and brown children need preparation for employment and political engagement of the most basic type suitable for the lowest rung of the socioracial ladder. Poor educational facilities are an important characteristic of insular poverty. These schools prevent participation in economic life at a substantive level.[170] Poorly prepared in underfunded schools, Black children are often made fodder for a waiting criminal justice system.

Affirmative Action/Reverse
Discrimination: *Bakke* and *Grutter*

One hundred years after the Emancipation Proclamation and nearly ten years after the *Brown* decision, disfranchisement remained a reality for Black school children in America. A civil rights movement challenged post-*Brown* segregation. In March of 1963, hundreds of thousands of protesters marched through Washington, D.C., for jobs and freedom. Their hopes lay with President John F. Kennedy's call for social reform. However, President Kennedy was assassinated in 1963 leaving his vice president, Lyndon Baines Johnson, a Southerner, to usher in major civil rights legislation. President Johnson signed the Civil Rights Act of 1964 as well as the Voting Rights Act of 1965.

In September of 1965, Johnson issued Executive Order 11246. That order required government contractors to take "affirmative action" in hiring minority employees. His successor, President Richard Nixon, initiated the Philadelphia Plan, an experiment to guarantee the hiring of Blacks in construction and craft unions. The 1969 initiative did not impose quotas. But, it required affirmative action in meeting employment goals. The federal government recognized the connection between American history and present economic obstacles.

However, by 1978, the country was in economic distress brought about by a global recession. America's economic woes made it difficult to recall the connection between the history of American racism and the need for affirmative action. In the North, busing Black school children in Boston led Whites to riot. In the South, Black parents grew frustrated with recalcitrant school systems relying on a time factor of "all deliberate speed" to stall integration. Legal decisions such as those in Denver, Georgia, and Oklahoma promised desegregation, only to disappoint in practice.[171]

In California, a White applicant, Allen Bakke, was denied admission to the medical school of the University of California at Davis. Bakke claimed he was denied admission based on "reverse discrimination" in violation of the equal-protection clause of the Fourteenth Amendment.[172] Under a special admissions program, Black and minority applicants were given an allotted sixteen out of a total of hundreds of spaces in the medical school. The school reasoned that Black doctors were needed and most likely to practice medicine in medically underserved areas. The Court had to decide whether voluntary measures at the University of California Medical School, intended to remedy the present effects of their past discrimination, were constitutional.[173] The Court found that the admissions policy prevented Whites from competing.[174]

The Supreme Court struck down the program, stating it could not support a remedy in the absence of judicial, legislative, or administrative findings of constitutional or statutory violations.[175] Unless the medical school could provide evidence of its own discrimination, the school could not provide a remedy for Black applicants. A plurality made up of Justices Stevens, Burger, Stewart, and Rehnquist held in *Bakke* that the admissions program violated Title VI of the Civil

Rights Act of 1964. Another plurality made up of Justices Brennan, White, Marshall, and Blackman dissented.[176] Justice Powell cast the critical vote approving the use of race in school admissions but only if there is a proven compelling government interest. He did not find such an interest, assessing the affirmative action program under challenge as an unconstitutional violation of Bakke's Fourteenth Amendment rights.

Despite a history replete with disfranchisement, the state must have a compelling reason to create an affirmative action plan and race can only be one factor in that plan.[177] The very hard-fought cases used to gain educational benefits for Blacks were now applied against affirmative action efforts.[178] In interpreting the Fourteenth Amendment, Justice Powell stated:

> Nothing in the Constitution supports the notion that individuals may be asked to suffer otherwise impermissible burdens in order to enhance the societal standing of their ethnic groups. Second, preferential programs may only reinforce common stereotypes holding that certain groups are unable to achieve success without special protection based on a factor having no relationship to individual worth.[179]

Powell's analysis would become the standard by which affirmative action policies in education would be judged.[180]

The Supreme Court was presented with a number of reverse discrimination cases not directly related to education. In *United Steelworkers of America v. Weber*, the Court upheld an affirmative action plan challenged by White steelworkers.[181] In *Fullilove v. Klutznick*, a set-aside program benefiting Blacks, Hispanics, Asians, Native Americans, and Eskimos was upheld by the Court in 1980.[182] In *Firefighters Local Union No. 1784 v. Stotts*, the Supreme Court found that Blacks recently hired under an affirmative action program could be laid off first because they lacked seniority.[183] In *Local 28 of the Sheet Metal Workers v. Equal Employment Opportunity Commission*, the Supreme Court upheld an affirmative action hiring plan challenged by White union members because the plan benefited more than the specific Blacks harmed by their discrimination.[184]

In *United States v. Paradise*, decided in 1987, the Supreme Court upheld a challenge to a court-ordered affirmative action plan. The plan required Alabama to promote Black state troopers. Prior to that decision, none of the 232 state troopers with a rank above corporal were Black.[185] However, Black teachers in Jackson, Michigan, would not fare as well. In *Wygant v. Jackson Board of Education*, the Supreme Court ruled in favor of White teachers challenging a collective bargaining agreement that allowed the Jackson School District to retain Black teachers during layoffs in order to maintain racial balances in the faculty.[186]

With the election of a conservative Republican, President Ronald Reagan, in 1980, the country entered an era of social conservatism. Reagan and his successor, George Bush, established an anti-affirmative action agenda. "Reverse discrimination" law suits were brought by Whites in education as well as employment and federal contracts. The legal standards that would allow affirmative action were made narrower in each case. In 1989, in *Croson v. City of Richmond*, the Supreme Court struck down an affirmative action program that set aside a percentage of government contracts for Black construction companies.[187] The Court determined that an affirmative action plan that could not be linked to specific acts of past governmental discrimination in that particular area was unconstitutional.[188] There must be a compelling governmental interest and a narrowly tailored plan. A government's attempt to address racism now must be directly linked to specific instances of past racism. Because the City of Richmond failed to identify a need for remedial action in the awarding of its public construction contracts, its affirmative action plan violated the equal-protection rights of White contractors.[189] America's socioracial hierarchy is conveniently forgotten. Attacks on affirmative action continue.

A few years later, Cheryl Hopwood, a White law school applicant, was denied admission to the University of Texas Law School. Hopwood argued that she had been discriminated against solely because of her race.[190] The trial court agreed. The law school appealed. The U.S. Court of Appeals ruled that the school's consideration of race in admissions violated Hopwood's equal protection rights.[191] The law school appealed to the U.S. Supreme Court. The school understood the need for an affirmative action plan. However, in 1992, the Supreme Court refused to review the decision. The Court let stand the appellate court's ruling as properly decided.[192] Despite the legacy of *Sweatt v. Painter*, the court found no justification for an affirmative action policy at the University of Texas Law School.[193] The threat of reverse discrimination had a chilling effect, preventing the development of affirmative action efforts in education.

Hopwood and *Croson* undermined efforts to create affirmative action plans. Colleges and professional schools feared protracted and costly reverse discrimination litigation. In public schools, busing and desegregation plans were challenged as a violation of the equal-protection rights of White students.[194] In 1995, the Supreme Court struck down another government affirmative action policy. A nonminority company, Adarand Constructors, Inc., challenged a federal government program that provided incentives to encourage contracts with minority-owned business enterprises.[195] The "strict scrutiny" legal standard, the Court's most rigorous, was applied.[196] Adarand won.

In a prior case, *Wygant v. Jackson Board of Education*, the Court decided that strict scrutiny must be applied in cases alleging race discrimination by a governmental entity.[197] In *Adarand*, Justice Sandra Day O'Connor indicated that the strict scrutiny theory did not necessarily doom affirmative action. Justice O'Connor explained that "the unhappy persistence of both the practice and the lingering effects of racial discrimination against minority groups in this country is an unfortunate reality, and government is not disqualified from acting in response to it."[198] However, the *Adarand* decision appeared only to embolden affirmative action opponents. As with any advancements by Blacks in America, the backlash was brutal.

In 1996, the State of California passed Proposition 209. This statewide referendum prohibited affirmative action in public education, public employment, and public contracting.[199] Once enacted, the anti-affirmative action legislation was challenged by Blacks, Latinos, women, and coalitions comprising educators, unions, and public officials.[200] The Supreme Court denied a request for review. Thus, the decision was allowed to stand without review.[201] The number of Black and Latino students attending graduate school, law school, and colleges in California plummeted.[202]

In 2003, the Supreme Court was presented with two reverse discrimination cases against the University of Michigan. The Supreme Court had last addressed the use of race in public higher education over twenty-five years earlier in the *Bakke* case. The Michigan cases were brought by White applicants challenging their denial of admission to the University of Michigan.[203] Jennifer Gratz challenged the admissions program at the University of Michigan's College of Literature, Science and Arts.[204] The college admissions process awarded twenty points to applicants from underrepresented minority groups.[205] Barbara Grutter challenged the use of race in admissions at the University of Michigan Law School,[206] which used race as one factor among a list of criteria in admissions.[207] Black applicants as well as other candidates of color benefited from the program.

The Supreme Court, in a divided opinion delivered by Justice O'Connor, struck down the use of race by the college in *Gratz* as unconstitutional.[208] Giving points was deemed a "quota system," which allegedly shielded Black applicants from competing with their White peers.[209] In *Grutter*, the Supreme Court found that the University of Michigan School of Law had a compelling interest in having a diverse student body.[210] The Court reasoned that law schools are a training ground for our country's future leaders. The state of Michigan needed to expose law students "to widely diverse people, cultures, ideas, and viewpoints" in order to equip them for leadership in an increasingly global business world as well as a diverse American society.[211]

The divergence in the Supreme Court's decisions in *Grutter* and *Gratz* demonstrates the complexities of any efforts made to address centuries of racism and ongoing discrimination in education. Diversity is now the key word. Maintaining diversity is a compelling state interest. The handful of Black students who are admitted based on a formula where race is only a single factor are performing a civic function. Their classmates are future White leaders of the free world who need to associate with a diverse population. It brings an appearance of "legitimacy in the eyes of the citizenry."[212] The words are taken with sincerity in their support of diversity and affirmative action. However, despite numbing oppression, Blacks have presented their case to the courts century after century, yet, decades after *Brown* their presence through an affirmative action program is justified only because the presence of Blacks will benefit White students.

Affirmative action for Whites in America has taken many shapes. After World War II, the G.I. Bill provided Whites with low-cost mortgages and tuition grants, points on government examinations, and low-interest business loans.[213] Another such affirmative action program was introduced by President Franklin D. Roosevelt in the 1930s, called the New Deal.[214] The spoils of these affirmative action programs (homes, real estate, social position, corporations) are now the inheritance of generations of White offspring.

Affirmative action programs were provided to Whites at a time when Blacks were forcibly segregated and precluded from any direct benefit from the programs.[215] Given the abbreviated history of affirmative action for Blacks, Justice Harlan's words of dissent in the *Civil Rights Cases* of 1883 still ring true: "It is, I submit, scarcely just to say that the colored race has been the special favorite of the laws."[216]

Present-Day Vestiges: Segregated and Underfunded Public Schools

Governmental failures and entrenched racism continue to undermine the centuries-long effort of Black parents and White advocates to gain an equal education for Black children. Progress made by legal challenges is undermined by social upheaval and continued prejudice. White flight has left public schools across the country with a majority of minority students.[217] Historically, public schools attended predominantly by Blacks were underfunded. Racism endemic in systemic underfunding continues today. In 2004, Alabama held a referendum to repeal a provision of its constitution that mandates racially segregated schools. The vote was merely symbolic, given the decisions of the Supreme Court and Congressional acts. This is fortunate because the referendum was soundly defeated by those who would maintain segregated schools. *Brown* presented American society an opportunity for positive change, which has been consistently resisted. This worthy battle has continued into the new millennium with *Meredith v. Jefferson* and *Parents Involved in Community Schools v. Seattle School District, No. 1.* In 2007, the Supreme Court decided when it is legally appropriate to use race as a factor in public school admissions.[218]

Following emancipation, Herculean efforts were made by Blacks to become literate. But, a lack of political will, fear of competition, and racial prejudice stymied federal financial support for Black achievement in education. It is a tale retold with great consistency. Commencing with *Roberts*, Blacks have faced numerous obstacles in the struggle to obtain an equal education for their children. Despite *Brown*, governmental failures, social tradition, entrenched racism, and an uncertain Supreme Court have prevented the realization of *Brown*. For most Black children, the path to education still leads to segregated underfunded public schools. One is reminded of the Bible verse, "there is no straw given unto thy servants and they say to us, make bricks."[219] Blacks and other racial minorities, must continue the struggle against educational disfranchisement by law and tradition. The education of future generations of children depend upon it.

3

PROPERTY RIGHTS AND OWNERSHIP

The tragedy of Reconstruction is the failure of the Black masses to acquire land, since without the economic security provided by land ownership the freedmen were soon deprived of the political and civil rights which they had won.

Claude Oubre, *Forty Acres and a Mule*

I believe that the division of men into separate communities and their living in society and association with fellows...are both divine institutions...We have the right to determine who shall be members of our community, and...I do not see where it comes in that we are bound to receive into our community those whose mingling with us might be detrimental to our interests. I do not believe that a superior race is bound to receive among it those of an inferior race...

U.S. Senator Peter Van Winkle,
Cong. Globe 39th Cong., 1st Sess., 498 (1866)

Shelter. It is a basic human need. From the colonial period forward, Blacks have sought to overcome restrictions on where and with whom they could live. Examining Supreme Court decisions related to property rights and race reveals a long history of societal discrimination in land and property ownership that has had a great impact on present-day land ownership and the attainment of wealth. For much of this country's history, housing determined employment opportunities, access to education, and health care.[1] For centuries, the eligibility to vote was limited to land owners.

This chapter focuses on the development of legal protections against race-based discrimination in housing and property ownership that has been uneven at best. Too often, federal and state governments have colluded with private actors to preclude Blacks from purchasing land or restrict them to certain communities. Despite this fact, Blacks continued to press toward home ownership and cross racially designated geographical boundaries. The cases in this chapter evidence the obstacles—past and continuing conflicts—facing Blacks when they transcend from a sociolegal status of chattel to that of real property owners.

Forty Acres and a Mule:
The Start to Broken Promises

Enslaved Blacks were forced to live as laborers attached to the land of another. They were kept dependent on their slaveholders for food and shelter. Unlike servants, most enslaved persons could not own property. For more than two hundred years free Blacks were relegated to specific areas assigned to them by law. Although the Thirteenth Amendment abolished slavery, upon their emancipation the vast majority of the now free Blacks were without land or any means by which to purchase land. Over four million Blacks were left homeless. The Homestead Act of 1862 applied only to non-Confederate Whites giving them prized land in the South.

In 1865, General William T. Sherman of the Union Army issued Special Order #15 setting aside the Sea Islands of South Carolina and a tract of land on the southern coast of Charleston for Black ownership. Each Black union soldier was promised 40 acres of land and an Army mule to till the soil. This land as well as other abandoned land confiscated by the Union Army from members of the Confederacy was to be given to newly freed African citizens. General Oliver Otis Howard, for whom Howard University in the District of Columbia is named, chaired the Freedmen's Bureau, a federal government agency established to assist the newly emancipated Africans in their transition to freedom. However, Black land ownership under Sherman's plan of 40 acres and a mule was quickly terminated by President Andrew Johnson. Upon hearing of this Black land ownership plan, President Johnson issued an executive order returning the land to the ex-Confederates.

Despite the undermining actions of President Johnson and the failure of the Freedmen's Bureau, thousands of manumitted, free, and emancipated Blacks obtained land through various means. One such method was the Southern Homestead Act of 1866. Although this act was created to promote Black landownership, the Southern Homestead Act became a mechanism for Whites to secure the best land for themselves, leaving rugged hills and swampland for Blacks. Additionally, these Black land buyers, most of whom were illiterate, faced racial oppression and "confidence men or con artists" selling fraudulent deeds. Blacks lived under the constant threat of death in the hands of those Whites who envied them their land or refused to accept Blacks as full citizens. Despite these obstacles placed before them, by the 1870s Blacks held significant land acreage in South Carolina, Virginia, and Arkansas. By 1900, one quarter of Black farmers in the South owned farmland.[2] In 1870, 80 percent of Blacks lived in the rural South.[3]

However, racial oppression, the merciless sharecropping system, and a prospect of bettering their lives motivated hundreds of thousands of Blacks to migrate from the South to northern cities. The "Great Migration" of Blacks to the North transformed the racial composition of urban centers. However, racial segregation in housing remained an obstacle for Blacks in the North and the former Confederate South. Once in the cities, Blacks were relegated to substandard housing. Prevented from living in predominantly White communities, Blacks were designated to racially contained areas.

Real estate deeds with racially restrictive covenants, or contract provisions, precluded the transfer or sale of homes by Whites to Blacks and, sometimes, to Asians, Mexicans, and Jews. Certain restrictive covenants explicitly stated that Blacks could not own, lease, or occupy a home formerly occupied by Whites. In California, for example, Chinese immigrants were segregated into racially designated neighborhoods.[4]

Land ownership remains the foremost mechanism to obtain or determine wealth in American society. In 1896, the *Plessy v. Ferguson* decision upheld a state's right to enact laws racially segregating social interaction, including housing.[5] In rural areas, "Black Codes" were enacted to entrap Blacks with rental agreements for barren land.

Predictably, the crops failed, leaving the tenant in debt to the land-owner. One such Alabama statute of 1907 states:

[A]ny person who, with intent to injure or defraud his landlord, enters into any contract in writing for the rent of land and thereby obtains any money or other personal property from such landlord, and with like intent, without just cause, and without refunding such money or paying for such property, refuses or fails to cultivate such land, or to comply with his contract relative thereto, must, on conviction, be punished by a fine in double the damage suffered by the injured party, but not more than three hundred dollars, one-half of said fine to go to the county and one-half to the party injured.[6]

Failure to repay the owner resulted in criminal convictions. In *Bailey v. Alabama*, the U.S. Supreme Court upheld this pernicious statute.[7] Infused with the imprimatur of the Court, racism created legal obstacles for Blacks seeking to gain a foothold in the American economy through farming. In the cities, Blacks were relegated to property or homes in areas based on their race, law, and de facto racial discrimination in housing and property ownership.

State Discrimination: *Buchanan v. Warley*

Louisville, Kentucky, was the site of the earliest U.S. Supreme Court decision challenging racial discrimination in housing. A Kentucky statute restricted the conveyance or sale of property based on race. In *Buchanan v. Warley* (1917), a White realtor, Charles Buchanan, entered into an agreement to sell a property on the corner of Thirty-Sixth Avenue and Pflanz Street to William Warley, a Black postal worker who was also an officer in the Louisville branch of the NAACP.[8] The sale agreement contained a clause that allowed Warley to void the sale if he was unable to occupy the home due to Louisville's racial hous-ing restrictions.[9] Under the law, Blacks could not live on a residential block that was occupied by a majority of White residents.

Blacks could work constructing homes for Whites. However, Blacks were prohibited from living in a home on a street of majority Whites residents. Whites could not sell land to Blacks if the Black purchaser intended to build a residence on a block occupied by a majority of White residents. Under certain exceptions, Black servants and employees could work and live within the homes of Whites on the block. The statute was enacted to:

> prevent conflict and ill-feeling between the white and colored races... and to preserve the public peace and promote the general welfare, by making reasonable provisions requiring, as far as practicable, the use of separate blocks, for residences, places of abode, and places of assembly by white and colored people respectively.[10]

As the number of Blacks in the community grew, concerned White neighbors sought enforcement of the statute against Warley.

Warley was told he could not occupy the property he planned to purchase. He then refused to pay Buchanan for the land. Buchanan wanted to enforce the agreement, so he brought an action against Warley for breach of contract. Buchanan argued that the Louisville statute prevented him from completing the sale of his property to Warley. He alleged that the segregation statute violated his rights under the Fourteenth Amendment of the U.S. Constitution. The City of Louisville countered that a statute separating the races was a legal prerogative based on the *Plessy* decision. Additionally, a state's police power provided the authority to protect the general public welfare from violence that could erupt if the races lived in close proximity to one another. Moreover, the city argued, the statute was not discriminatory because it in turn precluded Whites from occupying a residence on a block where Blacks were predominant. Kentucky's courts had found in favor of the City of Louisville.

The U.S. Supreme Court received the case on appeal. The issue before the high court was whether the City of Louisville could prevent a White seller from conveying his property to a Black buyer based solely on the race of the buyer, given the Thirteenth Amendment, which abolished slavery, and the Fourteenth Amendment, which provided for full citizenship and equal protection and guaranteed due process as well as privileges and immunities. Both amendments include enforcement provisions that allow Congress to enact legislation protecting the rights of Blacks against governmental acts that hinder realization of these rights, as did the Civil Rights Acts of 1866 and 1870.

The Civil Rights Act of 1866 states: "All citizens of the United States shall have the same right, in every state and territory, as is enjoyed by white citizens thereof to inherit, purchase, lease, sell, hold and convey real and personal property."[11] The Civil Rights Act of 1870 states: "All persons within the jurisdiction of the United States shall have the same right in every state and territory to make and enforce contracts..."[12] The U.S. Congress relied on these federal statutes to protect the privileges and immunities and due-process rights of Blacks against discrimination by states. The Supreme Court found in favor of Warley and Buchanan. The Court held that the City of Louisville's housing segregation statute interfered with the conveyance of property to a Black purchaser. Additionally, the property rights of Buchanan were violated. Therefore, the statute was an unconstitutional restriction in violation of the Civil Rights Acts and the Fourteenth Amendment. *Buchanan v. Warley* remains a landmark case in the struggle for access to housing.

Blacks who confronted implicit racism based on state laws and local ordinances could now rely on *Buchanan*. Whites who wanted to assist in the desegregation effort could look to Buchanan's role in this case.[13] However, the legal obstacles inflicted by *Plessy* remained after *Buchanan*. In *Buchanan*, the injured party could litigate a Fourteenth Amendment case involving race discrimination in housing only if it turned on governmental interference with the property contract. The effect of *Buchanan* was confined to laws segregating or interfering with housing contracts based on race. Meanwhile, banks refused to provide home mortgages to Blacks, lynch mobs attacked Black families who moved into formerly all-White neighborhoods, and so-called "home improvement associations" were formed by White members of the community intent on driving Black families out of the neighborhood.[14] *Buchanan* did not reach these private acts of discrimination.

In Detroit, Dr. Ossian Sweet defended his house against an attack by a White mob determined to drive his family out of the community.[15] Sweet was raised in Barstow, Florida. He had graduated from Wilberforce College in Ohio and Howard University Medical School.[16] He completed a year of postgraduate work in Vienna and Paris, returning to Detroit in 1924.[17] In 1925, Sweet and his family moved into a Detroit neighborhood with covenants restricting home ownership to Whites.[18] Angry Whites formed the Waterworks Park Improvement Association.[19] Other Black families had been driven out of Detroit's White neighborhoods prior to the arrival of the Sweets.[20]

On September 9, 1925, a mob of Whites began throwing rocks at Sweet's home and screaming profanities.[21] Sweet and his brothers retrieved their guns.[22] Shots were fired. Six of the eleven people inside the Sweet home fired weapons. Two people in the mob were struck. Leon Breiner, a White former coal miner who lived half a block from the Sweets, was killed.[23] The police stormed Sweet's house and arrested everyone inside.[24] Judge Frank Murphy was assigned the adjudication of the case.[25] James Weldon Johnson of the NAACP assisted in Sweet's defense.[26] Clarence Darrow, famous for criminal cases and the *Scopes* monkey case, represented the Sweets at trial.[27] Eleven defendants, including Ossian Sweet, his brother Otis, and Ossian's wife Gladys, were charged with Breiner's murder.

The first criminal trial lasted seven weeks and ended in a mistrial.[28] At the second trial, Henry Sweet was charged with the murder of Breiner. Sweet admitted to firing into the mob as it approached the house.[29] Darrow defended the rights of Sweet to protect his family and home from a murderous mob.[30] The second all-White jury returned a verdict of not guilty by reason of self-defense and Sweet was acquitted.[31] *People v. Sweet* represented a rare moment in American justice. Far too often, race was the deciding factor in where a person could live. White communities created mechanisms to thwart Blacks who wanted a choice in where they lived. This rarely mentioned case is evidence of the extent to which Blacks and other racial minorities had to fight for this choice.

Restrictive Covenants: *Hansberry v. Lee* and *Shelley v. Kraemer*

Whites who opposed fair-housing opportunities created private agreements called restrictive covenants to preclude Blacks from residing in certain areas. In *Hansberry v. Lee* (1940),[32] Blacks in Chicago sought to invalidate a restrictive covenant imposed by Whites in the city's Washington Park community. Private home owners, not the government, created the segregation provisions precluding Blacks. The restrictive covenant prevented the sale or lease of land by the owners to any person of color if 95 percent of the home owners signed an agreement restricting the property to Whites only. In *Hansberry v. Lee*, a White property owner sought to sell his property to Blacks. His White neighbors filed suit to enforce the restrictive covenant. The Black potential buyers began a complex litigation strategy that focused on whether 95 percent of the property owners had indeed signed the contract. The White homeowners argued that the agreement "ran with the land" and bound all subsequent purchasers to the restriction barring Blacks from ownership.

The U.S. Supreme Court did not reach the merits of the case. Instead, the Court found that the present class of Black litigants was free to challenge the 95 percent rule.[33] Although the case is considered too fact specific to meet the needs of the millions of Blacks affected by restrictive covenants, it raised the visibility of housing discrimination. Lorraine Hansberry's internationally acclaimed Broadway play, *A Raisin in the Sun*, explores the tensions within a Black family forced to live in the slums of Chicago when their dream of home ownership in the suburbs is met with resistance by the White residents. The fictional version ended with more success than the real case.

The NAACP wrestled with a legal strategy to defeat private race segregation provisions in real estate contracts. In 1948, the Supreme Court decided *Shelley v. Kraemer*.[34] The Court's ruling provided the formulae for a successful test of that civil rights strategy. In that case, the Shelley family attempted to purchase property in St. Louis, Missouri, that was bound by a racially restrictive covenant. Under the private contract between homeowners:

> A property is...restricted...for fifty years...As a condition precedent to the sale...no part of said property...shall be...occupied by any person not of the Caucasian race, it being intended hereby to restrict the use of said property for said period of time against the occupancy as owners or tenants of any portion of said property for resident or other purpose by people of the Negro or Mongolian race.[35]

The Missouri Supreme Court upheld the restrictive covenant.

The Shelleys appealed. They argued that state courts were being used to enforce racially discriminatory agreements. The U.S. Supreme Court was forced to decide whether a state court that used its authority to enforce provisions of a restrictive covenant denying property rights to a person based on race or skin color violated the Civil Rights Acts of 1866 and 1870. Intriguingly, at the time of the creation of this discriminatory covenant, Black families lived in the designated "Whites-only" area. One Black family had lived in the community for decades prior to the arrival of Whites who, in turn, drafted the restrictions.

At about the same time in Michigan, the McGhees, a Black family, acquired title and moved into a home bound by a covenant restricting property ownership to the Caucasian race based upon the agreement of 80 percent of the White property owners in the proscribed area. The White neighbors who signed the agreement brought an action in state court to enforce the covenant and evict the Black family. The state trial court found in favor of the White neighbors and entered a decree giving the McGhee family ninety days to vacate the property. The McGhees appealed, arguing that the state court decree violated their Fourteenth Amendment rights. The Michigan State Supreme Court upheld the eviction.[36]

Due to the similar fact pattern, the U.S. Supreme Court consolidated the cases of *McGhee v. Sipes* (1947) with that of *Shelley v. Kraemer* to determine whether state enforcement of private agreements to discriminate violated the Fourteenth Amendment. First, it ruled that the Fourteenth Amendment does not reach private discrimination. Only governmental action can trigger the equal-protection clause, due process, and privileges and immunities protections of the Fourteenth Amendment. However, racial covenants precluding Blacks violated *Buchanan*. The government cannot enforce discriminant housing contracts.

A deed with a racially restrictive provision or an agreement between neighbors is a private contract. However, the enforcement of that contract by the state court violated the Civil Rights Acts of 1866 and 1870 and the Fourteenth Amendment. Chief Justice Vinson, who delivered the opinion of the Court, stated that, except for the active intervention of the state courts, supported by the full panoply of state power, petitioners would have been free to occupy the property in question without restraint.[37] State enforcement of private discriminatory agreements was struck down in 1948.

In *Hurd v. Hodge* (1948),[38] a companion case to *Kraemer*, the district court as well as the U.S. Court of Appeals for the District of Columbia had upheld a restrictive covenant that precluded Blacks from ever owning or occupying certain homes in the northwest section of the city. Violating the ban exposed Blacks to a $2,000 penalty in the form of a lien on the property that could be assessed against the violator. Hurd purchased a home in a racially restricted area, which resulted in legal action against him and his family. Although he maintained that he was "Mohawk Indian and not a Negro," the trial court directed him to vacate the property within sixty days. Upon appeal, the U.S. Supreme Court held that the trial court's enforcement of the restrictive covenant violated public policy and that the District of Columbia was governed by the Civil Rights Act of 1866, which is applicable "to every state and territory."

Restricting the Japanese: *Oyama v. California*

In 1948, the U.S. Supreme Court was presented with a case involving California's Alien Land Law,[39] which forbade aliens (in this case, Asians) from American citizenship and from acquiring, owning, occupying, leasing, or transferring agricultural land. This state legislation was deeply rooted in decades of animosity toward the growing Asian population in California. Beginning with the arrival of a substantial number of Chinese immigrants in 1850, White trade unionists feared competition and White politicians catering to unions enacted restrictive laws against Asian laborers.[40] Japanese immigration in the early 1900s led to renewed antipathy toward Asians.

The Empire of Japan's attack on Pearl Harbor on December 1, 1941, ignited long simmering conflicts over employment, land, and opportunities combined with cultural and language differences. Citizens, legal residents, and visitors of Japanese descent became the focus of anti-Asian laws.[41] Within months of the attack on Pearl Harbor, President Franklin D. Roosevelt signed Executive Order 9066,[42] giving the military authority to enact laws to protect the country against invasion and sabotage.[43] Using this authority, General John L. DeWitt issued Civilian Exclusion Order 34, which led to the evacuation of all persons of Japanese ancestry in the western United States to military camps for the duration of World War II. Property laws such as California's Alien Land Law were enacted during this time period. Plaintiffs Fred and Kaijiro Oyama resided in such a camp.

In *Oyama v. California* (1948),[44] Fred, a minor, was a property owner and U.S. citizen. However, the property in question was purchased by his guardian and father, Kaijiro, who was not a citizen and therefore ineligible to own property under the Alien Land Law. The Alien Land Act prohibited an ineligible person from using a relative to purchase or convey land. The original White seller of the property sought to repossess the land, alleging that Kaijiro purchased it by fraud using his son's identity. The United States–Japan Treaty of 1911, which guaranteed Japanese in this country the right to own and lease land for residential and commercial purposes, was repealed in 1945.[45] State laws also forbade Kaijiro from becoming a naturalized citizen and thus eligible to purchase land in his own name.

The U.S. Supreme Court received the case on appeal. The Court refused to rule on the constitutionality of the Alien Land Act. Instead, it focused on whether the land purchased by Kaijiro Oyama on his son's behalf was a fraudulent purchase in violation of the Alien Land Act. Led by Chief Justice Vinson, the Court found that to deny ownership of the land to Fred would violate his Fourteenth Amendment right to own property. Since Fred was an American citizen, California's attempt to deny his claim to the property was based solely on the fact that Kaijiro, his father, was of Japanese ancestry. The opinion stated that "the only basis for this discrimination against an American citizen...is the fact that his father was Japanese and not American, Russian, Chinese, or English."[46]

In his concurring opinion, Justice Murphy stated that "the Alien Land Law...assumes there is some racial characteristic, common to all Japanese aliens, that makes them unfit to own or use agricultural land in California,"[47] adding that the "Alien Land Law does violence to the high ideals of the Constitution...and the Charter of the United Nations."[48] The majority opinion addressed necessary limitations on a state's ability to control the conveyance of property to a citizen.

Race, Urban Renewal, and Eminent
Domain: *Berman v. Parker*

In 1954, the U.S. Supreme Court decided *Brown v. Topeka Board
of Education*, finding that racially segregated public schools are
inherently unequal.[49] In that same year, the Court decided *Berman v.
Parker* (1954).[50] In *Berman*, the Court was faced with a challenge by
Blacks who were evicted from their property based on urban renewal
imperatives. At issue was the use of local governmental police power
to take possession of privately owned land for public purposes. Under
the "takings clause" of the Fifth Amendment, the government can
take private property for public use by eminent domain, provided the
owner receives just compensation.[51] Berman, a store owner in Washington, D.C., challenged the district's Redevelopment Act of 1945
under which his thriving department store was condemned using the
takings clause. The Redevelopment Act was devised to raze blighted
slum residences and replace them with new property developments.
Berman argued that, although his store was in the designated area, such
a program was never intended to include his commercial business.

The Supreme Court upheld the constitutionality of the Redevelopment Act even if it meant destroying Berman's commercial business.
The power of eminent domain provided state and local governments
with the authority to determine which areas, commercial or residential,
could be condemned and whether the public use was a worthy one.
Following this case, Black communities across America were readily
condemned in order to build highways connecting sprawling, predominantly White suburbs with urban business centers. Urban renewal programs became synonymous with "Black removal." However, housing
litigation took a twist in *Kelo v. City of New London* (2005),[52] when the
U.S. Supreme Court, citing *Berman*, upheld the taking of private property by eminent domain in a White middle-class Connecticut community by the local government for a development project.

Maintaining Segregation
by State Referendum

The referendum is a voting mechanism utilized often by White-majority
communities to circumvent minority protections. In *Reitman v. Mulky*

(1967),[53] a grassroots movement of White property owners placed a referendum, Proposition 14, on the ballot to counter California's antidiscrimination laws. Proposition 14 passed, leading to the inclusion of Article 1, Section 26, in the state's constitution. Under Art. 1, Sec. 26, a property owner may include racially restrictive covenants in property deeds and leases without interference by the state government. Specifically, the State of California could not "deny, limit or abridge, directly or indirectly, the right of any person...to decline to sell, lease or rent such property to such person or person as he, in his absolute discretion, chooses."[54]

Mr. and Mrs. Mulky, who were denied rental of an apartment based on their race, brought an action. In a similar case, the Pendergasts, a Black couple, were threatened with eviction because of their race. The newly enacted statute was given as the basis for the property owner's decision to evict them. The U.S. Court of Appeals for the Ninth Circuit decided in favor of the injured Black couples and against the legalized discrimination inherent in the state's referendum-based constitutional amendment. The defendants and the other White property owners appealed to the U.S. Supreme Court, arguing that pursuant to Art. 1, Sec. 26, they had a right to discriminate based on race. The Supreme Court upheld the appellate court, ruling that a private property owner cannot force the state to be a party to race discrimination. The Court explained that the amendment to the state's constitution encouraged racism in housing and thus made the state a party to equal-protection violations.

In 1964, local fair-housing laws were challenged in an Akron, Ohio, referendum case. Many Blacks lived in abysmal housing in Akron. The city council enacted fair-housing legislation and then created a Commission for Equal Opportunity in Housing to enforce it.[55] However, the White-majority electorate in Akron succeeded in passing a referendum to undermine these fair-housing laws. The referendum, known as Akron Charter 137, stated:

> Any ordinance enacted by the Council of the City of Akron which regulates the use, sale, advertisement, transfer...of property...on the basis of race, color, religion, national origin or ancestry must first be approved by a majority of the electors voting on the question.[56]

This charter amendment required receipt of only 10 percent of the votes to pass.

Nellie Hunter, a Black resident of Akron, was informed by a White real estate agent that he could not show her the houses on his list because the White property owners "specified they did not wish their houses shown to negroes." When she sought redress under Akron's fair-housing laws, Hunter was informed by the city that the new Akron Charter 137 precluded any legal action against the realtor, property owners, or the city. Hunter brought an action against the mayor of Akron. She sought to have the city convene the Fair Housing Commission to hear her case, alleging that the city's failure to act on her behalf violated her equal-protection rights.[57] The state trial court upheld the racially restrictive charter. The supreme court of Ohio found the charter did not violate the equal-protection clause of the federal Constitution.

Hunter appealed to the U.S. Supreme Court. In *Hunter v. Erickson*, the Court ruled that the charter's provision violated Hunter's Fourteenth Amendment rights in that it took only 10 percent of the voters to pass discriminatory laws and a clear majority of voters to approve antidiscriminatory legislation.[58] The charter's language included religion and nationality as though "Negro and white, Jew and gentile" are treated in a like manner. The Court was not persuaded and spoke to the reality that the law's harshest effects would be on Blacks and other minorities.[59] In the face of admitted "segregated…sub-standard, unhealthful,…overcrowded conditions [due to] discrimination in the sale, lease, rental and financing of housing, the Court rejected the City of Akron's plea to move slowly toward better race relations."[60]

Some thirty years after the *Hansberry* decision, Chicago became the site of a landmark U.S. Supreme Court decision involving the development of housing for low-income residents. At issue before the Court was the standard to determine when discrimination exists where the acts are not blatantly racist. In this case, the issue was whether the action of a predominantly White community denying a rezoning request to develop low-income housing constituted discrimination against people of color.

Obstacles to Racially Integrated
Housing: *Arlington Heights*

In *Arlington Heights v. Metropolitan Housing Development Corporation (MHDC)* (1977),[61] a wealthy civic group and religious organization

combined resources to assist in the development of racially integrated housing for residents with middle and low incomes. The group
requested rezoning of specific land within the Village of Arlington, a
predominantly White residential Chicago suburb, from single family
to multiple family classification. The rezoning request was denied by
the Village Council. The MHDC and three Black prospective residents of the planned housing units filed suit, alleging that the denial
was based on racial discrimination in violation of the Fourteenth
Amendment and the Fair Housing Act.

The decision of the Court of Appeals for the Seventh Circuit recognized the historical racial segregation as well as the effect the rezoning
denial had on the ability of Blacks to live in that area. The plaintiffs
provided evidence based on a 1970 census that only twenty-seven of
the village's sixty-four thousand residents were Black. However, the
U.S. Supreme Court was not persuaded and reversed the court of
appeals, finding that the evidence did not support a discriminatory
purpose behind the village's denial. The Court needed a "smoking
gun." Without a blatant racial action on the part of the municipality's
decision-makers, the plaintiffs were hard pressed to prove the village
intended to violate Fourteenth Amendment protections. The Court
provided an example of persuasive evidence that might support an
allegation of discriminatory intent, such as the quick change of the
zoning law to prevent the building of low-income housing or racially
integrated units. Without evidence of discriminatory intent or purpose, MHDC's equal protection claim failed. The case was remanded
to the lower courts for a decision on the Fair Housing Act issues. The
case lingered to a drawn out and miserable demise.

In *Memphis v. Greene* (1981), Black litigants were placed in the
untenable position of proving a racist motive with circumstantial
evidence.[62] Whites wished to erect a cement barrier between their
neighborhoods. The Court needed to be persuaded that there was a
discriminatory purpose behind the White communities' request to
erect a barrier between them and their Black neighbors. Residents in
the all-White Memphis community of Hein Park requested the closure of their street to outside traffic. Specifically, they asked the city to
have a barrier placed on a street that "happened" to link Hein Park to
an area to the north that was predominantly Black.

The City of Memphis granted the revised request and closed the street. Mr. Greene, a member of the Black community near Hein Park, brought an action against the city, alleging that the street closure was racially motivated and therefore the city was enforcing racial discrimination in violation of 42 U.S.C., Section 1982, and the Thirteenth Amendment.[63] Greene's Thirteenth Amendment claim was grounded on the remnants of discrimination left by *Plessy*: The cement street barrier acted as a "badge of inferiority" on Blacks who were then segregated and prevented from freely interacting with Whites in the Hein Park neighborhood. Hein Park residents countered that the barrier was necessary to lessen noise, traffic, and pollution while increasing safety for their children to play. The trial court found in favor of the City of Memphis. The Sixth Circuit Court of Appeals reversed the trial court, finding that the closing would benefit Whites and damaged the Black community through the depreciation of property values. Memphis appealed to the U.S. Supreme Court.

Relying on their decision in *Arlington Heights,* the Court held that there was no proof of discriminatory intent on the part of Hein Park residents and therefore no violation on the part of the City of Memphis. Thus, the governmental action of closing the street did not violate the equal-protection clause. Without the most obvious discriminatory motive, a claim of discrimination under the Thirteenth Amendment failed. Justice Stevens, writing for the majority, stated that "inconvenience cannot be equated to an actual restraint on the liberty of black citizens that is in any sense comparable to the odious practice the Thirteenth Amendment was designed to eradicate."[64] The Court viewed the barrier as representing a mere drive of a few more blocks to go around it.

However, Justice Marshall, joined by Justices Brennan and Blackmun, dissented. Their dissent focused on the significant psychological effect of a barrier closing the main thoroughfare between an all-White enclave and a predominantly Black community, the residents of which were referred to as "undesirables." Marshall pointed to the Senate debate over passage of the Civil Rights Act of 1866 during which supporters of the act addressed the direct and indirect discrimination that the statute was meant to prevent. Referring to the majority's determination that there was no racial motive behind the barrier, Justice Marshall stated that "the evidence in this case, combined with a dab of common sense paints a far different picture...[A] group of white citizens has decided to act to keep Negro citizens from traveling through their urban 'utopia,' and the city has placed its seal of approval on the scheme."[65] Thus, the majority's opinion sustained the building of White community enclaves surrounded by high walls, which only furthered racial segregation and tensions.

Private Discrimination in Housing Associations: *Jones v. Alfred H. Mayer*

Conflicts erupted in the streets of America and in the courts as the Civil Rights Movement of the 1950s and 1960s brought the nation's racial disparities to the forefront. The Black community, in turmoil over the ongoing denial of equal rights, pushed for federal civil rights legislation. Federal statutes were guided through the U.S. Congress by President Lyndon Johnson following the assassination of President John F. Kennedy in 1962. The Civil Rights Act of 1964 provided anti-discrimination protections, making governmental discrimination based on race, color, gender, religion, ethnicity, and national origin illegal.[66]

However, the Civil Rights Act did not extend to housing. Although detailed research and funding by the U.S. Commission on Civil Rights determined that housing was perhaps "the most ubiquitous, deeply rooted civil rights problem in the nation," the 1964 Civil Rights Act did not include protections against housing discrimination.[67] In 1968, Congress corrected its mistake. The Fair Housing Act enacted that year prohibited discrimination by real estate agents, landlords, banks, municipalities, and homeowners' insurance companies based on race, color, religion, gender, or national origin and was later amended to include disability and familial status.[68]

Shortly after passage of the Fair Housing Act, the U.S. Supreme Court decided *Jones v. Alfred H. Mayer Company* (1968).[69] Petitioner Joseph Lee Jones, a Black man, attempted to purchase a home in Paddock Woods, a predominantly White section of St. Louis, Missouri. He was refused based on his race. Jones filed a complaint under the former Civil Rights Act of 1866. However, he could not allege governmental action because his case involved only private individuals who chose to discriminate. The lower courts dismissed the suit, concluding that federal statutes only applied to discrimination entailing governmental action, such as court enforcement of a restrictive covenant as in *Kraemer.* Upon appeal, the U.S. Supreme Court addressed whether the Civil Rights Act of 1866 was meant to prevent private discrimination as well as state-sanctioned discrimination.

In *Jones v. Alfred H. Mayer Company,* respondents Alfred H. Mayer, a real estate company, contended that the Civil Rights Act of 1866 was narrowly focused to curtail post-Civil War state laws or Black Codes that restricted the rights of the newly freed Blacks in the Confederate states of the South. The act was not to reach the actions of private persons. The Supreme Court disagreed, instead finding that the Civil Rights Act of 1866 has at its foundation the reality that Black oppression is nationwide. To this end, Section 2 of the Thirteenth Amendment provides Congress with the power to enforce the law against private individuals, thus alleviating racial barriers to the acquisition of real and personal property.

Racial discrimination in housing "herds men into ghettos and makes their ability to buy property turn on the color of their skin, then it too is a relic of slavery."[70] Justice Stewart, writing for the majority, ruled that "the exclusion of Negroes from whole communities became a substitute for the Black Codes."[71] The Civil Rights Act of 1866 was explicitly expanded to cover private acts of discrimination in housing. Justices Harlan and White dissented.

Having surmounted the obstacles present in purchasing a home in majority White communities, Blacks were presented with discriminatory conduct in the perquisites that would often come with living in that home and residential community. In *Sullivan v. Little Hunting Park, Inc.,* decided in 1969, Sullivan, a White homeowner, was expelled from membership in Hunting Park Inc.[72] Little Hunting Park's playground facility was constructed for the benefit of residents of Fairfax, Virginia. For a nominal fee, residents of suburban Fairfax received access to the park grounds. Sullivan owned two properties in Fairfax and leased one of them to T. R. Freeman, a Black man. However, when Freeman arrived at the park, he was denied access by the guard. Freeman challenged the racially restricted admission to the organization's board.

The board of Little Hunting Park, Inc., a nonstock corporation organized to operate the park facility, refused to provide Freeman access to the park. When Sullivan protested on behalf of Freeman, he was expelled from the corporation and refused access to the park. The courts upheld the racial restrictions. Upon appeal, the U.S. Supreme Court found that access to the park represented a property right. It ruled that the failure of Hunting Park to assign a share to Freeman was a violation of the Civil Rights Act of 1866. Interestingly, the Court determined that Sullivan, the White property seller, was adversely affected and that his expulsion provided standing for the lawsuit against Hunting Park. *Sullivan* demonstrates that there have been and continue to be White advocates for racial justice who have fought alongside Blacks in the struggle for property rights and ownership.

Similarly, in *Tillman v. Wheaton-Haven Recreation Association* (1973),[73] the housing association operated a community swimming pool limited to White members who lived in a prescribed Silver Spring, Maryland, area and their guests. Dr. Harry C. Press and his wife, a Black couple, bought a home in the area and sought admission to the pool. The couple was refused membership into the association, which would, in turn, provide access to the pool. During that same year, Murray and Rosiland Tillman, a White couple and members of the Wheaton-Haven Association, brought an African-American guest, Grace Rosner, to the pool. The next day the board of the association held a special meeting during which the guest policy was changed to restrict guests to relatives of the membership. Rosner was denied admission to the pool on a subsequent visit.

The Tillmans, Presses, and Rosner brought an action against the association and its officers under the Civil Rights Act of 1866 and 1870 (which re-enacted the 1866 act), and the Civil Rights Act of 1964. The federal trial court and Court of Appeals for the Eighth Circuit rejected their claims, finding that the Wheaton-Haven Association was a private club and exempt from nondiscrimination laws. The plaintiffs petitioned the U.S. Supreme Court. The Court, relying on its decisions in *Sullivan v. Little Hunting Park* and *Jones v. Alfred H. Mayer Co.*, found that the association was not a private club exempt from federal statutes. Additionally, the Court found the right to admission to the pool was linked to the purchase of the home. The facility was a benefit the denial of which affected the property value and the ability of the purchaser to enjoy full property rights.

In 2002, the Court decided a case involving an interracial couple precluded by a White real estate agent from purchasing a house based on race. In *Meyer v. Holley*, the Court was presented with whether the realty owner or the agent was liable for the discrimination.[74] The couple brought the action against the real estate agent who worked for the Triad, Inc. real estate firm as well as a separate action against the owner of Triad, Inc., David Meyer. The trial court consolidated the two cases, dismissing the action against Meyer because under the Fair Housing Act he could not be found vicariously liable for the discriminatory acts of his real estate agent. The U.S. court of appeals reversed the trial court. However, the U.S. Supreme Court agreed with the trial court and narrowly interpreted the Fair Housing Act to limit personal liability. Thus, Holley lost because the owner was not vicariously liable for the acts of the real estate salesman. The unsatisfactory message is that the realtor can escape direct responsibility for racist acts attributed to the agent.

Discriminatory Lending

The Fair Housing Act provides procedures for individual as well as class action pattern and practice claims. In 2004, a complaint was filed in Michigan against the Old Kent Financial Corporation and Old Kent Bank for refusing to provide loans and services to the predominantly Black Detroit area. Old Kent Bank opened thirty-five new branches in predominantly White suburbs, but did not open a branch in Detroit until it was investigated for unlawful behavior.[75] Under a settlement agreement, additional branches were created in Black communities and provided with full lending services.

Racial discrimination in housing has progressed from "only White" to "mainly White" policies. In 2004, a complaint and consent decree was filed in the Northern District of Illinois to First American Bank's discriminatory policies, which limited residential loans primarily to White customers in Chicago.[76] Lending institutions demarcated high-risk geographic areas of the city. Too often, communities of color are redlined based on discrimination. Mortgages in areas labeled as high risk come with higher interest rates. Redlining by banks remains a legal issue against which people of color must contend. Redlining causes Blacks to pay higher interest rates because prime lenders refuse to do business in Black communities. These communities then become vulnerable to subprime lenders charging higher interest rates. The Fair Housing Act offers certain legal protections against redlining. However, for many years, the federal government played a role in the perpetuation of racially segregated housing by refusing to investigate discrimination in lending or enforce Fair Housing protection in public housing.

Public Property and Accommodations: *DeCuir* and *Mitchell*

Blacks have paid first-class fare and received second-class treatment in every area of American life. However, in regard to public accommodations, Blacks have met numerous obstacles to receiving their place in first class. The initial Civil Rights Acts, passed during Reconstruction, were enacted to protect the rights and privileges of Blacks. The test of those protections was immediate as Whites refused to acknowledge those rights and privileges. In *Hall v. DeCuir*, decided in 1878, the Court ruled that a Louisiana-based steamboat traveling interstate could not restrict first-class cabins to Whites when Mrs. DeCuir, a Black passenger, paid full fare for first-class accommodations. Under the commerce clause of the U.S. Constitution, the federal government can reach racial segregation on vehicles within interstate commerce.[77] Political changes in Congress brought about a retreat by the Court now filled with a complement of conservative justices. Southern Democrats played a pivotal role in the presidential elections of Rutherford B. Hayes, James A. Garfield, and Chester A. Arthur undermining further civil rights protections.

The rise in Southern power and dissipation of Northern resolve further undermined Black progress. In 1883, the Court ruled in the *Civil Rights Cases* that Congressional protections under the Civil Rights Acts would not apply to privately owned businesses such as theaters, hotels, or restaurants.[78] It was a blow to racial justice felt by Blacks in all stations of life. Well before *Plessy*, in 1894, Ida B. Wells-Barnett refused to move from a ladies car to the overcrowded smoking car reserved for Blacks, she was dragged from the train.[79] The fact that Wells-Barnett had purchased a first-class ticket meant nothing. As the conductor attempted to pull her out of the seat, Wells-Barnett bit his hand. Three White men physically picked her up and removed her from the train.[80] She brought a successful action against the railroad and was awarded damages.[81] However, the supreme court of Tennessee overturned the verdict and ordered Wells-Barnett to pay court costs.[82] She pointedly surmised the meager justice afforded Blacks after the decimation of the Civil Rights Bill, "[left to] the State courts for redress of grievances...I was given the brand of justice Charles Sumner knew Negroes would get when he fathered the Civil Rights Bill during the Reconstruction period."[83] W. E. B DuBois's suit challenging his placement in a soot-filled car after the purchase of a first-class ticket would be similarly dismissed.

By 1896, the decision in *Plessy v. Ferguson* upheld Louisiana's Separate Car Act, which segregated passengers on its intrastate railroad, creating the doctrine of "separate but equal." The Supreme Court made clear that the states controlled social interaction between the races in private as well as public spaces. When this power was granted to the states, social separation became racial segregation in all aspects of American life. In the early twentieth century, public accommodations cases were filed in state courts and summarily dispatched in a fashion predicted by Ida B. Wells-Barnett. Although the tentacle of legal segregation spread quickly because of the prior decision in *Hall vs. DeCuir*, *Plessy's* reach was somewhat limited in the area of interstate accommodations: cross-country trains.

In *Mitchell v. United States*, decided in 1941, the Court held once more that racial segregation on interstate transportation violated the Constitution.[84] The Interstate Commerce Act had prohibited such discrimination despite the custom of a state that the train had entered *en route* to a destination. Arthur W. Mitchell, a resident of Chicago and the first Black Democrat elected to the U.S. House of Representatives, brought legal action after being forced into a segregated interstate rail car.[85] On April 20, 1937, Mitchell left

Chicago on the Illinois Central Railroad Company. He requested a sleeping car but none was available. Shortly after leaving Memphis and crossing the Mississippi River into Arkansas, the car filled to capacity with White passengers.

The conductor, in accordance with custom, forced Mitchell, under threat of arrest, to move into the car reserved for Blacks. "This was in purported compliance with an Arkansas statute requiring segregation of colored from white persons by the use of cars or partitioned sections providing 'equal, but separate and sufficient accommodations' for both races."[86] The car for Whites was air-conditioned and had hot and cold running water and separate flushable toilets for men and women. The car for Blacks was "filthy and foul smelling," not air-conditioned, and only the toilet in the women's section was equipped for flushing; there were no wash basins, soap, towels, or running water.[87] Mitchell filed a complaint that was dismissed for lack of jurisdiction.

On appeal to the U.S. Supreme Court, Chief Justice Hughes, on behalf of the Court, found that Mitchell could bring such an action. Hughes wrote:

> We have repeatedly said that it is apparent from the legislative history of the [Interstate Commerce] Act that not only was the evil of discrimination the principal thing aimed at, but that there is no basis for the contention that Congress intended to exempt any discriminatory action or practice of interstate carriers affecting interstate commerce which it had authority to reach.[88]

A new train with a partition separating the White and Black passengers was discriminatory as well.

In 1950, the Supreme Court was once again presented with discrimination on interstate rail transportation. In response to complaints about racial discrimination in the dining car, the railroad assigned one table exclusively for Blacks and ten tables for Whites. The trial court dismissed the action, ruling that "racial segregation is not, per se, unconstitutional."[89] On appeal, the Supreme Court ruled, in *Henderson v. United States*, that the Interstate Commerce Act made it unlawful for a railroad to subject any person to unreasonable prejudice.[90]

In 1960, the Supreme Court ruled in *Boynton v. Virginia* that the restaurant serving interstate bus customers could not discriminate.[91] However, these decisions were ignored; little changed. In 1961, Freedom Riders challenged the segregation of interstate transportation. Interracial groups of men and women organized by James Farmer of the Congress of Racial Equality (CORE) rode public buses into the Deep South. After brutal attacks in the Alabama towns of Anniston and Birmingham, the federal government was forced to protect the Freedom Riders against rabid White mobs. In *Lewis v. Greyhound*, the court again ordered compliance with federal transportation laws.[92]

Segregation in Public Places

The *Brown v. Board* decision in 1954 provided the Court and Blacks much needed legal leverage in race discrimination cases. Challenges to segregated education and housing provided the groundwork for legal action against segregation in public accommodations. Protests and sit-in demonstrations drew media attention to racial segregation in restaurants, libraries, and public parks. Blacks brought legal challenges against exclusion from public spaces and private restaurants that catered to the public. In *Muir v. Louisville Park Theatrical Ass'n*, decided in 1954, the City of Louisville owned and maintained an amphitheater, which excluded Blacks, within Iroquois Park, a public park.[93] Blacks could only enjoy the parts of Iroquois Park that were maintained by public funds. They could play golf, walk in the woods, and fish at the lake. But, the Louisville Park Theatrical Association, a privately operated enterprise that leased the amphitheater from the city, excluded Blacks.

Five years earlier, James W. Muir and his family were denied entrance to the amphitheater because of race. Muir and other Black residents of Louisville brought an action under the Fourteenth Amendment.[94] The state courts found that there was no constitutional violation in excluding Blacks in the summertime from the amphitheater because the government did not directly or indirectly operate that section of the park.[95] On appeal, the U.S. Supreme Court ruled that the *Brown* decision prevented such segregation. Government control over a park built with public funds was not abdicated by a private lease.[96] However, for other cases of racial segregation in public accommodations that were without a clear connection to governmental action, Black patrons had little legal recourse.

The Court required a clear governmental nexus between the discrimination and the property in question. Prior to passage of the Civil Rights Act of 1964, the Supreme Court could do little to reach private discrimination in public accommodations. In *Wolfe v. North Carolina*, decided in 1960, the Court ruled that a golf course could discriminate against Blacks.[97] However, in 1961, in *Burton v. Wilmington Parking Authority*, the Supreme Court reversed the highest court of Delaware, finding that a public restaurant operated as part of a state-owned parking garage could not exclude William H. Burton, based only on his race.[98] However, the Court ruled in Burton's favor only because there was a finding of state action that violated the Fourteenth Amendment. Racial segregation or a "Whites-only" policy alone did not give rise to legal recourse in a public accomodation, such as a privately owned restaurant. A business may select its clientele. As Justice Brennan noted in 1963, "Apartheid, however, is barred by the common law as respects innkeepers and common carriers."[99]

Despite prior decisions and the ruling in *Brown v. Board*, Blacks were forced to bring legal action to gain equal access to public accommodations. In *Watson v. Memphis*, decided in 1963, the City of Memphis refused to desegregate its municipal parks and swimming pools without intervention by the highest Court. By 1964, the Supreme Court recognized the similarities between discrimination in private housing and racially segregating public accommodations such as hotels and restaurants. In *Bell v. Maryland*, the Court opined that "the property involved is not, however, a man's home or his yard or even his fields. Private property is involved, but it is property that is serving the public."[100]

After the passage of the Civil Rights Act of 1964, public accommodations, such as the public library, continued to be racially segregated by tradition.[101] *Georgia v. Rachel*, decided in 1966, involved a racially segregated library in Atlanta, Georgia, that was integrated only after sit-in protests and the ruling of the U.S. Supreme Court.[102] In *Brown v. Louisiana*, decided that same year, Blacks were arrested for refusing to leave the Whites-only public library in Clinton, Louisiana.[103] Blacks were directed to borrow and return books at a designated blue bookmobile or by mail.[104] They were prohibited from using the public libraries.[105] Library cards were stamped with the race of the borrower.[106] Justice Fortas lamented that a library—"this hallowed place…[—]bore the ugly stamp of racism."[107] The Court reversed the convictions of Brown and others arrested while protesting the library's segregation practice.

Jackson, Mississippi, closed its swimming pools, arguing that the pools could not be operated peacefully, safely, and economically on an integrated basis.[108] Black patrons challenged closing the pools to avoid integration arguing the closure created a badge of inferiority in violation of the Thirteenth Amendment. In *Palmer v. Thompson*, decided in 1971, the Court ruled in favor of the City of Jackson. Justice White dissented and was joined by Justices Marshall and Brennan. The dissent recounts the many discrimination cases brought by Blacks against the City of Jackson and the State of Mississippi and states that "it is untenable to suggest that the closing of the swimming pools—a pronouncement that Negroes are somehow unfit to swim with whites—operates equally on Negroes and whites.…[T]he closed pools stand as mute reminders to the community of the official view of Negro inferiority."[109]

The Civil Rights Act prohibits discrimination or segregation in public accommodations affecting interstate commerce.[110] In 1964, the owners of Heart of Atlanta Motel, a large facility located in downtown Atlanta, brought an action against the United States and Attorney General Robert F. Kennedy to enjoin the government from applying the Civil Rights Act to its motel. In *Heart of Atlanta Motel v. United States*, the owners alleged that the act should not apply to them because it was a privately owned business and, as such, had the right to exclude guests based on race.[111] The motel owners argued that the government violated their constitutional rights in forcing them to accept Black patrons.[112] On appeal, the U.S. Supreme Court upheld the commerce clause section of the Civil Rights Act, finding that the motel did substantial interstate business when it accepted out-of-state guests. The decision resulted in the desegregation of privately owned businesses with clear connections to interstate commerce. The Court also decided *Katzenbach v. McClung* (1964).[113] In that case, the connection to interstate commerce was not as clear.

In *Katzenbach*, Ollie McClung, owner of Ollie's Barbeque, a Birmingham, Alabama, restaurant, brought an action against U.S. Attorney General Nicolas Katzenbach to enjoin the enforcement of the Civil Rights Act.[114] Ollie's Barbeque served only White customers inside the facility.[115] Blacks were served from a take-out window in the back of the restaurant.[116] The restaurant had refused to serve Blacks in the dining room since its original opening in 1927.[117] McClung argued that the Civil Rights Act did not apply to his restaurant because it was a local business without any substantial ties to interstate commerce.[118] On appeal, the Supreme Court ruled that the approximately $70,000 worth of food McClung purchased from outside the state affected interstate commerce.[119] Thus, Ollie's Barbeque could not exclude Blacks from its dining facilities. *Katzenbach* and *Heart of Atlanta Motel* provided Blacks and other minorities with the ammunition to contest segregation in privately owned businesses located in the most remote parts of the country. Very few businesses were without some connection to interstate commerce. Additionally, Blacks have challenged discrimination in public accommodations under Title II of the Civil Rights Act of 1964.[120] Title II provides:

> All persons shall be entitled to the full and equal enjoyment of the goods, services, facilities, privileges, advantages, and accommodations of any place of public accommodation, as defined in this section, without discrimination or segregation on the ground of race, color, religion, or national origin.

As racism took a subtle turn, more complex legal methods were needed to defend against it. Direct proof of racist intent was more difficult to obtain. As in other cases, discrimination in public accommodations became a matter of perspective. Perhaps the waiter or waitress took the order of White patrons while Blacks who arrived earlier waited. Perhaps White servers ignored the requests of Black customers for great lengths of time until the Black customers left in frustration.

In cases lacking direct proof of intentional discrimination, the courts apply the burden-shifting test developed in *McDonnell Douglas Corp. v. Green*, 411 U.S. 792 (1973).[121] Based on *McDonnell Douglas*, a plaintiff in a public accommodation case must first establish a prima facie case of discrimination.[122] Specifically, Black plaintiffs must prove that they attempted to contract for services and enjoy the benefits of a public accommodation; they were denied the right and full benefits or enjoyment of a public accommodation; and the services were given to similarly situated White persons.

Once the prima facie case is established, the burden of production shifts to the defendant to demonstrate a legitimate, nondiscriminatory reason for the alleged racist behavior.[123] If the defendant meets this burden, then the plaintiff must present sufficient evidence to demonstrate that the proffered reason is merely a pretext for discrimination.[124] If the defendant fails to provide a persuasive reason, then the plaintiff has proven racism without direct evidence of intentional discrimination. However, racial bias in treatment in public restaurants and hotels remains an issue.

Even into the twenty-first century, private plaintiffs as well as the Justice Department were forced to bring legal action against hotels and restaurants that choose to discriminate based on race. Suits were brought against Cracker Barrel restaurants,[125] Denny's restaurants,[126] Waffle House restaurants,[127] and Adam's Mark hotels.[128]

The Federal Role in Unfair Housing: *Hills v. Gautreaux*

Created in 1934 during the Great Depression, the Federal Housing Administration (FHA) has as its mission access to home ownership through federally subsidized mortgages. However, these FHA loans and accompanying mortgage interest rates were based on a discriminatory grid that labeled Black communities as "undesirable." Resources provided to Whites through the FHA as well as the Veterans Administration "G.I. Bill" expanded the racial divide in home ownership. "Less than 2 percent of the housing financed with federal mortgage assistance from 1946 to 1959 was available to Negroes."[129] The government's Federal Housing Administration continued to provide loans on properties with racially restrictive covenants even after the *Shelley v. Kraemer* decision. Its broad-brush label of "undesirable" diminished the value of homes in Black communities. The diminished value of their homes in turn restricted Black property owners' accumulation of wealth.

The federal government sanctioned the creation of all-White suburbs. Levittown is a notable example of restrictive covenants sanctioned by the government's Federal Housing Administration. Levittown, New York, was a suburb constructed during the post-WWII housing boom with Federal Housing Administration subsidies. However, the FHA allowed developers to exclude Blacks and discriminate against them based on skin color. As late as 1960 not a single one of the eighty-two thousand residents of this Long Island town was Black.[130] The Court dismissed a lawsuit brought by the NAACP to integrate Levittown.

In *Hills v. Gautreaux*, decided in 1976, Blacks challenged the federal government's discriminatory site decisions for subsidized housing.[131] Black residents of Chicago brought class action suits against the Chicago Housing Authority and Federal Housing and Urban Development (HUD), alleging racial discrimination in government-subsidized housing. Evidence at trial substantiated their claims that between 1950 and 1965 almost 99 percent of Chicago's public housing was located within Black, low-income communities. Only four public housing units were located in White areas. The Chicago Housing Authority operated the four units in White communities under a "Whites-only" policy in violation of the Civil Rights Act of 1964 and the Fourteenth Amendment, with tacit federal agreement.

During trial, the Chicago Housing Authority revealed that it had long been aware that certain White politicians prevented the building of integrated public housing in their electoral districts. At best, the Chicago Housing Authority stood by and allowed the discrimination to take place. At worst, the Authority was duplicitous in these discriminatory practices. The trial court found in favor of the Black plaintiffs. The court developed a remedy for the distribution of public housing around the City of Chicago and its suburbs. On appeal to the U.S. Supreme Court, HUD and the Chicago Housing Authority argued that the trial court's redistribution remedy should not include the suburbs. The Supreme Court did not accept that argument. Instead, the Court found that the prior discriminatory practices and the housing market options made it necessary to provide Black residents with housing remedies that extended beyond Chicago. However, the struggle to implement this decision is decades long.

Subsidized and Low-Income Housing: *HUD v. Rucker*

A public housing case forced the Court to balance the property needs of an elderly resident living in subsidized housing with the government's need to enforce its drug-free policy. The federal government's antidrug statute resulted in the eviction of an innocent tenant from a public housing apartment building that had become a place with incidents of high crime in California. In *Department of Housing and Urban Development v. Rucker*, decided in 2002, tenants in public housing brought an action on behalf of themselves and Pearlie Rucker, a grandmother and resident.[132] Rucker, who is African American, was evicted from her government-subsidized apartment under the Anti-Drug Abuse Act of 1998 based on the actions of a young relative. The federal statute authorized local public housing officials to evict a tenant if a member of the household or a guest was involved in drug-related activity.

At her eviction hearing, Rucker testified that she was innocent. There was no evidence to support that she participated in any drug use or that drug activity was taking place in her apartment. Upon appeal, the Court had to decide whether the eviction provision of the federal statute applied to an innocent tenant who was unaware of drug activity conducted by a relative two streets away from the housing unit in which she lived. In one of the few unanimous housing decisions of the Supreme Court, the statute was upheld. In order to "provide public housing that was decent, safe, and free from illegal drugs"[133] even an innocent tenant such as Rucker could and would be evicted. She was evicted.

Housing developments that provide opportunities for low-income residents often face resistance based on race as well as class. In *Cuyahoga Falls, Ohio, v. Buckeye Community of Hope Foundation* (2003),[134] the Cuyahoga community filed a petition to halt the planned construction of a low-income housing development. The petition required that the building of the development be placed on the ballot as a referendum item. The majority of the town voted against the project. The building permit was denied. Prior to the vote, public sentiment arose that this low-income housing development would cause an increase in crime and drug activity and "attract a population similar to the one on Prange Drive, the city's only African-American neighborhood."[135]

The Hope Foundation brought an action under the equal-protection clause of the Fourteenth Amendment and the Fair Housing Act. The trial court, finding scant support for the race claims, denied them. The court of appeals reversed the trial court, finding that city officials instigated the negative public sentiment that led to the defeat of the housing development initiative. Also, the appellate court found that the building permit was arbitrarily denied. In the midst of the litigation, the Ohio Supreme Court voided the referendum on due-process grounds. On appeal, the U.S. Supreme Court addressed the remaining issues.

Relying on *Arlington Heights v. Metropolitan Housing Development Corp.*, the Supreme Court ruled against the plaintiffs. The Court once again required proof of intentional racial discrimination or evidence of a discriminatory purpose. Additionally, the Court found that a First Amendment right protected the racist comments. Lastly, the Court would not see that the city played a role in fomenting the negative public sentiment and the petition to stop the project. Without direct state action or unequivocal proof, the Hope Foundation's equal protection claim failed. Recalcitrant defendants in housing cases had found a way around *Shelley v. Kraemer.*

Fighting for Black Farmers:
Pigford v. Veneman

In rural communities, Black farmers waged a valiant effort to maintain their farms in the face of private and governmental discrimination. In 1997, they brought several lawsuits against the U.S. Department of Agriculture (USDA), alleging systematic discrimination in the administration of the department's farm loan programs.[136] Black farmers were denied loans and subsidies, charged higher interest rates, and made to provide increased collateral.[137] In 1999, the USDA entered a consent decree settling *Pigford v. Veneman*.[138] The federal government agreed to pay Black farmers $300 million in damages and other relief.[139] A reverse discrimination lawsuit was immediately filed by White farmers claiming that they, too, should have a part of the settlement money.[140] Their case was dismissed. However, the monetary settlement is delayed justice for most Black farmers. In 1920, they owned 14 percent of farmland.[141] By 1992, the share of Black farm ownership decreased to a mere 1 percent of all American farms.[142]

Present-Day Vestiges

The terms "inner city" and "urban area" have replaced the history-laden "ghetto." Blacks have advanced economically. However, comparable obstacles remain. Race acts to locate people by their color rather than by the proximity to employment or resources.[143] Black communities struggle to maintain undervalued homes located in areas of limited employment, crime, and overcrowded schools.[144] De facto housing segregation and discriminatory mortgage rates continue to limit the options of Blacks who choose to move.[145]

From 2002 to 2005, allegations of racial discrimination were second only to disability in complaints filed under the Fair Housing Act.[146] The overall number of housing complaints filed with the Department of Housing and Urban Affairs decreased between fiscal years 2002 and 2005 (averaging 2,576 complaints).[147] However, the percentage of complaints of racial discrimination in housing remained the same. In 2002, the number of complaints involving race discrimination was 977, or 39 percent.[148] In 2003, those complaints numbered 1,110 (40 percent), and in 2004 the number was 1,130 (40 percent).[149] However, in 2005, even when the number of overall complaints diminished, the percentage of race-based complaints remained 41 percent.[150]

Property ownership is a major indicator of wealth.[151] Thus, discrimination in property ownership has limited the opportunity of Blacks to achieve wealth. In Chicago, for example, Blacks comprise 36.8 percent of the population.[152] Yet, Whites in Chicago own and occupy twice as many of the housing units.[153] Although over 66 percent of Whites in America are home owners, less than half of Blacks and Latinos own their homes.[154] The majority of them live in racially segregated and densely populated areas.

The ten largest American cities account for 20 percent of the total Black population.[155] In 2000, Chicago was the ninth most racially segregated urban city.[156] St. Louis, Missouri, ranked fourth on the list of racially segregated cities.[157] New York was eighth. Cincinnati and Cleveland were sixth and third, respectively.[158] Philadelphia was tenth.[159] Segregated urban neighborhoods receive a diminished distribution of public services and amenities, while these neighborhoods have increased incidents of asthma or industry-related illnesses.[160] Gary, Indiana, was not considered racially segregated but it is 85 percent Black. In 2005, Whites represented 98 percent of Levittown's population while the entire Black population measured 0.5 percent.[161] Latinos, now 6 percent of the town's population, are heralded as the changing face of Levittown, although "skin color would have kept them out fifty years ago."[162]

Not all Black urban areas are economically deprived and poor White rural communities abound. "Urban Appalachia," filled with low-income Whites, exists in cities such as Philadelphia, Chicago, New York, and Los Angeles. However, certain Black urban areas are historically racially segregated by the consequences of law. Racial isolation is a vestige of segregated housing, restricted property ownership, and government-sustained discrimination. Every generation of Blacks has faced this form of discrimination. As did their forebears, Blacks must continue to combat discrimination in housing. It is a Herculean battle fought for one of life's most basic necessities: shelter.

4

CIVIL LIBERTIES AND RACIAL JUSTICE

Let us march on 'til victory is won.

       James Weldon Johnson (1887–1938), "Lift Ev'ry Voice and Sing"

I would rather die on my feet than live on my knees.

       Judge A. Leon Higginbotham (1988)

Live free or die.

       General John Stark (1809)

The protest strategies utilized by Blacks in America have been emulated by disenfranchised groups around the world. However, the determination, brilliance, and self-sacrifice of Blacks waged in this life-and-death struggle for human rights are often forgotten. This chapter examines the age-long fight waged for fundamental freedoms and first-class citizenship. This battle began during slavery and manifested after slavery in legal challenges, demonstration marches, sit-ins, and urban uprisings. The three hundred fifty-year journey through American history bears testimony to an intent to live free. America extols its Constitution, along with the promise of liberty and democratic government that the Constitution establishes. However, Blacks forced the Court to face many of these legal hypocrisies regarding liberty.

"Although the Court has not assumed to define 'liberty' with any great precision, that term is not confined to mere freedom from bodily restraint. Liberty under law extends to the full range of conduct which the individual is free to pursue."[1] Ratified in 1791, the

First Amendment to the U.S. Constitution provides the right to assembly, protest, speech, and religion, and to petition the government with grievances.[2] In pressing this country to recognize and protect their rights as human beings and then as citizens, Blacks strengthened fundamental freedoms, liberties, and protections for all peoples in this country.

Life without Liberty: *Bailey v. Poindexter*

An examination of civil liberties in the context of slavery and Reconstruction presents many challenges. Enslaved Blacks were prevented from exercising individual will. The Virginia case of *Bailey v. Poindexter* best illustrates this point.[3] In 1854, Richmond T. Lacy died, leaving a will that provided his slaves with the choice of remaining with his wife in slavery or emancipation. Lacy wrote that "the negroes loaned my wife, at her death I wish to have their choice of being emancipated or sold publicly. If they prefer being emancipated, it is my wish that they be hired out until a sufficient sum is raised to defray their expenses to a land where they can enjoy their freedom."[4] John Poindexter was appointed executor of Lacy's will.

The court, however, refused to execute the will. It was argued that slaves have no free will to determine whether they should be free or remain enslaved. "[T]he legal status of a slave is that of a personal chattel; that he is mere property; that he can do no legal civil act, can make no contract, &c.: and all this for the purpose of showing that he cannot make himself free by his own choice; that he can have no effectual will on the subject, and cannot be invested with any power of emancipating himself."[5] Counsel for Bailey stated that "all civil rights may be reduced to three principal or primary articles—the right of personal liberty, the right of personal security, and the right of private property...But which of these civil rights has the slave?"[6] None. Virginia's highest court ruled that slaves did not possess free choice. Lacy could not legally give free choice to his slaves in a will or otherwise. Only his heirs could manumit (free) them from slavery.

As property, slaves in America were forced by law to do the bidding of the White owner. Work began and ended upon the command of the slaveholder. When slaves were allowed off property, a letter was required with the owner's detailed instructions. Slaves had no right to privacy. A South Carolina statute required slaveholders to search the living quarters of all Blacks every fourteen days in search of stolen food, weapons, and plans for escape.[7] Enslaved Blacks were bred like animals without any choice of mate or lover. They had no legal rights over their bodies. A form of marriage was developed by slaves and tolerated by Whites. The master had to give permission to allow the union and the marriage was not recognized by law. Slave marriages did not create property rights or rights of inheritance. Slave owners could rape or sell enslaved spouses. The owner could and did rape slaves without legal repercussions. Children of slave women and White masters did not inherit property. Slave children were sold away from their parents. In the throes of these infringements of basic human rights, slaves were forbidden by law to protest or act in self-defense.

Slaves were prohibited from meeting in groups because associations between slaves were considered dangerous by Whites and hotbeds for insurrections. For example, a Virginia law stated that "to prevent insurrections no master or overseer shall allow a Negro slave of another to remain on his plantation above four hours without leave of the slave's own master."[8] Slaves could only meet for specific purposes permitted by the owner in a letter of permission providing the time of return and with whom the slave could associate. Slaves caught in clandestine meetings faced severe punishment.

Slaves could not practice their religion freely; any practice of religion was limited to Christianity. African religious practices were denigrated as pagan and heathenish. Initially, a slave could gain freedom with conversion to Christianity. However, the value of slave labor soon ended this practice. Slaves were encouraged to follow Christian doctrines of obedience. Only Bible passages that could be interpreted to support Black debasement and inferiority were allowed. God's will was interpreted as requiring Blacks to be laborers for Whites. Blacks took the opportunity provided by those religious services to find spiritual sustenance, exchange information, and plan revolts.

Manumitted or free Blacks lived an uneven and precarious existence.[9] Their liberty was subject to the jurisdictional laws of the particular town or state of residence. The fears of Whites, real and imagined, led to legislation that could remove them from the state or prohibit their ability to earn a living. In the North as well as the South, free Blacks were only allowed interstate travel upon the whim of White society. Free Blacks in the North and South lived in fear of marauding bands of White bounty hunters who could kidnap any Black person and sell them into slavery.

Protesting Slavery by Petition

Blacks have a long history of protest.[10] Free Blacks in the North and South petitioned state legislatures protesting slave-holding and the ill-treatment of free Blacks. In 1788, Prince Hall presented a petition to the Massachusetts legislature protesting the slave trade and the kidnapping of free people into slavery.[11] Hall's petition begged the question, "What then are our lives and Lebeties [*sic*] worth if they may be taken a way in shuch [*sic*] a cruel & unjust manner as these…"[12] That year, Blacks and Whites protested the kidnapping of several Black men from Massachusetts who were taken to the island of Martinique, a French colony, and sold into slavery. John Hancock, governor of Massachusetts, protested to the governor of the island. The men were returned. The success of Prince Hall's petition led to the passage of Massachusetts' Anti-Slave Act in 1788.[13]

In 1791, Blacks in South Carolina submitted a petition to the state legislature to protest their treatment. "[Free Blacks] have been and are considered as free citizens of this state, they hope to be treated as such."[14] Blacks in Massachusetts petitioned the government to desegregate public schools in 1844.[15] *The Ethiopian Manifesto, Issued in Defence of the Blackman's Rights, in the Scale of Universal Freedom* was published by Robert Alexander Young in 1829.[16] The *Manifesto* was an attack on slaveholding. "Hearken, therefore, oh! Slaveholder, thou task inflicter against the rights of men, the day is at hand, nay the hour draweth nigh, when poverty shall appear to thee a blessing, if it but restore to thy fellow-man his rights…"[17] That same year David Walker disseminated a petition seeking Black unity against oppression. In *Walker's Appeal*, he asked, "Can our condition be any worse?—Can it be more mean and abject? If there are any changes, will they not be for the better, though they may appear for the worst at first?"[18] Slaves escaped to free states and to Canada. As states such as Pennsylvania enacted laws abolishing slavery, recalcitrant slaveholders lobbied for more restrictive fugitive laws.

In 1842, the U.S. Supreme Court upheld an expansion of fugitive-slave laws.[19] *Prigg v. Pennsylvania* allowed bounty hunters to apprehend an escaped slave and return her and her children, including the children born in freedom, to slavery in Maryland. The Supreme Court ruled that the rights of slave owners to regain "property" superseded Pennsylvania's attempt to abolish slavery.[20] In 1850, harsher fugitive slave laws were passed by Congress. The new laws gave far-reaching authority to slave owners and bounty hunters to retrieve fugitive slaves. In response, a fugitive-slave convention was held in Cazenovia, New York, to propose strategies for slaves to defend themselves against a return to bondage.[21] The convention's proposal spoke to the vulnerability of free Blacks who could be kidnapped into slavery without legal recourse. Free and fugitive Blacks attending the convention drafted militant resolutions rebuking the enactment of laws that relegated their race to the lowest level of society.

Such a resolution opposing racial oppression was adopted at a meeting in Springfield, Massachusetts, in 1850:

> 2. *Resolved*, That we will repudiate all and every law that has for its object the oppression of any human being, or seeks to assign *us* degrading positions. And, *whereas*, we hold to the declaration of the poet, "that he who would be free, himself must strike the blow," and that resistance to tyrants is obedience to God, therefore,

> 3. *Resolved*, That we do welcome to our doors every one who feels and claims for himself the position of a man, and has broken from the Southern house of bondage, and that we feel ourselves justified in using every means which the God of love has placed in our power to sustain our liberty.[22]

Blacks and White activists defied the Fugitive Slave Law. Their acts of civil disobedience assisted escaped Blacks in obtaining their freedom from slavery. During slavery, Blacks created platforms for protest. Frederick Douglass, an escaped slave, rose from slavery and racial discrimination to be an internationally recognized abolitionist speaker, writer, and publisher of the *North Star*, an abolitionist newspaper. However, antislavery protesters also turned to violence as a means of retaliation against human bondage.

Slave Revolts: The Cases of Denmark Vesey, Nat Turner, and John Brown

Revolts are acts of protest. Enslaved Africans, free Blacks, and White advocates protested the brutality of slavery and the many laws enacted to enforce it. Their protests took many forms. Slaves ruined meals, sabotaged tools, and even poisoned the food of slave owners. Slaves escaped. Those slaves who failed in their attempts to escape were whipped and branded.[23] Repeated escape attempts could lead to castration.[24] Despite the laws and punishments, slaves escaped, planned insurrections, and staged uprisings (large and small) against perpetual servitude.

Slave revolts, real and imagined, led to greater restrictions. A mysterious fire or illness flamed hysteria and paranoia among Whites of a slave protest or act of sabotage. In 1741, New York City was the site of several unexplained fires. Whites viewed the fires as acts of slave protest. Following a show trial, dozens of slaves were found guilty. There remain questions as to whether the slaves were the tools of a White conspiracy, innocent of any crime, or guilty as charged. In the end, thirteen slaves were burned alive.[25] Eighteen were hanged and seventy banished.[26] There was little evidence to support slave involvement with these fires. The cruelty of the verdict in this case underscores a manifest fear of slave revolt and the brutal manner in which Whites would deal with Black protest. Despite the threat of torture and death, Denmark Vesey, Nathaniel Turner, and John Brown planned insurrections.

Denmark Vesey was born in Saint Domingue (now Haiti) in 1767. He was enslaved in South Carolina. In 1800, Vesey won a lottery and used the proceeds to purchase his freedom.[27] Vesey was influenced by the French Revolution (1789–1799) as well as the slave uprisings in Haiti led by Toussaint L'Ouverture (1791–1804).[28] Haitian slaves rose up to defeat General Napoleon Bonaparte's army and gain their independence. Once in the United States, Vesey followed the fierce congressional debates surrounding the creation of free states under the Missouri Compromise.[29] The lack of political will in the North and the obstinance of Southern slaveholders made him aware that Black freedom would not come through the Courts. Prior to the uprising, Denmark Vesey led a relatively prosperous life for a Black man as a carpenter. Then, God inspired him to lead an attack against slavery.[30] Vesey and his compatriots developed an elaborate plan of revolt.[31] However, in 1822, Vesey was betrayed by a slave with mixed loyalties.[32] He and seventy-two others were tried and convicted of the crime of attempting to overthrow slavery.[33] Although many others were involved in the plot, Vesey refused to divulge their names.[34] He and thirty-five co-conspirators were hanged.[35] Thirty-seven co-conspirators were deported to plantations on Caribbean islands.[36] Vesey's revolt terrified slaveholders and other Whites. Stricter state laws were enacted to prevent additional slave uprisings.

Nathaniel Turner led the first successful American slave revolt on a large scale. He was born in 1800 to slave owner Benjamin Turner of Southampton, Virginia.[37] Nat Turner's mother was born in Africa. She despised slavery and taught her son disdain for it, as well. Turner believed God meant for him to lead an uprising against slavery.[38] He awaited a sign from God to begin the revolt. In 1831, he was sold to Joseph Travis. During that year, an eclipse convinced Turner that it was time to revolt against slavery.[39] On August 21, 1831, Turner led a revolt.[40] He and his compatriots killed the Travis family and fifty other Whites.[41] They escaped into the woods. Over three thousand White soldiers were deputized to capture him and his accomplices.

After Turner was apprehended on October 30, 1831, hundreds of innocent slaves were tortured and murdered in retaliation for the revolt.[42] Turner stood trial in Southampton County Court and was found guilty. While imprisoned, he dictated a statement to Thomas Gray in which he provided details of the insurrection.[43] But, Turner refused to provide the names of co-conspirators. He and thirteen other Blacks, including a woman, were executed on November 11, 1831.[44,45] The malevolence shown him even after death once again evidenced the fear and animosity felt by many Whites for Blacks who protested slavery. Turner was hanged, skinned, and beheaded. His head was placed on a pole and left to rot as a warning to anyone who sought to challenge slavery.

In the wake of Nat Turner's revolt, Virginia and many other states enacted more restrictive laws against enslaved Blacks.[46] The limited civil liberties of free Blacks were further restricted. Following Turner's execution, Maryland enacted a law forbidding free Blacks from entering the state.[47] Free Blacks who lived in Maryland could not possess weapons.[48] Religious meetings were suspect. In Virginia, "no slave, free negro, or mulatto, whether he shall have been ordained or licensed, or otherwise, shall hereafter undertake to preach, exhort, or conduct, or hold any assembly or meeting, for religious or other purposes either in the day time, or at night."[49] Violating this law would result in thirty lashes.[50] Slaves were whipped, hanged, or tortured in the presence of other slaves to inspire terror against protest.[51] Whites watched all gatherings of Blacks. Religious meetings created great unease.[52]

In June of 1859, John Brown, a White abolitionist, broke into an armory in Harper's Ferry, Virginia. Brown planned to arm Blacks and mobilize a national slave revolt. Accompanied by twenty-one men, including his son, sixteen Whites, and five Blacks, Brown successfully entered the armory. However, he inadvertently alerted the town. Thousands of militia surrounded the armory. Brown was captured. His son was killed. He was tried and found guilty of treason and sentenced to hang. Born in 1800 to a deeply religious abolitionist family, John Brown believed violence was necessary to end the grip of slavery in America. On the date of his execution, Brown stated: "Now, if it is deemed necessary that I should forfeit my life for the furtherance of the ends of justice, and mingle my blood further with the blood of my children and with the blood of millions in this slave country whose rights are disregarded by wicked, cruel, and unjust enactments, I submit; so let it be done!"

An Uprising at Sea: The *Amistad*

Slave revolts at sea were frequent, despite the brutal consequences and certain death facing the captives. African men, women, and children rose up against their fate as human cargo. In anticipation of a revolt, the crew of a slave ship would murder selected captives as a warning against insurrection. For the captives aboard the Spanish schooner *Amistad*, rebellion meant freedom. The story of the *Amistad* revolt is told in the Supreme Court case of *United States v. the Libellants*.[53] In 1839, the *Amistad* was en route from Havana, Cuba, to Puerto Principe, Cuba, when the slaves revolted against their oppressors.[54] An enslaved African named Sengbe Pieh led the mutiny. The captain, Ramon Ferrer, and a member of the *Amistad* crew were slain.

Sengbe demanded that the ship turn around and sail back to Africa. The White surviving members of the crew misled the slaves. For two months, the ship sailed to Africa by day. At night, the ship was turned back toward Cuba. Gale force winds drove the ship to Long Island Sound in New York. The *Amistad* traveled the East Coast in search of food and supplies. The U.S. Navy brig *Washington* seized the *Amistad* and forced it to dock in Connecticut. Sengbe and thirty-seven others were captured and charged with murder and piracy. Sengbe's name was changed to Jose Cinque, a Spanish name, by a surviving crew member in an attempt to deceive the court as to Sengbe's African heritage and status as a slave.

The trial of Cinque (Sengbe) placed the issue of slavery before the Connecticut court and on the world stage when the government of Spain demanded the return of the ship and its human cargo, arguing that the ship and the slaves belonged to Spain. Spain also claimed that Sengbe and his men must stand trial in Spain for the murder of Captain Ferrer, a Spanish subject, in Spanish waters. At the time, Cuba was a Spanish territory. However, slavery was illegal based on the Anglo-Spanish Treaty of 1820, which prohibited the transatlantic slave trade.

The status of Cinque, as freedman or slave, would determine his fate. At trial, abolitionists argued that Cinque was a free man sold into slavery in violation of the Anglo-Spanish Treaty. Therefore, he was not property. As a free man, Cinque had the right to defend himself, whereas a slave was forbidden self-defense. As a man, Cinque was the lawful owner of the *Amistad*. The U.S. government did not have authority to commandeer the ship. If Cinque was deemed a human being, then the Spanish government had no right to the ship or control over the African men aboard it because they were African, not Spanish, subjects. Freedom or certain death in Spain turned on the captives' status or place.

The first trial ended with a verdict in favor of Cinque. Evidence revealed that the Africans were illegally captured. However, U.S. President Van Buren would not allow the men to go free. He was running for reelection and wanted the Southern vote. Van Buren promised the South that the ship and Africans would be returned to Spain. The case was retried. The abolitionists enlisted the assistance of former U.S. President John Quincy Adams. The second, favorable verdict was appealed by the government. Cinque remained imprisoned pending all appeals. On appeal to the U.S. Supreme Court, Adams was forceful and eloquent in his defense of their freedom. The Supreme Court ruled in favor of Cinque. In 1841, Cinque and his fellow captives were at last repatriated to Sierra Leone, Africa.

Escape as Protest: *Strader v. Graham*

Although the punishment was brutal if caught, escape remained a relatively common method of protesting enslavement. Intricate state and federal laws meted out civil and criminal liability for anyone intentionally or inadvertently assisting slaves to escape. In *Strader v. Graham*, an 1851 case, three slaves named George, Henry, and Reuben escaped aboard the steamboat *Pike*.[55] Dr. C. Graham, the owner of the slaves, sued the owners of the steamboat, Jacob Strader and James Gorman, as well as John Armstrong, the commander of the vessel, for $3,000.[56] Strader, Gorman, and Armstrong were sued under an 1824 Kentucky statute that provided that the master of a vessel was liable when his vessel was utilized by slaves as a means of escape.[57] The ship could be condemned and sold for damages. The escaped captives were talented musicians allowed to travel by permission of their owner for concert performances and training. While their owner remained in Harrodsburg, Kentucky, the slaves traveled nationally as a musical troupe. Having tasted freedom, George, Henry, and Reuben decided to escape. They traveled to Ohio, a free state, and then to Canada, never to return to Graham or slavery in Kentucky.

Graham's case turned on the status of George, Henry, and Reuben. Ohio and Indiana were part of the Northwestern Territory. In 1787, an Ordinance of the Northwestern Territory was enacted that declared that "there shall be neither slavery nor involuntary servitude" in the territory.[58] Graham allowed these Black men to travel to Ohio. Strader, Gorman, and Armstrong argued that George, Henry, and Reuben became free when Graham gave them permission to travel to a free state and play concerts. However, the substance of the suit against the vessel's owners never reached the Court.

Strader v. Graham was dismissed on jurisdictional grounds; the Court ruled that the case was not properly before it and therefore it would not render a decision on the merits. Justice Roger B. Taney delivered the Court's opinion. Although the Court could have stopped at this point, it went further to determine that the Northwestern Territory ordinance was preempted by the U.S. Constitution and acts of Congress.[59] Therefore, a slave from Kentucky would not become free in Ohio. Some six years later, Justice Taney would deliver the infamous opinion in *Dred Scott v. Sandford* (1857) denying rights to all Blacks.

The *Strader* decision would act as a precursor to *Dred Scott* in which an enslaved man, taken to a free state and then returned to a slave state, argued that under the Missouri Compromise he was free. That Court dismissed the claims of Scott, stating that as a noncitizen he could not bring an action in any court. Scott's case was also dismissed for lack of jurisdiction. However, there, too, the Court went further and found that the Missouri Compromise was without legal foundation. The *Strader v. Graham* decision undermined efforts of enslaved Blacks to change their status by escaping into free states. The Court's ruling also ignored the inherent right of a state to abolish or restrict slavery.

Jim Crow Freedom: Protesting Postslavery Segregation

Slavery was abolished in 1865. In 1868, Congress ratified the post-Civil War Amendments to provide full rights of citizenship to Blacks. However, by 1871, the Ku Klux Klan became an active force in maintaining the socioracial hierarchy established during slavery. States in the North and South enacted laws segregating the races. These laws were referred to as "Jim Crow" laws. States enacted Black Codes—criminal laws that discriminated against Blacks by providing harsher punishments than those given to Whites who committed the same crimes. Homer Plessy's

decision to sit in the car designated for Whites-only was an act of protest. Ida B. Wells-Barnett and W. E. B. DuBois participated in similar
protests of racial segregation in public accommodations. History has
focused on the Supreme Court's decision in *Plessy*, which entrenched
inequality as opposed to the constant press of Blacks to end it. Blacks,
acting individually and within formal associations, planned the defeat
of *Plessy* and the hundreds of segregation laws that mandated separate
treatment. Blacks protested against America's racial caste system using a
myriad of methods. Blacks lobbied Congress and presidents for change
through legislative action. Civil rights litigation continued. Protests
against unequal treatment took place across America as Blacks held fast
to their demand for full citizenship including the freedom to protest
against governmental wrongs.

Civil Disobedience: Protest
Marches and Sit-Ins

On July 28, 1917, thousands of African Americans participated in a
silent march in New York City. That year, Blacks were murdered with
impunity by lynch mobs in Waco, Texas; East St. Louis, Illinois; and
Memphis, Tennessee. Blacks were made victims of race riots in five
other American cities. The silent march protested this national wave
of violence against Blacks as well as the abject failure of law enforcement and the courts to provide protection against such lawlessness.

Protest marches were used to bring attention to racial injustice
and to demonstrate the unity and power of the masses. In 1941, A.
Philip Randolph,[60] leader of the first Black labor union, planned a
protest march of one hundred thousand Black persons through Washington, D.C., if President Franklin D. Roosevelt did not desegregate U.S. defense plants.[61] It was World War II and the segregated
defense plants refused to employ Blacks. After Randolph threatened
to march, Roosevelt signed Executive Order 8802 desegregating the
defense industry.[62] Randolph's campaign against segregation in the
military led President Harry S. Truman to sign Executive Order 9981
desegregating America's military.[63]

Civil disobedience entails defying "unjust" laws for "just" reasons;
it is a means of nonviolent protest. Marching without a permit has

long been used as a form of civil disobedience. Modern acts of protest by civil disobedience is attributed to Mahatma Gandhi. Born in 1869, Gandhi organized thousands of protesters across India in nonviolent protests, sit-ins, and work stoppages that eventually led to independence from Great Britain.[64] A sit-in involves remaining seated in a place where one is prohibited to be as an act of civil disobedience.

The American sit-in began on February 1, 1960, in Greensboro, North Carolina. Blacks organized sit-in protests at stores and restaurants where racial discrimination was practiced. After Black college students attending North Carolina A&T College were refused service at the F. W. Woolworth Company lunch counter, they were told to leave the store.[65] The students, Joseph McNeil, Franklin McCain, David Richmond, and Ezell Blair, Jr., refused to leave, remaining at the counter until the store closed. They returned the next day accompanied by a larger group of students. The civil rights organizations Congress for Racial Equality (CORE) and Southern Christian Leadership Conference (SCLC) took note and joined their protest. Activist Bayard Rustin persuaded Martin Luther King, Jr., to confront the oppressor's violence using Gandhi's philosophy of civil disobedience.[66] King, with other civil rights leaders, further developed the modern sit-in by applying nonviolence and economics within a protest strategy.[67] King understood that neither America's economy nor its international image could afford the disruptions caused by civil rights protesters in stores and restaurants.[68]

Blacks, many of whom were students, who were refused service in segregated restaurants and stores refused to leave. Sit-ins took place in Alabama, Louisiana, and Kansas City, Missouri, and Northern cities such as New York. The sit-in led to the arrest of hundreds of nonviolent protesters who refused to post bail. As with Gandhi, the arrests overwhelmed law enforcement and created havoc for a criminal justice system that relied (and still relies) on 90 percent of defendants pleading guilty or refusing jury trials. The arrest of dozens of protesters overburdened the jails and brought media attention to the struggle against apartheid in the United States. Protesters participating in acts of civil disobedience undertook a risk of great physical harm to themselves and their families. The reactions to civil disobedience by Whites in the South as well as in the North were often violent.[69] As part of an ongoing protest strategy, in 1963, A.

Philip Randolph and Rustin organized the March on Washington for Jobs and Freedom at which over half a million people demanded the end to racial segregation in America.

Young people continued their sit-ins despite beatings and arrests. States were determined to maintain the racial segregation sanctioned by the Supreme Court in *Plessy*. However, the change in composition of the Supreme Court meant the states no longer held carte blanche freedom to discriminate based on race or prohibit protest against that discrimination. Protesters now heavily relied on the Supreme Court to address their demands for civil rights and American liberties.

In *Lombard v. Louisiana* (1963),[70] four students, three Blacks and one White, staged a sit-in at a segregated New Orleans restaurant that served Whites only. They were convicted of criminal mischief. Although the state law did not require segregation, the management of the restaurant refused to serve Blacks. The manager informed Black patrons: "We have to sell to you at the rear of the store where we have a colored counter."[71] The students refused to leave.[72] Instead, they sat quietly at the counter. The police arrived. The students were led out of the store and taken away in a patrol wagon.[73] Each student was convicted and sentenced to serve sixty days in the parish prison and pay a fine of $350.[74] Another sit-in had taken place in a Woolworth store in New Orleans one week earlier.[75]

The mayor of New Orleans issued a statement condemning sit-in demonstrations and "directed the superintendent of police that no additional sit-in demonstrations will be permitted...regardless of the avowed purpose or intent of the participants..."[76] The students appealed their convictions to the Supreme Court. The Court reversed their convictions, finding a violation of the Fourteenth Amendment. Although the restaurant was not explicitly segregated by state law, the Supreme Court ruled that the government played a role in enforcing the tradition of segregation. The pressure of the mayor and police superintendent constituted governmental support of segregation in violation of the Fourteenth Amendment.[77]

In 1961, Black high school and college students protested at the South Carolina State House. The student protesters expressed their dissatisfaction with discriminatory actions "against Negroes...and

[we] would like for the laws which prohibited Negro privileges in this state to be removed."[78] The students sang "The Star-Spangled Banner" while walking peaceably around public grounds.[79] They carried signs with the messages such as "I am proud to be a Negro" and "Down with segregation."[80] They were ordered to disperse by the city manager. They refused. The students were charged with and convicted of breach of the peace.

Their criminal sentences ranged from a fine of $10 or five days in jail to a $100 fine or thirty days in jail.[81] The protesters appealed their convictions. The state courts upheld the convictions. However, the U.S. Supreme Court reversed the decision. Since the students had not blocked traffic and there was no violence on their part or on the part of any member of the crowd.[82] Therefore, it was the mere protest against injustice that caused their arrest. The Court found the arrest and conviction violated the student protesters' constitutionally protected rights of free speech, free assembly, and freedom to petition for redress of their grievances.[83] South Carolina could not criminalize a peaceful expression of unpopular views.[84] Blacks had gained footing in their effort to exercise fundamental freedoms ratified in the U.S. Constitution in 1791.

In 1965, the Supreme Court decided the case of *Cox v. Louisiana*.[85] The Reverend B. Elton Cox was field secretary for the local chapter of the Congress of Racial Equality (CORE), a civil rights organization. Cox and two thousand students from Southern University, a historically Black college, assembled at the state capital of Baton Rouge, Louisiana. The group was there to protest the arrest and detainment of some of their fellow students. The group walked toward the courthouse carrying signs reading "Don't buy discrimination for Christmas," which spoke to the racial segregation practiced by Baton Rouge stores and restaurants. The protesters sang "God Bless America" and "We Shall Overcome." The group remained peaceful and orderly. The demonstrators then turned their protest to the segregated lunch counters.

At this point, White deputies approached the students. Police officers exploded tear gas into the crowd. None of the protesters was arrested that day. However, the next day Cox was arrested. He was convicted of breach of the peace and unlawfully obstructing public passages.[86] The Louisiana statute provided that

Whoever with intent to provoke a breach of the peace, or under circumstances such that a breach of the peace may be occasioned thereby... crowds or congregates with others...in or upon...a public street or public highway...and who fails to refuse to disperse and move on when ordered to do so by any law enforcement officer...shall be guilty of disturbing the peace.[87]

Similar laws were enacted across the South to prevent sit-ins and peaceful demonstrations for racial justice. During the trial, the judge determined Cox must be convicted, stating that:

[It is] inherently dangerous and a breach of the peace to bring 1,500 people, colored people, down in the predominantly white business district...and congregated across the street from the courthouse and sing songs...such as "black and white together" and urge those 1,500 people to descend upon our lunch counters and sit until they are served. That has to be an inherent breach of the peace.[88]

Cox was convicted and sentenced to serve four months and to pay a $200 fine for disturbing the peace, five months and a $500 fine for obstructing public passages, and one year and a $5,000 fine for picketing before the courthouse.[89]

Cox appealed his conviction. The Louisiana courts upheld the conviction. However, the U.S. Supreme Court reversed the conviction, finding the state law unconstitutional. The Court relied on its decisions in the protest case of *Edwards v. South Carolina* and the public parks segregation case of *Watson v. Memphis*.[90] The Supreme Court upheld the protesters' freedom of speech and assembly under the First Amendment as applied to the states by the Fourteenth Amendment's due-process clause.[91] Under that amendment, no state could deny any person life, liberty, or property without due process of law. The conviction for obstructing public passages was overturned because the statute was applied to Cox in an attempt to restrict his freedom of speech and assembly.

However, the Supreme Court ruled in favor of the state and against Black protesters in *Adderley v. Florida* (1966).[92] Harriett Adderley and thirty-one students from Florida A&M University in Tallahassee demonstrated in front of the county jail. They were protesting the segregated jail facilities and the prior detainment of several students arrested for protesting against segregated theaters.[93] The A&M students marched to the site of the jail, sat down in the driveway, and refused to leave. The police gave orders to move away and then arrested Adderley and two other students. They were convicted of blocking municipal property.[94] The convictions were upheld by the state courts.

Upon appeal to the U.S. Supreme Court, Justice Hugo Black, a former Klan member turned "liberal" justice, wrote on behalf of the Court, which upheld the convictions. The Court distinguished its decisions in *Cox* and *Edwards* from *Adderley*.[95] The protesters in *Cox* were on public property where Adderley was on municipal property. A state can control its property even in the face of the exercise of free speech and assembly.[96] Justices William O. Douglas and Abe Fortas and Chief Justice Brennan dissented, believing that the Court erred in treating Adderley as a regular trespasser. The dissenting justices would elevate the status of the jailed student protesters to that of political prisoners. They stated:

> The jailhouse, like an executive mansion, a legislative chamber, a courthouse, or the statehouse itself is one of the seats of government, whether it be the Tower of London, the Bastille, or a small county jail. And when it houses political prisoners or those who many think are unjustly held, it is an obvious center for protest.[97]

The dissenters spoke passionately about the historical basis for protest rights in America grounded in the Magna Carta of England in 1215 through the First Continental Congress in 1774 and the Declaration of Independence in 1776.[98] Interestingly, the justices failed to note that most Blacks in America were enslaved during this time of alleged democratic development.

In California in 1965, Cesar Chavez organized Hispanic farmworker protests for better wages, safe working conditions, and unionization.

In 1968, Dr. Martin Luther King, Jr., was assassinated in Memphis, Tennessee. King was in Memphis as part of the Southern Christian Leadership Conference's Poor People's Campaign. King planned to lead a march on behalf of Black sanitation workers involved in a labor strike for decent wages and safe working conditions. As had been the case with previous nonviolent demonstrations King led, the planned march was met with violent opposition by local government officials and the majority White population.

The year after King's death, the Rev. Ralph Abernathy of the SCLC joined Chavez to protest the use of outside labor to undermine a farmworkers' strike for higher wages.

Urban Uprising as Protest

Blacks forced to live in Northern ghettos due to housing and unemployment discrimination were turning from civil disobedience to urban uprisings. On August 11, 1965, in the Watts section of Los Angeles, a questionable arrest of three Blacks by White police officers led a Black community frustrated with police brutality, the assassination of Malcolm X earlier that year, and racial injustice to unleash its fury. The Watts riot lasted six days and cost the lives of at least forty people and injured over a thousand. Entire city blocks were destroyed by fire and hundreds were arrested. The Watts riots ushered in a different type of protest: the urban uprising. Blacks rioted against the seemingly invisible hand of racial oppression by burning whatever was within their power to destroy. The war in Vietnam brought additional urban unrest. College students protested President Richard Nixon's expansion of the war into Cambodia and Laos. In May of 1970, student protesters were killed for protesting at Kent State University in Ohio and Jackson State University in Mississippi.[99]

With the assassination of Martin Luther King, Jr., on April 4, 1968, the role of nonviolence became overshadowed by violent urban uprisings. Blacks, in pain and shock over King's murder, struck out against the hypocrisy and injustice manifested in the murder by Whites of a Black man who stood for peace. Their grief and rage led to urban uprisings in every major city in America. With justice routinely denied in state courts, Black uprisings became the response to manifest injustice. Violent uprisings followed the deaths of Blacks at the hands of White police officers. Miami, Ohio, Seattle, Detroit, Chicago, Harlem, and Los Angeles have been the sites of urban uprisings against police brutality. On the evening of March 2, 1991, Rodney King, a Black motorist, was beaten by members of the Los Angeles Police Department following a high-speed chase on the Altadena highway.[100] When the White police officers charged with the brutal beating were acquitted, the Black community there erupted in mass uprisings.[101]

King had been handcuffed and was lying on the ground when officers beat him with clubs, stomped on him, and shocked him with electric tasers. The brutality was captured by an amateur videographer. Property damage resulting from the uprisings exceeded $1 billion; there were at least forty fatalities with over 13,000 arrests, and 2,000 people injured.[102] Mayor Tom Bradley, Los Angeles's first Black mayor, activated the California National Guard and President George H. Bush deployed federal troops to Los Angeles.[103] Later, the U.S. Justice Department brought an action in federal court under the Civil Rights Act, which found in favor of King.[104] However, the communities affected have yet to fully recover. A commission, chaired by Warren Christopher, formed to investigate police abuse in Los Angeles, found widespread evidence of racism and a failure to reprimand officers who used excessive force.[105] For urban Blacks impatient with the rhetoric of Whites (and the Black elite), these uprisings have all but replaced civil disobedience as the primary method of protest.

Protest and Public Officials:
New York Times v. Sullivan

A newspaper advertisement meant to protest civil rights abuses in Montgomery, Alabama, changed the legal standard for libel for the entire country. In *New York Times, Inc. v. Sullivan* (1964), four African-American ministers, seeking to bring national attention to discrimination in Alabama, placed a full-page advertisement in the *New York Times* newspaper.[106] The advertisement, *Heed Their Rising Voices*, protested the treatment of Black students at Alabama State University in Montgomery, Alabama.[107] The harassment of Martin Luther King by police officers and their failure to fully investigate the bombing of King's home were also addressed in the advertisement.[108] L. B. Sullivan, Commissioner of Public Affairs of the city of Montgomery, filed a libel action against the ministers and the *New York Times.*[109]

Sullivan was not mentioned by name in the advertisement. However, he alleged that the statements in the advertisement damaged his reputation as a public official and defamed him in the community.[110] Additionally, certain statements in the advertisement were not completely accurate. Dr. King was purportedly arrested seven times when, in fact, he was arrested four times.[111] Under Alabama's libelous *per se* statute, created to deter civil rights protesters, a public official could be awarded damages by merely proving a written statement had caused an injury.[112] The state trial court found in favor of Sullivan, awarding him $500,000 in damages.[113]

The *New York Times* appealed. However, the Alabama Supreme Court upheld the verdict and damage award, stating that "where words published tend to injure a person...in his reputation, profession, trade or business...or tend to bring the individual into public contempt they are libelous per se."[114] The *New York Times* and the ministers appealed to the U.S. Supreme Court. The Court reversed the Alabama court's verdict and damages award.[115] Justice Brennan delivered the opinion on behalf of the Court, which held that the Alabama statute unfairly restricted freedom of speech and press and the freedom to criticize public officials in violation of the First and Fourteenth Amendments.[116] The Court ruled that public officials must prove actual malice in a libel case.[117] The Court also made clear that commercial advertisements were protected by the First Amendment. This civil rights case changed the legal standard in libel cases involving protest speech and public officials and expanded freedom of the press.

Freedom of Association: *Bates v. Little Rock*

There is power in numbers. Civil rights groups and grassroots activists shared resources and created strategies as coalitions to defeat racial oppression.[118] As Blacks gathered to plan and protest, states enacted laws to prevent organized activism. Members of organizations, clubs, or groups exercised freedom of association in the face of racial oppressors who sought to defeat concerted efforts of Black organizations to gain civil liberties and civil rights. Freedom of association is a civil liberty grounded in First Amendment rights; it falls within freedom of assembly and speech. When proponents of civil rights, from beleaguered farmers in Alabama to college students in Michigan, worked together, they became an effective mechanism for justice attempts. Their effectiveness triggered retaliation from Southern legislatures. Alabama enacted a state law banning the NAACP and other civil rights organizations.

In 1955, Rosa Parks was secretary of the Montgomery, Alabama, chapter of the NAACP when she was arrested for refusing to surrender her seat on a public bus to a White male passenger. Alabama's segregation laws required Blacks on public transportation to move to accommodate standing White passengers or suffer arrest. Represented by civil rights attorney Fred Gray, Parks appealed her arrest. The arrest of Parks ignited the Women's Political Council, which initiated the 381-day boycott of Montgomery's segregated public buses.[119] The appeal of Parks's conviction reached the U.S. Supreme Court. In *Gayle v. Browder* and *Owen v. Browder*, decided in 1956, the Court held that racially segregated public transportation violated the Constitution.[120]

Following the bus boycott, a victory in *Brown*, and the forced desegregation of the University of Alabama, the attorney general of Alabama, without a hearing or trial, barred the NAACP from doing business in the state.[121]

In *NAACP v. Alabama* (1958), the attorney general required the National Association for the Advancement of Colored People to provide membership lists.[122] The Alabama chapter of the NAACP had been granted a corporate charter to do business in the state in 1918.[123] However, it was during the 1950s that the organization began expanding its regional offices, recruiting substantial numbers of members, and conducting boycotts of segregated facilities.[124] The NAACP refused to provide the membership list. The civil rights organization argued that Alabama's request violated the First and Fourteenth Amendment rights of its membership.[125]

The group was threatened with contempt. The trial court ordered the group to provide its membership list or risk a fine of $10,000.

The fine would increase to $100,000 if the NAACP did not comply within five days of the court's order.[126] The NAACP argued that its members had the right to associate freely and advance their beliefs and ideas without intimidation. During the trial, the organization presented incontrovertible evidence that members who revealed their identity were exposed to economic reprisals, loss of employment, threats of physical harm, and public hostility.[127] Alabama refused to protect NAACP members threatened with harm, stating that it was not responsible for the actions of its private (White) citizens.[128]

Alabama demanded the NAACP's membership lists. The state argued that the list of names and addresses would reveal whether the NAACP was conducting business activities in violation of Alabama law.[129] Additionally, Alabama contended that the NAACP must comply given that the Supreme Court had forced the Ku Klux Klan to provide its membership list in *Bryant v. Zimmerman* (1928).[130] In that case, the state of New York sought the membership list of the Buffalo chapter of the Knights of the Ku Klux Klan. The KKK refused, arguing it was similar to the Elks and Masons and therefore exempt from such a demand. The Klan lost because the Supreme Court found a real and substantial distinction between the Masons and a Klan group that conducted a "crusade against Catholics, Jews and Negroes."[131] Alabama's association of the NAACP with the KKK resulted in a favorable state court ruling for Alabama.

The NAACP appealed to the U.S. Supreme Court. Writing on behalf of the Court, Justice John M. Harlan, grandson of the Justice Harlan who had filed the famous dissent in *Plessy v. Ferguson*, reversed the state court.[132] The Court held that providing the membership lists was not a requirement within the statute, especially given that Alabama's attorney general had not requested lists of any other organizations. The "chilling effect'" or fear of reprisals for members of the NAACP outweighed the curiosity of the attorney general's office. In deciding in favor of the NAACP, the Supreme Court also considered the character of the organization.[133] In contrast, the KKK in *Bryant* refused to furnish any of the requested information. The NAACP furnished all requested information except for the membership list.[134]

Alabama defied the Supreme Court's ruling. The NAACP remained in contempt.[135] *NAACP v. Alabama* was appealed to the Supreme

Court on three separate occasions.[136] This case illustrates the bitterness between state courts and the more progressive federal courts during the modern civil rights era. State courts and state legislatures in the South adamantly refused to recognize the rights of Blacks. In turn, they refused to respect the primacy of the Supreme Court when it ruled against segregation and race discrimination.

It was a test of wills. The Court ruled in 1958 that the NAACP was not required to submit the names and addresses of its members to the state of Alabama. The Alabama state court, in defiance, scheduled a trial on the issue of whether the NAACP had complied with the membership disclosure requirement.[137] The trial court ruled against the NAACP and permanently forbade the organization from doing business in the state. The Alabama Supreme Court refused to hear the appeal of the NAACP because of an alleged error in the format of the group's court briefs.[138] The NAACP appealed to the U.S. Supreme Court.

Alabama argued that the activities of the NAACP undermined the people's right to racially segregate. The complaint against the organization stated in part that the NAACP:

1) furnished legal counsel to represent Autherine Lucy in proceedings to obtain admission to the university [of Alabama]; ...

3) engaged in organizing, supporting, and financing an illegal boycott to compel a bus line in Montgomery, Alabama, not to segregate passengers according to race; ...

9) encouraged, aided, and abetted the unlawful breach of the peace in many cities in Alabama for the purpose of gaining national notoriety and attention to enable it to raise funds under a false claim that it was for the protection of alleged constitutional rights; ...

10) encouraged, aided, and abetted a course of conduct within the state of Alabama, seeking to deny to the citizens of Alabama the constitutional right to voluntarily segregate.[139]

The U.S. Supreme Court remained adamant.

Once again, the Supreme Court found that the Alabama regulation did not support the ouster of the NAACP.[140] The Court made clear that an organization could not be prohibited from doing business in the state based only on its advocacy for racial justice.[141] Precluding the NAACP from maintaing a chapter in Alabama was a mechanism to restrict the freedom to associate for the collective advocacy of ideas. The Court stated that "freedoms such as [these] are protected not only against heavy-handed frontal attack, but also from being stifled by more subtle government interference."[142]

While the Court was addressing the issue of membership in *NAACP v. Alabama*, a similar case arose in Arkansas. In *Bates v. Little Rock*, decided in 1960, Daisy Bates and Birdie Williams were convicted of failing to disclose the names of the members of the Little Rock branch of the NAACP.[143] In 1957, after civil rights organizations began fighting against segregation, Little Rock amended its Arkansas occupation license tax ordinance to require an organization operating within the municipality to supply information about its membership, officers' salaries, dues, contributors, and net income.[144] Additionally, the records of the NAACP chapter were required to be open to the public.[145]

Bates was president of the NAACP of Little Rock and Williams was president of the North Little Rock NAACP.[146] Both women acted as custodians of the records and provided all information except the names and addresses of members.[147] They were both arrested and held in contempt. Bates and Williams based their refusal to provide the names on the anti-NAACP climate in Arkansas.[148] Public disclosure of the names could lead to harassment, economic reprisals, and even bodily harm.[149]

The City of Little Rock countered that it enacted the ordinance to reach certain organizations that were abusing their nonprofit status. The ordinance sought organizations in Little Rock, Arkansas which claimed immunity from the payment of occupation licenses.[150] Arkansas claimed it needed the names to ensure that the NAACP was not engaged in commercial business. The Arkansas Supreme Court upheld the contempt convictions of Bates and Williams.[151] On appeal to the U.S. Supreme Court, the convictions were overturned.[152] Justice Potter Stewart wrote the opinion on behalf of the Court. In its decision, the Court questioned the relationship between the stated purpose of the ordinance and the effect of the law on the First Amendment rights of the NAACP's members.[153] The Court ruled that disclosure of the NAACP's membership lists would significantly interfere with the freedom of association of its members.[154] Additionally, the Court found that the NAACP had not requested nonprofit organization status. Therefore, it did not fall within the scope of the ordinance.

The Supreme Court's decisions in *NAACP v. Alabama* and *Bates v. Little Rock* strengthened First Amendment protections for all advocacy organizations. Consequently, any membership organization benefited from these decisions. States responded to the advancement of constitutional protections of Blacks and other minorities by enacting statutes to deter civil rights activists from organizing. The tactics changed; the goal of preventing Blacks from realizing full citizenship remained.

In 1961, Louisiana sued the NAACP under a statute requiring an out-of-state organization to file an affidavit stating that none of its officers was a member of a Communist, Communist-front, or subversive organization on the grounds that organizations with connections to the Communist Party were prohibited from doing business in Louisiana.[155] Another state law required the names and addresses of members and officers.[156] The law, allegedly passed in 1924 to restrict the Ku Klux Klan, was only enforced against the NAACP.[157] Using the guise of investigating Communists and subversives was yet another mechanism for preventing Blacks from fighting against racial oppression. To demonstrate patriotism, Blacks complied. However, members of the NAACP chapters complying with the order were immediately fired from their jobs.[158]

The case was moved from state to federal court. Relying on the decision in *Bates v. Little Rock* and *NAACP v. Alabama*, the federal district court entered an injunction prohibiting Louisiana from enforcing the anti-Communism statute. The state of Louisiana appealed. The U.S. Supreme Court upheld the injunction, finding that the disclosure of the membership list was not required if it resulted in hostility against the members on the list.[159] Additionally, statutes that infringed on First Amendment rights had to be more narrowly drafted to achieve their stated purpose of detecting Communists.[160] The states retaliated against the success of the NAACP and other civil rights advocates.

In *NAACP v. Button*, decided by the Supreme Court in 1963, Virginia enacted legislation to prohibit any organization from retaining a lawyer from outside the state.[161] The law required that an out-of-state attorney hired by a resident of the state could have no pecuniary or financial interest in the case.[162] The NAACP was headquartered in New York.[163] The organization's attorneys represented clients in civil rights cases around the country. This law was meant to stop the NAACP from receiving any money if it was the victor in those cases. The NAACP sued to stop the enforcement of this law as a violation of its members' Fourteenth Amendment rights.[164] The Virginia courts ruled against the NAACP. On appeal, the U.S. Supreme Court reversed the Virginia Supreme Court.

The Supreme Court ruled in *Button* that litigation was a form of speech protected by the First Amendment.[165] Freedom of speech is protected against state action by the Fourteenth Amendment and advocating for civil rights is a mode of expression and association.[166] Virginia could not prohibit the civil rights advocacy of the NAACP, its affiliates, or legal staff.[167] Thus, *NAACP v. Button* expanded constitutional protections for the entire legal profession.

Freedom to be in an Interracial Relationship: *Pace v. Alabama*

Selecting one's intimate partner is a basic liberty. However, the freedom to enter a relationship with a person of another race is merely decades old. Blacks had never been fully free to choose their partners. Dating back to slavery, laws restricted with whom a Black person could socialize, mate, or marry. Colonial laws forbade marriage between the races. In 1705, a Massachusetts law stated that "none of her Majesty's English or Scottish subjects, nor of any other Christian nation...shall contract matrimony with any negro or mulatto."[168] The Massachusetts law forbade performing a marriage ceremony that united a man and woman of different races on penalty of fifty pounds.[169]

The Court, in *Dred Scott v. Sandford*, referred to these laws to support its denial of personhood to Black people. The deep societal animus toward marriage between the races is evidenced in the Court's pernicious words:

> A perpetual and impassable barrier was intended to be erected between the white race and the one which they reduced to slavery, and governed

as subjects with absolute and despotic power, and which they then looked upon as so far below them in the scale of created beings, that intermarriages between white person[s] and negroes or mulattoes were regarded as unnatural and immoral, and punished as crimes....And no distinction in this respect was made between the free negro or mulatto and the slave, but this stigma, of the deep degradation, was fixed upon the whole race.[170]

The Court placed Blacks outside the human species with respect to marriage. Although the Fourteenth Amendment was meant to provide Blacks with full rights of American citizenship, that citizenship did not entail the freedom to marry or choose a partner.

In 1883, the Supreme Court decided *Pace v. Alabama*, its first case involving an interracial relationship.[171] Tony Pace, a Black man, and Mary J. Cox, a White woman, were arrested and convicted of violating a statute prohibiting interracial cohabitation, physically living together, under the same roof. Under Section 4189 of an Alabama statute:

If any white person and any negro, or the descendent of any negro to the third generation, inclusive, though one ancestor of each generation was a white person, intermarry or live with each other, each of them must, on conviction, be imprisoned in the penitentiary or sentenced to hard labor for the county for not less then two nor more than seven years.[172]

Pace argued that the punishment was harsher for an interracial couple consisting of Black and White races. Under Section 4184, a conviction for fornication without marriage between two Whites was punishable by a $100 fine and two years of hard labor or confinement in the state penitentiary.[173]

Pace appealed the sentence. He argued that the difference in punishment was race discrimination and a violation of his equal-protection rights under the Fourteenth Amendment. The Alabama State Supreme court denied his appeal, stating that the fact that the punishment when committed by a Black person and a White person is different from that when committed by two White persons or two Black persons was not discrimination.[174] However, the Alabama court added that the "evil tendency of the crime of living in adultery or fornication is greater when it is committed between persons of the two races, than between persons of the same race."[175] Pace and Cox were sentenced to two years in the Alabama state penitentiary. Pace appealed to the U.S. Supreme Court.

Justice Stephen J. Field delivered the opinion in *Pace v. Alabama*. The U.S. Supreme Court upheld Alabama's decision.[176] The Court did not compare the provisions of the law, each with a different punishment based on race. Instead, the Court stated that there was no discrimination because the Black person and White person, within the interracial relationship, received a similar punishment.[177] The Court's message was clear. States could criminalize interracial relationships. The damage was not limited to relationships. For the next fifty years, *Pace v. Alabama* was used by states across the South to support differences in sentences based on race.[178]

Miscegenation is the cohabitation, sexual relationship, or marriage between persons of different races. In 1896, the Supreme Court relied on state laws prohibiting interracial marriage to support the "separate but equal" doctrine in *Plessy v. Ferguson*.[179] "Laws forbidding the intermarriage of the two races may be said in a technical sense to interfere with the freedom of contract, and yet have been universally recognized as within the police power of the State"; miscegenation is prohibited to prevent a violent response from Whites.[180] After *Pace* and *Plessy*, antimiscegenation laws were enacted across the country.

The laws were not limited to the states in the South. In 1899, Utah placed an antimiscegenation provision in its marriage laws prohibiting marriage between any White person and a person considered Negro, mulatto, quadroon, octoroon, Mongolian, or Malay.[181] States amended their constitutions to prohibit interracial relationships. The Alabama constitution states that "the legislature shall never pass any law to authorize or legalize any marriage between any white person and a negro, or descendent of a negro."[182] The Supreme Court would not decide the next case involving interracial relationships until well after the *Brown v. Board of Education* decision of 1954.

Antimiscegenation after
Brown: *Loving v. Virginia*

Antimiscegenation laws remained long after the country prohibited racial segregation in the armed forces, education, public accomodations, and housing. In 1964, the Supreme Court decided *McLaughlin v. Florida*, a miscegenation case involving a married interracial couple.[183] Dewey McLaughlin, a Black man, and Connie Hoffman, a White woman, were arrested for violating Florida's adultery and fornication statute.[184] Under the statute, "if any white person and negro, or mulatto, shall live in adultery or fornication with each other, each shall be punished by imprisonment not exceeding twelve months, or by fine not exceeding one thousand dollars."[185] McLaughlin argued that he was not Negro and that he and Hoffman were in a common-law marriage, not merely cohabitating. At trial, the arresting officer testified that McLaughlin appeared to be Black.[186] That statement satisfied the trial judge.

The couple was convicted. McLaughlin appealed on equal-protection grounds to the state's highest court. Once again, an interracial couple would receive harsher punishment for the same offense if committed by White couples. The Florida State Supreme court upheld the conviction based on the decision in *Pace v. Alabama*.[187] McLaughlin appealed his conviction to the U.S. Supreme Court. He also argued that miscegenation laws violated the U.S. Constitution. The Supreme Court reversed the conviction. Justice Byron White delivered the opinion. "Nothing in this legislative purpose...makes it essential to punish promiscuity of one racial group and not that of another."[188] However, the Court refused to address McLaughlin's request to find miscegenation laws unconstitutional. That issue would soon be confronted in *Loving v. Virginia*.

Richard Loving, a White man, and his wife Mildred, a Black woman, were arrested for violating Virginia's antimiscegenation law. The couple was married in Washington, D.C., in 1958 and returned to Virginia. Soon, three White police officers entered their bedroom and arrested the couple for violating Virginia's Racial Integrity Act of 1924. Neither knew that Virginia had antimiscegenation laws dating back to 1619.[189] The Lovings pled guilty to violating the statute and were convicted for leaving the state in order to marry. Under the law, "if any white person and colored person shall go out of this State, for the purpose of being married and with the intention of returning, and be married out of it, and afterwards return to and reside in it, cohabiting as man and wife, they shall be punished."[190] The punishment was confinement in the penitentiary for not less than one and no more than five years.[191] There was an exception, however. Descendants of John Rolf and Pocahontas were excluded. As late as 1967, Virginia was one of sixteen states that prohibited and punished marriages on the basis of racial classification.[192]

The Lovings were sentenced to one year in jail. The sentence was suspended provided the couple leave Virginia and not return together or at the same time for twenty-five years.[193] The Lovings complied and moved out of the state. However, several years later the couple wanted to return to Virginia to be close to Mildred's family.[194] With the assistance of the American Civil Liberties Union, they appealed their conviction and sentence of exile on equal-protection and due-process grounds.[195] Virginia's trial court judge, Leon Bazile, made clear at the rehearing that marriage is a relationship within the police power and control of the state.

Bazile upheld the conviction, declaring that "Almighty God created the race white, black, yellow, [Malay] and red, and he placed them on separate continents. And but for the interference with his arrangement there would be no cause for such marriages."[196] The Virginia state courts affirmed the convictions.[197] The Lovings appealed to the U.S. Supreme Court. Chief Justice Earl Warren delivered the opinion that would finally overturn *Pace v. Alabama*. The Court could find no legitimate overriding purpose for Virginia's antimiscegenation law independent of invidious racial discrimination.[198] Virginia's statue only prohibited interracial marriages between White and non-White persons, not between others races, for example, Asians and Blacks.

The Court made clear that antimiscegenation laws were merely thinly veiled "measures designed to maintain White supremacy."[199] States were prohibited from infringing upon the freedom to marry a person of another race.[200] Virginia's antimiscegenation statutes violated the Lovings' equal-protection and due-process rights.

Modern Antimiscegenation:
Bob Jones University v. United States

Although the Court prohibited state antimiscegenation laws, centuries of legal sanction proved more difficult to remove. Societal intransigence was demonstrated in a myriad of ways with numerous implications. Alabama's constitution contained a provision prohibiting interracial marriages until it was repealed by state referendum in 2000. In *Bob Jones University v. United States*, a 1983 decision, the Supreme Court was presented with a case of racially discriminatory conduct at a private religious school.[201]

Founded in 1927, Bob Jones University is a fundamentalist school of about five thousand students located in South Carolina. All teachers and students must be devoutly religious Christians. Their public and private conduct is scrutinized by the school's administrators. The university leadership believes that the Bible forbids interracial dating and marriage. "To effectuate these views, Negroes were completely excluded until 1971. From 1971 to May 1975, the university accepted no applications from unmarried Negroes, but it did accept applications from Negroes married within their race."[202]

In 1973, Bob Jones University inserted an exception to this rule. Unmarried Blacks who had been members of the university staff for four years or more were allowed to apply for admission.[203] In 1975, after the Supreme Court prohibited segregation in private schools, unmarried Blacks were allowed to apply.[204] But, the university continued to prohibit interracial dating and marriage:

1. Students who are partners in an interracial marriage will be expelled.
2. Students who are members of or affiliated with any group or organization which holds as one of its goals or advocates interracial marriage will be expelled.
3. Students who date outside of their own race will be expelled.
4. Students who espouse, promote, or encourage others to violate the University's dating rules and regulations will be expelled.[205]

Bob Jones University was also a tax-exempt, nonprofit organization. In 1970, the Internal Revenue Service changed its rules, denying tax-exempt status to colleges that practiced such race discrimination.[206]

In 1971, Bob Jones University sued the Internal Revenue Service.[207] The university argued that segregation of the races was part of its religious practice. Therefore, the university's First Amendment right to exercise its religion was violated when the IRS, referring to the school's racial segregation policy, revoked the tax-exempt status.[208] *Bob Jones University v. United States* was consolidated with *Goldsboro Christian School v. United States* because the cases posed similar legal questions involving antimiscegenation. Founded in 1963, Goldsboro Christian School advances the principle that "race is determined by descendance [*sic*] from one of Noah's three sons—Ham, Shem, and Japheth. Based on this interpretation, Orientals and Negroes are Hamitic, Hebrews are Shemitic, and Caucasians are Japhethitic."[209] According to Goldsboro, cultural or biological mixing of the races was regarded as a violation of God's command.[210]

The Internal Revenue Service changed its religious tax policy and permitted the schools' racist practices. The agency was under great political pressure from the Reagan administration, religious fundamentalists, and other conservative Republicans.[211] Civil rights organizations protested the agency's policy change, which would allow schools with antimiscegenation policies to maintain tax-exempt status.[212] After many years of litigation, the cases were accepted for review by the U.S. Supreme Court.[213] In 1983, Chief Justice Warren Burger delivered the opinion on behalf of the Court. The Court ruled that the Internal Revenue Service had the power to revoke the tax-exempt status of an educational institution that practiced racial discrimination.[214] The government's interest in eradicating race discrimination outweighed the religious beliefs practiced at the school. Justice William Rehnquist was the lone dissenter.[215] The Court made clear if an educational institution insisted on segregating students by race or instituting antimiscegenation policies, it would do so while paying federal taxes.

Present-Day Vestiges

Civil liberties are maintained by virtue of vigilance and exercise. Protest was a tool used to gain the right to protest. Protest remains a necessary component of the twenty-first century civil rights movement. Together with legal, grassroots, and political strategies, protest provides a proven weapon in the struggle for equal rights under law. During a time of war or peace, exercise of civil liberties is fundamental to a democracy and ensuring equal rights. American society has greatly benefited from the African-American quest for civil liberties. The proliferation of civil rights and civil liberty organizations across this country demonstrates the impact of Court decisions in which Blacks challenged societal racism and discrimination. Their victories have deepened fundamental rights for all persons in America.

Unfortunately, the efficacy of civil disobedience, outside of a larger strategy for change, is now questionable. There must be a strategy to shed light on mounting inequities. Race discrimination flourishes while issues of incarceration, unfair drug laws, racial profiling, societal discrimination, and limited opportunities are silently devastating Black and Latino communities. That destruction is all but ignored by lawmakers. As occurred during slavery, frustration with the *status quo* has led to violent revolts and uprisings. Nonviolent demonstrations and acts of civil disobedience have lost their attractiveness simply because their effectiveness as change mechanisms has become suspect. Violence has become a popular tool for social change for those who remain outside of the Black "talented tenth" or any mainstream channels through which they can effect change.[216] Bayard Rushton stated, "The tragedy is that those who are in deepest revolt are responding not only to [their] frustrations, but more fundamentally to the morality of a society which is teaching them that violence is the only effective force for social change."[217] Coalitions comprised of all members of society, and specifically including those most oppressed, are the greatest weapon for change. Proactive protest meant to secure a better society for future generations is the core of any progressive change.

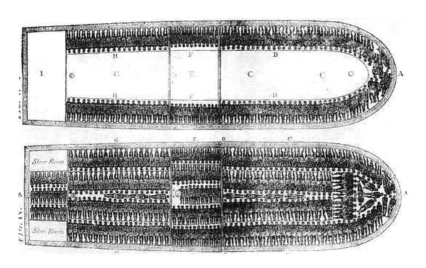

Figure 1 The decks of the slave ship Brooks were divided into sections for women, men, and children. The people were chained together, lying on their backs, without headroom to stand. Millions of Africans succumbed to disease, suicide, and murder on this hundred-day voyage from Africa to the Americas known as the "Middle Passage." (Courtesy of the Warder Collection, New York)

Figure 2 A fugitive slave bulletin on behalf of attorney Thomas Allen for the return of a family of escaped slaves. (October 1, 1847)

Figure 3 A chain gang of prisoners working on the railroad. Prison labor was leased to private businesses. (Postcard, circa 1910)

Figure 4 A military police officer awaits orders in Columbus, Georgia. Prior to Executive Order 9981, the U.S. military was racially segregated at home and abroad. (1942; courtesy of the National Archives)

Figure 5   Paul Robeson, actor, singer, and activist, was forced to testify before the House Committee of Un-American Activities. An international spokesperson for human rights, Robeson was often attacked for his support of the Soviet system as an option to lynching and discriminatory treatment in the United States. (June 12, 1956)

Figure 6 Rosa Parks was arrested in 1955 for refusing to relinquish her seat on a public bus to a White male passenger as required by law in Montgomery, Alabama.

Figure 7 White spectators at the lynching of Thomas Shipp and Abraham Smith in Marion, Indiana. (August 7, 1930)

Figure 8a   Emmett Till, at age 14, with his mother, Mamie Till, in Chicago.

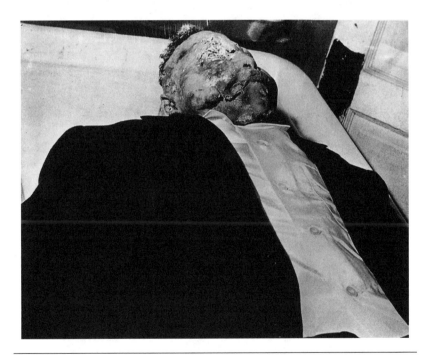

Figure 8b   The tortured body of 14-year-old Emmett Till was brought back to Chicago from Money, Mississippi, where he was lynched for talking to a White woman. (September 3, 1955; courtesy of *Chicago Defender*)

Figure 9 Public accommodations available to bus and train passengers were segregated by race. Federal laws prohibiting segregation of interstate passengers were ignored. Freedom Riders risked their lives to challenge segregated buses and depots across the South. (Circa 1961)

Figure 10 The all-White jury in the Emmett Till murder case prior to acquitting defendants Roy Bryant and his half-brother J.W. Milam of Till's murder. The deliberations took less than one hour. Tallahatchie County, Mississippi. (September 23, 1955)

Figure 11 Reprisals against U.S. Supreme Court Chief Justice Earl Warren followed the Court's decision in *Brown v. Board of Education of Topeka.*

Figure 12   A crowd torments an interracial group of students during a sit-in to protest racial segregation at Woolworth's lunch counters. Restaurants were segregated in the North as well as the South. (Circa 1960s)

Figure 13   Rev. Martin Luther King, Jr., (center) walks with protesters. Blacks were prohibited from being seated and served inside White-owned restaurants.

Figure 14   Black families were discouraged from residing in suburban communities. Restrictive covenants and "right of first refusal" clauses precluded many Blacks from moving out of urban areas.

Figure 15 This elderly woman was a victim of Hurricane Katrina and government neglect. In August 2005, two hurricanes struck the Gulf Coast of the United States. Following an evacuation, thousands of Blacks in New Orleans, referred to as "refugees," were left stranded at the Superdome sports arena without food, water, electricity, or medical attention. (September 2005; courtesy of Allen Chin)

5

VOTING RIGHTS AND RESTRICTIONS

[I]t is too plain for argument, that [Blacks] have never been regarded as a part of the people…nor supposed to possess any political rights which the dominant race might not withhold or grant at their pleasure.

Dred Scott v. Sandford, 60 U.S. 393, 412 (1857)

Power concedes nothing without demand; it never has and it never will.

Frederick Douglass (1857)

The very visible position of racial minorities in America's elected offices evidences progress. However, at the same time, the number of Black political officeholders belies a history of disfranchisement.[1] Voting is power. Proponents of second-class citizenship for Blacks have crafted a myriad of obstacles intended to prevent full exercise of this power. Blacks and Latinos have lost their lives, families, livelihoods, and homes in their quest for the vote. This chapter examines the journey of Blacks, Asians, Latinos, and Native Americans from political disfranchisement to voting rights.

In 1670, the Virginia colony restricted the privilege of voting to landholders.[2] By 1705, Blacks in Virginia were prohibited from holding political office.[3] Free Blacks paid taxes but most were prohibited from voting and those free Blacks who could vote did so wholly upon the whim of White state legislators. For example, in 1723, Virginia enacted a statute prohibiting free Black landholders from voting in any elections. Of course, enslaved Blacks, as nonpersons, were precluded from voting; however, the Delaware legislature passed a statute that prohibited Blacks from even being present when voting was in progress.[4] Once the U.S. Constitution was ratified in 1789, Southern politicians found they needed Black bodies to gain power in the U.S. Congress. Counting Blacks as three-fifths of a person, instead of discounting them completely, allowed the South to gain additional seats in the House of Representatives. In 1831, the U.S. Supreme Court ruled that Native Americans were part of a "domestic dependent nation" and thus each state could decide their level of suffrage or exclude them from voting. In *Dred Scott v. Sanford*, the Supreme Court decided that Blacks were never meant to be a part of the political community.[5] As slavery was in its death throes, the issue of Black suffrage was hotly contested in Congress and within state legislatures.

The Civil War, while at its core was a political and economic conflict between White men in the North and the South, also demonstrated the power of armed Blacks. The North, embracing the Industrial Revolution and its factories, could turn against slave farm labor. But, to gain a primary political as well as economic position over the South, it needed the Black vote. Heretofore, counting Blacks as three-fifths of a person only served to benefit Southern politicians. The defeat of the Confederate Army set the stage for Black political participation, albeit reluctantly given. Native Americans were deemed members of tribal nations and precluded from U.S. citizenship and voting.

Gaining the Vote

After slavery was abolished in 1865 and Blacks were made full citizens, the political backlash against giving Blacks the right to vote was immediate. The Ku Klux Klan was formed as well as other White terrorist organizations—in part, because they recognized that the number of potential Black voters was large enough to change the outcome of local and national elections. The South retaliated against the Republican Party and Abraham Lincoln for abolishing slavery. Southerners, once stalwart Republicans, renounced their party allegiance and registered as Democrats. Congress enacted the Civil Rights Act of 1866 granting citizenship to Blacks over the veto of

President Andrew Johnson.[6] Soon after, the Fourteenth Amendment of the U.S. Constitution was passed to better secure the rights granted in the Civil Rights Act of 1866 and formally rid the country of the *Dred Scott* ruling.[7]

The Fourteenth Amendment provided Blacks with equal protection under law and due process, as well as the privileges and immunities enjoyed by all citizens.[8] Additionally, the amendment provides every person born in the United States with citizenship as a birthright.[9] Former Confederate states were not allowed readmittance to the Union without amending their constitutions from a White male–only franchise to recognize the rights of Blacks. The issue of suffrage—the right to vote—for Blacks was a highly contested issue in the North as well as the South. There was a general view among Whites that Blacks could not grasp political issues or understand the power of their vote. However, the viewpoint was unfounded and often utilized as a justification for inequality and disfranchisement.

After a tangle of spirited Congressional debates, the Fifteenth Amendment was passed securing Blacks the right to vote.[10] It states: "The right of citizens of the United States to vote shall not be denied or abridged by the United States or by any state on account of race, color, or previous condition of servitude."[11] The second paragraph of this amendment states: "Congress shall have power to enforce this article by appropriate legislation."[12] The need for legislation was immediate. The rise of the Ku Klux Klan and other terrorist organizations led to the enactment of the Enforcement Act of May 31, 1870 (known as the Civil Rights Act of 1870) to protect these newly gained rights.[13]

Within the Enforcement Act of 1870, Section 5508 protected against conspiracies to deprive Blacks of their rights.[14] A subsequent provision, Section 5520, protected against any conspiracies to prevent Blacks from voting in national elections for offices of president, vice-president, or congressman. The law also laid down hefty sanctions for deprivation of African-American voting rights: no less than a $5,000 fine and six years imprisonment.[15] Section 5519 provides a similar punishment for depriving a person of equal protection of the laws.[16] The Ku Klux Klan Act of 1871 (known as the Civil Rights Act of 1871) was enacted in response to the Klan's terrorism against Blacks.[17]

Early Victories and Defeats:
U.S. v. Reese and *Ex Parte Yarbrough*

As Black men sought to exercise their voting rights, states enacted elaborate laws to prevent Blacks from voting. In Kentucky, two inspectors of a municipal election in Lexington refused to receive the vote of William Garner, a Black man. Reese, the inspector, demanded a receipt demonstrating that Garner had paid a $1.50 capitation tax the preceding year.[18] Garner had not known of the tax. The inspectors were convicted of violating the Enforcement Act of 1870.[19] They appealed their conviction and, in 1876, the U.S. Supreme Court, in *United States v. Reese*, ruled in their favor. Chief Justice Morrison Remick Waite wrote the opinion on behalf of the Court. First, the Court found that the Fifteenth Amendment does not confer the right to vote upon anyone.[20] It merely prevents the states from giving preference to one citizen over another on account of race, color, or previous condition of servitude.[21]

A fine distinction was made with catastrophic results. The Court determined in *Reese* that the right to vote was derived from the states. However, the right of a person to vote, free from racial discrimination, was protected by the federal government. Thus, the state had the power to enact legislation limiting who was qualified to vote and under what particular circumstances voting would take place. The Court presumed the voting tax was applied to everyone equally. Blacks had no legal support for allegations of race discrimination if the law was racially neutral on its face despite its intended effect. Second, the Court, in narrowly interpreting the Enforcement Act, found that it was not intended to punish Kentucky's inspectors of elections for refusing to break the law and count the votes of Black voters who had not paid the requisite tax.[22]

In 1876, the Court also decided *United States v. Cruikshank*.[23] In *Cruikshank*, Blacks were attacked at a civil rights strategy meeting in Grant Parish, Louisiana.[24] This became known as the Colfax Massacre. In 1872, Louisiana's gubernatorial contest between regular Republicans and a coalition of liberal Republicans and Democrats led to riots. Whites attacked supporters of the winning candidate, refusing to obey a ruling of the federal court or the troops deployed by President Ulysses S. Grant. Instead, White mobs attacked Blacks and any others who supported the winning Republicans. Blacks met at the local courthouse. Rumors spread among Whites that Blacks at the meeting were planning an assault. On April 13, 1873, Whites attacked Blacks housed in the courthouse. In the end, two White men were killed, probably by friendly fire, and nearly three hundred Blacks were dead. Hundreds of others were wounded.

Over one hundred White men were charged under the Enforcement Act of 1870.[25] Two of the counts alleged intent to prevent Blacks from voting. Upon appeal, the Supreme Court found in favor of the defendants. "It does not appear...that the intent of the defendants was to prevent these parties from exercising their right to vote on account of their race."[26] The Court found that the Civil Rights Act did not protect Blacks against violations of their First Amendment right to freedom of assembly. All charges were dismissed and the defendants ordered discharged.

The Supreme Court refused to uphold the federal protections intended under the Enforcement Act. Despite the failure of the Court and faintheartedness of Congress, Blacks demonstrated remarkable political participation. Hiram Revels, from Mississippi, was the first Black U.S. senator. Revels, a minister in the African Methodist Episcopal Church, served in the Senate from February 25, 1870, to March 4, 1871. Pickney Benton Stewart Pinchback was the first Black elected to the Louisiana State Senate.[27] After the death of the lieutenant governor, Pinchback served as acting governor from December 9, 1872, to January 13, 1873.[28] He was elected to the U.S. Senate in 1873. However, Whites refused to allow Pinchback to assume his office.[29]

A challenge by women to gain the right to vote would have ramifications on court claims based on race. The women's movement, under the leadership of Elizabeth Cady Stanton, placed suffrage for women as its principal platform issue. Certain factions of the movement had actively supported voting rights for Blacks. By 1870, the movement had evolved into a national force from a small meeting in Seneca Falls, New York, in 1848.[30] In 1872, Virginia Minor, a White woman in Missouri, attempted to register to vote in the national election. The judge of elections refused Minor's registration because she was not male. Minor sued under the Fourteenth Amendment. Upon appeal, the U.S. Supreme Court, in *Minor v. Happersett,* failed to find a constitutional violation and reinforced the state's right to determine who is legally eligible to vote.[31]

The Supreme Court ruled in 1875 that a person can be a citizen and deprived of the right to vote.[32] The Fourteenth Amendment was not violated because states were charged with deciding issues of suffrage. Chief Justice Waite, writing on behalf of a unanimous Supreme Court, wrote that the "Constitution of the United States does not confer the rights of suffrage upon any one…[it is] the constitutions and laws of the several States which commit that important trust to men alone…"[33] Despite this ruling, women across the country continued to press for the right to vote.[34]

Less than ten years after *Minor v. Happersett,* the Court decided a nonvoting case that would have a great impact on Black suffrage. In *United States v. Harris* (1883), Black men held in protective custody in a Crockett County, Kentucky, jail were beaten by a White lynch mob.[35] R. G. Harris, leader of the mob, and his fellow defendants were convicted under Section 5519 of the Enforcement Act. The defendants appealed their convictions. Subsequently, the U.S. Supreme Court overturned the convictions, holding that federal legislation did not apply to private persons. Specifically, the Court found that the duty of protecting citizens rests with states and not the federal government. The only obligation resting upon the United States is to see that the states do not deny these rights of protection.[36] Without state action or nonaction, the protections under the Enforcement Act and similar federal legislation did not apply. The *Harris* ruling weakened the Ku Klux Klan Act. Attacks by White mobs composed of private citizens acted with near impunity against Blacks who sought to vote or run for political office.

After *Reese,* violence against Blacks escalated as the federal government turned its back on any obligation toward Blacks in the American South. By 1884, the Court was presented with *Ex Parte Yarbrough.*[37] Jasper Yarbrough and seven others from Fulton County, Georgia, were convicted, under the Enforcement Act of 1870, of beating Berry Saunders, a Black man, because he voted in a U.S. Congressional election.[38] Yarbrough and his co-conspirators were sentenced to two years of hard labor in the Albany penitentiary in New York State.[39] They filed a writ of habeas corpus challenging the Enforcement Act as unconstitutional. The Supreme Court denied their writ.[40] In doing so, the Court revisited *Reese* and explained what was meant by "the Constitution of the United States does not confer the right of suffrage upon anyone."[41] The Court distinguished *Reese*.[42] In certain cases, the Fifteenth Amendment *does* confer the right to vote on Blacks. The amendment must confer this right in those cases involving recalcitrant states that refuse to recognize Black suffrage. Furthermore, Congress had the power to protect and enforce that right.

In 1896, *Plessy v. Ferguson* provided states with an opportunity to legally separate the races.[43] The *Plessy* decision was meant to draw a nuanced "distinction between laws interfering with the political equality of the negro and those requiring the separation of the two races in schools, theatres..."[44] However, Whites understood the clear message of Plessy—Blacks were outside the protection of the law. Lawlessness against Blacks increased for those who sought political participation. The Ku Klux Klan and other terrorist organizations, in conjunction with duplicitous government actors and discriminatory voting laws, served to diminish much of the great progress made by Blacks. Where 130,344 African Americans had been registered voters in Louisiana in 1896, by 1900 only 5,320 registered voters remained.[45] Then, in *Giles v. Harris* (analyzed next), the Supreme Court offered an opinion that further eroded efforts of Blacks to challenge discriminatory conduct.[46]

Grandfather Clauses: *Giles v. Harris* and *Guinn and Beal v. United States*

Justice Oliver Wendell Holmes, Jr., delivered the opinion in *Giles v. Harris*, a case that upheld racially pernicious grandfather clauses. Alabama lawmakers amended their constitution to allow persons registered before January 1, 1903, to gain the right to vote for life.[47] To do so, a potential voter needed to have served honorably in any of America's wars or to be a descendant of a person who served in the war, *or*, they needed to be of good character.[48] After January 1, 1903, among the new requirements, a person must have been able to read and write any article of the Constitution and have lawful employment for twelve months.[49] Alternatively, a person must have owned at least forty acres of land or land assessed for taxation at $300 or more.[50] The amendments were intended to "let in all whites and [keep] out a large part, if not all, of the blacks."[51]

Jackson W. Giles filed a class-action suit on behalf of himself and five thousand Blacks in Montgomery, Alabama. He and others applied for registration August 1, 1902, well before the deadline, and were turned away.[52] His action alleged violations of the Fourteenth and Fifteenth Amendments.[53] The federal trial court dismissed the suit for lack of jurisdiction, citing a technicality.[54] Giles had not indicated monetary damages of $2,000 or more.[55] On appeal, the U.S. Supreme Court upheld the ruling of the trial court ultimately denying Blacks in Alabama the right to vote for a lifetime.[56] Justice Holmes wrote that "[u]nless we are prepared to supervise the voting in that State by officers of the court, it seems to us that all that the plaintiff could get from equity would be an empty form."[57] Justices David J. Brewer and Marshall Harlan dissented, finding that a person could be damaged when he was precluded from voting.[58]

Blacks and White advocates for justice gathered in Niagara, Canada, to plan a strategy to combat racial discrimination. The Niagara Movement would result in the formation of the National Association for the Advancement of Colored People. Challenging state racist voting legislation inspired by *Plessy v. Ferguson* was of primary importance. Grandfather clauses, which often allowed voting only if one voted during slavery, were drafted to prevent Blacks from registering. If the grandfather held the right to vote, then the applicant for voter registration could vote as well. Of course, Blacks were precluded from full citizenship and suffrage prior to 1870. Thus, many of the grandfather clauses related back to that time period.

Oklahoma devised several plans to preclude Black voters. When Oklahoma became a state in 1907, a condition of statehood was a constitution free of racially discriminatory provisions. However, by 1910, Oklahoma amended its constitution to require suffrage and literacy tests to disfranchise Blacks. The state imposed a test of reading and writing a section of the state constitution as a condition to voting. The requirement only applied to persons who, on or prior to

January 1, 1866, were entitled to vote in the United States or under some form of government.[59] The caveat "some form of government" vested White immigrants from Europe with the vote while precluding the vast majority of Blacks, who were enslaved prior to 1866 or free but prohibited by racism from voting.

The attorney general brought an action under Section 5508 alleging a violation of the Fifteenth Amendment.[60] Frank Guinn and J. J. Beal, two state election officials, were convicted. The electors appealed, arguing that states had the right to fix standards for suffrage and that power was not taken away by the Fifteenth Amendment. The Court found in *Guinn and Beal v. United States*, a 1915 decision, that Oklahoma's grandfather clause was discriminatory.[61] Justice Edward Douglas White, writing on behalf of the Court, stated, "We have difficulty in finding the words to more clearly demonstrate the conviction we entertain that this [amendment] has the characteristics which the Government attributes to it..."[62] The convictions were upheld. Moorfield Storey, of the NAACP, was the attorney of record.[63] It was the first court case of the NAACP. A strategy to fight back through the courts had its first victory.

However, Oklahoma attempted to obviate the ruling in *Guinn v. United States*. In 1939, the U.S. Supreme Court was presented with Oklahoma's recalcitrance in *Lane v. Wilson*.[64] Oklahoma's legislature enacted a statute in which an application for voter registration was limited to the time period between April 30, 1916, and May 11, 1916.[65] Failure to register during this time period precluded a person from voting for an entire lifetime. (In case of illness or absence from the state, one could register between May 10, 1916, and June 30, 1916.)[66] Lane, a Black resident, attempted to register in Wagoner County, Oklahoma, within the time period and was turned away.[67] He brought an action for $5,000 in damages in federal court under Section 1979 of the Civil Rights Act:[68]

> Every person who, under color of any statute...of any State or Territory, subject, or causes to be subjected, any citizen of the United States... within the jurisdiction thereof to the deprivation of any rights, privileges, or immunities secured by the Constitution and laws, shall be liable to the party injured in an action at law.[69]

Section 1979, enacted by Congress, was designated to facilitate enforcement of the Fifteenth Amendment.[70]

At trial, Lane argued that a conspiracy existed between county and precinct registrars and the county election boards to prevent "the registration of negro voters solely on account of their race, color and previous condition of servitude."[71] James Nabrit, a Black attorney and professor of law at Howard University Law School, argued the case on behalf of Lane. The trial court found that Lane could not substantiate that he had registered. The court of appeals upheld the trial court. In 1939, Justice Felix Frankfurter, a recent appointee to the highest court, authored the opinion reversing the lower courts. Frankfurter wrote: "The [Fifteenth] Amendment nullifies sophisticated as well as simple-minded modes of discrimination."[72] Yet, the Court's decision would not end the discrimination faced by Blacks who sought access to the voting ballot.

In *Myers v. Anderson*, Blacks in Annapolis, Maryland, were precluded from registering to vote, tax assessments, and a grandfather clause.[73] The Maryland Statute of 1908 restricted qualifications for voting to: (1) taxpayers assessed at least $500; (2) naturalized citizens; and "(3) "[a]ll citizens who, prior to January 1, 1868, were entitled to vote in the State of Maryland or any other State of the United States...and the lawful male descendants of any person who prior to January 1, 1868, was entitled to vote."[74] John Anderson, William Howard, and Robert Brown each brought an action against Charles Myers and other registration officers, alleging a race-based violation of the Fifteenth Amendment and requesting damages under Section 1979. The plaintiffs were victorious at trial. However, Myers appealed the decision. The Supreme Court upheld the trial court, citing *Guinn*. The Court recognized that Maryland attempted to "recreate and reestablish a condition which the [Fifteenth] Amendment prohibits."[75] Grandfather clauses were conspicuous examples of efforts by Whites to use the law to maintain a hierarchy in which Blacks are subjugated to a place without power or protection. Unfortunately, relatively few Blacks were free to fully exercise their right to vote without threats of terrorism or abject refusal to accept their ballot. Native Americans were not granted the right of citizenship as a birth right until 1924. President Calvin Coolidge signed the Indian Citizenship Act providing full rights, including the right to vote, to Native Americans. With each positive measure, opponents of democracy instituted new obstacles.

Restricted Political Primary:
Nixon v. Herndon and *Smith v. Allwright*

In 1927, the Court ruled in *Nixon v. Herndon* that a political primary was state action within the auspices of the Fourteenth Amendment.[76] In this El Paso, Texas, case, the judges of elections refused to permit Dr. L. A. Nixon to vote at a primary election on July 26, 1924.[77] Nixon was denied the right to vote based on a Texas statute of May, 1923, Article 3093a.[78] The statute provided that "in no event shall a negro be eligible to participate in a Democratic party primary election held in the State of Texas."[79] Nixon brought an action under the Fourteenth and Fifteenth Amendments.[80] The trial court dismissed his suit on grounds that political matters were not within the jurisdiction of the court.[81] Justice Holmes redeemed himself, writing on behalf of the Court. He stated: "States may do a good deal of classifying that it is difficult to believe rational, but there are limits, and it is too clear for extended argument that color cannot be made the basis of a statutory classification."[82] The court ruled the Texas statute denying Blacks the right to vote in the Democratic primary unconstitutional.

Despite the clarity of the Court's decision, Texas remained determined to preclude Blacks from the political process. Less than five years later, in *Nixon v. Condon*, the Court was forced to confront the intransigence of racism.[83] The Texas legislature enacted Article 3107 to defeat the ruling in *Nixon v. Herndon*. The statute provided that every political party in the state, through its state executive committee, should have the power to prescribe the qualifications of its own members.[84] The executive committee adopted a resolution that only White Democrats could participate in the primary elections.[85] Nixon brought the action against the Texas Democratic primary election judges. The federal trial court as well as the Court of Appeals for the Fifth Circuit dismissed Nixon's case.[86] Upon appeal, the U.S. Supreme Court found that the control exercised by the Texas legislature over the executive committees was state action. Justice Benjamin

Cardozo wrote that "[d]elegates of the State's power have discharged their official functions in such a way as to discriminate invidiously between white citizens and black."[87] Thus, a Fourteenth Amendment violation could be alleged by Nixon.

Then, in 1935, the U.S. Supreme Court ruled that Texas could legally exclude Blacks from membership in the Democratic Party.[88] In *Grovey v. Townsend*, Justice Owen Roberts, writing on behalf of the Court, found no violation of the Fourteenth or Fifteenth Amendments. Roberts reasoned that voting as a Democrat in a political primary was not covered under the Fifteenth Amendment or considered state action under the Fourteenth Amendment. In this case, the White clerk of Harris County, Texas, Albert Townsend, refused to give R. R. Grovey, a Black man, a ballot for a Democratic Party primary election. A resolution of the Democratic Party, adopted May 24, 1932, restricted eligibility to membership in the Democratic Party in Texas to White citizens.[89] Grovey brought suit. On appeal, a unanimous Supreme Court held that neither *Nixon v. Herndon* nor *Nixon v. Condon* applied to voting in a primary election of a particular political party.[90] Democratic primaries were considered private and beyond the reach of congressional control. The decision was considered a controversial departure from the *Nixon* cases.

Nearly ten years later, the Court corrected the error of *Grovey*. In *Smith v. Allwright*, once again, Harris County, Texas, was before the highest Court. In *Smith v. Allwright*, the Supreme Court held that Democratic primary elections restricted to only White citizens violated the Fourteenth and Fifteenth Amendments. Thurgood Marshall and William Henry Hastie were among the NAACP attorneys representing a Black dentist, Lonnie Smith.[91] Smith sued after he was denied a ballot to vote in the Democratic Party primary by the judge of election, S. E. Allwright. Smith brought an action. The Court had found in *Grovey*, membership in the Democratic Party was analogous to a voluntary association. Thus, there was no state action found in the party's exclusion of Grovey from voting in the Democratic primary.

However, in *Smith v. Allwright*, the Court acknowledged the interconnection between the primary and general election. A refusal of a Democratic primary ballot resulted in a limited role in selecting the candidates presented in the general election.[92] The Court overturned *Grovey*, ruling that the primary and general election are subject to congressional sanction when integrally connected.[93] Justice Owen Roberts dissented, preferring to cling to *Grovey* as a symbol of consistency even in the face of injustice.[94] The composition of the Supreme Court had changed drastically since the *Grovey* ruling. Only Justice Roberts remained of that Court. The nation was at war. After pressure from A. Philip Randolph and other civil rights leaders, President Harry Truman desegregated the military July 26, 1948.[95] However, the Court would not address major issues involving voting rights for well over ten years.

Blacks' expectation of equality was quickly diminished. Protest and demand for rights, especially the right to select members of the government, led to heightened civil rights litigation.

Racist programs as well as legislation precluded millions of Blacks, Asians, and Latinos from voting in state and national elections. The Japanese were prohibited from becoming citizens or naturalized residents. The Chinese in American had only recently become citizens after nearly one hundred years of political exclusion by local laws and the federal Chinese Exclusion Act. In the southwest, Hispanics attempting to access the political process met virulent opposition. Cesar Chavez, the Mexican-American labor leader, organized Latino farmworkers to press for better wages and access to the ballot. The Supreme Court, led by Chief Justice Earl Warren, was now noted for the *Brown* decision. In 1958, the attorney general brought a civil rights action against deputy registrars in Terrell County, Georgia, charging discrimination against Black voters.[96] James Griggs Raines, Dixon Oxford, Roscoe Radford, registrars of Terrell County, Georgia, F. Lawson Cook, Sr., and Mrs. F. Lawson Cook, Sr., deputy registrars of Terrell County, Georgia, were charged under the Civil Rights Act of 1957. The act provided that all qualified voters in any state, territory, or municipality should be entitled to vote at all elections, regardless of race, color, or previous condition of servitude.

In *United States v. Raines*, the deputies claimed that their actions were purely private and beyond the reach of the revised Enforcement Act.[97] On appeal, the Supreme Court revisited *United States v. Reese*. Justice Brennan, writing on behalf of the Court, refused to follow the dictates of *Reese*.[98] Brennan wrote: "Discrimination by state officials, within the course of their official duties, against the voting rights of

United States citizens, on the grounds of race or color—is 'state action' and the clearest form of it."[99]

Gerrymandering: *Gomillion v. Lightfoot*

Gerrymandering—drawing voting districts to conform to political exclusion—has a long history. To contravene Black political power, districts were redrawn, or gerrymandered, to dilute the Black vote. In *Gomillion v. Lightfoot* (1960), White legislators redrew the boundaries of Tuskegee, Alabama, into an irregular twenty-eight-sided figure. The redrawn district eliminated all but four or five of its four hundred Black voters without eliminating any White voters. Attorneys Fred Gray and Robert Carter represented C. G. Gomillion and the class of Blacks who challenged the changed boundaries.[100] At trial, the district court dismissed the complaint, stating that the court could not intervene in state political matters without clear racial animus relying on *Colgrove v. Green*, where the Supreme Court had earlier granted local governments great latitude in political matters.[101]

On appeal, the Supreme Court reversed the trial court. The Court found that, prior to redistricting, the City of Tuskegee was square shaped. After the city passed Act 140 in 1957, the redefined boundaries resulted in discriminatorily depriving Black voters the right to vote in municipal elections.[102] Lightfoot, the White mayor of Tuskegee, "never suggested, either in [his] brief or in oral argument, any countervailing municipal function which Act 140 is designed to serve."[103] The Court distinguished the case here from *Colgrove*. There, the state did not use its power to circumvent a federally protected right.[104] It ruled that the redistricting here was an unlawful gerrymandering designed to dilute the Black vote: The "inescapable human effect of this essay in geometry and geography is to despoil colored citizens, and only colored citizens, of their theretofore enjoyed voting rights."[105]

Race and the Ballot: *Anderson v. Martin*

In 1964, the Court ruled in *Reynolds v. Sims* that the right to vote was a fundamental right.[106] The Twenty-fourth Amendment, ratified in 1964, provides:

Section 1. The right of citizens of the United States to vote in any primary or other election for President or Vice-President, for electors for President or Vice-President, or for Senate or Representative in Congress, shall not be denied or abridged by the United States or any State by reason of failure to pay any poll tax or other tax.[107]

Despite the ratification of this amendment invalidating poll taxes, a three-judge federal court in *Harper v. Virginia Board of Elections*, released the very same year, upheld the provision in Virginia's constitution requiring a poll tax.[108] On appeal, the Supreme Court held that wealth or payment of fees as a measure of a voter's qualification was capricious.[109] The Court overturned *Breedlove v. Suttles*, a 1937 case that upheld state poll taxes.[110]

Race was a factor in every aspect of voting. In Louisiana, in *Anderson v. Martin* (1964), Blacks challenged a statute that required ballots to specify the race of the candidates running for office. Louisiana defended its measure as necessary information for the electorate and, moreover, "the labeling applies equally to Negro and white."[111] However, the history of racism in America would undermine the chances for Black, as opposed to White, candidates. The Supreme Court struck down Louisiana's statute as a violation of the equal-protection clause.[112] In Virginia, voting records and property tax assessments were segregated by race. In *Hamm v. Virginia State Board of Elections* (1964), the Supreme Court affirmed the trial court's decision to desegregate this basic information.[113]

Students and civil rights workers from across the nation converged on the South to register Blacks to vote. These volunteers, as well as the Black attendees, suffered harassment, beatings, and murder.[114] Their sacrifice brought about immense change. On June 12, 1963, civil rights leader Medgar Evers was murdered to end his voter registration campaign.[115] Evers was state field secretary with the Mississippi branch of the NAACP. Byron De La Beckwith's fingerprint was found on the telescopic gunsight of the sniper's rifle.[116] De La Beckwith was indicted and acquitted by two all-White juries in 1964,[117] but was retried in 1994 and this time convicted of murder.[118]

Andrew Goodman, James Chaney, and Michael Schwerner, voting-rights activists, were murdered in Philadelphia, Mississippi, in 1964. Their tortured bodies were found months later. Edgar Killens, a Klansman and ringleader of the plot to murder the voting rights workers, was arrested along with his co-conspirators. The murder of the three men followed by the brutal attack against civil rights marchers by White state troopers on the Edmund Pettus Bridge in Selma, Alabama, impelled Congress to act against the recalcitrant South. Killens's trial in 1967 ended with a mistrial. However, he was retried and convicted of manslaughter in 2005.

The murder of Viola Liuzzo in 1965 was another among the many acts of terrorism, assault, and murder perpetrated against voting-rights workers. Liuzzo, a White homemaker, moved from Michigan to Alabama to register Blacks to vote.[119] She was shot and killed by three Klan members while driving to a voter registration meeting.[120] At their first trial, Eugene Thomas, William Orville Eaton, and Collie LeRoy Wilkins, Jr., were acquitted of first-degree murder in state court by an all-White, male jury.[121] However, the federal government indicted the men. All three were found guilty of violating Liuzzo's civil rights and sentenced to ten years in the federal penitentiary.[122]

Organizations such as the Student Non-Violent Coordinating Committee (SNCC), the Congress of Racial Equality (CORE), and the Council of Federated Organizations informed Blacks throughout the South of their voting rights.[123] Before the arrival of these college students from the North, the Fifteenth Amendment meant little in Mississippi. It was 1962. Fannie Lou Hamer was a forty-four-year-old sharecropper when she learned Blacks had the right to vote.[124] SNCC workers needed volunteers who were willing to register. Hamer joined. However, when Hamer and other Blacks attempted to register, they were arrested. After her release from jail, Hamer was evicted from the land where she and her family had lived and worked for eighteen years.[125] She was hired by SNCC and became their most effective organizer. Mississippi forced Blacks to qualify to vote by passing a literacy test. Hamer was successful on her third attempt. Afterwards, she was arrested and beaten for registering to vote.[126] The beating she received in jail was so severe that complications stemming from it would eventually shorten her life. Yet, Hamer continued to register Blacks to vote.

Blacks who passed the literacy test and registered were still excluded, by race, from membership in the Democratic Party of Mississippi.[127] Hamer helped create the alternative Mississippi Freedom Democratic Party (MFDP).[128] In 1964, she, along with members of the MFDP, attended the Democratic National Convention in Atlantic City. At the convention, Hamer spoke of the beating she received in retaliation for registering to vote.[129] She gave a nationally televised speech critical of a country that would allow the convention's Mississippi delegation to exclude Blacks and a political party that would not seat the MFDP.[130]

The Democratic Party's Executive Committee offered two at-large seats. Hamer turned them down as mere tokens. Hamer had been beaten, threatened, and fired upon while working as an advocate for voting rights. When asked why she persisted, Hamer responded, "All my life I've been sick and tired. Now I'm sick and tired of being sick and tired."[131] Regarding the law, she stated, "[W]e learned the hard way that even though we had all the law and all the righteousness on our side—that white man is not going to give up his power to us. We have to build our own power."[132]

Protest, murder, and internationally televised violence against Black voters in the midst of the Cold War finally led to federal voting legislation. On August 6, 1965, President Lyndon B. Johnson signed the Voting Rights Act.[133] Section 2 of the act states: "No voting qualification or prerequisite to voting, or standard, practice, or procedure shall be imposed or applied by any State or political subdivision to deny or abridge the right of any citizen of the United States to vote on account of race or color."[134] Section 5 of the act requires preclearance of districting plans affecting racial minorities. The Voting Rights Act of 1965 was passed in the aftermath of murder and protest. One will never know the true number of lives lost and shattered in the quest by Blacks for voting rights.

In 1968, Hamer attended the Democratic Convention in Chicago and became the first Black delegate to a national political convention since Reconstruction.[135] She was applauded inside the convention. However, outside, civil rights demonstrations, student antiwar protesters, and police violence resulted in mass arrests. In Brooklyn, New York, a legal challenge to the voting districts led to the election in 1972 of the first Black woman, Shirley Chisholm, to the U.S. House of Representatives. Chisholm then made a bid for the presidency.

The country was in the midst of great social change. However, the Supreme Court was changing in the opposite direction. Moderate and radical conservatives began to replace the "social engineers" who had reluctantly arrived at understanding the need for racial justice under law. Chief Justice Earl Warren, author of the *Brown v. Board* opinion, retired in 1969. Richard Nixon, a Republican, was elected president and, in 1971, nominated the ultraconservative William Rehnquist to the Court. Justices Warren Burger, Lewis Powell, and Harry Blackmun soon followed as Nixon nominees. But, it would be the conservative Justice Rehnquist who ascended to chief justice of the Supreme Court in 1986. His tenure would be marked by stymied progress toward racial justice over a twenty-year period.

Vote Dilution: *Mobile v. Bolden*

By 1980, abject terrorism was replaced as an obstacle to the voting booth with legislative machinations. However, the structure of elections presented a challenge to realizing the power of the Black vote. In *Mobile v. Bolden*, the at-large voting system instituted in the City of Mobile prevented Blacks from electing the candidates of their choice for mayor or city council.[136]

Despite the relatively large size of the Black population in the city, under the at-large voting system their vote was consistently diluted by the majority White vote.[137] Wiley E. Bolden brought a class action challenging the at-large electoral system as a violation of the Fourteenth and Fifteenth Amendments.[138] Bolden sought an electoral system with single member districts. A minority group could be a majority in a single member district.[139] The trial and appellate courts ruled in favor of the Black plaintiffs.[140] However, the U.S. Supreme Court reversed, refusing to strike down the at-large electoral system.[141] Instead, the Court ruling in favor of the City of Mobile demanded that Black plaintiffs provide evidence of intentional racial discrimination. Disproportionate effects alone were insufficient.

In *Thornburg v. Gingles*, Blacks in North Carolina challenged the state's redistricting plan, which diluted Black voting strength. Section 2 of the Voting Rights Act was amended after the ruling in *Mobile v. Bolden*. In *Gingles*, the Supreme Court instituted a totality of the circumstance's dual-pronged approach to determine whether voting districts were discriminatorily drawn. In 1993, the Court, in *Shaw v. Reno*, defeated Attorney General Janet Reno's plan to reapportion districts in North Carolina in favor of historically disfranchised Black voters.[142] On the heels of *Shaw*, the Court decided *Holder v. Hall* in 1994 and *Miller v. Johnson* in 1995.[143] In *Holder v. Hall*, Black residents of Bleckley County, Georgia, as well as the NAACP, challenged the multimember commission replacing the single commissioner system.[144] The trial and appellate courts found in favor of the Black plaintiffs. However, the Supreme Court reversed.

Equitable voting plans remain under attack as "reverse discrimination." The Court, in *Miller v. Johnson* and *Shaw v. Reno*, applied a strict scrutiny standard. The Court's highest standard must be satisfied whenever race becomes the overriding predominant factor. A history of race discrimination is no longer relevant. Under strict scrutiny, there must be a compelling state interest and a narrowly tailored plan to meet those interests or the plan will be unconstitutional. The era of reform had passed. Blacks must navigate a conservative Supreme Court and reverse discrimination lawsuits brought on behalf of Whites threatened by Black progress with little concern for nearly three hundred years of brutality, discrimination, and disfranchisement.

The Voting Rights Act removed barriers to registration. Following the ratification of the act, Black registration in Mississippi increased from 6.7 percent to 59.8 percent within two years.[145] In Alabama, registration increased from 19.3 percent to 51.6 percent by 1967.[146] In cities such as Atlanta, New Orleans, Detroit, Newark, Kansas City, and Chicago, White flight provided opportunities for Black politicians. White flight to the suburbs contributed to an increase in the concentration of Blacks within certain American cities corresponding to concentrated Black voting strength, which resulted in a higher number of Blacks elected to political office.

Ex-Felon Disenfranchisement:
Richardson v. Ramirez

Unfortunately, the incarceration rate of Blacks and Latinos increased as well. Ramirez and two others in California were refused registration to vote because of their felony convictions. They sued Viola Richardson and the other county clerks and registrar of voters, arguing that disenfranchising felons who have completed their sentences and parole violated the equal-protection clause of the Fourteenth Amendment. Article XX Section 11 of the California constitution was adopted in 1879.[147] It excludes from voting persons convicted of bribery, perjury, forgery, malfeasance in office, and other high crimes.[148] In 1972, Proposition 7 amended the California constitution to also exclude any mentally deficient person, insane person, and person convicted of an infamous crime, embezzlement, or misappropriation of public money.[149] A pardon by the governor of California was the only mechanism of rehabilitating the right to vote.[150]

Ramirez argued that of the 34,262 persons released from state prisons from 1968 to 1971 only 282 were granted pardons.[151] The California Supreme Court ruled that California may no longer exclude felons who had completed their sentences and paroles.[152] On appeal, Chief Justice Rehnquist, writing on behalf of the U.S. Supreme Court, reversed.[153] Justice Rehnquist relied on early nineteenth century instances in which states disfranchised Blacks and prisoners. Upon ratification of the Fourteenth and Fifteenth Amendments (1868 and 1870, respectively), Blacks were franchised, on paper. However, states continued to disenfranchise persons convicted of felonies or infamous crimes.[154]

Justice Thurgood Marshall dissented. In his dissent, Marshall questioned whether the Court should have taken the appeal. It appeared the Court was anxious to rule against enfranchisement for ex-felons. On September 21, 2000, Florida citizens Thomas Johnson, Derrick Andre Thomas, Eric Robinson, Omali Yeshitela, Adam Hernandez, Kathryn Williams-Carpenter, Jau'dohn Hicks, and John Hanes filed a class-action lawsuit.[155] Johnson and the others were convicted felons who had successfully completed their terms, probation, or parole. But, they were still ineligible to vote under Florida's felon disenfranchisement law.[156] The Florida constitution provides that "no person convicted of a felony...shall be qualified to vote or hold office until restoration of civil rights or removal of disability."[157] Johnson and the other plaintiffs sued Florida Governor Jeb Bush and Florida's Clemency Board, alleging that the disfranchisement law violated the First, Fourteenth, Fifteenth, and Twenty-fourth Amendments to the United States Constitution and Sections 2 and 10 of the Voting Rights Act of 1965.[158] The defendants lost at the appellate level.[159] On appeal to the U.S. Supreme Court, in 2005, the Court let stand the lower court's decision without an oral argument.[160]

In 2000, the highly contested presidential election between Democrat Albert Gore and Republican George W. Bush featured allegations of disenfranchisement of Black as well as White voters in Florida, Missouri, and Ohio. Bush was declared the winner of the election. Gore brought a legal action.[161] A manual recount was ordered by the Florida Supreme Court. Bush appealed the state's decision to the U.S. Supreme Court, giving rise to *Bush v. Gore*.[162] On expedited appeal, the Court reversed the Florida Supreme Court and found in favor of Bush.[163] The Supreme Court held that the Florida Supreme Court violated Bush's equal-protection rights when it ordered a manual recount of the state's presidential votes.[164] The former governor of Texas, George W. Bush, became the forty-third president of the United States.

Following the 2000 presidential election, Black plaintiffs in Florida challenged the disenfranchisement of their vote. In *NAACP v. Harris*, a class-action, Blacks argued that over fifty-seven thousand Black voters were wrongfully purged from Florida's voting lists and that Black communities were provided with defective voting mechanisms.[165] The case settled. However, had their vote not been disenfranchised, the presidential election would have resulted in a victory for Albert Gore. The efficacy of the Voting Rights Act is constantly questioned by those politicians who benefit most from disenfranchisement of Black voters. Given the intransigent nature of racism, the Voting Rights Act remains a necessary legal protection.

Present-Day Vestiges: Voting Disenfranchisement in the Twenty-First Century

Nearly a century of Black disfranchisement undermined the progress of Blacks in America. In 1970, a mere five years after passage of the Voting Rights Act, there were 1,469 Black elected officials. By 2001, there were over nine thousand Black elected officials. A similar rise in Black political participation took place following the abolition of slavery.

However, terrorism and discrimination prevented Black enfranchisement. If Blacks had been allowed to participate in federal and state elections freely during the eighteenth century, there would have been an extension of the Reconstruction era, a different composition of the U.S. Supreme Court, and federal antilynching legislation. A fully franchised Black constituency would have resulted in more instrumental civil rights legislation enacted earlier and strengthened when necessary.

Black voters remain disenfranchised. Approximately 15 percent of all Black men are disenfranchised due to criminal justice violations[166] (see Chapter 7). In 2004, there were 5.3 million disenfranchised felons in the United States.[167] Other countries, such as Canada, Spain, Sweden, Israel, The Netherlands, and Switzerland, place no restrictions on the voting rights of ex-felons.[168] Legal, political, and grassroots advocacy continues toward the rehabilitation of voters disenfranchised by America's criminal justice system.

After much debate as to its relevance, Section 5 of the Voting Rights Act was reauthorized in 2006 retaining desperately needed voting rights protections.[169] However, with more than two million people incarcerated and more than half of that population compromised of people of color, voter rehabilitation remains a grave concern. As with the three-fifths provision of the U.S. Constitution, politicians benefit politically from the increased prison population provided by the prison industrial complex in rural areas. However, there is little corresponding benefit to the inmates within that political district. Inmates need to have the ability to vote. Those who retain that right should request and utilize the absentee ballot, which then allows that vote to benefit their home community.

6

RACE AND THE MILITARY

Once let the black man get upon his person the brass letters *U.S.*; let him get an eagle on his button, and a musket on his shoulder and bullets in his pocket, and there is no power on earth which can deny that he has earned the right to citizenship in the United States.

Frederick Douglass (1863)

May – 1947 – *Sardis*, Georgia. Joe Nathan Roberts, 23-year-old veteran, was shot to death when he failed to say "yes sir" to a white man. A student at Temple University in Philadelphia on the G.I. Bill, Roberts was in Georgia visiting relatives. No one was tried for the killing.

We Charge Genocide **(1951)**

If the duty of the soldier is to risk his life, the responsibility of his leaders is not to spend that life in vain.

Colin Powell, *My American Journey* **(1996)**

Blacks have served honorably in every U.S. military conflict.[1] However, from its inception, they have had to fight for an opportunity to defend their country. This chapter examines the legal obstacles facing full inclusion of Blacks in the American military as well as the momentous efforts to overcome those obstacles. An analysis of Supreme Court decisions, federal statutes, and state laws illuminates the evolving treatment of Black soldiers from the colonial period to modern times. In the beginning of this nation's history, all men, free and enslaved, were expected to help protect the homeland. Then, as now, the military option was viewed as a method of gaining education, prestige in the community, financial benefits, and freedom.

However, White colonists' fear of slave insurrections limited a Black man's ability to bear arms. Even in the face of outside danger, Whites resisted arming Blacks "lest slaves when armed might become masters."[2]

Fighting for Humanity

Although Blacks arrived in Jamestown in 1619, the first slave codes were not enacted until 1680.[3] In the Northeast under Dutch rule, New Netherlands allowed free Blacks to join the militia and bear arms.[4] However, the Dutch colony fell to England in 1664, leading to the renaming of that city to New York and the enactment of the more restrictive English slave laws. In the South, early colonial limitations on the freedom of Blacks precluded self-protection. Such legal restrictions all but denied Blacks participation in the colonial armed forces.

The following Virginia statute of 1680 exemplifies the kinds of restrictions upon Blacks in the South during the colonial period.

> 1680. Act X. Whereas the frequent meetings of considerable numbers of Negro slaves under the pretense of feast and burials is judged of dangerous consequences [it is] enacted that no Negro or slave may carry arms, such as any club, staff, gun, sword, or other weapon, nor go from his owner's plantation without a certificate and then only on necessary occasions; the punishment twenty lashes on the bare back, well laid on. And further, if any Negro lift his hand against any Christian he shall receive thirty lashes, and if he absent himself or lie out from his master's service and resist lawful apprehension, he may be killed and this law shall be published every six months.[5]

The colonial militia was used to protect against attacks by Native Americans and to maintain social control over Africans in the colony. In the Georgia colony, the militia received special orders to "disperse, suppress, kill, destroy...any Company of Slaves, who shall be met together, or who shall be lurking in any suspected places, where they may do Mischief or who shall have absented themselves from the Service of their Owners."[6] Slave-control patrols trolled the highways in search of runaway slaves or secret slave meetings. In 1700, Blacks in Pennsylvania could not carry weapons or meet in groups of four or more; at night, Blacks were made to carry tickets from their masters detailing the route and time of travel.[7]

However, Georgia's vulnerable military position necessitated recruitment of dependable slaves for its local militia. Able-bodied male slaves from sixteen to sixty could join the militia, without pay. However, the total number of slaves in a company of soldiers could not exceed one third of the total number of Whites.[8] Disabled slaves, freemen, and servants were paid nine pounds annually if unmarried and thirteen pounds if married. A threat of a possible slave uprising brought stricter slave codes after 1765. At the same time, the colonists were forced to decide how to respond to the demands of Great Britain. The colonists chose war with regard to both.

Hoping for freedom, Blacks offered their services to both sides.[9] Abigail Adams wrote that "it always appeared a most iniquitous scheme to me to fight ourselves for what we are daily robbing and plundering from those who have as good a right to freedom as we have."[10] Although some Blacks who sought to fight for the American colonies enlisted, most were turned away. In 1775, General George Washington issued an order prohibiting Black enlistment.[11] That same year, too, the Massachusetts colony determined that having anyone other than a freeman fight for the colonial principles of freedom "reflect[ed] dishonor on [the] Colony, and that no slaves be admitted into this army upon any consideration whatever."[12] However, as would become the case throughout American history, the need for additional soldiers necessitated the inclusion of Blacks. The scarcity of recruits and cruelty of the winter of 1776 forced the colonial militia to accept Blacks into the ranks. Black soldiers eagerly fought for their country and their humanity.

In 1779, Sir Henry Clinton, the British commander, authorized the inclusion of slaves on the side of the British army.[13] However, Black soldiers were treated poorly, "marked, like a piece of military equipment, with the number of the regiment or initials of the department to which he was attached."[14] In response, a desperate colonial army levied its influence and in 1781 the New York General Assembly authorized the enlistment of slaves into the Revolutionary Army: "[S]uch slave…who shall serve for a term of three years, or until regularly discharged, shall, immediately after such service or discharge be, and is hereby declared to be a free man of this state."[15]

Moreover, the "Article 7" provision of the slave statute prohibited the taking of slaves from the state. But, the British made the slaves free Negroes upon enlisting them to fight. Thus, Black Loyalists—those Blacks who fought on the side of the British—could be transported to Nova Scotia, Canada, as free persons with promises of land. Unfortunately, a secondhand freedom awaited most of them there. The land allotted to Blacks in Birchtown, Nova Scotia, was rocky and nearly useless. Other Black Loyalists arrived in Canada only to be enslaved again.[16]

Abolitionists extolled the Black soldiers who fought in the Revolutionary War and the War of 1812.[17] The war included the first woman to fight in the American military as a Black soldier. Deborah Gannett served eighteen months in the army as Robert Shurliff before her gender was discovered.[18] She was praised by the commonwealth of Massachusetts for demonstrating an "extraordinary instance of female heroism."[19] Black soldiers displayed countless other incidents of bravery. Expectations were high after America's defeat of Britain. However, immediately following the war, "Negros, Indians and Mulattos" were once again precluded from militia.[20]

The Civil War

Blacks wanted to fight. But on what terms? The government was entreated to allow Negro troops to fight on equal terms with the White soldiers.[21] Blacks formed civilian regiments, trained with sticks, and begged for duty. But, their requests to join the battle were forcefully rejected and ultimately maligned. Abraham Lincoln and Republican leadership feared freeing and arming Blacks to fight against the Confederate army.[22] Frederick Douglass published "Men of Color, to Arms!" to motivate Black men to continue their push for inclusion in the military. In the words of Douglass, "Action! action! not criticism, is the plain duty of this hour."[23]

Governor John Andrew of Massachusetts obtained authorization to form a Black regiment. The men of the 54th Massachusetts Volunteers formed the first military regiment of Black soldiers in America. The troops were recruited from around the country. However, fearing the reaction of Whites to Black officers, positions as commissioned officers of the 54th and other Black regiments were restricted to Whites. Although promised equal pay by Lincoln, Blacks were given manual labor and unequal pay. The Militia Act of 1862 provided White soldiers with $13 per month plus an extra $3.50 for a clothing allowance, whereas Black soldiers received $10 per month and had $3 deducted for clothing. Black soldiers rebelled.[24]

Democrats and Republicans believed equal pay with Blacks to be an insult to the White soldier.[25] Congress hesitated. But, the Union army relied on Black soldiers in the North and South. In 1864, at the insistence of abolitionists, the U.S. Congress enacted legislation granting equal pay to Black soldiers, to be paid retroactively.[26] Unfortunately, the pay was differentiated based on the soldier's former status as free or enslaved at the time of recruitment. The Emancipation Proclamation provided for the enlistment of Blacks in the South to fight on the side of the Union Army. The first national draft, the Conscription Act of 1863, allowed a drafted man to hire a substitute or purchase his release from military service for $300. Poor Whites responded with savage riots against free and enslaved Blacks. New York City was the site of the worst conscription rioting. During the New York riot, hundreds of Blacks were murdered and thousands were assaulted by poor Whites angered by an unfair draft and the poverty that prevented them from avoiding it.[27]

Nearly four hundred thousand Blacks served the Union military as volunteers or enlisted men and women.[28] More than thirty-eight thousand died in that war.[29] The Civil War was won by the Union because Black regiments fought triumphantly for their freedom and the ideals of America.[30] However, after the war, Blacks were expelled from the service. The image of enslaved Black men fighting on behalf of the Union convinced leaders in Southern states to enact laws precluding Blacks from the militia.[31] South Carolina, for example, provided that persons of color could not serve in the militia of the state.[32] States in the North and South enacted laws dividing troops, companies, and regiments by race.[33] In West Virginia, Black soldiers who enlisted were "kept separate and apart from the other troops."[34]

Slavery was abolished in part because of the bravery shown by Black soldiers. During the Congressional debate on the passage of the Thirteenth Amendment, Blacks' sacrifices in laying down their lives for the Union army were recognized. Sergeant William H. Carney became the first Black to be awarded the Congressional Medal of Honor.[35] U.S. Congressman Henry Wilson, a Republican, pointed to feats of sacrifice and heroism of Black soldiers. Wilson recognized that the Union needed the Black soldier if it wanted to win the war against the Confederacy and that abolishing slavery would provide Blacks with an inducement to continue to fight for the North. Wilson said, "[W]e owe it to the course of the country, to liberty, to justice, and to patriotism to offer every inducement to every black man who can fight the battle of the country to join our armies."[36] On February 1, 1865, the Thirteenth Amendment, which abolished slavery, was passed.

In 1866, Congress reorganized the Black troops into the 9th and 10th Cavalries. The Black 24th and 25th Infantries were created by Congress in 1869.[37] Because of the fear of armed Black men and the segregationist animosity simmering in the South, these Black troops were assigned to the western frontier and would come to be known as Buffalo Soldiers.[38] They protected government property, established settlements, acted as scouts, and fought in the Indian Wars against Native Americans.[39] The 9th and 10th cavalries fought in Cuba, charging up San Juan Hill with Theodore Roosevelt during the Spanish American War of 1898.[40] During the Philippine insurrection of 1899, two Black regiments, the 48th and 49th Volunteers, were added to fight with the Buffalo Soldiers in the Pacific.[41]

Black soldiers fought overseas only to return to Jim Crow laws in the United States. Segregationist laws, fear of competition for jobs, and deep White resentment of their status as military heroes confronted Black soldiers at every turn. The fear of Blacks made "uppity" by world travel was given as a justification for lynching Black soldiers. Such terrorism was used to keep Blacks in their "place." The Southerners blamed the need for lynching on the federal government, which allowed social equality in Cuba, "where that race line which the Anglo-Saxon insists on does not exist."[42] The murder of Black soldiers returning home from battle continued without arrest or trial of perpetrators.

Brownsville Incident

Brownsville, Texas, was the site of the worst aggression toward Black soldiers. In 1906, the 25th Infantry's 1st Battalion of one hundred seventy Black men was sent to Fort Brown in Brownsville. Their arrival was met with hostility by White civilians and servicemen alike. One night soon after their arrival, shots were fired into the fort; the 25th Infantry returned fire.[43] One civilian was killed. With scant evidence against them, the men of the 25th were tried and found guilty of going on a murderous rampage against Whites. Blacks awaited support from Theodore Roosevelt, now president. Roosevelt fought with the Buffalo Soldiers in Cuba and could attest to their honor. Unfortunately, he refused to speak up on their behalf. The alleged Brownsville incident led to the dishonorable discharge of 167 soldiers.[44] Although it did not pass, Congress denigrated Black troops and attempted to pass legislation removing all Blacks from the army.[45] The Brownsville incident became the basis for excluding the 25th Infantry from action during World War I.

Camp Logan: The Houston Riots

In 1917, a racist riot erupted at Camp Logan in Houston, Texas, when members of the Third Battalion of the Black 24th United States Infantry fought back against racial harassment. The soldiers were heroes who had fought in Cuba and Mexico. Yet, their presence in Houston drew only racial epithets, harassment, and resentment. On August 23, 1917, two White Houston police officers pistol-whipped a Black woman. When Black military police intervened, they were also beaten and arrested. Rumors spread that Colonel Charles Baltimore, and exemplary Black soldier, had been shot while inquiring about the arrested soldiers. Black soldiers went on the offensive, securing weapons to defend themselves against an alleged White mob approaching Camp Logan. Armed, the Black soldiers went on the offensive against White attacks, real and imagined. Fifteen Whites and four Blacks were murdered. Military tribunals indicted 118 Black soldiers for mutiny and murder. Two White officers were indicted and later released. Military tribunals found 110 Black soldiers guilty. Nineteen were hanged and more than sixty received life sentences in federal prison. The Camp Logan military tribunal remains the largest murder trial in American history. Yet, few people are familiar with this trial or the reasons for the Houston riot.[46]

The Battles at Home and Abroad

World War I began in Europe in 1914. However, the United States would not enter the war until 1917. Black soldiers traveled to Europe on loan to the French military during World War I. The Black 369th regiment served on the front lines with General Henri Gouraud's Fourth Army. In 1918, U.S. General John Pershing sent a directive to the French government demanding that Black soldiers be treated as inferiors while in France to prevent "spoiling the Negroes."[47] The Black 371st and 360th and other regiments of Black soldiers in Europe fought bravely, lived with ridicule from White American soldiers, and were too often given the most menial tasks.[48] Sergeant Henry Johnson and Private Needham Roberts were the first Americans, Black or White, to earn the Croix de Guerre, the French medal of honor.[49] Charles Hamilton Houston, an Army officer during World War I, wrote:

> The hate and scorn showered on us Negro officers by our fellow Americans convinced me that there was no sense in my dying for a world ruled by them. I made up my mind that if I got through this war I would study law and use my time fighting for men who could not strike back.[50]

Following his honorable discharge from the army, Houston attended Harvard Law School and became dean of Howard University School of Law. Houston would become the architect of the twentieth-century civil rights movement.[51]

Despite the bravery of Black soldiers, the American military treated German prisoners of war with more respect than the Blacks who fought for American ideals. Humanitarian law, established under the Geneva Convention, protected German soldiers from abuse. No such legal protection was afforded the Black soldier abroad. Nor was there any such protection for the Black soldiers who confronted racism at home. Instead, they faced betrayal within the military and an armed enemy on the battlefield. Over three hundred fifty thousand Black men served in the First World War against Germany.[52] The return of Black soldiers after World War I sparked many sociopolitical changes and nationwide race riots. Soldiers of all races returned home following the end of the war. The American economy was so strong that military veterans were promised a bonus. But, many chose to support legislation that allowed a soldier to receive more than twice the bonus amount by waiting until 1945 to collect it.[53]

However, in 1932, with the collapse of the economy during the Depression, the destitute veterans demanded their bonus money early. Known as the "Bonus Veterans," they gathered in Washington, D.C., to lobby Congress to allocate the money. More than ten thousand veterans with their wives and children built a small, racially diverse town of scrap metal while awaiting their bonus money. At the time, it was the largest protest in American history. The area was ordered cleared of the protesters. General Douglas MacArthur attacked the protesters using soldiers on horseback, tear gas, and bayonets. One protester was killed and hundreds were injured. In 1936, Congress overrode the veto of President Roosevelt and paid the veterans their bonuses.[54] Black soldiers would have to fight another domestic battle.

The Red Summer

In 1919, race riots led to the murders of hundreds of Blacks. The "red summer" is so named because that summer blood ran through the streets of America. W. E. B. DuBois wrote in *The Crisis* magazine:

> [T]ens of thousands of black men were drafted into a great struggle. For bleeding France and what she means and has meant and will mean to us and humanity and against the threat of German race arrogance...
>
> But by the God of heaven, we are cowards and jackasses if now that the war is over, we do not marshal every ounce of our brain and brawn to fight a sterner, longer, more unbending battle against the forces of hell in our own land.[55]

Black soldiers returned home in 1919 to become the object of savage encounters with Whites.[56] Race riots erupted in cities across the country as Blacks trained in combat fought back. That year, at least, seventy-eight Black men and women were murdered by White lynch mobs. Eight Black men were murdered while wearing their military uniforms.[57] One Black man "was lynched *because of the fact* that he wore the uniform of a United States soldier."[58] Riots against any increase in Black social status occurred in Tulsa, Oklahoma; Chicago; Arkansas; and other American towns.

The exact number of lynchings of Black soldiers is unknown. Too often, members of law enforcement who were responsible for reporting these incidents ignored or were a participant in the murder. Blacks who had given complete loyalty fighting for democracy in Europe found Jim Crow laws and murder in America.[59] Evidence has shown that the rape of White women was often an excuse for murdering Black soldiers. However, according to Tuskegee Institute records for the years 1882 to 1951, most lynchings were a response to alleged assaults (self-defense) involving White men and acts such as arrogance toward a White person or attempting to register to vote.[60]

Segregated Military

During peacetime in the United States, the military formulated policies to "deal with" Black soldiers. The Navy attempted to have a vessel manned only by Black seamen, but it was too difficult to find enough recruits in the necessary specialties. The Great Depression of 1929 began a wave of interest in the military as a place of employment. However, the army forced most Blacks into menial jobs with the least opportunities. The Navy relegated Blacks to the lowest positions. The Air Corps explicitly prevented Blacks from enlisting.[61] Although Congress passed a law in 1939 to allow civilian aviation schools to train military pilots, the Air Corps refused to comply.[62] Congress passed other legislation such as H.R. 9850 that continued racial segregation, resulting in unequal treatment; leaders in the armed forces feared that "mixing the races" would demoralize the White units.[63]

By 1940, an election year, the full inclusion of Blacks in the military became the focal point of protests by the NAACP and other civil rights organizations. White politicians sought the Black vote. Black newspapers addressed the government's continued segregation or exclusion of Blacks in the military. Blacks were promised access to all branches of the military.[64] After years of being passed over for promotion, Colonel Benjamin O. Davis became the first Black person to achieve the rank of general.[65] Franklin D. Roosevelt won reelection. However, there remained dissatisfaction with a segregated military on the part of Blacks. William Hastie wrote that "the traditional mores of the South have been widely accepted and adopted by the Army as the basis of policy and practice affecting the Negro soldier."[66]

World War II

The onset of World War II brought changes to the military. The number of Blacks enlisted in the military climbed from a few thousand to over two hundred thousand. Activist groups continued to press for full inclusion and opportunity. Blacks were relegated into labor positions. A Black flying school was created in Tuskegee, Alabama.[67] However, the Black pilots were precluded from interacting with White pilots or White civilians.[68] In April 1945, over one hundred Black officers were arrested for leading a protest against segregation at Freeman Field Air Base in Indiana.[69] Miserable treatment by the military led one young Black soldier to write that he would rather "fight and die here for our rights as to do it on some foreign battlefield."[70]

Racial issues permeated the war. Hitler used racism and xenophobia to rise to power. However, America's image of proud democracy was undermined by racial segregation within the military. The United States came under great criticism by Europeans who did not understand or accept the depth of social segregation practiced in America. General Dwight D. Eisenhower found it difficult to maintain racial segregation in Europe. When Europeans embraced Black soldiers White Americans responded with violence against Blacks. "There were some shootings, most by whites against blacks and a few killings—all covered up by the army."[71]

At home, employment opportunities were limited. In 1941, A. Philip Randolph,[72] leader of the first Black labor union, planned a protest march of one hundred thousand Black persons through Washington, D.C., if President Franklin D. Roosevelt did not desegregate U.S. defense plants.[73] The defense plants refused to employ Blacks. After

Randolph threatened to march, Roosevelt signed Executive Order 8802 desegregating the defense industry.[74] After the death of Roosevelt, Randolph made a similar threat of protest to President Harry Truman. Presented with the political and logistical complexities of maintaining a segregated military, Truman agreed to desegregate.[75]

Executive Order 9981: Desegregation

On July 26, 1948, Truman signed Executive Order 9981, desegregating the military:

> It is hereby declared to be the policy of the President that there shall be equality of treatment and opportunity for all persons in the armed services without regard to race, color, religion or national origin. This policy shall be put into effect as rapidly as possible, having due regard to the time required to effectuate any necessary changes without impairing efficiency or morale.

The authority to sign this executive order falls within the presidential powers of Article II of the U.S. Constitution. An executive order does not require a vote of Congress.

President Truman recognized that Congress would not have passed legislation desegregating the armed forces. During this time period, Congress had repeatedly refused to pass the antilynching legislation in the face of race riots, savage murders, and pressure from the NAACP.[76] President Truman's executive order desegregated the troops in the United States and abroad. The order was met with resistance within certain areas of the military. While some Whites refused to accept Black equality, opportunities for Blacks expanded, as did the number of Blacks enlisting in the military.

However, as their numbers increased, Black enlisted personnel became targets of criminal allegations and court martial. Most serious are the cases involving a capital crime—a crime punishable by death. During World War II, Blacks comprised less than 10 percent of the Army. Yet, of that number, fifty-five Black men were executed, representing 79 percent of all executions.[77] After President Truman's Executive Order 9981, the number of accusations and executions increased.[78] Eighteen executions of American servicemen took place in Britain during World War II.[79] Of those men, eleven were African American and three were Latino.[80] All of the capital convictions of Black soldiers involved White victims. The case of Private David Cobb, a twenty-one-year-old soldier in the Army, was the first execution of a Black man serving in Europe during World War II. Cobb was found guilty of shooting a White officer. He was executed by hanging two months after being found guilty of the crime.[81]

The Port Chicago Incident

Black servicemen were often assigned the most dangerous and labor-intensive work. For Blacks, work that required special training was not given and special gear was never received. The Port Chicago explosion involved two ships docked at Port Chicago on the Sacramento River near San Francisco, California. Due to segregation and racial prejudice, Black servicemen were assigned the dangerous task of loading ammunition onto the ship. On July 17, 1944, an explosion occurred while ammunition was being loaded onto two ships. The explosion killed 320 naval personnel and civilians, including 202 Black servicemen.[82] Hundreds were injured.[83] It was the worst domestic loss of life during World War II.[84] Blacks were denied the usual thirty-day leave provided to their White peers.

Within weeks of the explosion, the survivors were ordered back to work loading ammunition. Without any improvement in safety conditions and fearing for their lives, 258 men refused to return. The men were arrested. Most returned to the dangerous work. But, fifty of the men refused to unload any more ammunition and were tried and found guilty of mutiny by naval court martial.[85] They were given sentences of five to fifteen years of hard labor and dishonorable discharges. Thurgood Marshall of the NAACP Legal Defense Fund launched a campaign to overturn the convictions, which resulted in the eventual release of forty-seven of the men.[86] On appeal, the dishonorable discharge was changed. However, the convictions remained on their records. Modern attempts to clear the names of the Port Chicago "mutineers" had been unsuccessful. Upon the request of Black naval veterans, President William Clinton pardoned one lone survivor in 1999.[87]

Asians and the Military:
Korematsu v. United States

Another example of racism in the military was demonstrated in the treatment of Japanese Americans during World War II, discussed next. Racial bigotry against Asians affected the manner in which they were treated in America's military. A foundational discussion of Asian immigration to the United States in the nineteenth century will illuminate the racial obstacles they feared in the twentieth century. Chinese émigrés arrived in the United States as early as 1848. At that time, two Chinese men and one Chinese woman disembarked in San Francisco. In 1863, Ah Hang became the first Asian to serve in the military. He fought in the U.S. Civil War.

The Chinese population in America increased due to several factors. China fell to Britain in a battle and shortly thereafter the country faced a devastating crop failure. The economic turmoil in China led thousands to answer the invitation to a better life in America. However, the United States enacted legislation specifically to prohibit Chinese immigration. The preamble of the Chinese Exclusion Act of 1882 stated: "Whereas, in the opinion of the Government of the United States the coming of Chinese laborers to this country endangers the good order of certain localities within the territory thereof."[88]

Japanese émigrés arrived in California in the 1890s. Competition for jobs and land created animosity against Asians among many American Whites. Racial segregation based on Asian descent was legalized in California and other western states. Successful as farmers, people of Asian descent were precluded from owning land.[89] The Chinese and Japanese in America were denied the right to become naturalized citizens.[90] The plaintiff in *United States v. Wong Kim Ark* (1898), Wong, was born in San Francisco, California, but denied citizenship because his parents were foreign nationals from China.[91] Upon appeal, the U.S. Supreme Court ruled that the Fourteenth Amendment bestowed citizenship on all persons born in the United States.[92] Granting citizenship to non-Whites born in this country became a hotly contested issue. If citizenship was a birthright, then America would limit the number of émigrés allowed to enter the United States.

By 1907, federal laws restricted the number of Asian immigrants eligible to immigrate to America.

In 1923, the U.S. Supreme Court decided *U.S. v. Bhagat Singh Thind*. The Court ruled that only Caucasians could become naturalized citizens.[93] In this case, "Caucasian" was narrowly defined to mean only White Europeans; thus, any non-White applicants were precluded from becoming naturalized American citizens.[94] Eugenics buffs and enthusiasts claimed the "yellow peril" would lead to the destruction of the White race and American culture.[95] Entrenched social and legal discrimination against persons of Asian descent reached levels of hysteria when the Empire of Japan attacked the Pearl Harbor naval base in Hawaii on December 7, 1941. The United States declared war on Japan the following day.

Attack on Pearl Harbor

The attack on Pearl Harbor led to intense fear and increased anti-Asian sentiment across America, especially on the West Coast. On February 19, 1942, President Roosevelt signed Executive Order 9066 giving the military power to protect the West Coast from sabotage or espionage by restricting the movement of persons in proscribed areas.[96] General John L. DeWitt was given authority to secure the West Coast of the United States against sabotage from the Japanese. Initially, based upon a belief of possible sabotage, General DeWitt ordered a general curfew and divided the West Coast into military areas. By military order, persons of Japanese, German, and Italian ancestry residing in military areas were required to notify the government of any change of residence.

By March of 1942, military orders focused on persons of Japanese descent. All persons of Japanese origin were prohibited from leaving the area. Subsequent orders required evacuation and relocation of persons of Japanese descent.[97] America was concerned about the loyalty of some undisclosed number of Japanese, among the hundred thousand, who could sabotage the naval and airbases located in California and Washington state.[98] The Supreme Court stated, "Like the curfew, exclusion of those of Japanese origin was deemed necessary because of the presence of an unascertained number of disloyal members of the group, most of whom we have no doubt were loyal to this country."[99] Disloyalty was based on any refusal to swear an oath of "unqualified allegiance to the United States" and to renounce all ties to Japan.[100] In response to the fear of disloyalty by a relative few, Civilian Exclusion Order No. 34 required all persons of Japanese ancestry, alien as well as citizens, to leave their homes and report to an assembly center.[101]

Over one hundred thousand Japanese citizens and visitors were evacuated.[102] They were sent from the assembly centers to detention camps located as far away as Arkansas. Of the one hundred twenty-six thousand persons of Japanese descent in the United States, approximately one hundred twelve thousand resided in California, Oregon, and Washington.[103] Refusal to report to the assembly centers was deemed a criminal act that would result in arrest. The internment camps have been referred to as "concentration camps" by many Japanese and non-Japanese alike. Each camp was surrounded by barbed wire and guards armed with machine guns. One such camp was actually a horse stable. Men, women, and children would reside in these camps for the duration of World War II.

Legal challenges to military orders directed at persons of Japanese ancestry were unsuccessful. In *Hirabayashi v. United States*, the plaintiff, an American citizen, was convicted of violating the curfew order that directed all persons of Japanese ancestry residing in the military areas to be in their residences between the hours of 8 p.m. and 6 a.m. At the time of his arrest, Hirabayashi was a student at the University of Washington. He refused to report to the assembly center and instead stayed in his residence. He argued that the military curfew orders exceeded the authority of the War Powers Act and the authority of Congress and the president.

The Supreme Court found that the war power of the U.S. government extended to any conduct necessary to wage war successfully. In upholding his conviction, the Court found that the Fifth Amendment did not contain an equal-protection clause. Moreover, Justice Stone, speaking on behalf of the Court, found that the Japanese were targets for such orders because they were different; they were different because

...social, economic and political conditions which have prevailed since the close of the last century, when the Japanese began to come to this country in substantial numbers, have intensified their solidarity and have in large measure prevented their assimilation as an integral part of the white population. In addition, large numbers of children of Japanese parentage are sent to Japanese language schools outside the regular hours of public schools in the locality. Some of these schools are generally believed to be sources of Japanese nationalistic propaganda, cultivating allegiance to Japan.[104]

The orders were considered constitutional and necessary to protect the country.

An example of the complexities of race involves a Japanese American, Fred Korematsu, and America's war-time internment camps. Korematsu was an American citizen born in San Leandro, California. He was arrested and convicted for failure to report to the assembly center. Korematsu, a twenty-two-year-old welder, argued that the military orders were contradictory in that the curfew required him to stay in his residence and the evacuation order required him to report to the assembly center.[105] He went so far as to have plastic surgery in order to avoid the relocation camps. His loyalty was not in question; the government did not provide any evidence of his disloyalty. However, he was regarded as a threat due to his Japanese ancestry.

In *Korematsu v. United States*, Korematsu argued that the conflicting orders were confusing and led to his arrest. The Court used this due-process case to clarify its position on the segregation of American citizens of Japanese descent into camps. Justice Black, speaking for the Court, stated that "citizenship has its responsibilities as well as its privileges".[106]

Korematsu was not excluded from the Military Area because of hostility to him or his race. He *was* excluded because we are at war with the Japanese Empire. [M]ilitary authorities feared an invasion...the situation demanded that all citizens of Japanese ancestry be segregated from the West Coast temporarily. There was evidence of disloyalty on the part of some....[W]e cannot—by availing ourselves of the calm perspective of hindsight—now say that at that time these actions were unjustified.[107]

Justice Frankfurter referred to the Framers in his concurring opinion, noting that the orders are "reasonably expedient military precautions" in time of war and "to deny them constitutional legitimacy makes of the Constitution an instrument for dialectic subtleties."[108] Wartime provides the government increased powers and diminishes those of citizens as well as noncitizens.

Justices Roberts, Murphy, and Jackson provided excoriating dissents. Justice Roberts made clear that the orders were an unconstitutional violation based on race. Justice Murphy stated that there was no reliable evidence to support the fear of disloyalty among the Japanese. Tribunals such as those created in Britain at the onset of the war could have been established to determine the loyalty of each person. Moreover, the failure of the Japanese to assimilate was due primarily to prejudice against them. Justice Jackson stated that if Korematsu had been standing next to "a German alien enemy, an Italian alien enemy, and a citizen of American-born ancestors, convicted of treason," only Korematsu, based on his ancestry, would be in violation of General DeWitt's orders.[109]

Japanese-American Soldiers in World War II

Japanese Americans fought in World War II. A Nisei (first-generation U.S.-born person of Japanese descent) formed the 100th Battalion, which consisted of part of the Hawaiian National Guard. By 1943, the war effort required every available person. The federal government recruited from the relocation camps, forming the 442nd Regimental "Go for broke" Combat Team. The units were racially segregated and most of their officers were White. As with Blacks during prior wars, the request for volunteers from the camps was met with the desire to prove loyalty from some captives and fierce protest from others. The 442nd became one of the most decorated regiments of its size in the war.[110]

In 1983, Korematsu successfully challenged his conviction to obtain a writ of error *coram nobis*, which allows the overturning of a decision if evidence becomes available that, if known, would have led to a different outcome.[111] Information within the government revealed that evidence of disloyalty among the Japanese was fabricated. The curfew and exclusion orders were based on racial prejudice rather than military exigency and war department officials revised the report in several material respects.[112] In 1987, Hirabayashi successfully challenged his conviction as well.[113] However, the original U.S. Supreme Court ruling that upheld the federal government's authority to place citizens and noncitizens in detention camps without charge during a time of war remains undisturbed. In 1998, President Clinton presented Fred Korematsu with the Medal of Freedom, the highest honor the American government gives to a civilian. The U.S. government formally apologized to the survivors of the internment camps. Each survivor received $20,000 as reparation for his or her losses during internment.

Native Americans in the Military

Native Americans have had a conflicted relationship with a country that sought to destroy their culture and seemingly tolerate their continued existence. Native Americans, who once numbered in the tens of millions, are now less than two percent of the U.S. population, according to the 2000 Census. Their record of military service in World War I was a decisive factor in finally attaining U.S. citizenship. In 1919, Native American soldiers and sailors received citizenship in recognition of their importance as code-talkers. The American military employed members of the Choctaw tribe as part of the 142nd Infantry regiment because their native tongue was not decipherable by enemy forces.[114] In 1924, Congress passed the Snyder Act granting full citizenship to all Native Americans.[115] Navajo code-talkers were employed during World War II. Native Americans spoke twenty-six languages or dialects that were unknown to Europeans and essential to secure communications between the Allied Forces. The code-talkers were awarded medals for their service. However, the discrimination afforded them upon returning to the United States was quite similar to Blacks in America.

The Korean War

By the Korean War, a quarter of the American military was Black. Legal segregation of the military ended with Executive Order 9981. However, Black soldiers were targets if they "refused to submit meekly to white supremacy regulations."[116] The Korean War bore witness to de facto or tradition-based racial segregation practiced by Whites. Black soldiers were often trained in racially segregated troops, housed in segregated barracks, and assigned to labor battalions. White Americans spread the disease of racism to Europe and Asia. As far as Newfoundland and the Philippines, the local populations were infected with America's racial prejudice. White servicemen convinced owners of local hotels and restaurants around the bases to refuse to service Blacks.[117] Criminal allegations were disproportionately lodged against Black soldiers.

In 1951, Thurgood Marshall, lead attorney for the NAACP, traveled to Asia to protect the rights of Black soldiers in Korea on trial for capital crimes, thus giving substance to his statement to the effect that "the NAACP is ready to defend, with all of its resources, any of those servicemen upon determination that they are victims of racial discrimination."[118] Military justice operates by separate procedural rules from those used in civilian courts. In several cases, the "courtroom" is on the battlefield, with capital verdicts rendered after only a few hours of testimony. Despite heroic deeds on the battlefield, Blacks were disproportionately charged with cowardice under Article 75—misbehavior in the presence of the enemy.

Marshall's investigations uncovered racial discrimination. During a three-month period in 1950, thirty-two Black servicemen were convicted under Article 75, compared with only two Whites. One of the thirty-two Black men was sentenced to death, fifteen of the men to life imprisonment, and the others to a span of imprisonment of from five to fifty years.[119] Yet, of the Whites found guilty of the same offense, the harshest sentence was five years. The publication of Marshall's investigation and pressure from the Black community led General MacArthur to reduce or suspend the sentences of many Black servicemen unjustly accused of crimes. However, Blacks continue to be disproportionately subjected to capital sentences and court martial hearings.

After discharge from the military, many Blacks failed to receive promised veteran benefits established under the G.I. Bill. Introduced as part of President Roosevelt's New Deal, the G.I. Bill or Selective Service Readjustment Act provided military veterans with low-cost mortgages, additional points on government employment examinations, small business loans, and tuition for college.[120] The G.I. programs assisted veterans in the transition back into civilian life. By 1948, 15 percent of the federal budget was used to finance G.I. Bill programs.[121] However, segregation in education and housing, and discrimination in employment prevented Black veterans from receiving these benefits.[122]

The Vietnam War: *Bond v. Floyd*

The nexus between civil rights and the peace movement is complex. Prior wars brought a possibility of harm as well as opportunities for employment, military promotion, and travel away from racial oppression. Blacks have served honorably in every American war and conflict. Yet, for much of America's history, the military has treated Blacks abysmally. Too often, Black lives were lost without recognition of their sacrifice or heroism. Racism in politics excluded or minimized Black opinion on foreign policy. Some Blacks protested war while other Blacks carried a sense of superpatriotism during war in an attempt to prove their worth.

The Vietnam War divided the country and the Black community.[123] Turmoil over racial justice combined with political protest over the war in Vietnam, a country in Southeast Asia that became a staging ground for this conflict between the West and the East. The government of the Republic of Vietnam (South Vietnam) was an ally of the West. The Democratic Republic of Vietnam (North Vietnam) was an ally of the former Soviet Union. During the Cold War, the United States first became a military presence in this war-torn nation under President Dwight Eisenhower, a Republican. Later, President John F. Kennedy, a Democrat, steadily increased America's presence in Vietnam through military force, advisors, and economic aid.

President Kennedy was assassinated in 1963. His vice president, Lyndon B. Johnson, upon becoming president, escalated the level of aggression and number of American personnel in Vietnam. Bombing raids in Southeast Asia had considerable implications in America. More troops were needed. Costs rose. The government's strategies for victory appeared unworkable. As the death toll increased, college students protested America's continued involvement in the war. The war continued amid a complex web of cultures, political conflicts, and human loss.

The civil rights community was quite divided over Vietnam. Civil rights leader Martin Luther King, Jr., spoke out against the war in Vietnam. War was counter to King's philosophy of nonviolence. Additionally, he believed the war drew momentum away from the fight for racial justice in America.[124] As the death toll of soldiers and civilians increased, King openly protested against the war. Others in the Black community expressed patriotism and a desire to support armed conflict if it would lead to democracy in other countries.

In 1966, amid America's antiwar protests, the U.S. Supreme Court was presented with the case of *Bond v. Floyd*.[125] In this case, Julian Bond, a newly elected Black member of the Georgia House of Representatives, spoke in open opposition to the war in Vietnam.[126] Prior to his election to state office, Bond was communications director for the Student Non-Violent Coordinating Committee (SNCC), a civil rights organization.[127] SNCC had issued a statement denouncing the lynching of a Black civil rights activist, Sam Young, comparing the murder with the invasion of Vietnam by the U.S. military. An excerpt states:

> The murder of Samuel Young in Tuskegee, Al., is no different than the murder of peasants in Vietnam, for both Young and the Vietnamese sought, and are seeking, to secure the rights guaranteed them by law. In each case the United States government bears a great part of the responsibility for their deaths.[128]

The Georgia House of Representatives voted 184 to 12 to deny Bond his seat in government. Bond was not allowed to take the oath of office and accused of treason.[129]

Bond sued to gain his elected office arguing that the actions of the Georgia House of Representatives violated his First Amendment right of freedom of speech.[130] Bond believed that as a Black American treated as a second-class citizen and as a pacifist, he was not required to support the war.[131] The oath of the office required Bond to swear to uphold the Constitution of the United States. The Georgia State Legislature argued that Bond's antiwar stance violated the U.S. Constitution and the law. The state court ruled against Bond. While he was appealing that ruling, the Georgia House called a special election to fill his vacant seat.[132] Bond entered the race and won the seat a second time by an overwhelming majority.[133]

Bond adamantly refused to recant his prior statements about the war. Once again, he was denied the oath of office.[134] He appealed to the U.S. Supreme Court. Relying on their ruling in *New York Times v. Sullivan*, the Court upheld Bond's freedom to take a controversial position concerning the war. Chief Justice Warren, writing for the unanimous Court, found that Bond's statements about the war and racial prejudice in America fell within the right of free expression protected by the First Amendment.[135] Years later, Bond would go on to become chair of the NAACP.

At the same time, the relationship between Blacks and the military began to change.[136] Black soldiers faced discrimination from the military and hostility from the Black community.[137] Captain Norman Alexander McDaniel was held as a prisoner of war in North Vietnam. During his imprisonment, Martin Luther King was assassinated. McDaniel was instructed to "tell black soldiers not to fight because the United States is waging a war of genocide, using dark-skinned people against dark-skinned people."[138] He refused. As punishment, the interrogator decreased McDaniel's food rations and ridiculed him. McDaniel stated, "We deal with our problems within our country."[139]

President Johnson did not seek reelection. Richard Nixon, a Republican, was elected president in 1968. Under Nixon, the Vietnam War expanded into neighboring Cambodia and Laos. College campuses erupted in antiwar protests. The National Guard was activated to keep the peace. On May 4, 1970, four White student protesters were killed and nine wounded at Kent State University when National Guard troops opened fire on protesters. The shootings provoked over one thousand student protests on college campuses across the country and tens of thousands of antiwar protesters to converge on Washington, D.C. A week later, Black student antiwar protesters were fired upon and two were killed at Jackson State University in Mississippi. National protests continued. College students protested President Nixon's expansion of the war into Cambodia and Laos.[140]

Conscientious Objector

In *Clay, aka Ali, v. United States* (1971), the Supreme Court decided the appeal of Muhammad Ali,[141] who was born Cassius Marcellus

Clay, Jr., in Kentucky.[142] Clay was world heavyweight champion when he converted to Islam and changed his name to Muhammad Ali. In 1967, when Ali was called for military service, he refused to be inducted into the army. His request for an exemption as a conscientious objector was rejected.[143] Ali based his antiwar sentiments on the religious beliefs of the Qur'an, the Muslim holy book.[144] Ali is reported to have said, "I ain't got no quarrel with Vietnam congress; no Vietnam congress ever called me a nigger." The New York State Athletic Commission suspended his license to box.

The Kentucky draft board denied Ali's appeal.[145] He was convicted of willfully refusing to submit to induction in the military and sentenced to five years for draft evasion.[146] The Selective Service Appeal Board upheld the decision without a stated reason.[147] Ali's championship boxing title was revoked and he was expelled from boxing. He appealed to the U.S. Supreme Court. The Court reversed the conviction, granting Ali conscientious objector status. Muhammad Ali would regain his heavyweight championship and become a respected world figure. He remained a fighter who abhorred the violence of war.

By 1973, a peace agreement was signed and the United States withdrew from Vietnam. In 1975, the South Vietnamese government fell to troops from North Vietnam. Although a peace treaty was negotiated, the Vietnam War represents America's first major military defeat. An unpopular war meant many Vietnam War veterans were not embraced upon their return home. This was also the case for Black soldiers who fought in Vietnam, who faced a racist American military and racism in America and found a cold reception because of an unpopular war.

The Vietnam War further exposed the racial discontent in the military. The Congressional Black Caucus held hearings on racism in the military that brought national attention to the situation.[148] Black Panthers and other Black leaders for social change were vocal in their criticism of the military system.[149] Once again, America was advocating democracy around the world without protecting the rights of Blacks in uniform. In response, equal opportunity and racial awareness programs were created by the military.[150] However, military commitment to reform was uneven.[151] In 1973, a peace accord was reached between the United States and North Vietnam. In 1975, South Vietnam was invaded and fell to the North Vietnamese. Over seven thousand Black soldiers lost their lives in the Vietnam War.[152] Questions concerning the treatment of Black soldiers and a disproportionate Black injury and casualty rate persisted.[153] Too often, Blacks already facing higher unemployment rates returned from Vietnam to find few job opportunities, discrimination, and many war-related medical needs.[154]

The Iraq Wars

Racial bias within America's criminal justice system has led to a disproportionate number of Black and Latino convictions. The incarceration of nearly one in four Blacks has, in turn, reduced the pool of eligible people for military service. The result is evident in the Iraq Wars fought with one of the lowest levels of military personnel in American history.

Present-Day Vestiges: Bending the Brass Ceiling

Blacks continue to serve in America's military courageously and honorably. The military offers access to basic opportunities for Black enlisted personnel.[155,156] In 1970, Blacks were 11 percent of all U.S. military personnel.[157] When the draft ended in 1973, Blacks represented 12 percent of the all-volunteer force.[158] In 1983, during the throes of economic uncertainty, that number increased to 19 percent.[159] Blacks accounted for 17 percent of military personnel in 2004.[160] Black women represent 28 percent of female servicemembers.[161] Black civilian unemployment remains between 9.1 and 8.9 percent as compared with about 4.1 percent for Whites.[162] Given the crisis in Black civilian employment, the military becomes an attractive alternative for education and employment opportunities. For many Blacks, it is a Hobsian choice: Risk life and health by joining the military or face unemployment as a civilian.

For those who choose the military for its prestige and honor, racial discrimination remains an obstacle to promotion.[163] The increase in Black enlisted personnel has not led to a corresponding increase in the number of Black military officers.[164] In 1976, only 3.4 percent of all U.S. military officers were Black.[165] By 2003, the number of Black military officers had risen to only 9.1 percent.[166] Success of the Tuskegee Airmen in World War II has not translated into opportunities for Blacks as pilots. Sixty years later, the Air Force has 12,000 pilots, of which only 245, or approximately 2 percent, are Black. In the Navy, only 2.5 percent of all pilots are Black. There are only 196 Blacks in the legendary Green Berets, fewer than 5 percent of the 4,278 enlisted persons in that elite unit.[167]

Concerns of disproportionate injury and casualty rates persist. Blacks are 13 percent of the U.S. population. However, since 1980, Black men represent 18.4 percent of male active-duty military casualties.[168] Black women represent 25.8 percent of female military casualties.[169] For Black veterans, life after military service is difficult. Black veterans comprise 35 percent of inmates in state and federal correctional facilities as well as over 36 percent of those incarcerated in local jails.[170] The incarceration rates for Blacks in the military are also disproportionate to their number in the U.S. population.[171] Whether to support or protest America's wars remains a controversial question within the Black community.

The immediate domestic issues facing Blacks in America are so vast as to restrict the time or energy to focus on foreign policy.[172] Yet, Blacks continue to find the time and inclination to follow foreign policy and debate the issues. When the debates rise to the level of protest, Blacks are rejecting the hypocrisy inherent in a society that talks of human rights abroad and practices discrimination domestically. Black soldiers remain invested in an American ideal of democracy and justice under law. As in centuries past, these men and women have sworn to give their lives to protect this country.[173] Their sacrifices must not be made in vain.

7

RACE, CRIME, AND INJUSTICE

My Dear Friend:

You remember the old fable of The Man and the Lion, where the lion complained that he should not be so misrepresented when the lions write history.

Letter to Frederick Douglass from Wendell Phillips, Esq. (1845),
from *Narrative of the Life of Frederick Douglass*

Neither slavery nor involuntary servitude, *except as punishment for crime whereof the party shall have been duly convicted,* shall exist within the United States, or any place subject to their jurisdiction.

Thirteenth Amendment to the U.S. Constitution

Today, our criminal justice system incarcerates Black men, women, and children in astounding numbers. Blacks comprise 13 percent of the U.S. population, but of America's more than two million incarcerated persons, over half are men and women of color. Twice as many Whites as Blacks are arrested.[1] Yet, seven times as many Blacks as Whites are convicted of crimes.[2] Black women represent the fastest growing segment of incarcerated persons.[3] Black juveniles are disproportionately represented at every stage of juvenile justice proceedings.[4]

This chapter examines the monumental challenges Blacks have faced from slavery to the present period within the criminal justice system. As victims of crime, jurors, witnesses, suspects, and defendants, the struggle of Blacks to access justice and defeat institutionalized discrimination has been arduous.

Crimes without Punishment

As captives, Blacks were victims of kidnapping and torture. Their legal right of self-defense was abrogated. As early as 1639, Virginia enacted a statute that stated: "Act X. All *persons except Negroes* are to be provided with arms and ammunition."[5] In 1669, the Virginia legislature enacted the following statute, titled "An Act about the casual killing of slaves."[6] The law declared that "if any slave resist his master…and by the extremity of the correction should chance to die, that death shall not be accompted by felony…"[7] A slaveholder who failed to beat or mutilate a recalcitrant slave could be fined or even forfeit his slave.[8] Laws protected slave owners upon the death of their property during a corrective beating. For the enslaved person, these were crimes without punishments.

Criminal laws and punishments were intended to assist in subjugation of Blacks into a labor class benefiting Whites. Thus, slaves and free Blacks were prosecuted without benefit of due-process protections.[9] However, Whites comprised the majority of the inmate populations in the Deep South where slave laborers were too valuable to imprison. For free Blacks accused of a crime, conviction was nearly certain to be followed by punishments of death, banishment, or lengthy incarceration. In states such as Maryland and Virginia, free Blacks represented over a third of the inmate population.[10] Free Blacks convicted of crimes in 1850s Virginia could be sold into slavery or hanged. A more profitable option involved leasing these Black inmates to work on canals, roads, and bridges. Jails and prisons were segregated. White politicians considered housing Black prisoners with Whites an insult to the White prisoners and bad for morale.

Slaves could not testify against Whites or legally defend themselves against attacks by Whites. The magnitude of these due-process deprivations are evidenced in the case of Celia. In 1855, Celia, an enslaved woman, was hanged for the murder of her owner, Robert Newsom, a wealthy White farmer in Fulton, Missouri, whom she killed after he attempted to rape her.[11] Newsom's murder was precipitated by years of rape, beginning when she was purchased at the age of fourteen. On the night of the murder, Celia had warned Newsom to leave her alone. When he entered her room and lunged for her, Celia beat him to death. She cut up his body and burned the pieces in the fireplace.

The state of Missouri charged her with murder.[12] Celia admitted she struck Newsom but only to end his sexual attacks; she did not mean to kill him.[13] Under Missouri law, a woman is permitted to protect herself against rape.[14] However, in Celia's case, the law would not apply to her because a slave had no right of self-defense or grounds upon which she is allowed to resist her master.[15] Missouri law prohibited Blacks from testifying in court against Whites. Thus, Celia could not take the witness stand and testify in her own defense. On October 10, 1855, the jury of White men, four of whom were slave owners, found Celia guilty of murder; she was sentenced to death by hanging.[16] The execution was delayed until December 21, 1855, long enough for Celia to give birth to Newsom's stillborn child conceived by rape.

Even after slavery was abolished, the courtroom remained a hostile place for Blacks who sought to defend their rights, testify against Whites, or seek justice. The rule of law offered little for aggrieved Blacks, especially in criminal cases. America had grown accustomed to ignoring the rights of Blacks and dismissing Black litigants, witnesses, jurors, or spectators. With the passage of the Civil Rights Act of 1866, Congress provided another avenue for Blacks who were denied justice in state courts. Specifically, the act provides, in pertinent part, that all persons shall have the same right to:

> ...make and enforce contracts, to sue, be parties, and give evidence, to inherit, purchase, lease, sell, hold, and convey real and personal property, and to full and equal benefit of all laws and proceedings for the security of person and property as is enjoyed by white citizens, and shall be subject to like punishment, pains, and penalties, and to none other, any law, statute, ordinance, regulation, or custom to the contrary notwithstanding.[17]

The act is triggered by crimes and offenses committed against the provisions of the act "and of all causes, civil and criminal, *affecting persons* who are denied, or cannot enforce in the courts or judicial tribunals of the State, or locality, where they may be, any of the rights secured to them by the first section of the act."[18] The Civil Rights Act of 1866 provides for the removal from state court into federal court any suit or prosecution, civil or criminal, which had been, or might hereafter be, commenced against any such person for any cause whatever.[19]

Congress did not trust the states to fairly adjudicate criminal cases involving Blacks. As the Supreme Court stated in *Blyew v. United States*: "We cannot be expected to be ignorant of the condition of things which existed when the statute was enacted, or of the evils which it was intended to remedy."[20] Historically, the criminal justice system has shown a blatant disregard for protecting the rights of Blacks or providing equal justice under law. Disparate treatment and unfair criminal convictions, as well as the failure to protect Black communities, demonstrate societal efforts to restrict the freedom and economic mobility of people of color.

Fugitive Slave Patrols: *Prigg v. Pennsylvania*

Escape was a crime punishable by beating, torture, or death. States enacted rigid laws to punish slaves who attempted to escape. The harshness of those laws was intended to discourage anyone from considering escape or revolt.[21] Yet, slaves faced these risks for the sake of freedom. To reduce escape attempts, slave patrols were used to scrutinize all activities of Blacks, both free and enslaved.[22] The Fugitive Slave Act of 1850 extended criminal punishment to the person escaping as well as to those who assisted an enslaved person with an escape. Bystanders could be implicated as well.[23] A $1,000 fine was imposed on marshals who refused to capture and return runaway slaves.[24]

In *Prigg v. Pennsylvania*, an 1842 case, the U.S. Supreme Court found unconstitutional a Commonwealth of Pennsylvania law criminalizing bounty hunters who captured Blacks to return to slavery.[25] Escaped slave Margaret Morgan and her children were captured by bounty hunters in Pennsylvania and taken to Maryland. Edward Prigg, one of the bounty hunters, was convicted under the Pennsylvania statute. The Court overturned the conviction. Although Morgan's children were born in Pennsylvania, the Court maintained that as children of a "slave for life," they, too, were property of the slaveholder, Margaret Ashmore. The fugitive slave laws enacted by Congress in 1793 were enforcement mechanisms for Article IV of the U.S. Constitution, which provides slave owners with a right to have escaped persons "delivered up on Claim of the Party to Whom Service or Labour may be due."[26] The rights of slave owners to regain "property" superseded Pennsylvania's attempt to abolish slavery.

Slave patrols acted with near impunity. Freed Blacks were sold into slavery with little redress. The Fugitive Slave Act was utilized as a mechanism for kidnapping and enslaving free Blacks.[27] There was little legal recourse for them. A White person could kidnap a Black person and claim him as a fugitive slave.[28] The owner need only present an affidavit to a U.S. judge or commissioner. There was no trial by jury. A $10 fee was required if the captured Black person was determined to be a fugitive. A $5 fee had to be paid by the bounty hunter or alleged owner if the captured person was determined to be free. A captured Black person determined by the court to be free had little recourse against the fraudulent owner. Attempts to protect or harbor an escaped slave were deemed criminal acts.[29] The fugitive slave clause of the U.S. Constitution and fugitive slave legislation were promulgated to protect the rights of the slave owner even after escape to a free state or Canada.[30]

Blacks were deemed nonpersons by the Supreme Court in *Dred Scott v. Sandford*.[31] The Court determined Dred Scott was not a citizen of the United States or a person with legal rights protected by law.[32] Without personhood, a slave was precluded from accessing the courts for justice based solely on his race. Even after slavery was abolished, Blacks remained outside the halls of justice. Blacks learned how to use the courts to fight laws enacted to intentionally prevent their social, economic, and political mobility. They fought in spite of the hostility and prejudice accorded them by the courts, law enforcement, lawmakers, and American society.

Black Codes/Black Labor: *Bailey v. Alabama*

After slavery, Black Codes were criminal laws enacted by states to maintain the socioracial hierarchy of slavery. These laws were enacted "to make Negroes slaves in everything but name."[33] Slavery was abolished except as punishment for a crime. In the words of political compromise found in the Thirteenth Amendment, "Neither slavery nor involuntary servitude, *except as a punishment for crime whereof the party shall have been duly convicted,* shall exist within the United States, or any place subject to their jurisdiction."[34] This clause invoked freedom and revoked it simultaneously. The legacy of the criminal component to the Thirteenth Amendment is evident in modern prison populations. Homeless Blacks were subjected to vagrancy laws enacted to criminalize homelessness. The vagrancy laws also restricted the ability of Blacks to travel. As in slavery, Blacks were forced to produce documents, when requested by Whites, to prove that they were viably employed or had a home—or they could be charged with vagrancy or trespassing and jailed. Unable to pay the fine, Blacks became prisoners of a convict labor system.[35] For many Blacks, the criminal justice system was simply a mechanism for enslavement.

"Jim Crow" laws and prejudice meant Blacks were more susceptible to imprisonment. Black Codes subjected Blacks to harsher punishments and longer sentences for similar offenses.[36] Without counsel, the right to testify, or Blacks serving on the jury, the Black defendant stood unarmed before a court of law and injustice. The Supreme Court noted that "in many quarters prejudices existed against the colored race, which naturally affected the administration of justice in the State courts, and operated harshly when one of the race was a party accused."[37] Once he was convicted, the state could use the prisoner as free labor. Black defendants were convicted on the most minor infraction of the law and sentenced to hard labor.[38]

Convict lease systems relegated Blacks to the status of indentured laborers without rights or protections.[39] The prison or jail officials leased out convict labor to businesses or farms. The profits accrued to prison officials and politicians. Convict work camps were scattered across the South.[40] Convict lessees worked the mines, railroads as well as the fields.[41] Both Blacks and Whites were subject to convict leases. However, the prison conditions for Blacks were consistently worse.[42] Once convicted, Black inmates were reduced to free labor for any municipality or business owners willing to lease the labor from the correctional facility. Blacks were subjugated, disfranchised, and made to labor for economic profit of the more politically powerful for yet another hundred years. This system of arrest under Black Codes and sham trials with sentences of hard labor bore a remarkable similarity to the gulag labor system of the former Soviet Union.[43]

Farm labor contracts placed Blacks and their children back into indentured servitude. Once signed, insidiously worded labor contracts made it a crime for the laborer to refuse or escape.[44] Blacks were tricked or forced into signing land lease contracts that relegated them into involuntary servitude. The property was uninhabitable and the land useless for farming, leaving the lessee in debt and enslaved as was the intent of the diabolical lessor. Sharecropping poor land would then lead to inescapable debt to the general store, landowner, and employer. The occurrence was known as peonage and, simply defined, debt slavery.[45] Once the contract was signed, breaking the agreement became a criminal offense punishable by heavy fines. If the laborer or tenant refused or was unable to pay the fine, then he was imprisoned and forced to "work off" the debt.

The labor required under the contract was arduous work under horrendous conditions. The local courts enforced the contracts. Failure to complete the contract was a criminal offense. A contract may require the signatory to become an "apprentice" in conditions similar to slavery.[46] Blacks under these contracts were denied the right to trial by jury.[47] Defendants were summarily sentenced to hard labor and the convict lease system.

In *Bailey v. Alabama*, Bailey entered into a labor contract that in actuality reduced him to involuntary servitude.[48] The Alabama statue enforced the peonage contract. It provided:

> Any person who, with intent to injure or defraud his employer, enters into a contract in writing for the performance of any act or service, and thereby obtains money or other personal property from such employer, and with like intent, and without just cause, and without refunding such money or paying for such property, refuses or fails to perform such act or service, must, *on conviction*, be punished by a fine in double the damage suffered by the injured party, but not more than three hundred dollars, one-half of said fine to go to the county and one-half to the party injured.[49]

Refusing to work as a servant or sharecropper and the inability to refund money that may or may not have been given by the employer were considered prima facie evidence of the intent to injure or defraud an employer.[50] Bailey refused to be enslaved. Under Alabama law, his refusal to work constituted a criminal act.[51] He was arrested. After a preliminary trial before a justice of the peace, he was imprisoned for obtaining $15 under a contract in writing, with intent to injure or defraud his employer.

Bailey appealed his conviction.[52] He filed a writ of habeas corpus seeking his release. The Supreme Court of Alabama upheld his conviction. Bailey appealed to the U.S. Supreme Court. He argued that Alabama's statute violated his Thirteenth and Fourteenth Amendment rights. He made clear that the statute forced him into involuntary servitude. The U.S. attorney general filed an amicus or friend of the court brief in support of Bailey. Justice Oliver Wendell Holmes, Jr., writing for the majority, upheld the Alabama statute under which Bailey was imprisoned. In the opinion, Justice Holmes briefly referred to the illegitimacy of the statute. But, he quickly decided that there were not enough facts upon which the Court could base a decision. Bailey was left without justice and precluded from the basic right of testifying in court regarding his intent.[53]

Murder by Lynch Mob: *United States v. Shipp*

Lynching was the crudest form of resistance to Black progress. This killing by torture became a mechanism of control that involved Black women and children and foreign nationals as well as Black men.[54] A lynch mob has as its goal subjugating the victim and spreading terror. For Blacks in America, lynching was an attempt to prevent their ascension, thus forcing a perpetual labor class relegated to America's bottom rung socially, politically, and economically.[55] Despite efforts to undermine their success, Blacks pressed forward and sometimes even thrived.

In the South, as Blacks advanced, rural Whites lost economic ground. Between 1900 and 1930, the number of White tenant farmers increased by 61 percent.[56] During that same period, the number of Black tenant farmers increased by only 27 percent. Blacks were the obvious competitors.[57] Given the failure of the criminal justice system, Blacks were made vulnerable targets. Mob violence and terrorism became an outlet for White frustration and jealousy in rural communities.[58] Photographs bear witness to Whites, male and female, children and elders, standing in approval next to the mutilated body of a lynched Black person who forgot his or her "place" at the bottom.[59]

White lynch mobs attacked Blacks with impunity.[60] Law enforcement offered little or no protection against the lynching of Black women, men, and children.[61] Too often, law enforcement was implicated in the murders. Federal and state courts offered scant protection. Living with the intimidation produced by White lynch mobs became a way of life for Blacks in America.[62] Black women who fought against White rapists were lynched.[63] In certain cases, Black women were raped and then lynched.[64]

White Slave-Traffic Act

Lynching became a social phenomenon.[65] Members of a lynch mob were swept into a vicious hysteria of racism. Whites attacked Blacks arbitrarily or based on vendetta.[66]

White mobs attacked when their boxing champion lost to Jack Johnson, a Black fighter. Prior to 1908, boxing was segregated. White fighters were assumed to be physically superior to Blacks. Johnson challenged the reigning White heavyweight champion, Canadian Tommy Burns. Burns was in search of a lucrative match and agreed. The fight was held in Australia. Johnson defeated Burns to become the first Black heavyweight champion. White audiences and boxing promoters, assured the victory over Burns was a fluke, persuaded White former champion Jim Jeffries to leave retirement to fight Johnson. In 1910, in Reno, Nevada, Johnson defeated the "Great White Hope" Jeffries. Riots broke out among lower-class Whites.[67] Whites retaliated by attacking Blacks and burning their homes.[68] Scores of Blacks were injured and many were killed. In the midst of rabid racism, Johnson maintained an entourage of White girlfriends.

Three years after his victory over Jeffries, Johnson became the first person convicted under the White Slave-Traffic Act of 1910.[69] It was a racially motivated charge. The White woman at the center of the charge, Belle Schreiber, had been a prostitute for several years before meeting Johnson.[70] To avoid arrest, Johnson fled to Cuba and lost his title. He later returned and spent one year in federal prison. Johnson was the "prototype of the independent black who acted as he pleased and accepted no bar to his conduct. As such…[he] threatened America's social order."[71] The criminal justice system was used to wreak social vengeance on Johnson. Yet, those who harmed Blacks following Johnson's victory against Jeffries were not prosecuted.

Police Powers

Racial interaction was presumed to be so volatile it was placed under a state's police powers. In *Plessy v. Ferguson*, Justice Brown, speaking on behalf of the Court, stated: "Laws permitting, and even requiring, their separation in places where they are liable to be brought into contact do not necessarily imply the inferiority of either race to the other, and have been generally, if not universally, recognized as within…[state] police power.[72] Mobs used lynching as punishment for Blacks who violated the racial divisions sanctioned by *Plessy*. In essence, *Plessy* exonerated the mobs' actions by supporting the notion that Whites hated Blacks too much to control their own actions. Racial animosity was considered a natural response to racial interaction. Thus, law enforcement abdicated its responsibility to stop a mob from assaulting Blacks.

Given this undercurrent of animosity, any minor provocation could cause violence. Racial hatred on the part of Whites was supposedly so strong an emotion that little could prevent the killing of Blacks encountered under civil circumstances. However, violence was presumed necessary for Blacks who left their place of lower rank through achievement, confidence, or refusal to acquiesce to White demand. Torturing an emboldened Black person was intended to send a threatening message to all Blacks to remain obsequious.

Too often, any dispute between Whites and Blacks could result in the forming of a lynch mob. A dispute over back wages between Sam Hose, a Black laborer, and Alfred Cranford, his White employer, led to murder.[73] In this case, Cranford lay dead. Hose fled the scene. A lynch mob tracked him down. They seized him and the torture began. First, his ears were sliced off, followed by his fingers and genitals.

The torture and murder of Sam Hose was reported in the *New York Tribune*, April 24, 1899:

> Sam Hose (a Negro who committed two of the basest acts known to crime) was burned at the stake in a public road, one and a half miles from here. Before the torch was applied to the pyre, the Negro was deprived of his ears, fingers and other portions of his body with surprising fortitude. Before the body was cool, it was cut to pieces, the bones were crushed into small bits and even the tree upon which the wretch met his fate was torn up and disposed of as souvenirs. The Negro's heart was cut in several pieces, as was his liver. Those unable to obtain the ghastly relics directly, paid more fortunate possessors extravagant sums for them. Small pieces of bone went for 25 cents and a bit of the liver, crisply cooked, for 10 cents.[74]

No one was prosecuted for murder or abuse of the corpse. Despite these threats, Blacks intensified their challenge to the brutal torture and murder of Blacks by lynch mobs.[75]

Lynching and the Supreme Court: *U.S. v. Shipp*

In *U.S. v. Shipp*, the U.S. Supreme Court tried a sheriff in Tennessee for aiding and abetting the lynching of a prisoner.[76] It is the only case in U.S. history in which the Court tried an individual for contempt.[77] The facts of this case involve acts of savagery. On January 23, 1906, Nevada Taylor was raped on her way home from work.[78] It was a late night in Chattanooga, Tennessee. Taylor, a White woman, never saw her attacker and could not describe him; she did not know if he was Black or White.[79] On January 25, "Captain" Joseph F. Shipp, sheriff of Chattanooga, arrested a Black man, Ed Johnson, and charged him with the crime.[80] Alibi witnesses placed Johnson across town in another part of the city at the time of the crime. Taylor never identified Johnson or accused him of rape. Johnson argued he was working at the time and had several witnesses to support his alibi.[81] Upon hearing of the arrest, residents of Chattanooga formed a lynch mob and approached the jail.[82] At first, Shipp and three of his deputies guarded Johnson from the mob.

On February 6, Johnson was convicted of the crime.[83] Following a trial before Judge Samuel McReynolds that lasted only two days, Johnson was sentenced to death. His execution was scheduled to take place on March 13. No appeal was made on Johnson's behalf by his court-appointed lawyers. It was the judgment of Johnson's counsel that due to the unrest in the community, "the defendant, *even if the wrong man,* could not be saved."[84] Johnson had the option of an appeal. But, his lawyers advised him against appealing the sentence.[85] He was told: "An appeal would so inflame the public that the jail would be attacked."[86] Johnson was given two choices: die by lynch mob or be executed "in an orderly manner" by the state of Tennessee.[87] His lawyers stated to the Court: "[T]he defendant, now that he had been convicted by a jury, must die by the judgment of the law, or else, if his case were appealed, he would die by the act of the uprising of the people."[88] Faced with these despicable choices, Johnson surrendered his right of appeal.[89]

Prior to the execution, extra guns were purchased by Shipp to protect the jail against a mob.[90] Johnson was taken to nearby Knoxville to avoid an attempt to lynch him in Chattanooga.[91] Noah Parden, a prominent Black attorney, entered the case.[92] Parden filed an appeal in state court on behalf of Johnson. That appeal was denied. On March 10, 1909, Parden filed an unsuccessful petition for habeas corpus in federal court.[93] He then traveled to Washington, D.C., to file a writ of habeas corpus in federal court alleging that Johnson's Fifth and Sixth Amendment rights to a fair trial before an impartial jury in state court had been denied.[94] Blacks were precluded by law from serving on the jury.[95] He also argued that the lynch mob intimidated jurors as well as the defense counsel, thus tainting the entire trial.[96] Parden met with U.S. Supreme Court Justice Harlan, the lone dissenter in *Plessy v. Ferguson.* Justice Harlan promised to consider Johnson's petition.

On March 19, 1909, Justice Harlan sent a telegram to Shipp staying Johnson's execution.[97] Shipp was informed by Harlan that Johnson was to be protected from harm while the Court reviewed the appeal.[98] Johnson was now a federal prisoner.[99] The local *Chattanooga News* published the telegram, inflaming the crowds.[100] When people read about the stay of execution granted by the Supreme Court, a lynch mob mentality enveloped Chattanooga.[101] Sheriff Shipp was aware of the mob. Johnson received a reprieve from state execution only to have Shipp and a lynch mob determine that he die extrajudicially. Shipp made no effort to call in the militia or alert the governor that reinforcements were needed.[102] Shipp gave no orders for additional deputies to guard the jail.[103] He left only one person, Jeremiah Gibson, in his seventies, to guard Johnson.

The door to the cell was probably left ajar. Upon hearing of the appeal and stay of execution, mobs formed. That night a White lynch mob attacked the jail.[104] They dragged Johnson to a bridge six blocks away.[105] His last words were: "I am not guilty and that is all I have to say. God Bless you all. I am innocent."[106] At the arc of the bridge, Johnson was hung twice (the first time the rope broke) and then shot dozens of times.[107] The murderers left a note to Justice Harlan pinned to Johnson's body: "To Justice Harlan: Come get your nigger now."[108] Shipp and his deputies did nothing to stop the crowd or protect Johnson. The *Chattanooga Times* headline read: "'God Bless You All—I Am Innocent' Ed Johnson's Last Words before Being Shot to Death by a Mob like a Dog."[109]

Justice Marshall Harlan was outraged that Shipp would allow the mob to attack Johnson.[110] The Supreme Court held Shipp and others in contempt for defying their order to stay any execution until a review of the case.[111] Shipp blamed the lynching on the Supreme Court. He declared the Court an alien intrusion of federal authority on state territory.[112] Shipp argued that had the Court not stayed the execution, Johnson would have died differently. Justice Harlan ordered the first and only criminal trial conducted by the U.S. Supreme Court.[113] The Court found Shipp and four others guilty of criminal contempt. Justice Fuller wrote the opinion on behalf of the Court. Fuller noted that, in *Shipp*, "a dangerous portion of the community was seized with the awful thirst for blood which only killing can quench, and that considerations of law and order were swept away in the overwhelming flood."[114] After the lynching, outraged Blacks rioted through the streets of downtown Chattanooga.[115] The *Shipp* defendants were sentenced to a mere ninety *days* in jail.[116] Whites in Chattanooga reelected Shipp by a wide majority, although Blacks voted against him.[117]

Mob Violence and Riots

Race riots increased against Black communities across the country. In Tulsa, Oklahoma, Chicago, Arkansas, and small villages, Blacks were murdered by lynch mobs and in race riots. A link could be established between the mob violence and the improved social status of Blacks. African-American servicemen who had defended their country overseas were shot, tortured, and mutilated by White American mobs.[118] Blacks were murdered for wearing their military uniforms.[119] Blacks, considered "uppity" for their desire for civil rights and equal treatment, were murdered by lynch mobs. Blacks were lynched for refusing to "stay in their place" as alleged inferiors to Whites.[120] Blacks were lynched while attempting to escape the racial oppression of the South by migrating North.[121] Without equal protection of the laws, the Black community was made vulnerable to these murderous mobs.[122]

Lynching intensified in the North as well as the South.[123] Black women and children were murdered by lynch mobs.[124] Black mothers were killed with their children.[125] A Black woman and her husband were burned at the stake in Doddsville, Mississippi.[126] Lynching of Black women and men took place with little provocation or evidence of wrongdoing.[127] Lethal mob violence for seemingly minor infractions of the caste codes of behavior was a fundamental mechanism for maintaining social control.[128] In Columbus, Mississippi, a Black woman was raped and lynched after the lynch mob could not locate her son to lynch.[129] A Black man was lynched for refusing to dance when ordered to do so by a White man.[130]

On July 28, 1917, thousands of African Americans participated in a silent march in New York City. That year, Blacks were murdered with impunity by lynch mobs in Waco, Texas, East St. Louis, Illinois, and Memphis, Tennessee. Blacks were made victims of race riots in five other American cities. The silent march protested this national wave of violence against Blacks as well as the abject failure of law enforcement and the courts to provide protection against such lawlessness. As Blacks migrated to the North for better employment opportunities, tensions rose. White immigrant groups fought against the influx of Black competition, resulting in race riots.[131] The red summer of 1919 was named for the numerous race riots across the country;

most notable were the riots in St. Louis, Chicago, Washington, D.C., and Arkansas.[132] In 1921, the alleged bumping of a White woman in Tulsa, Oklahoma, by a Black man in a crowded elevator led to a riot that ended with the deaths of one hundred fifty people, the use of U.S. military bombers, and the destruction of Greenwood, Oklahoma, a prosperous Black community[133] (see the list of race riots in Appendix B).

Anti-Semitic Violence: *Frank v. Mangum*

Although Blacks have long been the targets of lynching, Whites have also been murdered by lynch mobs. In *Frank v. Mangum*, a Jewish defendant, Leo M. Frank, was awaiting retrial in the rape and murder of Mary Phagan, a thirteen-year-old girl, when he became a victim of a lynching.[134] The homicide occurred in 1913.[135] Frank supervised the National Pencil Factory, a manufacturer of pencils, in Atlanta, Georgia, at which Phagan was an employee. Phagan's body was found in the basement of the factory. Angry mobs made anti-Semitic statements about Frank.[136] During the reading of the verdict, Frank was forced to leave the courthouse for fear an acquittal would lead to mob violence.[137] The jury deliberated for four hours. Leo Frank was convicted and sentenced to death the next day.[138] Frank appealed his conviction, arguing that the disorder in the courtroom during trial and the mobs gathered around the courthouse influenced the jury.[139] The Georgia Supreme Court upheld the verdict.[140]

On appeal, the U.S. Supreme Court affirmed the lower court, allowing the conviction to stand.[141] The Court recognized that mob violence could affect the fairness of a trial, thus causing a due-process violation. However, the Court failed to find any disruption rising to that level in this case. Following the decision affirming the conviction, Governor Frank Slaton commuted Frank's death sentence to life in prison. On August 17, 1915, a mob of twenty-five men stormed the prison. Frank was recovering in the prison hospital from having his throat cut by a fellow inmate. The mob forced Frank to a car and drove him to Marietta, Georgia, the hometown of Mary Phagan, which was over one hundred miles away. There they hanged Frank from a tree near the Phagan home. No one was convicted for this crime. It is believed that Leo Frank was the only known person of Jewish descent to be lynched in America.[142] In 1986, the Georgia Board of Pardons and Parole gave Leo Frank a posthumous pardon.[143]

Elaine Riots: *Moore v. Dempsey*

The threats of a lynch mob played a role in the rush to judgment in a riot case in Elaine, Arkansas, in 1919. On the night of September 30, Black residents of the town of Elaine located in Phillips County, Arkansas, gathered at their church. The farmers had been systematically paid below market prices for their crops by the White brokers in town. They met at the church to discuss joining the Progressive Farmers and Household Union of America and retaining an attorney to represent them in a lawsuit. They believed that membership in the union would allow them to sell crops without going through local White brokers. Whites, angered at the audacity of Blacks, circled the church and attacked. The Blacks defended themselves. A White sheriff was injured and a White railroad worker was killed. Rumor spread of a Black uprising in Elaine. Whites from other counties and bordering states converged on the town.

Blacks were hunted down and murdered. Clinton Lee, a White man, lost his life. Governor Hillman Brough requested assistance from the U.S. military. The estimated number of Blacks killed has ranged from eighty to over two hundred. Blacks were blamed for the riot and arrested in the hundreds. A grand jury was convened on which no Blacks were allowed to serve.[144] Little more than a month after the riot, 112 Blacks were charged with murder, conspiracy, and participating in an insurrection. Those who testified against other Blacks were freed. The Black prisoners who refused to confess were tortured. Walter White of the NAACP investigated as well. White, a Black man of very light complexion, freely walked among the White residents of Elaine without being detected. Governor Brough appointed a "Committee of Seven" to investigate and assign guilt.[145] The *Helena World Newspaper* published an article titled "Inward Facts about the Negro Insurrection" that presented the results of the committee's investigation.[146]

The newspapers inflamed White anger. The article in the *Helena World* reported that the race riot in Phillips County was "a deliberately planned insurrection of the negroes against the whites, directed by... Progressive Farmers and Household Union of America, established for the purpose of banding negroes together for the killing of white people."[147] The article was quite lengthy and among other things stated that Robert L. Hill, who organized the union, told Black people "to arm themselves in preparation of the day when they should be called upon to attack their white oppressors."[148] At trial, the defendants were represented by the renowned Black attorney Scipio A. Jones.[149] By November, twelve defendants were convicted of murder in the first degree and sentenced to death.[150] "The trial lasted about three quarters of an hour and in less than five minutes the jury brought in a verdict of guilty of murder in the first degree."[151]

There were several trials and appeals.[152] In 1923, the U.S. Supreme Court decided *Moore v. Dempsey*.[153] Frank Moore, named petitioner of the group of convicted Black men, argued upon a writ of habeas corpus that they were convicted of murder under pressure of mob violence without any regard for their rights and without due process of law.[154] The Supreme Court found that "no juryman could have voted for an acquittal and continued to live in Phillips County and if any prisoner by any chance had been acquitted by a jury he could not have escaped the mob."[155] The *Moore* defendants were finally pardoned by Governor McRae on January 13, 1925.[156]

Fighting Back: *People v. Ossian Sweet*

Blacks led a continuous fight against lynch mobs and riotous marauders. Dr. Ossian Sweet and his family fought a lynch mob angered by their purchase of a home in an all-White community. The mob of Whites approached Sweet's home, throwing rocks and screaming profanities. Shots were fired from inside the Sweets' home. Two people were struck by gunfire. Leon Breiner, a White neighbor who had joined the lynch mob, was killed.[157] Sweet admitted to firing his weapon into the crowd.[158] Attorney Clarence Darrow defended Sweet's right to protect his family and home from a murderous mob.[159]

An all-White jury returned a verdict of not guilty by reason of self-defense[160] and Sweet was acquitted.[161] Unfortunately, the legal outcome in *People v. Sweet* remains an exception. Efforts undertaken by Blacks to create legal protections against lynching were undermined by all three branches of the federal government. State prosecutors refused to bring cases against Whites involved in these murders. Blacks turned to the international arena and world opinion to place pressure on the United States to provide more than the promise of constitutional protections.

Antilynching Bills

In 1900, Black Congressman George White introduced the first antilynching bill.[162] It was purposely stalled in the House Judiciary Committee. Then, Congressman Leonidas Dyer, a White Democrat from Missouri, proposed an antilynching bill in 1918.[163] After tremendous lobbying on the part of the NAACP, the Dyer antilynching bill was passed by the House of Representatives in 1922.[164] However, it was defeated by a Senate filibuster of Southern Democrats.[165]

A reluctant president, Warren G. Harding, and an avowed Southern patrician, President Woodrow Wilson, refused to take a stand against the Southern Democrats in the Senate.[166] In 1932, Blacks hoped the newly elected president, Franklin D. Roosevelt, would press for antilynching legislation. They were disappointed once more. African Americans developed their own national campaign against lynching. Mary Church Terrell and Ida B. Wells-Barnett were joined by thousands of Black women and a handful of White Southern abolitionists who also opposed lynching and supported passage of federal protections. Senator Charles Sumner, an abolitionist, joined in the protests against lynching and racial discrimination.[167]

In 1935, an antilynching bill was proposed by U.S. Senators Edward Costigan and Robert F. Wagner.[168] The Costigan–Wagner Bill was defeated by the Senate.[169] The U.S. Senate refused to pass federal antilynching legislation and local antilynching laws were never enforced.[170] Riots and lynching continued for decades.[171] Black war veterans received unfettered hostility.[172] In 1946, a Black veteran in Louisiana was partially dismembered, castrated, and burned with a blow-torch for refusing to give a White man a war memento.[173] Eight Black men were murdered while wearing their military uniforms.[174] One Black man "was lynched *because of the fact* that he wore the uniform of a United States soldier"[175] (see Chapter 6).

Rosewood Riots: *Goins v. Florida*

In 1994, Florida paid reparations to Blacks terrorized by White mobs in 1923. In January 1923, a White mob attacked a community of Blacks in the town of Rosewood, Florida.[176] Rosewood was home to over twenty families. The year prior to the attack a White female school teacher has been murdered. Whites accused Blacks of the crime. Two Black men were lynched. A White woman in a nearby town accused a Black man of rape and a White mob began searching for the man. As the mob grew in number, it began to shoot any Blacks in its path and burn homes.[177] The death toll remains a topic of dispute.[178] Black residents claim twenty to thirty men, women, and children were murdered that night. Whites claim four Blacks (including a woman and child) and one White male lost their lives that night. It is not disputed that the homes, churches, and farms of Black residents were burned to the ground.[179] After the massacre, a special grand jury was convened by Governor Cary Hardee. However, the grand jury found insufficient evidence to prosecute.

No charges were brought. The community of Rosewood was never rebuilt. Later, it was discovered that the White female accuser has been beaten, not raped, by a White man.[180] Once again, the state and federal government failed to protect Blacks from flagrant criminal behavior perpetrated by Whites. Decades later, in 1994, the victims of the race riot in Rosewood, Florida, presented a claim for damages for $7.5 million. The case of *Arnett Goins, Minnie Lee Langley, et al. v. State of Florida* sought restitution for the losses in 1923.[181] Remedies were sought through the Florida legislature. The legislature came to acknowledge the harm committed in 1923 and the ensuing denial.[182] Congressional remedies were sought because the statute of limitations had expired on the crimes and the criminals involved were destitute or dead. The victims of Rosewood received their reparations for the harm in 1923. However, there has been no such financial recovery for the thousands of other Black victims of the brutality of America's lynch mobs and race riots.[183]

Modern Lynching: James Byrd, Jr.

Unfortunately, these occurrences carry through into recent periods. On June 7, 1998, James Byrd, Jr., age forty-nine, was tied to a pick-up truck and dragged to his death.[184] Byrd's throat was cut before his body was dragged over two miles behind the pick-up truck through the back country roads of Jasper, Texas. His skin, blood, arms, head, genitalia, and other parts of his body were strewn along the highway. His remains were then dumped in front of a cemetery traditionally used for Blacks. Three White men, John William King, age twenty-three, Shawn Berry, age twenty-three, and Lawrence Brewer, age thirty-one, with links to White supremacist groups were convicted of the crime. King and Brewer were attempting to ingratiate themselves into a White supremacist organization.[185] They received the death penalty. Berry received a sentence of life in prison. This case appears to be one of the few incidents, if not the only incident, in American history where White defendants received the death penalty for the murder of a single Black person.[186] The murder of Byrd led jurisdictions across the country to enact hate-crime legislation. Sadly, James Byrd's grave has been desecrated twice.[187]

In June 2005, the U.S. Senate apologized for decades of resisting the passage of antilynching legislation.[188] Senator Mary Landrieu introduced the apology bill after reading the book *Without Sanctuary*.[189] The official apology recognizes that the Senate was instrumental in blocking over two hundred proposed antilynching bills.[190] The legislation speaks to generations of loss and acknowledges the "crime of lynching succeeded slavery as the ultimate expression of racism in the United States following Reconstruction."[191] Over 4,740 persons have been murdered by lynching, the majority of whom were Black. Ninety-nine percent of perpetrators escaped punishment by state or local officials. The apology was supported by eighty-nine senators. However, eight U.S. senators refused to vote on behalf of the apology.

Lynching, Rape, and the White Woman
Myth: The Case of Emmett Till

The myth of the Black rapist of White women has been used to sanction lynching.[192] Ida Wells-Barnett directly confronted the myth of lynching Black men as punishment for the rape of White women. She also addressed the reality of a criminal system that wantonly failed to protect Black women from rape for centuries.[193] Lynching is a murderous act of intimidation and societal evil. To murder by lynch mob takes more than one angry person to hang a person from a tree or burn him alive and sell the ears and testicles as souvenirs.[194] Wells-Barnett said that the "real purpose of these savage demonstrations is to teach the Negro that in the South he had no rights that the law will enforce."[195]

Wells-Barnett gathered research giving rise to the act to refute the rape myth. According to Tuskegee Institute records for the years 1882 to 1951, lynchings were divided into: 41 percent for felonious assault, 19.2 percent for rape, 6.1 percent for attempted rape, 4.9 percent for robbery and theft, 1.8 percent for insult to White persons, and 22.7 percent for miscellaneous offenses or no offense at all.[196] Black men were lynched for disputing with a White man, attempting to register to vote, unpopularity, self-defense, testifying against a White man, asking a White woman in marriage, and peeping in a window.

Allegations of rape involving White women and Black men were made in less than one fourth of lynch murders. Of the 3,693 persons lynched between 1889 and 1930, the rape of a White woman was not given as the motivation.[197] The true motives for lynching were usually economic or political. Prosperous Blacks were lynched by Whites jealous of Black prosperity.[198] Lynching often took place in areas where Whites were mired in economic deprivation and Blacks represented a large numerical majority of the population.[199] Blacks were lynched to inhibit voter turnout or as a means of political intimidation or retribution.[200]

The night of July 19, 1935, Rubin Stacey was lynched in Fort Lauderdale, Florida. Stacey, a Black homeless man, was caught stealing food from the kitchen of a White family. Marion Jones, the wife of the house, screamed when she saw him in her house. She filed a complaint against him. Stacey was arrested. The rumor of rape and attack of a White woman led a lynch mob to search for him. Sheriff's deputies placed Stacey in custody. However, the White lynch mob brazenly broke down the door of the jail and dragged Stacey away. He was beaten and hanged from a tree beside the home of Marion Jones. The photos of Stacey were published in many local newspapers as a warning to Blacks to stay in their place.

One year after *Brown v. Board of Education*, Emmett Till was murdered. On August 28, 1955, the civil rights movement was galvanized by the lynching of fourteen-year-old Chicago native Emmett Till in Money, Mississippi.[201] The entire facts of the murder are still unknown. Till was visiting relatives in Mississippi. His offense was to speak directly to or whistle at a White woman, Carolyn Bryant, in a country store. The interaction took place during broad daylight. There was no allegation of rape. A few nights later, two White men abducted Till from the house where he was staying. He was tortured and dumped into the Tallahatchie River.[202] Carolyn Bryant's husband, Roy Bryant, and his half-brother, J. W. Milam, were arrested for the crime. Bryant and Milam were tried by an all-White jury in Sumner, Mississippi, and acquitted after less than two hours of deliberation. Reportedly, there were questions as to the identity of the body.[203] Bryant and Milam have since died.[204] However, new witnesses and additional suspects have been uncovered, leading the federal government to reopen the case in 2004. State criminal charges are still viable. Till's body was exhumed to quell questions of misidentification; he was positively identified on August 26, 2005.

Police Brutality

The criminal cases and controversies are too varied and the lives lost over these centuries number in heartbreaking digits that cannot all be recounted here. People of color have learned well to fear the police and with good reason.[205] It is not unheard of for police to attempt to save a Black life from lynching or mob violence.[206] However, the attempts are scant when compared to the history of complicity in racial violence and the continued failure of the state courts to render justice.

Robert Hall was arrested on January 23, 1943, for allegedly stealing a tire.[207] He was taken into custody by Screws, the sheriff of Baker County, Georgia. Screws had enlisted Jones, a police officer of the city of Newton, Georgia, and deputized a man named Kelley. All of the officers involved were White. At the time of his arrest, Hall was a thirty-year-old Black man in good health. Screws, Jones, and Kelley beat Hall to death that night. The details are as follows:

> As Hall alighted from the car at the court house square, the three petitioners began beating him with their fists and with a solid-bar blackjack about eight inches long and weighing two pounds. They claimed Hall had reached for a gun and had used insulting language as he alighted from the car. But after Hall, still handcuffed, had been knocked to the ground they continued to beat him from fifteen to thirty minutes until he was unconscious. Hall was then dragged feet first through the court house yard into the jail and thrown upon the floor dying. An ambulance was called and Hall was removed to a hospital where he died within the hour and without regaining consciousness. There was evidence that Screws held a grudge against Hall and had threatened to "get" him.[208]

Screws, Jones, and Kelly were indicted and each charged with violating Hall's civil rights[209] and conspiracy to violate his civil rights.[210]

The Fourteenth Amendment needed a criminal component to reach police brutality. Under the amendment, a state could not deprive a person of life, liberty, or property without due process. Screws was employed by the state. Hall was deprived of the right to a trial and, if convicted, a reasonable sentence. However, the amendment did not provide criminal sanctions and offered no punishment for those who, like Screws, violated those protections and then hid behind a state's failure to bring a criminal action. Historically, states had failed to protect Blacks "from the cruelties of bigoted and ruthless authority....But, where, as here, the states are unwilling for some reason to prosecute such crimes the federal government must step in unless constitutional guarantees are to become atrophied."[211] Thus, Congress enacted a criminal statute to enforce the protections under the Fourteenth Amendment.[212]

Screws and his accomplices were tried under the federal statute in district court.[213] The federal statute provided:

> Whoever, under color of any law, statute, ordinance, regulation, or custom, willfully subjects, or causes to be subjected, any inhabitant of any State...to the deprivation of any rights, privileges, or immunities secured or protected by the Constitution...or to different punishments, pains, or penalties, on account of such inhabitant being an alien, or by reason of his color, or race...shall be fined not more than $1,000, or imprisoned not more than one year, or both. Color of law means acting under governmental authority or in their official capacity as officers.[214]

Screws, Jones, and Kelley were convicted. They were never charged or tried for murder under state law. Screws and his accomplices appealed their convictions. The officers argued that the federal statute was unconstitutional and it should not apply to them. Screws et al. reasoned that the phrase "color of law" only applied to the actions of governmental officials who were behaving appropriately.[215] The murder of Hall, while handcuffed, was inappropriate behavior for law enforcement officers. Thus, they were not acting under color of law. Thus, the statute should not apply to their actions. The federal appellate court upheld the convictions.[216] However, upon appeal to the U.S. Supreme Court, their convictions were overturned.[217]

In *Screws v. United States*, the U.S. Supreme Court rejected the color of law argument.[218] But, the Court found that there was no evidence that Screws, Kelley, and Jones intended to kill Hall.[219] The Court overturned the convictions and ordered a new trial. Screws was retried. This time he was found not guilty of the murder of Hall. He later ran for office and was elected to the Georgia State Senate. Repeatedly, Blacks would find little protection from police brutality. The *Screws* requirement of proving intent to do harm while acting under "color of law" would remain an obstacle to justice for many years.[220] However, the civil rights legislation enacted during the post-Civil War era continues to provide the basis for a remedy when state prosecutors refuse to take legal action. Blacks are in an ongoing struggle with those elements in law enforcement who take a position similar to that of the overseer responsible for maintaining racial boundaries.[221]

Unreasonable Search and
Seizure: *Mapp v. Ohio*

In *Mapp v. Ohio* (1961), the Supreme Court was presented with a case of unreasonable search and seizure that changed criminal law.[222] Dollree Mapp, a Black single parent, rented a room in her home to a boarder. The man was secretive about his travel and plans. He told her he was leaving for a long trip. Mapp stored his belongings in the basement. On May 23, 1957, three Cleveland, Ohio, police officers arrived at her home.[223] The police wanted information about a person hiding out in her home who was wanted for questioning in connection with a recent bombing. The officers demanded admittance to the home. Mapp telephoned her attorney who advised against it. Mapp refused the officers admittance to her home. Three hours later the officers returned with additional force.

The officers pried open the screen door, kicked in and broke the glass in the door, and reached in and turned the lock. Mapp demanded to see a search warrant. She was shown a piece of paper and told it was a warrant. At trial, no warrant was produced by the prosecution. Mapp grabbed at the paper and managed to hold on to it long enough to place it in the bosom of her clothing. The officers grabbed Mapp and knocked her to the floor, retrieving the paper from her bosom. They handcuffed her and began a search of her home. The officers dragged her upstairs where they searched her dresser, closet, suitcases, photo album, and personal papers. Their search led to the basement. While searching a chest in the basement, the officers found pornographic materials. Dollree Mapp was arrested and charged with possession of obscene literature.

Mapp was convicted of possession of pornographic materials. Section 2905.34 of Ohio Revised Code read, in part: "No person shall knowingly...have in his possession or under his control an obscene, lewd, or lascivious book...print, [or] picture." The Ohio statute provides a fine of "not less than $200 nor more than $2,000 or imprison[ment] not less than one nor more than seven years, or both."[224] She was sentenced to imprisonment in the Ohio Reformatory for Women for an indeterminate period. The material did not belong to Mapp and she offered evidence to prove that these books and pictures belonged to a man who had rented from her and occupied a room in her home.[225]

When she learned he was not going to return or use the room for the balance of the last month for which he had rented it, she decided to use the room for herself and to pack up his belongings and store them until he came for them.

Mapp found the boarder's books and pictures and packed them in a box with his other belongings. She never looked at these books and pictures again before they were seized by the police. Her appeals were denied.[226] The police violated Mapp's Fourth Amendment protection against unreasonable search and seizure. The amendment states:

> The right of the people to be secure in their persons, houses, papers, and effects, against unreasonable searches and seizures, shall not be violated, and no Warrants shall issue, but upon probable cause, supported by Oath or affirmation, and particularly describing the place to be searched, and the persons or things to be seized.

Based on an earlier case, *Weeks v. United States* (1914), federal courts punished officers who obtained evidence in violation of the Fourth Amendment by suppressing that evidence.[227] If evidence had been obtained unconstitutionally, it could be suppressed or excluded from a federal trial. At this time, the exclusionary rule was not mandatory in state courts.[228] Thus, if evidence were obtained unconstitutionally, it would not necessarily be suppressed or excluded from use in a state court trial. The trial court judge determined what, if any, sanction may be given to a police officer who abused his authority in obtaining evidence. In *Mapp*, the trial judge determined that the end, finding the evidence, justified the means. The officers brutalized her during their unlawful search for the boarder. There was little evidence that a search warrant ever existed.[229] Yet, the Ohio Supreme court upheld her conviction.[230] This Black woman's defiance led police officers and the state courts to punish her with indefinite imprisonment for possession of lewd materials belonging to her absent male boarder.

The U.S. Supreme Court was shocked by the arrogance of the police and state court. It did not examine whether the material was obscene. Instead, the Court reviewed the manner in which the officers obtained the evidence. The Court had previously decided in *Wolf v. Colorado* that it would not mandate the suppression of evidence in cases of Fourth Amendment violations.[231] However, the times and composition of the Supreme Court had changed since *Wolf* was decided in 1949. Moreover, the states had not made sufficient effort to address the abuse of overzealous officers.

The Supreme Court decided in *Mapp v. Ohio* that a mandatory exclusionary rule must be extended to states. The Court stated: "Since the Fourth Amendment's right of privacy has been declared enforceable against the States through the Due Process Clause of the Fourteenth Amendment, it is enforceable against them by the same sanction of exclusion as is used against the Federal Government."[232] The exclusionary rule suppressed the unconstitutionally obtained evidence in Mapp's home and her conviction was overturned.[233] The exclusionary rule acts as a sanction. Without evidence, the prosecution has little support against a defendant.

Mapp v. Ohio was a landmark Supreme Court case and a major victory for Dollree Mapp, a Black woman abused by Ohio police officers. It is rare for a police brutality case to reach the U.S. Supreme Court. Countless cases of abuse by law enforcement remain unreported or are summarily dispatched without a written record.[234] With the availability of videotaping, the offending actions of police officers are now recorded more frequently. Testimony by victims can be supported with videotape evidence. Rapid media response to police brutality cases means greater national attention and in-depth coverage by newspapers, radio, and cable and network television programs. In the more recent past, certain police abuse cases have captured national headlines and had an impact on American society. The cases of Rodney King, Alberta Spruill, and Abner Louima are three distinct examples of police violence against Blacks.

Rodney King

On the evening of March 2, 1991, Rodney King, a Black man, was suspected of driving under the influence. King was beaten by members of the Los Angeles Police Department following a high-speed chase on the Altadena Highway.[235] He pulled the car over in a park area. Upon exiting the car, King initially refused to lie prone on the ground as instructed by the police officers. They used force to get him to lie down. After he was handcuffed and still lying on the ground, the officers beat him with clubs, stomped on him, and shocked him with electric tasers. The excessive force used by police officers against King was captured on an amateur videotape. Officer Laurence Powell wrote: "I havent [*sic*] beaten anyone this bad in a long time."[236] King was treated for a fractured leg, multiple facial fractures, and numerous bruises and contusions.[237] Officers Stacey Koon, Ted Briseno, Roland Solano, and Powell were charged with assault with a deadly weapon and excessive use of force by a police officer. However, even with the videotape evidence of abuse, a jury comprising eleven Whites and an Asian acquitted the officers.[238]

The acquittals were met with outrage from the Black community. Mass uprisings erupted, resulting in more than $1 billion in property damage, at least forty fatalities, over thirteen thousand arrests, and two thousand people injured.[239] Mayor Tom Bradley activated the California National Guard and President George H. Bush deployed federal troops to Los Angeles.[240] The U.S. Justice Department brought an action in federal court under the Civil Rights Act.[241] Once again, the lack of justice for Blacks in state courts required dependence on the Civil Rights Act in federal courts. In April of 1993, after a trial in U.S. District Court for the Central District of California, the verdicts were announced. The jury convicted Koon and Powell, but acquitted Wind and Briseno. There were no riots. Rodney King brought a successful civil action that resulted in a monetary settlement.[242] A commission, chaired by Warren Christopher, was formed to investigate police abuse in Los Angeles.[243] The Christopher Commission found widespread evidence of racism and a failure to reprimand officers who used excessive force.[244]

Officers Koon and Powell were sentenced to 30 months in prison.[245] However, the U.S. court of appeals rejected the reduced sentences. Koon and Powell appealed the ruling of the appellate court.[246] The U.S. Supreme Court granted review of the case to determine the standard of review governing appeals from a district court's decision to depart from the sentencing ranges in the sentencing guidelines. The U.S. Sentencing Guidelines established ranges of criminal sentences for federal offenses and offenders. In *Koon v. United States*, the Supreme Court held that special circumstances could lower the sentence from the seventy to eighty-seven months of imprisonment as provided under the guidelines.[247] However, the Court gave a jumble of reasons and rationale in a split decision that ultimately ended with a remand of the decision back to the trial court for resentencing. The Rodney King beating remains a symbol of police abuse.

Alberta Spruill

Alberta Spruill, age fifty-seven, was attacked by the police in her home on May 16, 2003. Spruill was in her apartment in Harlem, New York, preparing to go to work at the Department of Citywide Administrative Services. At 5:50 in the morning, her door was kicked in by members of the New York City Police Department. A stun grenade was thrown into the living room. Twelve police officers searched her apartment looking for drugs. Spruill was handcuffed to a chair. Her complaints of shortness of breath and chest pains were ignored. The officers had been granted a "no-knock" warrant, which allows the police to break into a home or business without notice. But, the police had raided the wrong apartment. The raid, based on information from a drug informant, did not uncover any criminal activity. It was the fifth no-knock raid on the wrong home. All of the victims were Black. After a fruitless search of her apartment, Spruill was taken to the hospital. She died two hours later of a heart attack. Police Commissioner Raymond Kelly offered an apology to Spruill's family and ordered an investigation. The City of New York entered into a private settlement with the Spruill family and ceased using the no-knock warrant. However, there was no public admission of racial bias in the execution of no-knock warrants.

Abner Louima

Abner Louima, a Haitian émigré, was a victim of horrendous abuse. On August 9, 1997, Louima was arrested for allegedly participating in a fight at a night club in Brooklyn, New York. He was taken in a police car to the 70th precinct in Brooklyn. While handcuffed in a restroom of the precinct, Louima was beaten by police officers and sodomized with a broken wooden handle of a toilet plunger.[248] The officers then pushed the stick into Louima's mouth, breaking several of his teeth. He was then dragged through the precinct as the officers bragged about having beaten him. Louima was later taken to the hospital with severe damage to his spleen, intestines, and bladder. Police Officer Justin Volpe pleaded guilty and was sentenced to thirty years in prison. Louima brought a civil action against the New York Police Department. The case was settled for $8.75 million. Louima's award is the largest award for a police brutality case in New York history.

Abuse in Prison: *Hudson v. McMillian*

Blacks are disproportionately represented in the prison system. The majority of corrections officers are White. Given the history of racism in the administration of justice, the correctional facility is a combustible arena for discrimination and violence. In *Hudson v. McMillian*, Keith J. Hudson brought an action against White corrections officers Jack McMillian, Marvin Woods, and Arthur Mezo.[249] At the time, Hudson, a Black inmate, was serving his sentence in Angola, a state penitentiary in Louisiana. During the morning of October 30, 1983, Hudson and McMillan became engaged in an argument.[250] Hudson was placed in handcuffs and shackles. McMillian then punched and kicked him in the mouth, eyes, chest, and stomach while Woods held him in place. Mezo, the supervisor on duty, watched the beating and told the officers "not to have too much fun."[251]

As a result of the beating, Hudson suffered bruises and swelling of his face, mouth, and lip. The blows to his face loosened his teeth and cracked his partial dental plate. This type of violence was not an isolated incident.[252] Hudson brought a successful action in federal court, arguing that the officers violated his Eighth Amendment protection against cruel and unusual punishment.[253] The magistrate awarded him damages in the amount of $800.[254] However, the court of appeals reversed the judgment.[255] The appellate court agreed that the officers' use of force was unreasonable, clearly excessive, and a wanton infliction of pain. However, Hudson could not prevail on his Eighth Amendment claim because, according to the court, his injuries were minor. Upon appeal, the U.S. Supreme Court found in favor of Hudson. The Court recognized that the power over prisoners must have some limit. The intentional infliction of pain does not always result in medical treatment. Moreover, the standard applied to medical necessity in a correctional facility is much lower than that applied to private persons.[256] A corrections officer is not free to harm an inmate without sanction.

As in *Screws v. United States*, too often a case of police brutality ends with the death of a Black or Latino victim at the hands of White officers. Those cases include, but are not limited to Cornel Young, Jonny Gammage, Anthony Baez, Richard Brown, Patrick Dorismond, Tyisha Miller, Amadou Diallo, Anthony Dwaine Lee, and Prince Jones. As with decades past, all of these cases ended without an indictment of the officers involved or their acquittal. Once again, the victims were forced to pursue justice under the Civil Rights Act. The cases of Amadou Diallo, Tyisha Miller, and Sean Bell are examined here as examples of police brutality with fatal results.

Amadou Diallo

Shortly after midnight on February 4, 1999, four members of New York City's Street Crime Unit knocked on the door of Amadou Diallo's apartment in the Bronx, New York.[257] Diallo was born in Liberia in western Africa to middle-class parents. He moved to New York City from the French-speaking country of Guinea. He was a legal resident of the United States. The officers, all White, were Sean Carroll, Edward McMellon, Richard Murphy, and Kenneth Boss. The officers wanted to question Diallo regarding several rapes, although they had absolutely no evidence against him. Diallo answered the door. Upon seeing the men, he reached inside his jacket to retrieve a wallet for identification. Without any other provocation, the officers began shooting. They shot at Diallo forty-one times, riddling his body with nineteen bullets. Amadou Diallo, age twenty-two, died on the vestibule floor outside his apartment. His murder led to protests in New York and news coverage around the world.

Hundreds of protesters demanded justice for Diallo. Politicians and celebrities joined with advocates and concerned citizens in national protest marches and acts of civil disobedience to demonstrate their anger with the Diallo shooting. The officers were indicted on two counts of murder in the second degree and reckless endangerment in the first degree.[258] Citing negative pretrial publicity, the officers requested a change of venue. They believed it was not possible to receive a fair trial in the Bronx. The request was denied by Patricia Williams, the Black female judge appointed to the case. However, the officers appealed. Their request was granted by the New York Appellate Court. The trial was moved to Albany County in upstate New York. A new judge, Joseph Teresi, a White male, presided. The officers testified that the shooting was an accident. Moreover, they argued that Diallo contributed to his death by not obeying their orders.

The jury of four Black women and seven White men found in favor of the officers. The jury deliberated three days and delivered twenty-four verdicts of not guilty on the six charges each against the four officers. When asked about the not guilty verdicts, Arlene Taylor, a Black juror in the case, stated, "It has nothing to do with race." A White juror, Helen Harder, said, "Race wasn't even discussed." The family of Diallo filed a civil action against the officers and the City of New York.[259] The case was settled prior to trial. The family agreed to a $3 million settlement. The controversial Street Crime Unit of the New York Police Department was disbanded.[260] Since no criminal liability was found, the police officers were free to resume their roles in law enforcement.[261] Diallo's body was returned to Africa for burial. A commission created to study the incident found the officers had not overreacted.[262] The commission deemed forty-one bullets an appropriate response to Diallo's reaching into his pocket.

America's history of racial bias and denigration of Blacks continues to play a role in police brutality cases. In particular, the murder of Amadou Diallo evidences the learned assumptions of race, power, and place. First, there is an assumption that a Black man should have known that the unknown White men in the vestibule of his apartment building in a predominantly Black community must be conducting official business or participating in some illegal enterprise. It matters not. Whatever their business, a Black person is assumed to realize immediately that these White men bring with them the inherent power of life and death and therefore Blacks bow down and seek the lowest position possible. The appropriate Black behavior, based on slavery and *Plessy*, is to genuflect. Diallo, an African, did not know to fall to the ground upon seeing White men at his door. A Black man who does not genuflect immediately to White men is presumed to be dangerous. Therefore, the officers feared for their lives when confronted with this slender twenty-two year old Black man and shot him nineteen times.

Tyisha Miller

On December 28, 1998, Tyisha Miller, a Black young woman of nineteen, was headed home to Rubidoux, a small, predominantly Black town in California, when the tire on her car went flat. She drove to a convenience store in the predominantly White city of Riverside to get air for the tire. However, the air pump at the convenience store was out of order. She tried to drive to a nearby gas station. The tire was quickly losing air. Miller called her friends for help. While waiting in the car for her friends to arrive, she fell asleep. Miller placed a loaded .380 semiautomatic pistol in her lap for protection. It was dark and the neighborhood where she was parked was somewhat dangerous. About an hour later, one of Miller's cousins and a friend arrived to assist her. However, Miller was locked in her car asleep with music playing on the radio. They saw the gun on her lap. But, Miller would not respond to the knocks on the window. The cousin and friend thought Miller was foaming at the mouth and needed medical attention. They called 911, reporting Tyisha to be unconscious and in need of a doctor; they also stated that she had a gun.

Four police officers from Riverside arrived, as well as an ambulance. The police were called because of the 911 report of Miller having a gun. Police knocked on the windows of Miller's car. She did not respond. They broke the windows in an effort to retrieve the gun. Two of the officers say Miller reached for her pistol; two said they were not sure whether she reached for the gun. The four Riverside officers—Daniel Hotard, Paul Bugar, Michael Alagna, and Wayne Stewart—fired twenty-seven shots into the car. Twelve bullets hit and took the life of Miller. All four officers were White. Two officers were still on probation as "rookies" at the time of the shooting.[263]

The Riverside police have not released tapes or transcripts of the 911 call or of the radio communication among the officers. However, the City of Riverside released the autopsy report showing that Miller was legally drunk. On May 6, 1999, the Riverside District Attorney's Office stated that it had elected not to prosecute the officers. The officers were terminated after a review by the Riverside Office of Internal Affairs. They appealed the terminations.

Sean Bell

On November 26, 2006, in an incident reminiscent of the Amadou Diallo case, Sean Bell, a twenty-three-year-old Black man, was shot fifty times by undercover police officers and struck four times. Bell was leaving a bachelor party with three friends the night before he was to marry the mother of his two children. Bell was killed and two of his friends in the car was wounded, one critically. Joseph Guzman, thirty-one, was seated in the front seat and shot at least eleven times. Trent Benefield, twenty-three, was in the back seat and shot three times. One of the officers involved in the shooting fired his weapon thirty-one times, emptying a full 9 mm magazine and reloading. The officers claim there was an imminent threat. However, the evidence indicates that Bell and the others in the care were unarmed.

Excluded from Juries: *Strauder v. W. Va.*

Special slave courts adjudicated civil issues involving other slaves and free Blacks. In 1791, free Blacks in South Carolina petitioned the state legislature to repeal provisions of the Negro Act, which deprived free Blacks in South Carolina of

> rights and privileges of citizens by not having it in their power to give testimony on oath in prosecutions on behalf of the state; from which culprits have escaped the punishment due to their atrocious crimes, nor can they give their testimony in recovering debts due to them, or in establishing agreements made by them within the meaning of the Statue of Frauds and Perjuries...whereby they are subject to great losses and repeated injuries without any means of redress. [T]hey are debarred

of the rights of free citizens by being subject to a trial without the benefit of jury...[264]

Any legal issue involving Blacks during slavery was litigated before state and federal courts. Blacks were voiceless in all three branches of the federal government. Federal and state courts adjudicated cases involving issues of slavery and those of concern to free Blacks without providing them due-process rights.

Whites had long before concluded that Blacks were not capable of standing in judgment of Whites. Even after the Thirteenth and Fourteenth Amendments were passed, Blacks were disfranchised from the court system because these rights were sporadically enforced by the Supreme Court. Justice for Blacks was a brilliant idea on paper that rarely ever manifested in practice. The Court revealed:

> Slavery, when it existed, extended its influence in every direction, depressing and disfranchising the slave and his race in every possible way. Hence, in order to give full effect to the National will in abolishing slavery, it was necessary in some way to counteract these various disabilities and the effects flowing from them. Merely striking off the fetters of the slave, without removing the incidents and consequences of slavery, would hardly have been a boon to the colored race.[265]

In *Strauder v. West Virginia*, the Court held that a law of West Virginia limiting jury selection to White male persons, twenty-one years of age, and citizens of the state was a discrimination that implied a legal inferiority in civil society, "lessened the security of the right of the colored race, and was a step toward reducing them to a condition of servility."[266] The Court could define the problem and elaborate the principle. In *Carter v. Texas*, decided in 1900, the Court stated, with respect to grand juries:

> Whenever by any action of a State, whether through its legislature, through its courts, or through its executive or administrative officers, all persons of the African race are excluded, solely because of their race or color, from serving as grand jurors in the criminal prosecution of a person of the African race, the equal protection of the laws is denied...[267]

Unfortunately, state courts continued to exclude Blacks from juries.

In *Swain v. Alabama* (1908), Robert Swain, a Black man, was indicted in Talladega County, Alabama, for the rape of a seventeen-year-old White girl, convicted by an all-White jury, and sentenced to death.[268] Swain appealed the conviction, arguing that he was denied equal protection by the state's exercise of peremptory challenges to exclude Blacks from the petit jury.[269] The prosecutor in *Swain* used his peremptory challenges—challenges that may be used to strike potential jurors from the jury pool without indicating any particular cause, to strike the six Black potential jurors. The Alabama courts affirmed the conviction as did the U.S. Supreme Court. According to the Supreme Court, Swain needed to prove purposeful discrimination. The Court noted that the equal-protection clause placed certain limits on the state's exercise of peremptory challenges. Unfortunately, those limitations did not rise to the level of a violation in Swain's case.[270]

The Supreme Court held that a prosecutor may use peremptory strikes to eliminate all members of the accused's race from the jury and said that the fact that "no Negroes had ever served on a petit jury in Talladega County did not show a perversion of a peremptory strike system…where the record failed to show when, how often, and under what circumstances the prosecutor" excluded the potential jurors.[271] The Court sought a balance between the prosecutor's historical privilege of peremptory challenge free of judicial control and the constitutional prohibition against excluding persons from jury service on account of race.[272] In the end, despite America's history of racial discrimination, the Court chose not to scrutinize the prosecutor's actions.[273] The burden on the defendant to prove intent to discriminate effectively undermined arguments alleging racial discrimination in jury selection.

The Court was forced to grapple with the wholesale exclusion of Blacks from juries by recalcitrant state trial court judges and court officials. When Black defendants challenged the exclusion of Blacks from grand and petit juries, court officials testified to the paucity of qualified Blacks fit to serve on a jury in their counties.[274] In *Norris v. Alabama*, the clerk of the jury commission had been given wide discretion to determine who was a qualified juror.[275] However, no person of color had ever served as a juror during the entire history of Jackson County.[276] The Supreme Court, in *Norris*, noted that the population consisted of "a large number of negroes in the county... Men of intelligence, some of whom were college graduates...including many business men, owners of real property and householders."[277] The Court reversed the conviction of Norris and remanded the case back to the trial court for a second trial. Despite numerous decisions of the Supreme Court denouncing exclusion of Blacks from juries, the practice continued.

Modern Jury Exclusion: *Batson v. Kentucky*

In *Batson v. Kentucky*, decided in 1985, the Court was once again faced with the exclusion of Blacks from a criminal jury.[278] Blacks have struggled to secure their rightful place on American juries for nearly a century.[279] In *Batson*, the trial court of Jefferson County, Kentucky, allowed the prosecutor to strike all of the Blacks from the jury. James Kirkland Batson, a Black man, was charged with second-degree burglary and receipt of stolen goods. The defense counsel representing Batson and the prosecutor were allowed to strike potential jurors for cause if they demonstrated bias.[280] However, counsel were provided with a mechanism referred to as the peremptory strike, which allowed an attorney in the case to strike a potential juror without cause.[281]

The prosecutor in *Batson* used his peremptory challenges to strike all four Black persons, which resulted in a jury composed only of White persons. Defense counsel moved to discharge the jury, partly on the ground that the prosecutor's actions violated Batson's right to equal protection of the laws under the Fourteenth Amendment. The trial court judge denied the motion. The "judge observed that the parties were entitled to use their peremptory challenges to 'strike anybody they want to.'"[282] Batson was tried and convicted on both counts. He appealed. The Kentucky appellate courts, relying on *Swain v. Alabama*, affirmed the trial court. Batson had not provided any evidence of purposeful discrimination.

Finally, the U.S. Supreme Court overruled *Swain v Alabama*.[283] The Court held that the equal-protection clause forbids a prosecutor from using the peremptorily challenge to reject potential jurors solely on account of their race or on the assumption that Black jurors as a group would be unable to consider the prosecution's case against a

Black defendant impartially.[284] The Court also stated that a criminal defendant did not have to prove repeated instances of discriminatory conduct. Moreover, once a defendant made a prima facie showing, the burden shifted to the prosecution to present a neutral explanation for striking that juror. The Court reaffirmed the principles of *Strauder v. West Virginia*.[285] Despite the ruling in *Batson*, Blacks continue to wrestle with racial discrimination in jury selection.[286]

Black Witnesses: *Blyew v. United States*
and *Hamilton v. Alabama*

As with the case of Celia, Blacks were precluded from the witness box during slavery as well as after slavery was abolished. Whites considered themselves beyond the judgment of Blacks or any other race of people. Thus, the testimony of a Black, Asian, or Native American witness could not convict or bind a White party in a legal matter. In *Blyew v. United States*, the U.S. Supreme Court affirmed this position. The Court acknowledged that the crimes in *Blyew v. United States* were atrocious.[287] On the evening of August 29, 1868, two White males, Blyew and Kennard, set out to murder Black people. These murders were committed in response to the passage of the Fourteenth Amendment on July 20, 1868.[288]

Blyew and Kennard arrived at the cabin of Jack Foster, a Black man, and his family.[289] They then took an axe and brutally murdered Foster, his wife, Sallie Foster, their seventeen-year-old son, Richard Foster, and Sallie Foster's ninety-year-old blind mother, Lucy Armstrong.[290] "Lucy Armstrong was wounded in the head, which was cut open. Jack Foster and Sallie, his wife, were cut in several places, almost to pieces."[291] Richard Foster died two days after the attack. While he lay dying, Foster gave a dying declaration accusing Blyew and Kennard of the crimes. Two young girls, one aged ten years and the other thirteen, escaped. Laura Foster was a witness.[292]

The State of Kentucky did not allow Blacks to testify against Whites. The Kentucky law stated: "That a slave, negro, or Indian, shall be a competent witness in the case of the commonwealth for or against a slave, negro, or Indian, or in a civil case to which only negroes or Indians are parties, but in no other case."[293] The Kentucky statute forbade "the testimony of colored persons either for or against a white person in any civil or criminal cause to which he may be a party."[294] Blyew and Kennard were indicted in Kentucky for the murder of Lucy Armstrong. The case was removed from state court to federal court under authority of the Civil Rights Act. Blyew and Kennard were found guilty of murdering Lucy Armstrong. They appealed, arguing that the Civil Rights Act did not apply and that evidence provided by Lucy Foster was inadmissible under the Kentucky statute.

The Court found that the federal government did not have jurisdiction and removed the case back to the courts of Kentucky. Under the Civil Rights Act, the United States had exclusive control of certain race cases. Specifically, the act is triggered by crimes and offenses committed against the provisions of the act "and of all causes, civil and criminal, *affecting persons* who are denied, or cannot enforce in the courts or judicial tribunals of the State, or locality, where they may be, any of the rights secured to them by the first section of the act."[295] The act then provides for removal into the federal courts of any suit or prosecution, civil or criminal, which had been, or might hereafter be, commenced against any such person for any cause whatever.

The U.S. Supreme Court recognized all of these federal protections. However, the Court narrowly interpreted the statute's language— "affecting persons." In doing so, the Court reasoned that the Civil Rights Act was applicable only to parties because they were directly affected by a crime. Witnesses were not covered within the "affecting person" provision. Thus, Laura and Richard Foster, as witnesses, were not affected persons within the meaning of the statute. Without an affected person involved in the case, the Civil Rights statute was not applicable. Since the Court determined that the Kentucky law did not violate the Civil Rights Act, the case had to be moved back to Kentucky for trial. However, under the Kentucky law, Laura Foster could not testify against Blyew and Kennard.

The Court decided the deceased victim, Lucy Armstrong, was not an affected person. In fact, the Court stated: "In no sense can she be said to be affected by the cause. Manifestly the act refers to persons in existence. She was the victim of the frightful outrage which gave rise to the cause, but she is beyond being affected by the cause itself."[296] Therefore, Laura Foster, the only living witness to the murder of her family, was precluded by state law from testifying because she was Black. Richard Foster's dying declaration was inadmissible evidence under that same law because he was Black. Essentially, the Supreme Court undermined the Civil Rights Act and supported a state's ability to preclude witness testimony based on race. Blyew and Kennard murdered four persons in cold blood and were never punished for the crime. For nearly a century following the *Blyew* case, Blacks remained unable to testify against Whites in state courts across the South.

By the mid-twentieth century, Blacks gained access to the witness stand. However, discriminatory treatment by judges, prosecutors, and court personnel became an obstacle to justice. In *Hamilton v. Alabama* (1963), the Supreme Court was faced with another relic of slavery. Mary Hamilton, a civil rights organizer, was before an Alabama court on criminal charges[297] and took the stand to testify in her own defense. In addressing her, the prosecutor referred to her as "Mary," her first name. The cross examination was as follows:

Cross examination by Solicitor Rayburn:
Q.: What is your name, please?
A.: Miss Mary Hamilton.
Q.: Mary, I believe—you were arrested—who were you arrested by?
A.: My name is Miss Hamilton. Please address me correctly.
Q.: Who were you arrested by, Mary?
A.: I will not answer—
Attorney Amaker: The witness's name is Miss Hamilton.
A.: —your question until I am addressed correctly.
The Court: Answer the question.
The Witness: I will not answer them unless I am addressed correctly.
The Court: You are in contempt of court—
Attorney Conley: Your Honor—your Honor—
The Court: You are in contempt of this court, and you are sentenced to five days in jail and a fifty dollar fine.[298]

Mary Hamilton was found in contempt, fined, and jailed. The trial court applied a state law that allowed a finding of contempt if a witness diminished or disrespected a judicial tribunal.[299]

Hamilton filed a writ of habeas corpus to gain her freedom. The Alabama Supreme Court denied her appeal and ignored the attorney's disrespect in calling Hamilton only by her first name. She appealed. The U.S. Supreme Court reversed her conviction for contempt. The Court referred to this disrespect as a relic of slavery. During slavery and segregation, Whites refused to refer to Blacks by their full names or acknowledge their professional titles. Only White witnesses were given the dignity of being called by their first and last names.

Segregated Courtrooms: *Johnson v. Virginia*

Blacks had to attack the blatant disrespect shown them under law and by court officials. Courthouses were segregated places. Spectators were required to sit in the section designated for their race. In 1963, Ford T. Johnson, Jr., a Black man, refused to sit in the "colored section" of the traffic court of Richmond, Virginia.[300] When Johnson arrived at traffic court he sat in the section of the courtroom reserved for Whites only.[301] The bailiff requested him to move to the section of the courtroom designated for him. Instead, Johnson said he preferred to stand and then stood in front of the counsel tables with his arms folded. The traffic court judge directed Johnson to be seated. He refused. Johnson was found in contempt of court, arrested, and convicted.

Johnson appealed. The Virginia appellate courts upheld the conviction. Johnson appealed to the U.S. Supreme Court. In *Johnson v. Virginia*, the Court stated: "Such a conviction cannot stand, for it is no longer open to question that a State may not constitutionally require segregation of public facilities."[302] This 1963 case led to the desegregation of courthouses and other state government facilities. Peolpe of color were no longer physically segregated in court. However, discrimination in the treatment of Blacks within the court system continued unabated.

Segregated Prisons—Then and Now:
Lee v. Washington and *Johnson v. California*

Jails and prisons remain a vestige of government-imposed racial segregation. During slavery, enslaved Blacks convicted of crimes were not imprisoned because their labor was too valuable. Instead, convicted slaves were beaten and returned to their labor.[303] The jail and prison populations comprised White inmates.[304] After slavery was abolished, Blacks were imprisoned in great waves, especially in the South. Prison officials believed that White inmates should not suffer the insult of being housed with Blacks. Moreover, racial segregation was thought essential to preventing Whites from harming Blacks. *Brown v. Board of Education*, the Supreme Court's school desegregation decision of 1954, had little effect on racial segregation in jails and prisons.[305]

In *Lee v. Washington*, the constitutionality of racially segregated prisons was placed before the Supreme Court for the first time.[306] As late as 1968, Alabama's prisons, jails, and medical facilities for male and female inmates were racially segregated. Inmate Caliph Washington brought an action against the prison system.[307] Washington led a class action alleging that an Alabama statute requiring racial segregation of inmates violated the equal protection clause of the Fourteenth Amendment.[308] Alabama's Commissioner of Corrections Frank Lee argued that racial tensions in maintaining security, discipline, and order required the separation of the races.[309] On appeal, the Supreme Court ruled in *Lee v. Washington* that Alabama's statute segregating the races in prisons and jails violated the Fourteenth Amendment.[310] The Court ordered that "[a]ll facilities in the minimum and medium security institutions, including Draper Correctional Center and Julia Tutwiler Prison for Women...[be] completely desegregated within six months."[311] The maximum-security prisons were allowed a more gradual desegregation.

The desegregation process actually took many years. On September 9, 1971, inmates at Attica Correctional Facility in Attica, New York, begin a four-day uprising. Forty people died, including hostages. Racially prejudiced correctional officers, overcrowding, and ill treatment of inmates led to the riot and brought national attention to racial issues within America's prison system.

In 1973, the Court of Appeals for the Eighth Circuit decided the Kansas City, Kansas, prison case of *U.S. v. Wyandotte*.[312] The correctional system in Wyandotte County segregated inmates based on race. Inmates were separated into the West Tank and East Tank areas of the prison facility. Whites were assigned to the West Tank and Blacks to the East Tank.[313] The U.S. Department of Justice brought an action against the facility calling for the termination of segregation in the prison because it violated the Fourteenth Amendment. The Wyandotte Correctional facility, a state entity, argued that racial segregation was necessary to maintain order in the prison.[314] The appellate court ruled: "We need not labor the point that a State may not constitutionally require segregation of public facilities...the principle is as applicable to jails as to other public facilities."[315] The Supreme Court rejected this argument and affirmed the decision of the appellate court.[316] Prisons are public places and must be desegregated. The threat of violence between the races does not justify segregating inmates.

Racial segregation in jails and prisons remains a controversial issue. The U.S. Supreme Court addressed the issue as recently as 2005. The California Department of Corrections maintained an unwritten policy of racially segregating male prisoners. The prisoners were placed in double cells for up to sixty days each time they entered a correctional facility as a new prisoner or a transferee. Garrison Johnson had been incarcerated since 1987 and, during that time, had been housed at a number of California prison facilities.[317] Upon his arrival at Folsom Prison in 1987 and each time he was transferred to a new facility thereafter, Johnson was double-celled with another African-American inmate. Johnson, an African-American inmate in the custody of the California Department of Corrections, brought a pro se race discrimination action in federal court. He alleged that the segregation policy violated his equal-protection rights under the Fourteenth Amendment.[318] After years of attempting to access justice, Johnson's argument was heard and dismissed.[319]

As in prior decades, the California Department of Corrections argued that its racial segregation policy was necessary to prevent violence.[320] The trial court found in favor of the Department of Corrections.[321] Johnson appealed. The appellate court ruled in favor of the correctional facility as well.[322] Johnson then appealed to the U.S. Supreme Court. He argued that the trial court erred in failing to use the strict scrutiny standard. Strict scrutiny is the most rigorous legal test to overcome. It is applied to determine whether the use of race by a governmental entity is constitutional. The trial court in *Johnson v. California* applied a test known as the *Turner* standard.[323] Under *Turner*, the correctional facility needed only to demonstrate that there was no "common-sense connection" between the segregation policy and prison violence. The state appellate court upheld the use of the *Turner* test. However, the Supreme Court rejected the argument of the California Department of Corrections and reversed the lower court.

The Court ruled that the strict scrutiny test must be applied in *Johnson v. California*.[324] The *Turner* test was appropriate mainly for adjudicating prisoner cases involving issues such as inmate-to-inmate communication, freedom of speech issues, and inmate marriages.[325] However, strict scrutiny is the proper standard of review for cases involving a governmental use of race.[326] Prison officials also argued that deference should be shown to those officials managing the prison; their experience with handling inmate matters and "common sense" judgment placed them in a better position than the Court to know when racial segregation was appropriate.[327] This argument was rejected by the Supreme Court as well because, given America's history of race discrimination, racial segregation by a governmental entity was immediately suspect.[328] However, the Court would not render a decision on the merits of the case.[329] Instead, *Johnson v. California* was remanded back to the trial court for a new trial. The Supreme Court directed the trial court to adjudicate the matter in light of the requirements under the strict scrutiny analysis.

Stop and Frisk: *Terry v. Ohio*

Racial profiling is far from a recent phenomenon. During slavery, patrols of deputies and bounty hunters searched for fugitive slaves. Slaves on plantations were watched closely for any signs of escape plans or uprising. State laws limited interaction between free and enslaved Blacks. Laws also restricted the number of enslaved Blacks allowed to legally assemble at any given time. Written permission was required for slaves to travel off the plantation. White overseers and, after slavery, local law enforcement kept watch over Blacks to ensure that they stayed "in their place" (see Chapter 4). Incarceration under discriminatory Black Code laws and even lynching were punishments awaiting Blacks accused of making trouble for Whites. In the late twentieth century, law enforcement was given inordinate power over Black communities in the form of the "stop and frisk" activity established in *Terry v. Ohio*.[330]

On October 31, 1963, John Terry and Richard Chilton, two Black men, were standing on a corner in downtown Cleveland, Ohio, at 2:30 in the afternoon. McFadden, an undercover police detective, watched Terry and Chilton look into a store window and then confer several times at the corner.[331] They were joined by a third Black man, Katz. McFadden testified later that the men alternately looked into the store window and then returned to the corner approximately a dozen times.[332] McFadden had been a policeman for thirty-nine years and a detective for thirty-five years.[333] At the time, he had patrolled that vicinity of downtown Cleveland for thirty years. He was assigned specifically to look for shoplifters and pickpockets. McFadden testified at trial that he had developed a routine habit of observing people in the area. He stated that Terry and Chilton "didn't look right to me at the time."[334] McFadden had never seen these three Black men prior to this encounter.

McFadden suspected the two men of "casing a job, [for] a stick-up."[335] He added that he feared "they may have [had] a gun."[336] McFadden followed Chilton and Terry and saw them join Katz down the street. He approached the three men, identified himself as a police officer, and asked their names.[337] The men had not committed any crime. He had not received any complaints from the store.[338] He was unable to say what drew his eye to them.[339] After McFadden asked their names, the men "mumbled something," at which point McFadden grabbed Terry, spun him around, and patted down his clothing.[340] McFadden felt a pistol. He ultimately removed a .38-caliber revolver from Terry's pocket.

McFadden proceeded to pat down Chilton and Katz. He discovered another revolver in Chilton's overcoat, but no weapons were found on Katz. The men were arrested. Terry and Chilton were charged with carrying a concealed weapon.[341] The trial court judge denied the motion of Terry and Chilton to have the weapons suppressed.[342] Terry and Chilton were convicted and sentenced to three years in prison.[343] Terry appealed his conviction, arguing that McFadden acted without probable cause in violation of the Fourth Amendment,[344] which protects against unreasonable searches and seizures by government officials.[345]

Upon appeal, the Supreme Court affirmed Terry's conviction. Although McFadden did not have probable cause that a crime had been committed, the Court supported his search of Terry. The Court confirmed the conviction using the rationale of fear. As the population of major cities became mainly composed of minorities, they were seen as growing in dangerousness. The Supreme Court stated: "In dealing with the rapidly unfolding and often dangerous situations on city streets, the police are in need of an escalating set of flexible responses..."[346]

Based on the *Terry* decision, a person can be stopped and frisked by law enforcement "upon suspicion that he *may* be connected with criminal activity."[347] Having police officers pat down a Black adult woman, man, and their children is considered by the Court to be "a mere 'minor inconvenience and petty indignity,' which can properly be imposed upon the citizen in the interest of effective law enforcement."[348] The trigger for a "stop and frisk" is merely the police officer's suspicion that he or the public may be in danger of imminent harm.[349] Given the segregated backgrounds of Blacks and Whites in America, a feeling of "reasonable suspicion" may simply be an officer's discomfort with being a minority within the Black community or basic fear of other races and ethnic groups.

With this new-found authority would come police abuse. The Court summarily dismissed arguments that unfettered power to stop and frisk a suspicious looking person would increase tensions between the Black community and police officers.[350] Humiliating a countless number of Blacks with futile searches meant little to nothing when one such search might produce admissible evidence. Chief Justice Earl Warren, writing on behalf of the Court, stated: "The wholesale harassment by certain elements of the police community, of which minority groups, particularly Negroes, frequently complain, will not be stopped by the exclusion of any evidence from any criminal trial."[351] The Court accepted the premise that Blacks would be harassed as a consequence of granting police authority to stop and frisk.

Police authority to stop and frisk had little to no boundary. An officer needed only to state there was a reasonable suspicion of harm. The evidence found on the suspicious person would not be suppressed. Thus, a mainstay of the Fourth Amendment—the exclusionary rule—was not provided. This rule, long recognized as a deterrent to lawlessness in other cases, no longer applied.[352] Thus, the decision in *Terry v. Ohio* opened the floodgates for racial harassment and profiling. America's history of racism and police bias toward Blacks was ignored.[353] Instead, the *Terry* Court charged the judiciary to devise other remedies to curtail abuses of the stop and frisk procedure.[354] The reach of *Terry v. Ohio* has been extended.[355] In the Terry case, McFadden asked the men their names. Terry "mumbled something."[356] Police can now arrest any person who refuses to provide identification upon request by law enforcement.[357] Due to racial discrimination in housing and other economic factors, predominantly Blacks and other people of color live in concentrated areas within America's cities (see Chapter 3). Unfortunately, neighborhood demographics have enabled racial profiling by police. Once a community is labeled a "high crime area," walking or standing is considered suspicious behavior triggering a stop and frisk procedure by police officers.[358] In a "high drug area," the police are free to search the driver, passengers, and entire car even for the slightest traffic violation.[359]

Racial Profiling: *Chicago v. Morales*

In *Chicago v. Morales*, Blacks and Latinos challenged a Chicago "gang congregation" statute that prohibited two or more people from gathering together in any public place.[360] Conviction under this law was punishable by a fine of up to $500, imprisonment for not more than six months, and one hundred twenty hours of community service.[361] The law states:

> Whenever a police officer observes a person whom he reasonably believes to be a criminal street gang member loitering in any public place with one or more other persons, he shall order all such persons to disperse and remove themselves from the area. Any person who does not promptly obey such an order is in violation...[362]

In the statute, loitering was loosely defined as remaining in any one place with no apparent purpose.[363]

However, the city gave no indication what conduct constituted loitering. During the three years of the statute's enforcement (1992–1995), the police in Chicago issued over eighty-nine thousand dispersal orders and arrested forty thousand people.[364] The City of Chicago argued that the statute effectively lowered gang violence.[365] Defendants argued that they should be free to loiter. The Illinois Supreme

Court agreed with the defendants. Upon appeal, the U.S. Supreme Court ruled that the vagueness of Chicago's gang congregation statute violated the right to liberty under the due-process clause of the Fourteenth Amendment.[366] Additionally, the statute did not provide sufficient limits on police enforcement.[367] In essence, the law afforded "too much discretion to the police and too little notice to citizens who wish to use the public streets."[368] The Court apparently recognized that this gang statute, intended for urban communities of color, could potentially be applied to White middle-class communities as well. Of course, the Court noted that interactions anywhere else in the city would be "innocent and harmless."[369] Convictions under the statute were overturned.

Bias Drug Prosecutions: *U.S. v. Armstrong*

Black defendants in California challenged racial profiling in drug prosecutions. In 1996, the Supreme Court decided *United States v. Armstrong*.[370] Christopher Lee Armstrong, a Black man, argued that Blacks in Los Angeles were selectively arrested and charged with drug possession by federal prosecutors.[371] Armstrong challenged his arrest on charges of crack cocaine possession with intent to distribute and other charges.[372] He claimed that more Whites used drugs but more Blacks were targeted for prosecution on drug crimes.[373] Armstrong filed a motion for discovery requesting that the federal government provide him with documents and statistics concerning the race of persons arrested on federal drug offenses in Los Angeles. He relied on the case of *Oyler v. Boles*.[374] In that 1962 decision, the Supreme Court ruled that the government may not prosecute based on race or religion.

The trial court granted Armstrong's request for the information.[375] The government was ordered to provide a list of all cases from the last three years in which the government charged both cocaine and firearms offenses, identify the race of defendants in those cases, and explain its criteria for prosecuting those defendants. The government asked for reconsideration; it was denied.[376] The government then informed the court that it would not comply with the order.[377] The trial court dismissed the case.[378] An *en banc* ruling of the appellate court affirmed the decision to dismiss the case.[379]

Upon appeal, the U.S. Supreme Court reversed the appellate court. The Court ruled that in order to prove a selective-prosecution case based on race, Armstrong must show that the government declined to prosecute similarly situated suspects of other races.[380] Proof of discrimination need not be made available to the defendants by the prosecutor. The *Armstrong* defendants were defeated by the intransigence of the criminal justice system. The government refused to provide information that would probably demonstrate a failure to prosecute similarly situated suspects of other races. However, the *Armstrong* case brought national attention to one aspect of racial discrimination within the criminal justice system. Blacks continued to challenge unfair criminal laws and procedures.

Scottsboro Bays

Rape was a capital offense until 1977. However, the death penalty was reserved primarily for Blacks. For example, in Baton Rouge, Louisiana, from 1907 to 1950, not one White man charged with rape was put to death, "although 29 Negroes charged with rape had been executed in that period."[381]

In *Powell v. Alabama* (1932), nine Black young men were charged with the rape of two White women.[382] At this time, rape was a capital offense.[383] The young men were riding the Southern Railroad freight car from Chattanooga, Tennessee, to Memphis to find work when an altercation began with two White men in the freight car.[384] The Black youths won the fight and forced all but one of the White men off the moving train. One White man and the two White women, Ruby Bates and Victoria Price, were left on the train with the boys. The White men who lost the fight informed the local sheriff, who sent a radio message ahead to stop the train at the next town. When the train arrived in Scottsboro, Alabama, the boys were arrested and charged with gang raping the White women. The rape allegedly occurred on March 25, 1931. The defendants, who came to be known as the "Scottsboro Boys," were indicted in Alabama on March 31.[385]

The Scottsboro Boys were indicted on the very day they were arraigned. The defendants entered pleas of not guilty. They did not have counsel representing them at the arraignment.[386] The trial judge appointed all the members of the bar to represent the defendants at the arraignment. No individual attorneys were appointed.[387] The defendants were tried in three groups.[388] As each of the three cases was called for trial, each defendant was arraigned and, having the indictment read to him, entered a plea of not guilty.[389] Each of the three trials was completed within a single day. Under the Alabama statute, punishment for rape was decided by the jury and within its discretion may be from ten years' imprisonment to death. The juries found defendants guilty and imposed the death penalty upon all of them. The trial court overruled motions for new trials and sentenced the defendants in accordance with the verdicts. The judgments were affirmed by the state supreme court.[390]

Samuel Liebowitz, a New York attorney with the International Labor Defense, took on the case. Liebowitz appealed their convictions to the U.S. Supreme Court. They argued that the trial court had denied them due process of law and the equal protection of the laws under the Fourteenth Amendment, specifically: (1) they were not given a fair, impartial, and deliberate trial; (2) they were denied the right of counsel, particularly the ability to consult with an attorney and opportunity of preparation for trial; and (3) they were tried before juries from which Blacks were excluded. The Supreme Court chose to review only the Sixth Amendment denial of counsel. In clarifying its position regarding the need for counsel in a capital case, the Court provided the following hypothetical situation:

> Let us suppose the extreme case of a prisoner charged with a capital offen[s]e, who is deaf and dumb, illiterate and feeble minded, unable to employ counsel, with the whole power of the state arrayed against him, prosecuted by counsel for the state without assignment of counsel for his defense, tried, convicted and sentenced to death. Such a result, which, if carried into execution, would be little short of judicial murder...[391]

The Supreme Court found the failure to assign counsel in a capital case constituted a violation of the Sixth Amendment and the due-process clause of the Fourteenth Amendment. The Court held that states must appoint counsel to indigent defendants in cases involving a possible death sentence.

Later, Ruby Bates recanted her story about the rape and during the retrial became a witness for the defense.[392] The case was tried again and the Scottsboro defendants were again convicted and sentenced to death. Other legal issues arose involving the defendants. In 1935, the Court decided *Norris v. Alabama*, in which the exclusion of Blacks from the criminal jury was appealed to the U.S. Supreme Court.[393] In that case, the Supreme Court declared: "[T]his long-continued, unvarying, and wholesale exclusion of negroes from jury service… [has] no justification consistent with the constitutional mandate."[394] The justices reviewed the jury roles and found that the names of Blacks were added much later.[395]

The conviction of Clarence Norris was reversed and the case was remanded for another trial conducted without precluding Blacks from the jury box.[396] In 1937, Norris was retried and again sentenced to death. The other defendants were given sentences ranging from twenty to seventy-five years. In 1938, Governor Bibb Graves com-muted the sentence of Clarence Norris from death to life in prison. It would be nearly fifteen years before members of the Scottsboro Boys regained their freedom.

Forced Confession: *Chambers v. Florida*

In *Chambers v. Florida*, decided in 1940, the Supreme Court was faced with four Black men sentenced to death based on forced con-fessions.[397] On the night of May 13, 1933, Robert Darsey, an elderly White member of the Pompano, Florida, community was robbed and murdered.[398] The Pompano police arrested twenty-five to forty Black men on suspicion of his murder. The community was outraged. Mobs formed. The police transported the men to various towns to avoid lynch mobs.[399] J. T. Williams, a guard, interrogated the group for six days in the death cell of Dade County, Florida, in all-night vigils of torture and threats until confessions were produced from Esel Chambers, Jack Williamson, Charlie Davis, and Walter Woodward.[400] Based on their confession to the crime, the men were convicted and sentenced to death.

On appeal to the state appellate court, the men argued that their confessions should have been excluded. After four appeals to the Florida State Supreme Court, their death sentences were upheld.[401] That Court opined that a forcibly produced confession, although not approved, was not *ipso facto* illegal.[402]

In 1940, the U.S. Supreme Court overturned the convictions of Williamson, Chambers, Davis, and Woodward, holding that a death sentence could not be based on coerced confessions.[403] In reversing the convictions, the Court acknowledged that forcibly extracting a confession from a detainee was a widespread practice in this country.[404] The practice was frequently used against Blacks. Law enforcement could act with impunity because the state courts did not uphold the constitutional rights of Blacks and other people.

The Death Penalty

Prior to 1972, judges and juries had a great deal of discretion in giving death sentences. Socioeconomic position played a major role in who would receive a death sentence. In 1972, the Supreme Court decided *Georgia v. Furman*, in which the state's administration of the death penalty was found to be so arbitrary as to constitute cruel and unusual punishment.[405] Under the Eighth Amendment: "Excessive bail shall not be required, nor excessive fines imposed, nor cruel and unusual punishments inflicted."[406] Justice William O. Douglas found the discretion of judges and juries in imposing the death penalty enabled "the penalty to be selectively applied, feeding prejudices against the accused if he is poor and…a member of a suspect or unpopular minority, and saving those who by social position may be in a more protected position."[407] Justice Potter Stewart admonished that the Eighth and Fourteenth Amendments "cannot tolerate the infliction of a sentence of death under legal systems that permit this unique penalty to be so wantonly and so freakishly imposed."[408] The death sentences were commuted to life imprisonment.

However, by 1976, the Supreme Court reinstated the death penalty. In *Gregg v. Georgia*, the Court rejected the "standards of decency" argument and affirmed the death sentence of Troy Gregg.[409] The Court ruled that capital punishment is not cruel and unusual punishment when administered fairly.[410] Methods of execution include lethal injection, firing squad, gas chamber, electrocution, and hanging.[411] The most common method has become lethal injection. Not all states have enacted death penalty statutes. America is enveloped in a death penalty moratorium movement.[412] In 2000, George H. Ryan, governor of Illinois, temporarily ceased executions upon finding that thirteen death row inmates were innocent. Those exonerated inmates were released based on exculpatory evidence stemming from diligent investigation, scientific advancement in the analysis of DNA evidence, or witness testimony. Questioning the credibility of the state's death penalty statute, Governor Ryan commuted the sentences of the other prisoners from death to life imprisonment.

Blacks have long argued that the administration of the death penalty in America is skewed based on race. In *McClesky v. Kemp* (1987), Warren McClesky, a Black defendant, was convicted of murdering a White police officer during a planned robbery. His case was tried in a Georgia state court. The jury convicted McClesky and found that he should receive the death penalty. McClesky's initial appeals in state court were denied. Then, he filed a writ of habeas corpus in federal court arguing that the death penalty was meted out in a racially discriminatory manner. He presented a study by David C. Baldus that demonstrated that a Black defendant charged in a killing involving a White victim was 4.3 times as likely to receive a death sentence in Georgia as defendants charged with killing Blacks.[413] The district court and court of appeals denied his writ.

The U.S. Supreme affirmed the lower courts. The Court held that the racial disparities presented in the Baldus study did not establish that the administration of the death penalty in Georgia constituted a violation of a defendant's Fourteenth or Eighth Amendment rights. Specifically, the Court stated that:

> At most, the Baldus study indicates a discrepancy that appears to correlate with race, but this discrepancy does not constitute a major systemic

defect. Any mode for determining guilt or punishment has its weaknesses and the potential for misuse. Despite such imperfections, constitutional guarantees are met when the mode for determining guilt or punishment has been surrounded with safeguards to make it as fair as possible.[414]

The Court required McClesky to present evidence of discriminatory intent on the part of prosecutors who seek the death penalty. The Baldus study and its progeny continue to underscore the role of race in the administration of the death penalty. "In 82% of the studies, race of victim was found to influence the likelihood of being charged with capital murder or receiving a death sentence."[415]

In *Atkins v. Virginia*, the Supreme Court ruled, in 2002, that the execution of mentally retarded defendants convicted of capital crimes constituted cruel and unusual punishment.[416] In 2005, the Court held in the case of *Roper v. Simmons* that the execution of defendants who commit a capital offense while juveniles is a violation of the Eighth Amendment's protection against cruel and unusual punishment.[417] However, the Court has yet to fully recognize the role of race in the administration of the death penalty.

Present-Day Vestiges: Incarceration Rates and Debates

Vestiges of slavery and postslavery discrimination are rarely discussed in the context of criminal justice. Black Codes were enacted to intentionally discriminate against the newly freed Black citizen and prevent his rise above a labor class. These laws restricted travel and alliances and criminalized their behavior. Under the Black Codes, harsher punishments were meted out for Blacks. Although slavery was abolished, the prison system was used to maintain control over Blacks and continue to abuse their labor. Present-day racial profiling bears a remarkable resemblance to the work of fugitive slave patrols. The race to incarcerate young men of color has caused imprisonment to become a nearly normal urban experience.[418]

Black Codes have taken the modern form of drug laws. Under these laws, twice as many Whites as Blacks are arrested while seven times as many Blacks as Whites are convicted.[419] Blacks are almost three times more likely than Hispanics and five times more likely than Whites to be in jail.[420] In capital cases, death sentences for Black defendants are more likely when a White victim is involved.[421] Blacks comprise 13 percent of the U.S. population. However, in 2006, of the more than three thousand persons on death row in America, 42 percent are Black, 56 percent are White, and 2 percent are of other races.[422] Black women are now incarcerated at a faster rate than men.[423] Black, non-Hispanic women are five times more likely than White women to be incarcerated.[424] Black minors represent over half of incarcerated young people.[425]

In a capitalistic system, criminal justice is meted out with profit-making possibilities.[426] This is especially relevant as it concerns racial prejudice. The privatization of prisons and the panoply of extant services represent a multibillion dollar business scheme. Companies engaged in building and controlling private prison facilities trade their stock on the markets.[427] As with slavery, peonage, and prison labor, their profits are contingent upon continued growth in the market (i.e., Black prisoners). One corporation stated:

> We are a world leader in the privatized development and/or manage-ment of correctional facilities. The North American market is growing rapidly, and we are focused on expanding Federal procurement oppor-tunities. The Federal Bureau of Prisons is operating over capacity and Federal law now authorizes longer term contracts than ever before, resulting in more favorable financing alternatives for new privatized development.[428]

The "war on drugs" has become a war on the Black community. Too many in law enforcement are using this war as a vehicle for police harassment and racial profiling.[429] Possession of crack cocaine as com-pared to powder cocaine evidences America's continued discriminatory crime policies. Crack cocaine is less expensive and thus more readily available for the urban poor. Powder cocaine is more expensive and thus more readily available to suburban America. Of those charged with possession of powder cocaine, 80 percent are White. Under the Federal Omnibus Anti-Drug Abuse Act, anyone convicted of pos-sessing 5 grams of crack cocaine will receive a mandatory minimum prison sentence of five years. A person must possess 500 grams of powder cocaine to receive a mandatory five-year sentence.

Too often, criminal punishment depends on race. Whites are consistently charged under a state statute, whereas Blacks were charged under the harsher federal statute.[430] In a criminal justice system dependent on plea bargains and guilty pleas, demanding a jury trial would bring the procedure of injustice to a halt and send a strong message that racial profiling is an intolerable act of injustice. During the time of Jim Crow, Blacks were lynched with the explicit or implicit assistance of law enforcement.[431] Today, Blacks remain disproportionately victimized by crime and law enforcement. As long as these vestiges of slavery and *Plessy* remain, Blacks must live hypervigilantly, suspecting criminals as well as the criminal justice system.

8

RACE AND INTERNATIONALISM

We are able to do away with domestic tyranny and violence and aggression by those in power against the rights of their own people only when we make all men answerable to law.

**Robert Jackson, Supreme Court justice
and chief prosecutor of the Nuremberg Trials**

Prayers are made to the General Assembly [of the United Nations] for such action as will condemn and prevent the crime of genocide now being committed against the Negro people of the United States.

We Charge Genocide[1]

For centuries, Blacks in America have accessed and utilized the international arena as a device to bring external pressure against America's discriminatory policies.[2] Their struggle for justice under law was fought with every available tool including emigration international law, the United Nations, and the pressure of international public opinion. The issues have evolved with time. However, the need for international mechanisms remains. This chapter examines how Blacks in America utilized international venues to escape oppression and accessed the international stage to condemn slavery, lynching, and racial injustice.

Slavery and Internationalism

As early as the eighteenth century, Blacks placed their battle for human rights before the world in an effort to effect changes in American rule of law. Black enslaved and free persons in America fought against bondage and degradation by utilizing state courts and legislatures as well as the international arena. International law was in its infancy. During the colonial and postcolonial periods, the ideals of international law consisted mainly of customs and agreements or treaties between nations focused on national boundaries, cargo ships, and commercial trade. International law was based on a fundamental principle of the law of nations: national sovereignty.[3] Slavery or any abuse of populations within a country was considered a domestic matter within the sovereign rights of the nation.[4] Nation-states, or states in international parlance, could act with impunity against their own people. Intervention by other countries in the domestic affairs of a nation was, and still is, considered a violation of national sovereignty. The vast majority of human rights treaties, tribunals, and conventions that comprise present-day international public law were not developed until the twentieth century.[5]

The *Somerset* Case

The case of an escaped African enslaved in Britain would bring attention to the struggle of enslaved Blacks in America. Sovereignty aside, nations could impact domestic policy in another nation. The 1771 case of James Somerset provoked debate over the morality and political efficacy of slavery in Great Britain.[6] The court's opinion in *Somerset* remains a landmark decision of English law.[7]

Somerset was either chattel, without rights, or a human being based on whether he had attained freedom in England. Born in Guinea in West Africa, Somerset was stolen by slavers and taken to Virginia. Charles Steuart, a young Scottish businessman, purchased Somerset in 1749.[8] Somerset traveled with Steuart to Boston several times and then in 1769 to London, England. In 1771, Somerset escaped. Months later, Steuart's agent captured him. Somerset was forced aboard a ship to be sold as a slave in the West Indies. Before the ship could sail, a White attorney and friend, Jonathan Strong, obtained a writ of habeas corpus demanding the release of Somerset from the ship. A writ of habeas corpus requires the person having custody of another person to appear in court and give the reason for holding that person.

Somerset v. Steuart pitted the proponents of slavery against England's abolitionists.[9] The court was faced with deciding whether Steuart could imprison Somerset in England and force him to travel to Jamaica based on the powers given to a slave owner in Virginia. Jonathan Strong argued that the Virginia slave laws did not apply in England. After legal arguments on property rights and the rights of man, Lord James Mansfield entered a decision on behalf of Somerset.[10] In England, Somerset was deemed a man and therefore free.[11] Although the court did not extend its determination to the legality of slavery, the decision effectively changed public policy in England. Lord Mansfield declared:

> The state of slavery is of such a nature, that it is incapable of being introduced on any reasons, moral or political, but only by positive law, which preserves its force long after the reasons, occasion, and time itself from whence it was created, is erased from memory. It is odious, that nothing can be suffered to support it, but positive law...and therefore the black must be discharged.[12]

The *Somerset* decision inspired abolitionists in England.[13] The importation of slaves into Great Britain was banned shortly after the decision. But, there was little positive change in the slavery laws of the American colonies.

Slavery in America continued despite the ruling in *Somerset*. The United States ended only its direct participation in the international slave trade as of 1808. America was victorious against England. However, slavery remained the center of controversy at the Continental Congress. The leaders of this new nation refused to acknowledge the *Somerset* decision. They also refused to abolish slavery. Certain provisions of the Constitution reflect a compromise between abolitionists and slaveholders.

A $10 tax would be levied on each slave illegally brought into the United States.[14] The tax was imposed only if the slave traffickers were apprehended, tried, and convicted of the offense. This provision did not end slavery in America—only importation into the country. The institution of slavery would continue until the Thirteenth Amendment was ratified. The Framers also included a fugitive-slave clause in the U.S. Constitution. Under this provision, any escaped slave must be delivered back to the owner upon claim.[15] The provision was enforced through state laws, federal legislation, and bounty hunters. Thus, free and enslaved Blacks crossed national borders in search of freedom.

Settlement in Canada

The Declaration of Independence denounced the tyranny of King George. "We hold these truths to be self-evident that all men are created equal, that they are endowed by their Creator with certain unalienable Rights, that among these are Life, Liberty and the pursuit of Happiness."[16] These bold and noble words did not apply to Africans in the newly formed United States. During the Revolutionary War, Britain promised land and freedom in its Canadian territories to enslaved Africans who fought on the side of England.[17] Blacks had to choose between England's promise of freedom and the ideals of America's unspoken promise.[18]

Those Blacks who accepted the offer were referred to as Black Loyalists.[19] They fought on behalf of Britain's King George in return for their freedom and a promise of land in British Canada.[20] Thousands of Black Loyalists became émigrés to Shelburne and Birchtown, Nova Scotia.[21] However, the conditions were inauspicious, and many died of disease and the harsh weather. Slavery in Canada, racial discrimination, and bitterly cold weather limited the immigration of Blacks to Canada.[22] The land promised to Black Loyalists failed to materialize[23] and Blacks were in only a slightly better position in Canada than in the United States.[24] Nova Scotia did not officially abolish slavery until 1800.

In 1829, David Walker wrote his *Appeal to the Colored Citizens of the World* in which he advocated Blacks leaving America for England. However, due to its proximity and less oppressive race laws, Canada continued to be viewed as a more accessible "promised land." When racially restrictive laws or Black Codes were enacted in Cincinnati, Ohio, in 1829, dozens of Blacks fled to Canada. With the assistance of Quakers, those Black expatriates from Cincinnati created a settlement near Lucan, Canada.[25] The settlement, named Wilberforce, hosted over eight hundred Blacks intent on self-development[26] and offered a mitigated freedom to enslaved persons fleeing American oppression[27] Canada often defied extradition requests made by American slave owners demanding the return of escaped slaves.

Although slavery was practiced in parts of Canada, fugitive slaves found a modicum of solace in British Canada (later Nova Scotia).[28] In 1829, the Canadian government denied an official request from the American government for the return of a fugitive slave and his benefactor.[29] In 1831, the first Annual Convention of the People of Color was held in Philadelphia at Wesleyan Church. The convention's agenda included (1) study of conditions of free Negroes; (2) study of settlement options in Canada; (3) recommendation of annual conventions of free Negroes; (4) opposing the American Colonization Society.[30] The White financed American Colonization Society sought the forced transplacement of all Blacks in America.

An "underground railroad" was created to ferry slaves into Canada. Harriet Tubman escaped enslavement in Maryland to freedom in Canada via this means.[31] The underground railroad was actually safe houses owned by Blacks such as Tubman, White abolitionists, and Quakers who had long opposed slavery. The safe houses consisted of homes, barns, and stores along hundreds of miles leading from slave states into the North and often traveling to Canada. Escaping slavery alone, Tubman learned of the underground railroad while in Pennsylvania. She used it to bring her family up from slavery in Maryland to freedom in Canada. Tubman then brought others out of bondage to Ontario, Canada.

Tubman became known as the "Moses of the underground railroad." Although fugitive slave laws made any escape dangerous for the runaway slave as well as anyone assisting in the escape and bounty hunters were dispatched to apprehend Tubman, she successfully assisted over three hundred people to escape slavery. She was never captured. Nor were any of her "passengers" seized. Tubman stated, "When I found I had crossed that line [into Canada in 1845], I looked at my hands to see if I was the same person. There was such a glory over everything."[32] Tubman remained in Ontario, Canada, until 1857. By 1860, conservative estimates put the number of fugitive slaves and free Blacks residing in Canada at over sixty thousand.[33]

Returning to Africa

Blacks traveled to Africa to develop settlements. As early as 1815, Paul Caffe led a group of Blacks to Africa.[34] After the slave revolt led by Nat Turner in 1831, the state of Maryland enacted legislation encouraging free Blacks to emigrate to Liberia.[35] In1859, Martin R. Delany, a free Black and physician, led a group to the Niger Valley in Africa and entered into an immigration treaty with a king and seven chiefs at Abeokuta.[36] It was the first treaty between the people of African descent and Africans to create a Black settlement in Africa.[37] The treaty provided Blacks from America with land for a settlement in exchange for contributing their skills to the development of the area. Delany's plan to grow cotton would have provided the economic foundation for the colony to sustain itself and compete in the international marketplace.[38] These attempts at emigration were frustrated by the harsh environment, disease, and Europe's determined efforts to politically and economically dominate Africa.[39]

The Emigration Debate

Forced Black emigration had long been a topic debated by presidents and policymakers. President Thomas Jefferson pondered the place of Africans in America. Jefferson believed Blacks should be returned to Africa. President Abraham Lincoln proposed deporting former slaves to Haiti or Liberia upon the abolition of slavery.[40] The National Colonization Society of America was instrumental in moving free Blacks to a location in West Africa later renamed Liberia. Over thirteen thousand Blacks were settled in Liberia. The first president of the National Colonization Society was former U.S. President James Monroe. His influence is evident in that the capital of Liberia is Monrovia.

The Black community was divided on the issue of emigration. Frederick Douglass was a staunch opponent of forced colonization.[41] Even in the face of slavery and oppression, Douglass, as did many Blacks of the time, believed that Blacks had invested too much in the building of America to emigrate from it.[42] Others believed that that investment had been made to a consistently ungrateful nation. Bishop Henry M. Turner of the African Methodist Episcopal Church created the Colored Emigration League in an effort to return to Africa. Turner petitioned for financial assistance for emigration as well as reparations for slave labor.[43] His request was denied.

Trinidad and Jamaica (former British colonies) sought Black immigrants. Haiti was viewed as a possible site for emigration. However, civil conflicts within the country made it a less desirable destination. In 1829, Mexico abolished slavery. Settlers were permitted to emigrate to Mexico only if they agreed to abide by laws recognizing Blacks as free persons.[44] However, when America acquired northern Mexico, America's expansion of slavery undermined the incentive to emigrate to Mexico.[45]

International Pressure

In 1838, Great Britain banned slavery among its colonies around the world. American abolitionists looked to the United States to end slavery as well. That international pressure to end slavery intensified with the signing of the Quintuple Treaty in 1841. Under this treaty, England, France, Russia, Prussia, and Austria could seize and search vessels on the high seas to inhibit the importation of slaves.[46] Meanwhile, Black as well as White abolitionists traveled to Europe giving orations on the evils of slavery. As a sign of international pressure, in 1844, the British government sent a communication to U.S. Secretary of State Abel Upshur requesting an end to slavery in the United States.[47] The request was rebuffed as an inappropriate reach into U.S. domestic affairs.[48]

By 1845, Frederick Douglass, a former slave and internationally known orator, had traveled frequently to Europe and Canada to speak against slavery and gather support for the abolitionist movement.[49] Abolitionist and writer William Wells Brown, a former slave, traveled to Europe in 1849 to lecture on the cruelty of American slavery and gain international support for its abolition.[50] His book recounts over one thousand speeches given to European audiences before returning to the United States.[51] These abolitionists and many more would bring international attention to the horrific treatment of enslaved Blacks in America. Within America, the pressure mounted.

Yet, in 1856, the infamous *Dred Scott* case underscored America's resolve to maintain slavery. The case, brought in St. Louis, Missouri, and heard on appeal before the U.S. Supreme Court, pitted abolitionists against staunch slavery supporters. Chief Justice Roger Taney delivered the opinion of the Court, which held that Dred Scott was not a citizen and the basis for his challenge was an unconstitutional agreement referred to as the Missouri Compromise. As with the case of James Somerset, the decision held international implications. Few countries in the Western Hemisphere maintained a government-legislated slave system. Slavery had been abolished in the French and Danish colonies in 1848.

The U.S. Supreme Court recognized the international attention the case received. The Court rebuked the international community and its efforts to apply pressure on the United States to abolish slavery. Referring specifically to Europe's call to end slavery, the Court stated in *Dred Scott*:

> No one, we presume, supposes that any change in public opinion or feeling, in relation to this unfortunate race, *in the civilized nations of Europe* or in this country, should induce the court to give to the words of the Constitution a more liberal construction in their favor than they were intended to bear when the instrument was framed and adopted.[52] [emphasis added]

The Court refused to acknowledge the conflict between the Constitution's fundamental freedoms and slavery despite international pressure.

A Black man had no rights that a White man need respect—this was the expression summarizing the Court's position on Blacks, free and slave, within the United States. The country soon slipped into a consuming civil war.

Black soldiers played a pivotal role in the war between the North and South. The Union Army's success relied on Black troops. Slavery in the South was abolished before the end of the Civil War. The Thirteenth Amendment abolished slavery throughout the nation. However, soon after slavery was abolished, discriminatory laws called "Black Codes" were enacted to severely restrict the rights of Blacks. Terrorist organizations, such as the Ku Klux Klan, were responsible for murder and brutality across the country. Without federal protection, Blacks were made vulnerable to horrific violence.[53] That violence resulted in the need to once again access the world stage.

Lynching and International Criticism

The brutality of America's lynch mobs spurred the need for international assistance. America's social reform movement focused on the protection of home and family. However, the lynching of Blacks was condoned or ignored by local, state, and federal governments. Blacks entered the international arena to seek justice and to inform the world of the evils of lynching and racial segregation. Ida B. Wells-Barnett traveled nationally and internationally to garner international pressure against lynching in America.[54] Her fiery speeches denouncing the barbarity of lynching drew international attention and support.[55] As early as 1894, Wells-Barnett traveled to Great Britain to give lectures about the horrors of lynching in America.

At the same time, White women leaders of social reform were traveling the world decrying the horrors of "White slavery" or the kidnapping of White women for prostitution in Asia. This alleged practice had little substantiation outside of a fear of Orientalism. But, as Wells-Barnett pointed out, these women ignored the issue of lynching in America.[56] In a letter from Wells-Barnett to the editor of Britain's *Westminster Gazette* newspaper, she admonished Frances Willard, a noted leader of the women's reform movement, for her indifference to the lynching of Blacks:

> The fact is, Miss Willard is no better or worse than the great bulk of white Americans on the Negro question. They are all afraid to speak out, and it is only British public opinion which will move them, as I am thankful to see it has already begun to move Miss Willard.[57]

During that time, racial segregation, legal deprivation, and lynching were ignored by most White social reform leaders in America. Such indifference by White women suffragettes and social reformers was practiced by many Whites who believed the myth that Black men were lynched as punishment for raping White women.

America's rape myth was used to refute international appeals for assistance. Support for this myth continued with little basis in reality.[58] In fact, lynching was used as a method of controlling Blacks socially, politically, and economically.[59] Victims of lynch mobs included Black men as well as Black women, children, poor Whites, and foreign nationals.[60] In 1896, the U.S. Supreme Court's decision in *Plessy v. Ferguson* established racial apartheid in the United States.[61] In addition to the brutal beatings, torture, and murder at the hands of White lynch mobs, Blacks had to contend with restricted rights and freedoms caused by the *Plessy* decision.[62]

Blacks, as well as a small number of White advocates, organized international meetings to develop strategies to defeat *Plessy*. World opinion was needed to place pressure on the United States to provide more than the promise of constitutional protections. Without relinquishing the fight domestically, Blacks sought international alliances. In 1900, sociologist and noted civil rights advocate W. E. B. DuBois joined with Trinidadian barrister Henry Sylvester Williams to originate the Pan-African Congress. The meeting of the congress was held in London's Westminster Town Hall.[63] The congress examined mutual issues affecting Africans of the Diaspora and worked to address those issues.[64] The conference was attended by people of African descent from around the world, including heads of state, national leaders for civil rights, and scholars. It was discovered that similar obstacles precluded advancement by Blacks in America and the African Diaspora. DuBois is given credit for being among the first to grasp the international implications of the struggle for racial justice.[65]

In 1905, civil rights advocates met in Ontario, Canada. This interracial gathering, led by DuBois, inaugurated the Niagara Movement,[66] which took its name from the Niagara Falls nearby. It was attended by Black and White civil rights leaders working to better the conditions of Blacks in America. That meeting provided the framework for the formation of the National Association for the Advancement of Colored People (NAACP) in 1909.[67] Establishing full rights of citizenship, civil liberties, and civil rights for Blacks in America became the mission of the NAACP. Civil rights attorneys developed and executed their legal strategies to defeat apartheid. But, as World War I devastated Europe, Black leaders sought to show a united patriotic front and restrict international pleas to end lynching. Despite these efforts, lynching continued. Heroic Black soldiers returning from war in Europe were particular targets of this barbarism.

Back to Africa: *Marcus Garvey v. United States*

Not all would remain silent. Marcus Garvey led a subsequent stage of the repatriation-to-Africa movement similar to that initiated by Martin Delany a century before. Garvey's "Back to Africa" movement was larger and better organized. Born in Jamaica in 1887, Garvey traveled extensively as a young man. He studied the condition of Blacks around the world. Although not formally educated beyond high school, Garvey was well read. In 1914, he founded the Universal Negro Improvement Association and African Communities League to unite Blacks around the world in a political movement of self-determination.[68] By 1920, Garvey led an international organization of Garveyites with branches in forty countries. He chose the symbolic colors black, red, and green, and believed that Blacks must have a country of their own. At the time, except for Ethiopia, Africa was divided among the European colonial powers. Garvey turned to Liberia as a proposed homeland for Blacks.

Garvey's movement inspired Blacks who wanted more than American terrorism and disfranchisement.[69] Stock was sold to buy ships that would ferry Blacks back to Africa. The Black Star Line and other ships were acquired. The popularity of Garvey and his nationalist beliefs ran counter to integrationists such as W. E. B. DuBois, who considered Garvey reckless, grandiose, and a provocateur who would endanger the civil rights movement.[70] Garvey was a skilled leader of the people who, however, lacked business acumen and placed his trust in unscrupulous White businessmen. In 1924, he was arrested while in New York City and charged by the U.S. government with mail fraud for selling stock in the woefully undercapitalized and unseaworthy Black Star Line. Garvey was found guilty and he appealed. The Second Circuit Court of Appeals in New York affirmed the conviction. That court ridiculed Garvey's Back to Africa movement, stating:

> It may be true that Garvey fancied himself a Moses, if not a Messiah; that he deemed himself a man with a message to deliver, and believed that he needed ships for the deliverance of his people...if his gospel consisted in part of exhortations to buy worthless stock...he was guilty of a scheme...no matter how uplifting, philanthropic, or altruistic his larger outlook may have been.[71]

Garvey appealed to the U.S. Supreme Court, which refused to hear the appeal and let the conviction stand.[72] He was sentenced to five years in the federal penitentiary and was released in 1927. Since he was not an American citizen, Garvey was deported back to Jamaica upon his release from prison where he continued to promote Pan-Africanism and human rights for Blacks.

The League of Nations:
A Petition of the Negro Race

Europe suffered a horrific loss of life and property during World War I. That loss motivated President Woodrow Wilson and other leaders to create a society of nations working cooperatively around a code of international values that could be used to resolve disputes between nations peaceably.[73] The United States participated in the war from 1917 to its end in 1919. At war's end, the League of Nations was formed to promote international cooperation and to achieve peace and security.[74] For centuries prior to the League of Nations, countries acted in their own domestic interests based on treaties and customs of the time. Changes in international law evidenced the worldwide concern that, sovereignty aside, countries could no longer maintain the custom of noninterference in the affairs of other nations.[75] The original league members were victors of World War I.[76]

Although the United States refused to ratify the Treaty of Versailles, which was required to join the League of Nations, Marcus Garvey seized the league's existence as an opportunity to bring lynching and race discrimination to the world's attention.[77]

Garvey is credited with first bringing such a grievance to an international organization of nations. In 1928, he traveled to Geneva, Switzerland, and presented *A Petition of the Negro Race* to the League of Nations. The petition detailed the crimes against Blacks in the African Diaspora.[78] It impugned many of the league's most powerful members. Since it was not presented by a member, the league had no incentive to take it seriously and there is little evidence that it formally addressed Garvey's petition. As an institution, the League of Nations had neither the power nor inclination to address the issue of racial oppression within a nonmember country. However, individual members were in a position to make statements or bring pressure to bear on the United States.

Although it made positive contributions to the international community, the League of Nations' tenure was short-lived. The United States never joined the league. Despite strenuous efforts by Woodrow Wilson, the U.S. Senate would not agree to membership. The league was powerless to prevent major political catastrophes such as Italy's invasion of Ethiopia, the Spanish Civil War, and the militarization of Germany, which led to World War II.

The United Nations

As World War II progressed through Europe, member-states (nations) withdrew from the league. With little international support and limited resources, the league dissolved itself. It was during the war that President Roosevelt, a Democrat, is credited with coining the phrase "a united nations" in reference to the Allied Powers at war with Germany. In 1945, following the end of the war, the United Nations was formed from the structure of the League of Nations.[79] The creation of the United Nations provided another possible platform for racial justice against the atrocities suffered by Blacks in the United States. The international community sought justice against Hitler's forces. Treaties and customs in existence were not broad enough. Humanitarian laws such as the Geneva Convention were confined to the treatment of soldiers wounded during conflict[80] and prisoners of war.[81]

For millennia, a government's treatment of its populace remained firmly within the established right of sovereignty.[82] The International Military Tribunal of Nuremberg was created in 1945 and convened in Germany with U.S. Supreme Court Justice Robert Jackson as chief prosecutor.[83] This ad hoc, or temporary, tribunal tried German soldiers for crimes against humanity and genocide.[84] The Nuremberg Tribunal created legal precedent in international criminal jurisdiction by applying *in personam* jurisdiction, or jurisdiction over the person, to allow the trial of individual military officials accused of war crimes and crimes against humanity.[85] Prior to the Nuremberg Tribunal, individuals in the military were mostly immune to prosecution under international law.[86]

The Nuremberg Tribunal was the first legal forum to try soldiers for crimes against humanity.[87] Their crimes included genocide for their roles in the premeditated murder of civilian populations. The defendants' argument in response to the charges was that the state and not the individual soldiers should be held responsible. International criminal law jurisprudence had evolved. The international community had come to accept that, during war, the criminal acts performed on behalf of the state are committed by individuals. Soldiers convicted for crimes against humanity could not justify their criminal behavior with claims that they were just following orders of superiors.

The Japanese military was responsible for the deaths of over four million civilians during World War II.[88] The International Military Tribunal of Tokyo was created to address war crimes and crimes against humanity committed by the Japanese during World War II. The Tokyo Tribunal convened in 1946. Arguments of "nonresponsibility" similar to those of the Nuremberg defendants were raised at the International Military Tribunal of Tokyo. The Tokyo defendants were accused of a "kill all, burn all, destroy all" campaign of brutality.[89] Those arguments were also defeated. The world community recognized that although national acts of aggression and violence require state participation, the crimes were committed by individuals.[90] War crimes, crimes against humanity, and genocide are broadly defined to take into account heinous conduct committed on a large scale that shocked the moral conscience of the international community.

In 1945, the United Nations was created in response to the over sixty million people who died in World War II. Most of the casualties were civilians. The United Nations has as its mission, in part, to:

> ...save succeeding generations from the scourge of war, which twice in our lifetime has brought untold sorrow to mankind, and to reaffirm faith in fundamental human rights, in the dignity and worth of the human person, in the equal rights of men and women and of nations large and small...[91]

Only nation-states recognized by the United Nations can become members of the United Nations.[92]

Human Rights

One of the important initiatives of the new organization was the Office of the High Commissioner for Human Rights (OHCHR), a department of the U.N. Secretariat. The OHCHR was mandated to promote and protect the enjoyment and full realization, by all people, of all rights established in the charter of the United Nations and in international human rights laws and treaties. This included preventing human rights violations, securing respect for all human rights, promoting international cooperation to protect human rights, coordinating related activities throughout the United Nations, and strengthening and streamlining the U.N. system in the field of human rights.[93] It does not have an enforcement mechanism. However, the very existence of the United Nations provided an opportunity for Blacks in America to place lynching and racial discrimination on the international stage. Advocates needed access to the United Nations in order to present their argument to its membership.

Black advocates for equality under law viewed the United Nations as an appropriate forum for their grievances against the United States. Soilders who had fought to free Europe were met with unfettered hostility in the United States. Congress refused to pass antilynching legislation and the states would not prosecute Whites who attacked Blacks. In 1946, a Black veteran in Louisiana was partially dismembered, castrated, and burned with a blow-torch for refusing to give a White man a war memento.[94] It was the third failed attempt to enact antilynching legislation that led the National Negro Congress to seek assistance from the United Nations. The organization presented a document titled, "The Petition to the United Nations on Behalf of 13 Million Oppressed Negro Citizens of the United States of America," which set forth the lynching, racial segregation, disfranchisement, and economic oppression suffered by Blacks in America.[95] The petition presented the dates, facts, and crimes against Blacks to the OHCHR.

America was appalled. As Cold War tensions grew between the Soviet bloc countries and democratic countries led by the United States, the United States demanded a patriotic front for the international critics. The leadership of the NAACP and other Black organizations believed that their compliance would gain much needed federal support for antilynching legislation. However, the National Negro Congress would not comply with America's hypocrisy. Instead, the group pressed the United Nations to respond to its petition of grievances. When the U.N.'s Human Rights Commission requested additional evidence, America retaliated by labeling the National Negro Congress a Communist organization.

The stigma and forced "patriotism" among Blacks undermined any efforts of the National Negro Congress to garner widespread support for petition.[96] Financial support dwindled. Conflicts within the organization caused the congress to disband before it could provide the additional evidence requested by the Commission on Human Rights.[97] However, the organization's petition and the idea of alerting the world to lynching in America was taken up by the Civil Rights Congress and the NAACP.[98]

An Appeal to the World

Walter White, then president of the NAACP, W. E. B. DuBois, attorneys Robert Carter and Thurgood Marshall, and experts in sociology worked on a separate NAACP petition titled *An Appeal to the World*.[99] However, Eleanor Roosevelt, widow of the late President Franklin Delano Roosevelt and a member of the NAACP board of directors, was displeased with the organization's plan to expose America's horrendous treatment of Blacks to the world. Mrs. Roosevelt was known as a strong supporter of equal rights for Blacks and a member of the U.S. delegation to the United Nations. Given the Cold War, Mrs. Roosevelt refused to support the NAACP's *An Appeal to the World*, which laid bare the truth of racial hostilities in America.[100]

In 1948, members of the United Nations adopted the Convention on the Prevention and Punishment of the Crime of Genocide[101] and it was entered into force September 8, 1951. Under this treaty, certain acts are punishable as crimes of genocide under international law, including:

> [W]illful killing, torture or inhumane treatment, including biological experiments, willfully causing great suffering or serious injury to body or health, unlawful deportation or transfer or unlawful confinement of a protected person, compelling a protected person to serve in the forces of a hostile Power, or willfully depriving a protected person of

the rights of fair and regular trial prescribed in the present Convention, taking of hostages and extensive destruction and appropriation of property, not justified by military necessity and carried out unlawfully and wantonly.

This convention can be enforced by an international tribunal or a national court within the state committing the breach.[102] The devastation of World War II led to the adoption of such international human rights laws.

The vast majority of human rights laws are based on treaties. Treaties are agreements signed and ratified by nations. Upon signing a treaty agreement, the nation or state is bound by its terms. The Constitution addresses the role of treaties in Article 6:

> This Constitution, and the laws of the United States which shall be made in pursuance thereof; and all treaties made, or which shall be made, under the authority of the United States, shall be the supreme law of the land; and the judges in every state shall be bound thereby, anything in the Constitution or laws of any State to the contrary notwithstanding.[103]

This provision of the Constitution is referred to as the "supremacy clause." Ratifying a treaty requires a vote by the U.S. Congress and the signature of the president. Only then is the country bound by the terms of the treaty. The U.S. government chose not to ratify the Genocide Treaty until decades later.[104]

On December 10, 1948, the General Assembly of the United Nations adopted the Universal Declaration of Human Rights.[105] Eleanor Roosevelt played a pivotal role in the drafting of the Declaration of Human Rights.[106] International human rights law recognizes that all peoples have basic rights. The U.N. Declaration of Human Rights provides that:

> Article 4
>
> No one shall be held in slavery or servitude; slavery and the slave trade shall be prohibited in all their forms.
>
> Article 5
>
> No one shall be subjected to torture or to cruel, inhuman or degrading treatment or punishment.

Article 7

All are equal before the law and are entitled without any discrimination to equal protection of the law. All are entitled to equal protection
against any discrimination in violation of this Declaration and against
any incitement to such discrimination.[107]

These articles are the foundation of international human rights law.[108]

However, the words of the Universal Declaration of Human Rights
or the U.S. Constitution meant little to the Blacks in America deprived
of justice, opportunities, and equality and murdered with impunity by
lynch mobs. DuBois attempted several times to have the wanton murder
of Blacks placed before the world with the hope of ending lynching in
America. However, neither the Commission on Human Rights nor the
Universal Declaration of Human Rights has enforcement powers. International pressure on the United States was evident in President Harry
Truman's decision to create a committee on civil rights and publish its
report, *To Secure These Rights*.[109] The report was an effort to appease world
opinion critical of America's foreign policy touting democracy while segregation and terrorism of Blacks reigned domestically.[110]

Restricting Travel: *Kent v. Dulles*

The Cold War and fear of being labeled as Communists forced Blacks
to limit protest about lynching. Blacks were pressured to remain silent
about segregation and racial oppression.[111] Paul Robeson, internationally
renowned singer, actor, and scholar, chose to speak out about the oppression of Blacks in America. He and other Blacks, such as Josephine Baker
and W. E. B. DuBois, were labeled anti-American, investigated, and
harassed.[112] Denial of a passport prevented Robeson from traveling outside the country.[113] In 1957, the Supreme Court decided *Kent v. Dulles*.[114]
The U.S. State Department had unfairly classified Robeson's activism as
a threat to national security and rescinded his passport. At the same time,
the State Department drafted Blacks such as attorney Edith Sampson to
counter the international pressure by minimizing lynching.[115]

In the *Kent* case, Rockwell Kent initiated an action against Secretary of State John Foster Dulles.[116] Kent challenged a law promulgated by the State Department that denied a passport to anyone

with an affiliation with the Communist Party.[117] At the time, the federal government required a passport to travel outside the United States. The McCarran–Walter Act, Internal Security Act of 1950, Taft–Hartley Act, and Smith Act were used to restrict the rights of suspected Communists. Under these acts, the interest of national security required anyone considered a Communist to be prevented from receiving a U.S. passport.[118]

The United States twisted Robeson's advocacy for racial justice into un-American acts and promotion of Communism. Under the law, Communists were defined as[119]

(b) Persons, regardless of the formal state of their affiliation with the Communist Party, who engage in activities which support the Communist movement under such circumstances as to warrant the conclusion—not otherwise rebutted by the evidence—that they have engaged in such activities as a result of direction, domination, or control exercised over them by the Communist movement

(c) Persons, regardless of the formal state of their affiliation with the Communist Party, as to whom there is reason to believe, on the balance of all the evidence, that they are going abroad to engage in activities which will advance the Communist movement for the purpose, knowingly and willfully of advancing that movement.

Robeson had visited the Soviet Union in search of a country that did not brutalize Black people. The trial court agreed with the government, referring to *Korematsu v. United States*, which allowed the government to restrict the movement of Japanese citizens during World War II.[120] But, the United States was not engaged in a declared war when Robeson's passport was seized.

On appeal, the U.S. Supreme Court ruled that the right to domestic and foreign travel is a fundamental freedom.[121] The secretary of state did not have authority to restrict freedom of travel based on beliefs or associations.[122] The decision in *Kent v. Dulles* reinstated the passports of Paul Robeson and others. However, in Robeson's case, justice delayed was justice denied. By the time of the Court's decision in 1957, Robeson was suffering from several medical problems and his international career was devastated beyond recovery.

DuBois supported the Civil Rights Congress's petition, *We Charge Genocide*, and pressed to place *An Appeal to the World* on the agenda of the United Nations.[123] Eleanor Roosevelt once again threatened to resign from the board of the NAACP.[124] To appease Roosevelt, DuBois, scholar and a founder of the organization, was terminated from the NAACP.[125] The larger issue of the Cold War was deemed more important than the domestic issues affecting the lives of generations of Blacks in America.[126] However, the strategy of placing the treatment of Blacks in America on a world stage was not lost.

In 1951, in the midst of heightened Cold War tensions between the United States and the Soviet Union, a document presenting evidence of lynching, economic oppression, political disfranchisement, and racial segregation of Blacks was presented to the United Nations. Activist and artist Paul Robeson accompanied William L. Patterson of the Civil Rights Congress. The petition delivered to the U.N. office in New York is titled *We Charge Genocide: The Crime of Government against the Negro People.*[127] With it, the issue of lynching finally reached the world stage.

We Charge Genocide

We Charge Genocide substantiated charges of inhumanity with facts obtained by the NAACP, placing the evidence within the terms and meaning of the Genocide Convention of the United Nations.[128] One section of the petition stated:

> The policy of non-enforcement of basic American constitutional law, written and passed to protect the Negro people, has become a legal authorization of genocide. It is the enabling act for genocide. It is the foundation for segregation and other discriminatory practices in law and by the courts. Non-enforcement of the Fourteenth Amendment of the Constitution of the United States, which guarantees the Negro people "due process of law" and "equal treatment before the laws," obviously incites genocide. Non-enforcement as a matter of cardinal policy of the Civil Rights Act also drafted and passed notification that the Negro people have no rights that will be protected by the Government of the United States.[129]

However, the United Nations did not act on the petition because the United States was not a signatory to the Genocide Treaty.[130] That treaty was not signed by the United States due to a fear by the Department of State and some Southern politicians that Blacks would indeed access the United Nations and utilize the Genocide Treaty to enact federal antilynching legislation.[131]

However, international pressure caused by the petition affected U.S. laws and policies. Upon reading the petitions of the Civil Rights Congress and the NAACP, America's foreign policy of advocating freedom abroad and denying basic human rights to Blacks was highly criticized by the international community.[132] Staving off international criticism of America's "Jim Crow" policies provided a catalyst for the *Brown v. Topeka Board of Education* decision in 1954 desegregating public schools, among other civil rights efforts.[133] The U.S. Supreme Court held in *Brown* that racially segregated public schools were inherently unequal.[134] The manner in which civil rights advocates utilized the United Nations in the 1950s evidences its power as a vehicle for justice and social change, especially in addressing domestic issues such as race discrimination and minority rights.[135]

Treaties against Racism: Covenant
on the Elimination of All Forms
of Racial Discrimination

The twentieth century bore witness to the independence of African countries from European colonial rule. As Africa gained its sovereignty, those nation-states applied for admission to the United Nations. Between 1951 and 1968, thirty-eight African countries gained their independence from the rule of France, Britain, Portugal, Spain, and Belgium. At present, there are 191 member-states in the United Nations.[136] Just as the horrific events of World War II led to the development of the Universal Declaration of Human Rights and the Genocide Convention, the inclusion of newly independent African countries led to United Nations conventions on racial discrimination and minority rights.

In adopting the International Convention on the Elimination of All Forms of Racial Discrimination, the United Nations General Assembly set forth specific measures that states agree to undertake once the treaty is ratified. The Convention on the Elimination of All Forms of Racial Discrimination was enacted in 1965.[137] Under the convention, states' parties pledged:

to engage in no act or practice of racial discrimination against individuals, groups of persons, or institutions and to ensure that public authorities and institutions do likewise; not to sponsor, defend or support racial discrimination by persons or organizations

to review government, national, and local policies and to amend or repeal laws and regulations that create or perpetuate racial discrimination

to prohibit and put a stop to racial discrimination by persons, groups, and organizations

to encourage integrationist or multiracial organizations and movements and other means of eliminating barriers between races, as well as to discourage anything that tends to strengthen racial division

Afterwards, the U.N. General Assembly created the Committee on the Elimination of Racial Discrimination (CERD) to oversee the convention.[138]

CERD was the first body created by the United Nations to monitor and review actions by states to fulfill their obligations under a specific human rights agreement. CERD reviews the legal, judicial, administrative, and other steps taken by individual states to fulfill their obligations to combat racial discrimination. All states that ratify or accede to the convention must submit periodic reports to CERD. States may file complaints against another state. An individual or a group of persons who allege racial discrimination may lodge a complaint with CERD against their state. The United States signed the Convention for the Elimination of Racial Discrimination in 1966 and ratified the treaty in 1994.[139]

However, the United States included declarations and reservations to the treaty that limit its effectiveness by tying it to American constitutional case law.[140] Remedies under the treaty, such as reparations or affirmative action, are precluded if they conflict with U.S. Supreme Court precedent. To further restrict implementation in the United States, the convention's provisions are not self-executing, meaning that the United States must agree to accept litigation against it. Members of the U.S. Supreme Court have recognized that the convention could be quite beneficial to race issues in the

United States. In *Grutter v. Bollinger*, where an affirmative action program at the University of Michigan was attacked as "reverse discrimination," Justices Ruth Bader Ginsburg and Stephen Breyer recognized that the convention supported an affirmative action policy. The justices stated:

> The International Convention on the Elimination of All Forms of Racial Discrimination, ratified by the United States in 1994,...endorses "special and concrete measures to ensue the adequate development and protection of certain racial groups or individuals belonging to them, for the purpose of guaranteeing them the full and equal enjoyment of human rights and fundamental freedoms."[141]

The affirmative action policy of the law school was upheld by the Court.[142]

In addition to the Universal Declaration of Human Rights and the International Convention on the Elimination of All Forms of Racial Discrimination, other treaties comprise international human rights law:

- the International Covenant on Civil and Political Rights, enacted in 1966[143]
- the International Covenant on Economic, Social and Cultural Rights, enacted in 1966[144]
- the Convention on the Elimination of All Forms of Discrimination against Women, enacted in 1979[145]
- the Convention against Torture and Other Cruel, Inhuman or Degrading Treatment or Punishment, enacted in 1984[146]
- the Convention on the Rights of the Child, enacted in 1989[147]
- the International Convention on the Protection of the Rights of All Migrant Workers and Members of Their Families, enacted in 1990

As of this writing, the United States has yet to ratify the Convention on the Elimination of All Forms of Discrimination against Women and the Convention on the Rights of the Child.

International Tribunals

The charter of the United Nations gives the U.N. Security Council the power and responsibility to take collective action to maintain international peace and security.[148] For this reason, the international community looks to the Security Council to authorize peacekeeping operations. Most of these operations are established and implemented by the United Nations with troops serving under U.N. operational command. In other cases, the Council may authorize regional organizations such as the North Atlantic Treaty Organization, the Economic Community of West African States, or coalitions of willing countries to implement certain peacekeeping or peace enforcement functions.

In the 1980s, attacks by Serbs against Croats and Muslims in Yugoslavia led to civil war, mass killing, and allegations of ethnic cleansing. During the course of the conflict, over forty thousand persons were killed. In 1993, the U.N. Security Council established the International Criminal Tribunal for the Former Yugoslavia (ICTY) for the prosecution of persons responsible for serious violations of international humanitarian law committed in the territory of the former Yugoslavia since 1991.[149] The ICTY represents a significant development in international criminal law because, under its charter, governments as well as military leaders are individually liable for war crimes against civilian populations. This modern-day criminal law tribunal is based on the ideals of the Nuremberg Tribunal created in 1945.

In Rwanda, a country the size of the state of Vermont, nearly one million Tutsi were murdered in an act of genocide by Hutus. The massacre took place in 1994. That year, the U.N. Security Council established the International Criminal Tribunal for Rwanda (ICTR), located in Arusha, Tanzania, for the prosecution of persons responsible for genocide or other serious violations of international humanitarian law committed in the territory of Rwanda and Rwandan citizens responsible for genocide and other such violations committed in the territory of neighboring states, between January 1, 1994, and December 31, 1994.[150] Unlike Yugoslavia, which opposed the intervention of an international criminal tribunal, Rwanda supported the opportunity to try those who participated before international adjudicators.[151] With increased awareness of sexual assault as a weapon of war, the ICTR and ICTY charter provisions recognize rape as a crime of genocide. Civilians as well as military leaders are within the jurisdiction of ICTR.[152]

In 1991, an attempted coup supported by paramilitary forces from Liberia led to attacks on civilians and soldiers who supported the standing government in Sierra Leone. Crimes of murder, torture, mutilation, and burned villages were committed against tens of thousands of civilians during this civil war.[153] In 2002, the United Nations assisted in the creation of the Special Court for Sierra Leone to adjudicate crimes against humanity taking place in Sierra Leone after 1996. The special court has jurisdiction to hear allegations of international violations against humanity, Common Article 3 of the Geneva Conventions and Additional Protocol II, crimes against peacekeepers, and the recruitment of children, as well as violations of local Sierra Leone laws.[154] However, rape does not fall within its jurisdiction. A defendant may receive a prison sentence or the death penalty.

During the final battles of the Vietnam War, the Khmer Rouge, a political and military movement, rose to power in Cambodia. Led by Pol Pot, the Khmer Rouge executed elites, intellectuals, and certain ethnic groups using murder, scientific experimentation, forced labor, and torture.[155] Between 1975 and 1979, an estimated two million lives were lost and millions more were displaced.[156] Evidence of these crimes against humanity was received as early as 1979. Decades passed. Given the lapse of time, there was uncertainty as to whether the Khmer Rouge would ever be brought to justice. Pol Pot was finally tried by a national court and condemned to death. He was sentenced to life in prison after a subsequent trial that was viewed by many as procedurally flawed, thus renewing efforts for an international tribunal.[157]

In 2003, after years of negotiation, the United Nations and Cambodia signed an agreement establishing the Extraordinary Chambers in the Courts of Cambodia for Prosecution of Crimes Committed during the Period of Democratic Kampuchea. The Extraordinary Chambers will be a national tribunal financed by donor pledges from U.N. member-states placed in a trust fund. Due process is based on the Cambodian system, which has a death penalty. In sum, the

Extraordinary Chambers is unique in that it will be a national tribunal created in collaboration with the United Nations. The effectiveness of this tribunal will largely depend on the abilities of the Cambodian jurists, prosecutors, and investigators as well as the cooperation of the Cambodian government.

The International Criminal Court was established in 1998.[158] The Rome Treaty is the result of decades of international diplomacy and tragic inhumanity. The convention, held in Rome, Italy, led to enactment of the Rome Statute, which created the International Criminal Court. Previous criminal tribunals were ad hoc or temporary. The International Criminal Court is the first permanent criminal court to adjudicate crimes against humanity, genocide, and war crimes.[159] The Rome Statute entered into force in 2002 when the requisite states ratified the treaty. The jurisdiction of the International Criminal Court is complementary to national criminal courts; it does not usurp the powers of national domestic courts.[160] Complaints brought before the International Criminal Court cannot be brought before national courts. The creation of the International Criminal Court provides the international military and civilian communities with a legal standard for moral conduct during war and civil conflict.[161] The initial case before the court was filed by Uganda. The United States declined to ratify the Rome Treaty, which would have given the international criminal court jurisdiction over complaints involving international crimes in the United States and allegations against America's actions abroad.

Abolitionists and civil rights advocates understood the importance of world opinion. In the struggle for justice under law, international pressure proved a viable tool for changing domestic conditions. International human rights laws evolved over the last century. Disparaged in its early stages, the United Nations is still viewed by many as an unwelcome intruder on the integrity of a nation-state's sovereignty. War and conflict continue despite the United Nations and its Universal Declaration of Human Rights. However, the world situation would be made worse for its absence.

Presently, the Human Rights Commission of the United Nations receives requests for intervention on issues such as racial, ethnic, and criminal justice. The Convention on the Elimination of Race Discrimination, of which the United States is a member, requires each member-state to provide a progress report. Nongovernmental organizations may submit informational material to the commission. Yet, the United Nations remains a sporadically utilized tool of advocates for racial equality and social justice. Heavy reliance on the American justice system and an unquestioned patriotism may be at the center of the reluctance to access the international arena.

Present-Day Vestiges: Exported U.S. Racism

Television, movies, and books have transmitted American racism to the world. America's popular culture has been exported to even the smallest nation. America's racism has been exported, as well. The socioracial hierarchy that attempts to relegate Blacks to the bottom tier has seeped into the social fabric of other nations. On May 13, 2005, Vicente Fox, president of Mexico, gave a speech to Texas business owners in a resort hotel. In that speech, Fox hoped to persuade the audience members to support more conducive immigration policy for Mexican workers who wished to migrate to the United States.

Speaking in Spanish, President Fox said, "There is no doubt that Mexicans, filled with dignity, willingness and ability to work, are doing jobs that not even blacks want to do there in the United States."[162] His speech was meant to criticize the proposed U.S. immigration policies that would limit legal immigration from Mexico and deport illegal immigrants living in the United States. In making his comment, the president of Mexico embraced America's racial hierarchy and with it the presumption that Blacks must take the lowliest tasks.

The "Sambo" character is visible in various forms around the world. Mexico was criticized for publishing a national postage stamp featuring Sambo.[163] Japanese and Korean bands feature singers in blackface Sambo make-up as caricatures of Black Americans. In Italy, to work hard is to work "like a n----r." Transmitted internationally over decades, racism specifically maligning American Blacks unfortunately continues to spread. Therefore, challenges to American racism must extend beyond the borders of the United States.

In the face of these racist episodes, for many Blacks in America, the discrimination abroad is not comparable to the intransigence of racism at home. As in centuries past, debates rage over emigrating to another country. As others immigrate to the United States from Africa and the Caribbean, American Blacks remain in search of their "America." International travel provides temporary respite from America's dual standards. Frustrated Blacks can also choose to leave the United States and build lives elsewhere.[164] While expatriot status undermines the investment of generations of Blacks who fought on behalf of this country and died seeking their part of it, every émigré arriving on American shores has left behind generations of investment in a homeland abroad.

There is no utopia. Discrimination can be found in myriad forms and places near and far. However, given White America's desire to cling to an antiquated socioracial hierarchy, a dialogue on opportunities elsewhere is more than warranted. For Blacks, such a discussion is as appropriate today as it was two centuries ago.

Afterword

Power concedes nothing without demand. It never has and it never will.

Frederick Douglass

The problem of the new millennium remains the color line. That being said, researching and writing this book has been cathartic, intellectually and emotionally. There were many nights working alone in my office when the brutal facts of these cases became overwhelming. I was moved by a mixture of wonder and pride that people of color could continue despite the resistance that met their every move. Sometimes, outrage and indignation forced me to walk away. Yet, I returned to this work, sometimes grudgingly, because these stories needed to be told. In the end, I am a mere witness to the tenacity of spirit demonstrated by generation after generation of Black people in America.

Derrick Bell's foreword to this book speaks of a student's perspective on race in America. I, too, have a student's story to recall. My student assistants and I often discussed race issues while working on this book. Their intensity and compassion prevented me from becoming numb to the debacle made of the rule of law when applied to minorities in America. Nor did I want ever to treat racism with some antiseptic disconnection for the sake of self-protection. I know racism to be a live mutating organism that must be watched with a vigilant eye.

The viciousness of racism is most evident in the acts of a lynch mob. Our discussion was silenced by the photographs of hanging Black corpses surrounded by smiling White faces. One student, Amikar Herbert, turned to me and said, "White people don't want Blacks to have anything. Not even our lives." His statement started a discussion of race relations during slavery and afterward. Black life remained undervalued. We parted that evening pledging to remember the resilience of generations past, so essential to Black advancement then, as we confront obstacles to achievement today. But, I was drawn back to those photographs and the desperation to maintain a racial hierarchy that would motivate such savage acts. The law played an implicit role in each racist crime. For the law condoned murder with impunity as long as the murder victims were people of color. Justice came, albeit decades later, for murder victim Medgar Evers. But, for the Black men hanging from the trees in those photographs and their White murderers, justice died with them and the consequences of those brutal acts still linger in American society.

The burden is on all Americans to remove racial discrimination from the justice system. The disproportionate number of Blacks in prison is injustice at work. We may just as well take photographs of smiling White politicians and policymakers standing next to Black prisoners. Tragic events, gross incarceration rates, police brutality, undereducated children, and disenfranchised voters are accepted because the protagonists are Black, Asian, or Latino. It is assumed that bad things are supposed to happen to "those" people. The racial hierarchy dictates that if anyone should be in a position of vulnerability, then people of color, especially Blacks, are the likely candidates.

Why? Simply because at one point in this country's history Blacks had the least political and economic power. American society grew accustomed to this hierarchy. The Court in *Brown v. Board of Topeka* addressed segregation's badge of inferiority on Blacks. However, what of the illusion of superiority embraced by Whites in a segregated society? Far too many Whites continue to invest in this racial hierarchy. If one presumes Blacks are supposed to be at the bottom of the socioeconomic ladder, then anything they possess must be of lesser value than the Whites. Therefore, Blacks must earn less income than Whites. Their houses must be of lesser value. Blacks are presumed to be less educated and then require less education. They should be relegated to manual labor or, at least, not a supervisory position over Whites. They are presumed to be more culpable than Whites. Therefore, if Blacks have more, the social equilibrium is askew.

These presumptions buttress legal realities that, when challenged, are adjudicated using laws enacted under the same presumptions. New arrivals to this country seek a place above Blacks to prove they are truly "White" or American. If Blacks appear to be rising socially, economically, or politically, then they must be put back down in their "place." When Blacks have achieved more, such as in Tulsa, Oklahoma, or Rosewood, Florida, or the myriad examples across America from the time of slavery to present, a backlash of reprisal wiped the slate clean of those accomplishments. American history has denied achievements by Blacks. For what is the value of Whiteness when Blacks achieve parity? Would acknowledging the humanity of Black people expose the core flaws in American democracy? For how could this country maintain the duality?

American foreign policymakers chide other nations for their inability to accept modernity. However, America has failed to accept racial modernity. Despite poorly funded schools, crime traps, and restricted choices, Blacks have risen and continue to rise beyond social prediction. This book presented America's legal history as a tool from which we all may learn, as opposed to a place to dwell. Racial justice rides a continuum that ebbs and flows with urgency for betterment. The countless heroes and heroines of these cases thrust themselves in harm's way on behalf of freedom and American ideals. Their courage was an investment in a better society for all of us. We can ill afford to be reckless heirs.

What do we do now? Blacks must continue to rise. The litigants and victims in the preceding chapters faced opponents far greater than any foe within the present generation. To rise from slavery under law, to challenge Supreme Court-sanctioned segregation, to then defeat *de facto* segregation and remain standing is an historic feat. This is merely a glimpse into an epic story. I remain honored to have had the privilege of telling this one small part of it. The quest to remove present-day vestiges of slavery and the *Plessy* decision is before us. I am reminded of Fannie Lou Hamer who said, "The question for black people is not, when is the white man going to give us our rights, or when is he going to give us good education for our children, or when is he going to give us jobs."[1] Thus, it is time to reaffirm our conviction and obligation to achieve full racial justice under law despite any and all obstacles. We are the leaders for whom we have been waiting.[2]

Appendix A.1: Selected Decisions of the U.S. Supreme Court

Plessy v. Ferguson
(excerpt)
163 U.S. 537 (1896)

JUSTICE BROWN delivered the opinion of the court.

The petition for the writ of prohibition averred that petitioner was seven eighths Caucasian and one eighth African blood; that the mixture of colored blood was not discernible in him, and that he was entitled to every right, privilege and immunity secured to citizens of the United States of the white race; and that, upon such theory, he took possession of a vacant seat in a coach where passengers of the white race were accommodated, and was ordered by the conductor to vacate said coach and take a seat in another assigned to persons of the colored race, and having refused to comply with such demand he was forcibly ejected with the aid of a police officer, and imprisoned in the parish jail to answer a charge of having violated the above act.

A statute which implies merely a legal distinction between the white and colored races—a distinction which is founded in the color of the two races, and which must always exist so long as white men are distinguished from the other race by color—has no tendency to destroy the legal equality of the two races, or reestablish a state of involuntary servitude. Indeed, we do not understand that the Thirteenth Amendment is strenuously relied upon by the plaintiff in error in this connection.

The object of the amendment was undoubtedly to enforce the absolute equality of the two races before the law, but in the nature of things it could not have been intended to abolish distinctions based upon color, or to enforce social, as distinguished from political equality, or a commingling of the two races upon terms unsatisfactory to either.

One of the earliest of these cases is that of *Roberts v. City of Boston*, 5 Cush. 198, in which the Supreme Judicial Court of Massachusetts held that the general school committee of Boston had power to make provision for the instruction of colored children.

It is claimed by the plaintiff in error that, in any mixed community, the reputation of belonging to the dominant race, in this instance the white race, is property, in the same sense that a right of action, or of inheritance, is property. Conceding this to be so, for the purposes of this case, we are unable to see how this statute deprives him of, or in any way affects his right to, such property. If he be a white man and assigned to a colored coach, he may have his action for damages against the company for being deprived of his so called property. Upon the other hand, if he be a colored man and be so assigned, he has been deprived of no property, since he is not lawfully entitled to the reputation of being a white man.

So far, then, as a conflict with the Fourteenth Amendment is concerned, the case reduces itself to the question whether the statute of Louisiana is a reasonable regulation, and with respect to this there must necessarily be a large discretion on the part of the legislature. In determining the question of reasonableness it is at liberty to act with reference to the established usages, customs and traditions of the people, and with a view to the promotion of their comfort, and the preservation of the public peace and good order. Gauged by this standard, we cannot say that a law which authorizes or even requires the separation of the two races in public conveyances is unreasonable, or more obnoxious to the Fourteenth Amendment than the acts of Congress requiring separate schools for colored children in the District of Columbia, the constitutionality of which does not seem to have been questioned, or the corresponding acts of state legislatures.

We consider the underlying fallacy of the plaintiff's argument to consist in the assumption that the enforced separation of the two races stamps the colored race with a badge of inferiority. If this be so, it is not by reason of anything found in the act, but solely because the colored race chooses to put that construction upon it. The argument necessarily assumes that if, as has been more than once the case, and is not unlikely to be so again, the colored race should become the dominant power in the state legislature, and should enact a law in precisely similar terms, it would thereby relegate the white race to an inferior position. We imagine that the white race, at least, would not acquiesce in this assumption. The argument also assumes that social prejudices may be overcome by legislation, and that equal rights cannot be secured to the negro except by an enforced commingling of the two races. We cannot accept this proposition. If the two races are to meet upon terms of social equality, it must be the result of natural affinities, a mutual appreciation of each other's merits and a voluntary consent of individuals.

The judgment of the court below is, therefore,

Affirmed.

JUSTICE HARLAN dissenting.

The white race deems itself to be the dominant race in this country. And so it is, in prestige, in achievements, in education, in wealth and in power. So, I doubt not, it will continue to be for all time, if it remains true to its great heritage and holds fast to the principles of constitutional liberty. But in view of the Constitution, in the eye of the law, there is in this country no superior, dominant, ruling class of citizens. There is no caste here. Our Constitution is color-blind, and neither knows nor tolerates classes among citizens. In respect of civil rights, all citizens are equal before the law. The humblest is the peer of the most powerful. The law regards man as man, and takes no account of his surroundings or of his color when his civil rights as guaranteed by the supreme law of the land are involved. It is, therefore, to be regretted that this high tribunal, the final expositor of the fundamental law of the land, has reached the conclusion that it is competent for a State to regulate the enjoyment by citizens of their civil rights solely upon the basis of race.

In my opinion, the judgment this day rendered will, in time, prove to be quite as pernicious as the decision made by this tribunal in the *Dred Scott* case. It was adjudged in that case that the descendants of Africans who were imported into this country and sold as slaves were not included nor intended to be included under the word "citizens" in the Constitution, and could not claim any of the rights and privileges which that instrument provided for and secured to citizens of the United States; that at the time of the adoption of the Constitution they were "considered as a subordinate and inferior class of beings, who had been subjugated by the dominant race, and, whether emancipated or not, yet remained subject to their authority, and had no rights or privileges but such as those who held the power and the government might choose to grant them." 19 How. 393, 404. The recent amendments of the Constitution, it was supposed, had eradicated these principles from our institutions. But it seems that we have yet, in some of the States, a dominant race—a superior class of citizens, which assumes to regulate the enjoyment of civil rights, common to all citizens, upon the basis of race. The present decision, it may well be apprehended, will not only stimulate aggressions, more or less brutal and irritating, upon the admitted rights of colored citizens, but will encourage the belief that it is possible, by means of state enactments, to defeat the beneficent purposes which the people of the United States had in view when they adopted the recent amendments of the Constitution, by one of which the blacks of this country were made citizens of the United States and of the States in which they respectively reside, and whose privileges and immunities, as citizens, the States are forbidden to abridge. Sixty millions of whites are in no danger from the presence here of eight millions of blacks. The destinies of the two races, in this country, are indissolubly linked together, and the interests of both require that the common government of all shall not permit the seeds of race hate to be planted under the sanction of law. What can more certainly arouse race hate, what more certainly create and perpetuate a feeling of distrust between these races, than state enactments, which, in fact, proceed on the ground that colored citizens are so inferior and degraded that they cannot be allowed to sit in public coaches occupied by white citizens? That, as all will admit, is the real meaning of such legislation as was enacted in Louisiana.

The sure guarantee of the peace and security of each race is the clear, distinct, unconditional recognition by our governments, National and State, of every right that inheres in civil freedom, and of the equality before the law of all citizens of the United States without regard to race. State enactments, regulating the enjoyment of civil rights, upon the basis of race, and cunningly devised to defeat legitimate results of the war, under the pretence of recognizing equality of rights, can have no other result than to render permanent peace impossible, and to keep alive a conflict of races, the continuance of which must do harm to all concerned.

There is a race so different from our own that we do not permit those belonging to it to become citizens of the United States. Persons belonging to it are, with few exceptions, absolutely excluded from our country. I allude to the Chinese race. But by the statute in question, a Chinaman can ride in the same passenger coach with white citizens of the United States, while citizens of the black race in Louisiana, many of whom, perhaps, risked their lives for the preservation of the Union, who are entitled, by law, to participate in the political control of the State and nation, who are not excluded, by law or by reason of their race, from public stations of any kind, and who have all the legal rights that belong to white citizens, are yet declared to be criminals, liable to imprisonment, if they ride in a public coach occupied by citizens of the white race. It is scarcely just to say that a colored citizen should not object to occupying a public coach assigned to his own race. He does not object, nor, perhaps, would he object to separate coaches for his race, if his rights under the law were recognized. But he objects, and ought never to cease objecting to the proposition, that citizens of the white and black races can be adjudged criminals because they sit, or claim the right to sit, in the same public coach on a public highway.

The arbitrary separation of citizens, on the basis of race, while they are on a public highway, is a badge of servitude wholly inconsistent with the civil freedom and the equality before the law established by the Constitution.

I am of opinion that the statute of Louisiana is inconsistent with the personal liberty of citizens, white and black, in that State, and hostile to both the spirit and letter of the Constitution of the United States. If laws of like character should be enacted in the several States of the Union, the effect would be in the highest degree mischievous. Slavery, as an institution tolerated by law would, it is true, have disappeared from our country, but there would remain a power in the States, by sinister legislation, to interfere with the full enjoyment of the blessings of freedom; to regulate civil rights, common to all citizens, upon the basis of race; and to place in a condition of legal inferiority a large body of American citizens, now constituting a part of the political community called the People of the United States, for whom, and by whom through representatives, our government is administered. Such a system is inconsistent with the guarantee given by the Constitution to each State of a republican form of government, and may be stricken down by Congressional action, or by the courts in the discharge of their solemn duty to maintain the supreme law of the land, anything in the constitution or laws of any State to the contrary notwithstanding.

For the reasons stated, I am constrained to withhold my assent from the opinion and judgment of the majority.

JUSTICE BREWER did not hear the argument or participate in the decision of this case.

Appendix A.2: Selected Decisions of the U.S. Supreme Court

Brown v. Board of Education of Topeka (I)
347 U.S. 483 (1954)

CHIEF JUSTICE WARREN delivered the opinion of the Court.

These cases come to us from the States of Kansas, South Carolina, Virginia, and Delaware. They are premised on different facts and different local conditions, but a common legal question justifies their consideration together in this consolidated opinion.

In each of the cases, minors of the Negro race, through their legal representatives, seek the aid of the courts in obtaining admission to the public schools of their community on a nonsegregated basis. In each instance, they had been denied admission to schools attended by white children under laws requiring or permitting segregation according to race. This segregation was alleged to deprive the plaintiffs of the equal protection of the laws under the Fourteenth Amendment. In each of the cases other than the Delaware case, a three-judge federal district court denied relief to the plaintiffs on the so-called "separate but equal" doctrine announced by this Court in *Plessy v. Ferguson*, 163 U.S. 537. Under that doctrine, equality of treatment is accorded when the races are provided substantially equal facilities, even though these facilities be separate. In the Delaware case, the Supreme Court of Delaware adhered to that doctrine, but ordered that the plaintiffs be admitted to the white schools because of their superiority to the Negro schools.

The plaintiffs contend that segregated public schools are not "equal" and cannot be made "equal," and that hence they are deprived of the equal protection of the laws. Because of the obvious importance of the question presented, the Court took jurisdiction. Argument was heard in the 1952 Term, and reargument was heard this Term on certain questions propounded by the Court.

Reargument was largely devoted to the circumstances surrounding the adoption of the Fourteenth Amendment in 1868. It covered exhaustively consideration of the Amendment in Congress, ratification by the states, then existing practices in racial segregation, and the views of proponents and opponents of the Amendment. This discussion and our own investigation convince us that, although these sources cast some light, it is not enough to resolve the problem with which we are faced. At best, they are inconclusive. The most avid proponents of the post-War Amendments undoubtedly intended them to remove all legal distinctions among "all persons born or naturalized in the United States." Their opponents, just as certainly, were antagonistic to both the letter and the spirit of the Amendments and wished them to have the most limited effect. What others in Congress and the state legislatures had in mind cannot be determined with any degree of certainty.

An additional reason for the inconclusive nature of the Amendment's history, with respect to segregated schools, is the status of public education at that time. In the South, the movement toward free common schools, supported by general taxation, had not yet taken hold. Education of white children was largely in the hands of private groups. Education of Negroes was almost nonexistent, and practically all of the race were illiterate. In fact, any education of Negroes was forbidden by law in some states. Today, in contrast, many Negroes have achieved outstanding success in the arts and sciences as well as in the business and professional world. It is true that public school education at the time of the Amendment had advanced further in the North, but the effect of the Amendment on Northern States was generally ignored in the congressional debates. Even in the North, the conditions of public education did not approximate those existing today. The curriculum was usually rudimentary; ungraded schools were common in rural areas; the school term was but three months a year in many states; and compulsory school attendance was virtually unknown. As a consequence, it is not surprising that there should be so little in the history of the Fourteenth Amendment relating to its intended effect on public education.

In the first cases in this Court construing the Fourteenth Amendment, decided shortly after its adoption, the Court interpreted it as proscribing all state-imposed discriminations against the Negro race. The doctrine of "separate but equal" did not make its appearance in this Court until 1896 in the case of *Plessy v. Ferguson*, supra, involving not education but transportation. American courts have since labored with the doctrine for over half a century. In this Court, there have been six cases involving the "separate but equal" doctrine in the field of public education. In *Cumming v. County Board of Education*, 175 U.S. 528, and *Gong Lum v. Rice*, 275 U.S. 78, the validity of the doctrine itself was not challenged. In more recent cases, all on the graduate school level, inequality was found in that specific benefits enjoyed by white students were denied to Negro students of the same educational qualifications. *Missouri ex rel. Gaines v. Canada*, 305 U.S. 337; *Sipuel v. Oklahoma*, 332 U.S. 631; *Sweatt v. Painter*, 339 U.S. 629; *McLaurin v. Oklahoma State Regents*, 339 U.S. 637. In none of these cases was it necessary to re-examine the doctrine to grant relief to the Negro plaintiff. And in *Sweatt v. Painter*, supra, the Court expressly reserved decision on the question whether *Plessy v. Ferguson* should be held inapplicable to public education.

In the instant cases, that question is directly presented. Here, unlike *Sweatt v. Painter*, there are findings below that the Negro and white schools involved have been equalized, or are being equalized, with respect to buildings, curricula, qualifications and salaries of teachers, and other "tangible" factors. Our decision, therefore, cannot turn on merely a comparison of these tangible factors in the Negro and white schools involved in each of the cases. We must look instead to the effect of segregation itself on public education.

In approaching this problem, we cannot turn the clock back to 1868 when the Amendment was adopted, or even to 1896 when *Plessy v. Ferguson* was written. We must consider public education in the light of its full development and its present place in American life throughout the Nation. Only in this way can it be determined if segregation in public schools deprives these plaintiffs of the equal protection of the laws.

Today, education is perhaps the most important function of state and local governments. Compulsory school attendance laws and the great expenditures for education both demonstrate our recognition of the importance of education to our democratic society. It is required in the performance of our most basic public responsibilities, even service in the armed forces. It is the very foundation of good citizenship. Today it is a principal instrument in awakening the child to cultural values, in preparing him for later professional training, and in helping him to adjust normally to his environment. In these days, it is doubtful that any child may reasonably be expected to succeed in life if he is denied the opportunity of an education. Such an opportunity, where the state has undertaken to provide it, is a right which must be made available to all on equal terms.

We come then to the question presented: Does segregation of children in public schools solely on the basis of race, even though the physical facilities and other "tangible" factors may be equal, deprive the children of the minority group of equal educational opportunities? We believe that it does.

In *Sweatt v. Painter*, supra, in finding that a segregated law school for Negroes could not provide them equal educational opportunities, this Court relied in large part on "those qualities which are incapable of objective measurement but which make for greatness in a law school." In *McLaurin v. Oklahoma State Regents*, supra, the Court, in requiring that a Negro admitted to a white graduate school be treated like all other students, again resorted to intangible considerations: "...his ability to study, to engage in discussions and exchange views with other students, and, in general, to learn his profession." Such considerations apply with added force to children in grade and high schools. To separate them from others of similar age and qualifications solely because of their race generates a feeling of inferiority as to their status in the community that may affect their hearts and minds in a way unlikely ever to be undone. The effect of this separation on their educational opportunities was well stated by a finding in the Kansas case by a court which nevertheless felt compelled to rule against the Negro plaintiffs:

> Segregation of white and colored children in public schools has a detrimental effect upon the colored children. The impact is greater when it has the sanction of the law; for the policy of separating the races is usually interpreted as denoting the inferiority of the negro group. A sense of inferiority affects the motivation of a child to learn. Segregation with the sanction of law, therefore, has a tendency to [retard] the

educational and mental development of negro children and to deprive them of some of the benefits they would receive in a racial[ly] integrated school system.

Whatever may have been the extent of psychological knowledge at the time of *Plessy v. Ferguson*, this finding is amply supported by modern authority. Any language in *Plessy v. Ferguson* contrary to this finding is rejected.

We conclude that in the field of public education the doctrine of "separate but equal" has no place. Separate educational facilities are inherently unequal. Therefore, we hold that the plaintiffs and others similarly situated for whom the actions have been brought are, by reason of the segregation complained of, deprived of the equal protection of the laws guaranteed by the Fourteenth Amendment. This disposition makes unnecessary any discussion whether such segregation also violates the Due Process Clause of the Fourteenth Amendment.

Because these are class actions, because of the wide applicability of this decision, and because of the great variety of local conditions, the formulation of decrees in these cases presents problems of considerable complexity. On reargument, the consideration of appropriate relief was necessarily subordinated to the primary question—the constitutionality of segregation in public education. We have now announced that such segregation is a denial of the equal protection of the laws. In order that we may have the full assistance of the parties in formulating decrees, the cases will be restored to the docket, and the parties are requested to present further argument on Questions 4 and 5 previously propounded by the Court for the reargument this Term. The Attorney General of the United States is again invited to participate. The Attorneys General of the states requiring or permitting segregation in public education will also be permitted to appear as amici curiae upon request to do so by September 15, 1954, and submission of briefs by October 1, 1954.

It is so ordered.

Appendix A.3: Selected Decisions of the U.S. Supreme Court

Brown v. Board of Education of Topeka (II)
349 U.S. 294 (1955)

CHIEF JUSTICE WARREN delivered the opinion of the Court.

These cases were decided on May 17, 1954. The opinions of that date, declaring the fundamental principle that racial discrimination in public education is unconstitutional, are incorporated herein by reference. All provisions of federal, state, or local law requiring or permitting such discrimination must yield to this principle. There remains for consideration the manner in which relief is to be accorded.

Because these cases arose under different local conditions and their disposition will involve a variety of local problems, we requested further argument on the question of relief. In view of the nationwide importance of the decision, we invited the Attorney General of the United States and the Attorneys General of all states requiring or permitting racial discrimination in public education to present their views on that question. The parties, the United States, and the States of Florida, North Carolina, Arkansas, Oklahoma, Maryland, and Texas filed briefs and participated in the oral argument.

These presentations were informative and helpful to the Court in its consideration of the complexities arising from the transition to a system of public education freed of racial discrimination. The presentations also demonstrated that substantial steps to eliminate racial discrimination in public schools have already been taken, not only in some of the communities in which these cases arose, but in some of the states appearing as *amici curiae*, and in other states as well. Substantial progress has been made in the District of Columbia and in the communities in Kansas and Delaware involved in this litigation. The defendants in the cases coming to us from South Carolina and Virginia are awaiting the decision of this Court concerning relief.

Full implementation of these constitutional principles may require solution of varied local school problems. School authorities have the primary responsibility for elucidating, assessing, and solving these problems; courts will have to consider whether the action of school authorities constitutes good faith implementation of the governing constitutional principles. Because of their proximity to local conditions and the possible need for further hearings, the courts which originally heard these cases can best perform this judicial appraisal. Accordingly, we believe it appropriate to remand the cases to those courts.

In fashioning and effectuating the decrees, the courts will be guided by equitable principles. Traditionally, equity has been characterized by a practical flexibility in shaping its remedies and by a facility for adjusting and reconciling public and private needs. These cases call for the exercise of these traditional attributes of equity power. At stake is the personal interest of the plaintiffs in admission to public schools as soon as practicable on a nondiscriminatory basis. To effectuate this interest may call for elimination of a variety of obstacles in making the transition to school systems operated in accordance with the constitutional principles set forth in our May 17, 1954, decision. Courts of equity may properly take into account the public interest in the elimination of such obstacles in a systematic and effective manner. But it should go without saying that the vitality of these constitutional principles cannot be allowed to yield simply because of disagreement with them.

While giving weight to these public and private considerations, the courts will require that the defendants make a prompt and reasonable start toward full compliance with our May 17, 1954, ruling. Once such a start has been made, the courts may find that additional time is necessary to carry out the ruling in an effective manner. The burden rests upon the defendants to establish that such time is necessary in the public interest and is consistent with good faith compliance at the earliest practicable date. To that end, the courts may consider problems related to administration, arising from the physical condition of the school plant, the school transportation system, personnel, revision of school districts and attendance areas into compact units to achieve a system of determining admission to the public schools on a non-racial basis, and revision of local laws and regulations which may be necessary in solving the foregoing problems. They will also consider the adequacy of any plans the defendants may propose to meet these problems and to effectuate a transition to a racially nondiscriminatory school system. During this period of transition, the courts will retain jurisdiction of these cases.

The judgments below, except that in the Delaware case, are accordingly reversed and the cases are remanded to the District Courts to take such proceedings and enter such orders and decrees consistent with this opinion as are necessary and proper to admit to public schools on a racially nondiscriminatory basis with all deliberate speed the parties to these cases. The judgment in the Delaware case—ordering the immediate admission of the plaintiffs to schools previously attended only by white children—is affirmed on the basis of the principles stated in our May 17, 1954, opinion, but the case is remanded to the Supreme Court of Delaware for such further proceedings as that Court may deem necessary in light of this opinion.

It is so ordered.

Appendix B: Race Riots in the United States

1739	South Carolina (riots in response to the Black insurrection; also known as the Stono Rebellion)
1741	New York City (riots in response to suspected Black rebellion)
1829	Cincinnati, OH
1863	New York City (also known as the Civil War Draft riots)
1866	Memphis, TN.; New Orleans, LA
1868	New Orleans, LA
1870	Meridian, MS
1874	New Orleans, LA; Vicksburg, MS
1875	Yazoo City, MS
1878	Grant Paris, LA (also known as the Colfax massacre)
1898	Wilmington, NC; Lake City, NC, Greenwood County, SC
1900	New Orleans, LA; New York City
1904	Springfield, OH
1906	Springfield, OH; Greenburg, IN
1906	Brownsville, TX (also known as the Brownsville incident); Atlanta, GA
1908	Springfield, IL
1910	Riots nationwide in response to Jack Johnson's victory over White heavyweight champion
1917	East St. Louis, MO; Houston, TX; Chester, PA
1919	Chicago, IL (twice that year); Gregg County, TX; Washington, DC; Knoxville, TN; Elaine, AK; Longview, TX; Omaha, NB (26 riots nationwide; also known as the Red Summer)
1921	Tulsa, OK (military weapons used against Black civilian population)
1923	Rosewood, FL
1930	Watsonville, CA (Filipinos attacked by Whites)
1935	Harlem, NY

1942   Detroit, MI

1943   St. Louis, MO; Beaumont, TX; Philadelphia, PA; Baltimore, MD; Indianapolis, IN; Washington, D.C.; Harlem, NY; Mobile, AL; Los Angeles, CA; Detroit, MI; Columbia, TN; Los Angeles, CA (Mexicans attacked by White servicemen; also known as the Zoot Suit riots)

1946   Columbia, TN; Athens, AL; Philadelphia, PA

1951   Cicero, IL

1960   Chattanooga, TN; Biloxi, MS; Jacksonville, FL

1962   Mississippi

1964   Harlem, NY; Rochester, NY; Paterson, NJ; Philadelphia, PA; St. Augustine, FL

1965   Los Angeles, CA (also known as the Watts riot)

1966   Los Angeles, CA; Cleveland, OH (also known as the Hough riots)

1967   Newark, NJ

1967   Detroit, MI

1968   Riots nationwide in response to the assassination of Dr. Martin Luther King, Jr.

1969   York, PA

1970   Asbury Park, NJ

1980   Miami, FL

1989   Miami, FL

1992   Los Angeles, CA (also known as the Rodney King riots)

2001   Cincinnati, OH

Appendix C: Persons Lynched, by Race, 1882–1920[*]

YEAR	TOTAL	WHITE	BLACK
1882	113	64	49
1883	130	77	53
1884	211	160	51
1885	184	110	74
1886	138	64	74
1887	120	50	70
1888	137	68	69
1889	170	76	94
1890	96	11	85
1891	184	71	113
1892	230	69	161
1893	152	34	118
1894	192	58	134
1895	179	66	113
1896	123	45	78
1897	158	35	123
1898	120	19	101
1899	106	21	85
1900	15	9	106
1901	130	25	105
1902	92	7	85
1903	99	15	84
1904	83	7	76
1905	62	5	57
1906	65	3	62
1907	60	2	58
1908	97	8	89
1909	82	13	69
1910	76	9	67
1911	67	7	60
1912	63	2	61
1913	52	1	51
1914	55	4	51

[*] There are discrepancies in the number of persons lynched in this time period due primarily to the definition of lynching and the organizations or entities collecting the information. The Tuskegee Institute and the NAACP collected data during overlapping time periods. The federal government did not collect such information on a consistent basis.

YEAR	TOTAL	WHITE	BLACK
1915	69	13	56
1916	54	4	50
1917	38	2	36
1918	64	4	60
1919	83	7	76
1920	61	8	53

Source: United States Series H 1168–1170.

Appendix D: U.S. Military Conflicts*

American Revolutionary War (1776–1783)
War of 1812 (1812–1815)
Mexican War (1846–1848)
Civil War (1861–1865)
Indian Wars (1607–1890)
Spanish American War (1898)
World War I (1917–1918)
World War II (1941–1945)
Korean War (1950–1953)
Vietnam War (1962–1973)
Lebanon (1982–1984)
Grenada (1983)
Panama (1989)
Iraq War I (1990–1991)
Afghanistan (2001–2002)
Iraq War II (2003–ongoing)†

---

* Blacks served honorably in all military actions and also defended the United States in armed conflicts as well as U.N. peace missions not listed here.
† Ongoing as of this writing.

Appendix E: Cases

Adarand Constructors, Inc. v. Pena, 515 U.S. 209 (1995)

Adderley v. Florida, 385 U.S. 39 (1966)

Adickes v. S. H. Kress & Co., 398 U.S. 144 (1970)

Anderson v. Martin, 375 U.S. 399 (1964)

Arlington Heights v. Metropolitan Housing Dev. Corp., 429 U.S. 252 (1977)

Bailey v. Poindexter, 55 Va. 132 (1858)

Baman v. Parker, 348 U.S. 26 (1954)

Bates v. City of Little Rock, 361 U.S. 516 (1960)

Bell et al. v. Maryland, 378 U.S. 226 (1964)

Berea College v. Kentucky, 211 U.S. 45 (1908)

Blyew v. United States, 80 U.S. 581 (1871)

Board of Educ. of Ottawa v. Tinnon, 26 Kan. 1 (1881)

Bob Jones University v. United States, 461 U.S. 574 (1983)

Bolling v. Sharpe, 347 U.S. 497 (1954)

Bond v. Floyd, 385 U.S. 116 (1966)

Boynton v. Virginia, 364 U.S. 454 (1960)

Brandenburg v. Ohio, 395 U.S. 444, 446 (1969)

Brown et al. v. Louisiana, 383 U.S. 131 (1966)

Brown v. Board of Education of Topeka, 347 U.S. 483 (1954)

Brown v. Board of Education II, 349 U.S. 294 (1955)

Brown v. Texas, 443 U.S. 47 (1979)

Bryant v. Zimmerman, 278 U.S. 63 (1928)

Buchanan v. Warley, 245 U.S. 60 (1917)

Burton v. Wilmington Parking Authority et al., 365 U.S. 715 (1961)

Burton v. Wilmington Parking Authority, 365 U.S. 715 (1961)

Bush v. Gore, 531 U.S 98 (2000)

Campaign for Fiscal Equity, Inc. v. State of New York, 86 N.Y. 2d 307 (1995)

Chambers v. Florida, 309 U.S. 227 (1940)

Cherokee Nation v. Georgia, 30 U.S. 1 (1831)

Chicago v. Morales, 527 U.S. 41 (1999)

City of Richmond v. Croson Co., 488 U.S. 469 (1989)

Civil Rights Cases, 109 U.S. 3 (1883)

Clay, aka Muhammad Ali v. United States, 403 U.S. 698 (1971)

Clyatt v. U.S., 197 U.S. 207 (1905)

Colegrove v. Green, 328 U.S. 549 (1946)

Commonwealth v. Jennison, Mass. Rec. (1783)

Cooper v. Aaron, 358 U.S. 1 (1958)

Cox v. Louisiana, 379 U.S. 536 (1965)

Crawford v. Board of Education of Los Angeles, 458 U.S. 527 (1982)

Cumming v. Richmond County Board of Education, 175 U.S. 528 (1899)

Cuyahoga Falls v. Buckeye Community of Hope Foundation, 538 U.S. 188 (2003)

Department of Housing and Urban Development v. Rucher, 535 U.S. 125 (2002)

Dred Scott v. Sandford, 60 U.S. 394 (1856)

Edwards v. South Carolina, 372 U.S. 229 (1963)

Estelle v. Gamble, 429 U.S. 97 (1976)

Ex Parte Mitsuye Endo, 323 U.S. 283 (1944)

Ex Parte Yarbrough, 110 U.S. 651 (1884)

Firefighters Local Union No. 1784 v. Stotts, 467 U.S. 561 (1984)

Fullilove v. Klutznick, 448 U.S. 448 (1980)

Gainer v. Louisiana, 368 U.S. 157 (1961)

Gayle v. Browder and Owen Browder, 532 U.S. 203 (1956)

Georgia v. Rachel et al., 384 U.S. 780 (1966)

Georgia v. Stanton, 73 U.S. 50 (1867)

Giles v. Harris, 189 U.S. 475 (1903)

Goldsboro Christian Schools v. United States, 644 F. 2d 879 (4th Cir. 1981)

Gomillion v. Lightfoot, 364 U.S. 339 (1960)

Gomperts v. Chase, 404 U.S. 1237 (1971)

Gong Lum v. Rice, 275 U.S. 78 (1927)

Gore v. Harris, 779 So. 2d 270 (2000)

Gratz v. Bollinger, 539 U.S. 244 (2003)

Green v. New Kent County School Board, 391 U.S. 430 (1968)

Green v. Veneman, 159 F. Supp. 2d 360 (2001)

Griffin v. County School Board of Prince Edward County, 377 U.S. 218 (1964)

Grovey v. Townsend, 295 U.S. 45 (1935)

Grutter v. Bollinger, 539 U.S. 306 (2003)

Guey Heung Lee v. Johnson, 404 U.S. 1215, 1216 (1971)

Guinn and Beal v. U.S., 238 U.S. 347 (1915)

Hall v. De Cuir, 95 U.S. 485 (1878)

Hamm v. Virginia State Board of Election, 379 U.S. 19 (1964)

Hansberry v. Lee, 311 U.S. 32 (1940)

Harper v. Virginia, 383 U.S. 663 (1966)

Heart of Atlanta Motel, Inc. v. U.S. et al., 379 U.S. 241 (1964)

Henderson v. U.S. et al., 339 U.S. 816 (1950)

Hiibel v. Nevada, 542 U.S. 177 (2004)

Hill, Warden v. U.S. ex. rel. Weiner, 300 U.S. 105 (1937)

Hills v. Gautreaux, et al., 425 U.S. 284 (1976)

Hirabayashi v. United States, 320 U.S. 81 (1943)

Holder v. Hall, 512 U.S. 874 (1994)

Hood v. Kuhn, 407 U.S. 258 (1972)

Hopwood v. Texas, 78 F. 3d 932 (5th Cir. 1996)

Hudson v. McMillian, 503 U.S. 1 (1992)

Hunter v. Erickson, 393 U.S. 385 (1969)

Hunter v. Underwood, 471 U.S. 222 (1986)

Hurd v. Hodges, 334 U.S. 24 (1948)

Illinois v. William, 528 U.S. 119 (2000)

Jenkins v. Missouri, 515 U.S. 70 (1995)

Johnson v. Bush, 126 S. Ct. 650 (2005)

Johnson v. Bush, 353 F. 3d 1287 (11th Cir. 2003)

Johnson v. California, 543 U.S. 499 (2005)

Johnson v. Virginia, 373 U.S. 61 (1963)

Jones v. Alfred H. Mayer Co., 392 U.S. 409 (1968)

Katzenbach, Acting Attorney General v. McClung, 379 U.S. 294 (1964)

Kelo v. City of New London, 125 S. Ct. 326 (2005)

Keyes v. School District, No.1 Denver, CO., 413 U.S. 189 (1973)

King v. Gallagher, 93 N.Y. 438 (1883)

Koon v. United States, 518 U.S. 81 (1996)

Korematsu v. United States, 321 U.S. 760 (1944)

Lane v. Wilson, 307 U.S. 268 (1939)

Lee, Commissioner of Corrections of Alabama v. Washington, 390 U.S. 333 (1968)

Lee v. Washington, 263 F. Supp. 327 (MD. AL. 1966)

Lewis v. Greyhound, 199 F. Supp. 210 (M.D. AL. 1961)

Local 28 of the Sheet Metal Workers v. Equal Employment Opportunity Comm., 478 U.S. 421 (1986)

Lombard v. Louisiana, 373 U.S. 267 (1963)

Louisiana v. NAACP, 366 U.S. 293 (1961)

Loving v. Virginia, 388 U.S. 1 (1967)

Lucy v. Adams, 350 U.S. 1 (1955)

Mapp v. Ohio, 170 Ohio St. 427 (1960)

Mapp v. Ohio, 367 U.S. 643 (1961)

Marbury v. Madison, 5 U.S. (1 Cranch) 137 (1803)

McDaniel v. Barresi, 402 U.S. 39 (1971)

McDonnell Douglas Corp v. Green, 411 U.S. 792 (1973)

McLaughlin v. Florida, 379 U.S. 184 (1964)

McLaurin v. Oklahoma, 339 U.S. 637 (1950)

Meyer v. Holley, 537 U.S. 280 (2002)

Miller v. Johnson, 515 U.S. 900 (1995)

Minor v. Happersett, 88 U.S. 162 (1875)

Mitchell v. United States, 313 U.S. 80 (1941)

Mobile v. Bolden, 446 U.S. 55 (1980)

Monroe v. Board of Commissioners, 391 U.S. 450 (1968)

Muir v. Louisville Park Theatrical Association, 202 F.2d 275 (6th Cir. 1953)

Myers v. Anderson, 238 U.S. 368 (1915)

NAACP v. Alabama, 357 U.S. 449 (1958)

NAACP v. Alabama, 377 U.S. 288 (1964)

NAACP v. Button, 371 U.S. 415 (1963)

NAACP v. Cracker Barrel Old Country Store Inc., No. 4:01-CV-325-HLM (N.D. Ga. April 11, 2002)

NAACP v. Harris, No. 01-CIV-120 (SD Fla. filed Jan.10, 2001)

Memphis v. Greene, 451 U.S. 100 (1981)

New York Times, Inc. v. Sullivan, 376 U.S. 254 (1964)

Nixon v. Condon, 286 U.S. 73 (1932)

Nixon v. Herndon, 273 U.S. 536 (1927)

Oyama v. California, 332 U.S. 633 (1948)

Ozawa v. United States, 260 U.S. 178 (1922)

Pace & Cox v. Alabama, 69 Ala. 231 (1881)

Pace v. Alabama, 106 U.S. 583 (1883)

Palmer v. Thompson, 403 U.S. 217 (1971)

Pennsylvania v. Board of Directors of City Trust, 353 U.S. 230 (1957)

Pigford v. Glickman, 206 F. 3d 1212 (D.C. Cir. 2000)

Pigford v. Veneman, 355 F. Supp. 2d 148 (DDC. 2005)

Plessy v. Ferguson, 163 U.S. 537 (1896)

Powell v. Alabama, 287 U.S. 45 (1963)

Rachel v. Walker, 4 Mo. 350 (1836)

Reitman v. Mulky, 387 U.S. 369 (1967)

Reynolds v. Board of Education of the City of Topeka, 66 Kan. 672 (1903)

Reynolds v. Sims, 377 U.S. 533 (1964)

Richardson v. Ramirez, 418 U.S. 24 (1974)

Roberts v. City of Boston, 5 Cush. 198 (1850)

Runyon v. McCrary, 427 U.S. 160 (1976)

San Antonio School District v. Rodriguez, 411 U.S. 1 (1973)

Screws v. U.S., 325 U.S. 21 (1945)

Shaw v. Reno, 509 U.S. 630 (1993)

Shelley v. Kraemer, 334 U.S. 1 (1948)

Sipes v. McGhee, 316 Mich. 614 (1947)

Sipuel v. Board of Regents, 332 U.S. 631 (1948)

Slaughter-House Cases, 393 U.S. 385 (1873)

Smith v. Allwright, 321 U.S. 649 (1944)

Smith v. Tuner, 48 U.S. 283 (1849)

State of Missouri ex rel. Gaines v. Canada, 305 U.S. 337 (1938)

State of Ohio, ex rel. Garnes v. McCann, 21 Ohio St. 198 (1871)

Strader v. Graham, 51 U.S. 82 (1851)

Sullivan v. Little Hunting Park, Inc., 396 U.S. 299 (1969)

Swann v. Charlotte–Mecklenburg, 402 U.S. 1 (1971)

Sweatt v. Painter, 339 U.S. 629 (1950)

Thurman-Watts v. Board of Education of Coffeyville, 115 Kan. 328 (1924)

Tillman v. Wheaton–Haven Recreation Association, 410 U.S. 431 (1973)

U.S. v. Bhagat Singh Thind, 261 U.S. 204 (1923)

U.S. v. Wong Kim, 169 U.S. 649 (1898)

United States v. Cruikshank, 92 U.S. 542 (1876)

United States v. Harris, 106 U.S. 629 (1883)

United States v. Paradise, 480 U.S. 616 (1987)

United States v. Raines, 362 U.S. 17 (1960)

United States v. Reese, 92 U.S. 214 (1876)

United States v. the Libellants et al., 40 U.S. 518 (1841)

United States. v. Wyandotte County, 480 F. 2d 969 (10th Cir. 1973)

United Steelworkers of America v. Weber, 443 U.S. 193 (1979)

University of California Regents v. Bakke, 438 U.S. 265 (1978)

Virginia v. Rives, 100 U.S. 313 (1880)

Watson et al. v. City of Memphis et al., 373 U.S. 526 (1963)

Watson v. Memphis, 373 U.S. 526 (1963)

Weeks v. United States, 232 U.S. 383 (1914)

Whren & Brown v. U.S., 517 U.S. 806 (1996)

Williams v. Board of Education of Parson, 79 Kan. 202 (1908)

Wolf v. Colorado, 338 U.S. 25 (1949)

Wolfe et al. v. North Carolina, 364 U.S. 177 (1960)

Wygant v. Jackson Board of Education, 476 U.S. 267 (1986)

Yick Wo v. Hopkins, 118 U.S. 356 (1886)

Notes

Foreword

1. See Jamaica Kincaid, "The Little Revenge from the Periphery," *Transition*, 73, 68.
2. *Lochner v. New York*, 198 U.S. 45 (1905).

Preface

1. See Vernallia R. Randall, *Dying While Black* (Dayton, Ohio: Seven Principles Press, 2006).
2. The U.S. Supreme Court reviews cases on appeal from the state supreme courts as well as the federal courts of appeal. A petitioner requests review, or certiorari, by the Supreme Court. On average, the Court grants review to approximately 1% of all requests.

Introduction

1. See Winthrop D. Jordan, *White over Black: American Attitudes toward the Negro, 1550–1812* (Chapel Hill: University of North Carolina Press, 1968).
2. See Eric E. Williams, *Capitalism and Slavery* (Chapel Hill: University of North Carolina Press, 1944); Robert William Fogel and Stanley L. Engerman, *Time on the Cross: The Economics of American Negro Slavery* (New York: W.W. Norton & Company, Inc., 1974); John Henrik Clarke, *Christopher Columbus and the Afrikan Holocaust: Slavery and the Rise of European Capitalism* (Brooklyn, N.Y.: A&B Books, 1992).
3. See Joseph R. Washington, *Puritan Race Virtue, Vice and Values 1620–1820: Original Calvinist True Believers' Enduring Faith and Ethics Race Claims in Emerging Congregationalist, Presbyterian and Power Denominations* (New York: Pete Lang Publisher, 1998).
4. See Jordan, *White over Black: American Attitudes toward the Negro, 1550–1812*.
5. See Frances Cress Welsing, *The Isis Papers: The Keys to the Colors* (Chicago: Third World Press, 1991).
6. See Theodore W. Allen, *The Invention of the White Race: Racial Oppression and Social Control*, vol. 1 (London: Verso Press, 1994).

7. *Scott v. Sandford*, 60 U.S. 393, 413 (1856); *Plessy v. Ferguson*, 163 U.S. 537 (1896).

Chapter 1

1. Eric Williams, *Capitalism and Slavery* (New York: Capricorn Books/ G.P. Putnam's Sons, 1966), 7.
2. James Horn, *A Land as God Made It: Jamestown and the Birth of America* (New York: Basic Books/Perseus Books Group, 2005), 25.
3. Ibid., 37.
4. Hugh Thomas, *The Slave Trade: The Story of the Atlantic Slave Trade: 1440–1870* (New York: Simon & Schuster, 1997), 36, 196–205.
5. A. Leon Higginbotham, *In the Matter of Color* (New York: Oxford University Press, 1978; Africans captured from Spanish ships were brought to Virginia by Dutch), 20, 58. There is some dispute concerning the possible arrival of slaves from Angola later that year.
6. Paula Giddings, *When and Where I Enter: The Impact of Black Women on Race and Sex in America* (New York: Bantam Press, 1984), 34.
7. *Black Survival, 1776–1976: The Urban League Perspective* (Philadelphia: The Philadelphia Urban League, 1977), 2.
8. Higginbotham, *In the Matter of Color* (discussing Irish and Scottish immigrants as well as indentured servants), 33, 159–160.
9. Naomi Chazan et al., eds., *Politics and Society in Contemporary Africa* 340–49, 3rd ed. (New York: Lynne Reinner Publishers, Inc., 1999), 340–345.
10. For more on the Middle Passage, see Tom Feelings, *The Middle Passage: White Ships/Black Cargo* (New York: Dial Books, 1995).
11. Mario Azevedo, *Africana Studies: A Survey of Africa and the African Diaspora*, 3rd ed. (Durham, N.C.: Carolina Academic Press, 2005), 97.
12. From "Debate on Mr. Wilberforce's Resolutions Respecting the Slave Trade" in William Cobbett, *The Parliamentary History of England: From the Norman Conquest in 1066 to the Year 1803*, 36 vols. (London: T. Curson Hansard, 1806–1820), 28 (1789–1791), cols. 42–68.
13. Chazan et al., eds., *Politics and Society in Contemporary Africa*, 3rd ed., 340–349.
14. Philip Aka, "The Military, Globalization and Human Rights in Africa," *New York Law School Journal of Human Rights* 18 (Summer, 2002): 361–438.
15. Rene Dumont, *False Start in Africa* (London: Andre Deutsch, 1966), 35.
16. Chazan et al., eds., *Politics and Society in Contemporary Africa*, 3rd ed., 252.
17. Ibid.
18. See Dumont, *False Start in Africa*; Chazan et al., eds., *Politics and Society in Contemporary Africa*, 3rd ed., 340–49.

19. For more on Africa, see W. E. Burghardt Du Bois, *The World and Africa* (New York: International Publishers, Co., 1946); John Henrik Clarke, *Christopher Columbus and the Afrikan Holocaust: Slavery and the Rise of European Capitalism* (Brooklyn, N.Y.: A&B Books, 1992).

20. Thomas, *The Slave Trade: The Story of the Atlantic Slave Trade: 1440–1870*, 36, 201.

21. See Peter Kolchin, *American Slavery 1619–1877* (New York: Hill and Wang/Farrar, Straus, Giroux, 1993).

22. See Higginbotham, *In the Matter of Color*.

23. Ibid., 33, 58. The legal status was indefinite; for example, Virginia legislation of 1859 is the first reference to Africans as slaves.

24. See David Brion Davis, *Inhuman Bondage: The Rise and Fall of Slavery in the New World* (New York: Oxford University Press, 2006); Aka, "The Military, Globalization and Human Rights in Africa."

25. Francisco Chapman, *Race, Identity and Myth in the Spanish Speaking Caribbean: Essays on Biculturalism as a Contested Terrain of Difference* (Santo Domingo, Dominican Republic: Chapman & Associates, 2002), 125.

26. See Edmund S. Morgan, *American Slavery/American Freedom: The Ordeal of Colonial Virginia* (New York: W. W. Norton, Inc., 1976).

27. Horn, *A Land as God Made It: Jamestown and the Birth of America*, 286–288; Higginbotham, *In the Matter of Color*, 58–59, 75–78, 120–122, 161–163, 261–263 (discussing the colonial legal restrictions on Africans in Virginia, Massachusetts, New York, South Carolina, and Georgia).

28. Horn, *A Land as God Made It: Jamestown and the Birth of America*, 287.

29. Ibid.

30. Higginbotham, *In the Matter of Color*, 161 (discussing the enslaving and in some cases exporting of American Indians to the West Indies).

31. Ibid., 37.

32. Ibid., 34, 38, 53–55.

33. Ibid., 34.

34. Ibid., 25, 38.

35. See the writings of Lucretia Mott (1793–1880). See also Lucretia Mott, *American Sermons* (New York: Library of America/Penguin Putnam, 1999).

36. Kolchin, *American Slavery 1619–1877*, 67–69. See also Henry Mayer, *All on Fire: William Lloyd Garrison and the Abolition of Slavery* (New York: St. Martin's Press, 1998).

37. South Carolina, Preamble to the Act of 1712; A. Leon Higginbotham, *In the Matter of Color—Race & The American Legal Process: The Colonial Period* (New York: Oxford University Press, 1980), 167.

38. Higginbotham, *In the Matter of Color*, 50.

39. See Helen Tunnicliffe Catterall, *Judicial Cases Concerning American Slavery and the Negro* (Washington, D.C.: Carnegie Institution of Washington, 1926); Herbert Aptheker, *A Documentary History of the Negro People in the United States: From Colonial Times through the Civil War* (New York: Citadel Press, 1951), 26; Higginbotham, *In the Matter of Color*, 22.

40. See Catterall, *Judicial Cases Concerning American Slavery and the Negro*. The author advocates an expansion as follows:
English (with land)
White, non-English (with land)
English (without land)
White, non-English (without land)
White indentured servants
White servants (without indenture: voluntary and involuntary servants)
Christian Black servants
Indian servants
Mulatto servants
Indian slaves
Black slaves

41. See generally The Declaration of Independence, July 4, 1776.

42. Ibid., 1.

43. Higginbotham, *In the Matter of Color*, 138.

44. Preamble to U.S. Constitution.

45. *Smith v. Turner*, 48 U.S. 283 (1849).

46. Ibid.

47. See *George Smith v. Turner*, 48 U.S. 283 (1849).

48. U.S. Const., Art. I, Sec. 9.

49. *Prigg v. Pennsylvania*, 41 U.S. 539, 626 (1842).

50. U.S. Const., Art. IV, Sec. 2, cl. 2.

51. U.S. Const., Art. 1, Sec. 2.

52. Ibid.

53. *Scott v. Sandford*, 60 U.S. 393, 413 (1856). The correct spelling is Sanford. However, the error was made by the lower courts. The present spelling of Sandford is on record.

54. Ibid., 395–396 (1856).

55. *Rachael, a woman of color, v. Walker*, 4 Mo. 350 (1836).

56. Ibid.

57. *Scott v. Sandford*, 60 U.S. 393 (1856).

58. Original intent is a fundamentalist interpretation of the U.S. Constitution.

59. Lively, *The Constitution and Race*, 29. See *Marbury v. Madison*, 5 U.S. (1 Cranch) 137 (1803).

60. *Scott v. Sandford*, 60 U.S. 393, 413 (1856).

61. Donald E. Lively, *The Constitution and Race* (New York: Greenwood Publishing Group, Inc., 1992), 28–29.

62. *Scott v. Sandford*, 60 U.S. 393, at 426–427.

63. *Scott v. Sandford*, 60 U.S. 393, at 401.

64. David Levering Lewis, *W. E. B. DuBois: Portrait of a Race, 1869–1919* (New York: Henry Holt, 1993, discussing the Black migration North of the 1800s), 117–118.

65. Ibid.

66. Abraham Lincoln, August 22, 1862. "My paramount object in this struggle is to save the Union, and is not either to save or destroy slavery. If I could save the Union without freeing any slave I would do it, and if I could save it by freeing all the slaves, I would do it; and if I could save it by freeing some and leaving others alone I would also do that. I have here stated my purpose according to my view of official duty; and I intend no modification of my oft expressed personal wish that all men everywhere could be free."

67. *Jones v. Alfred H. Mayer Co.*, 392 U.S. 409, 439 (1968).

68. U.S. statutes at large, 38th Congress, Sess. II, Chapter 90, 507–509.

79. *Georgia v. Stanton*, 73 U.S. 50 (1867).

70. John Hope Franklin, *From Slavery to Freedom: A History of African Americans* (New York: Alfred A. Knopf, 2005), 248–253.

71. Christopher A. Bracey, *Louis Brandeis and the Race Question*, 52 Ala. L. Rev. 859, 871 (Spring 2001).

72. See 42 U.S.C.A. § 1981 (1994).

73. 1866 Civil Rights Act, 14 Stat. 27-30, April 9, 1866 A.D.CHAP. XXXI.

74. U.S. Const., Am. 14, Sec. 1.

75. Ibid.

76. Civil Rights Act of 1870, 16 Stat. 140 (1870).

77. U.S. Const., Am. 15, Sec. 2.

78. See 42 U.S.C. § § 1981, 1985 (1994).

79. See 18 U.S.C. 243 (1994).

80. *Civil Rights Cases*, 109 U.S. 3 (1883).

81. Due to the similarity of the issues involved, the Court consolidated the five cases.

82. *Civil Rights Cases*, 109 U.S. 3 (1883).

83. *Plessy v. Ferguson*, 163 U.S. 537 (1896).

84. Ibid., at 552.

85. Ibid., at 552.

86. Ibid., at 544.

87. Whites formed abolitionist organizations during slavery, assisted in the Underground Railroad, formed the NAACP, and acted as counsel in numerous civil rights cases.

88. *Scott v. Sandford*, 60 U.S. 393, 395–396 (1856).

89. *Plessy v. Ferguson*, 163 U.S. at 559.

90. Ibid., at 559–560.

91. Harry Blackmun, *Section 1983 and Federal Protection of Individual Rights—Will the Statute Remain Alive or Fade Away?* 60 N.Y.U. L. Rev. 1, 11 (1985).

92. Ibid.

93. *Garner v. Louisiana*, 368 U.S. 157 (1961).

94. Carl T. Rowan, *Dream Makers, Dream Breakers: The World of Justice Thurgood Marshall* (Boston: Little, Brown and Company, 1993), 27.

95. Lewis, *W. E. B. DuBois: The Fight for Equality and the American Century, 1919–1963*, 1–3.

96. Lewis, *W. E. B. DuBois: Portrait of a Race, 1869–1919*, 387.

97. Ibid.

98. Mark V. Tushnet, *Making Civil Rights Law* (New York: Oxford University Press, 1994), 6.

99. Constance Baker Motley, *Equal Justice under Law* (New York: Farrar, Straus and Giroux, 1998), 99–101.

100. *Brown v. Board of Education of Topeka*, 347 U.S. 483 (1954).

101. Civil Rights Act of 1964, Pub. L. No. 88-352, 78 Stat. 241 (July 2, 1964).

102. *Brandenburg v. Ohio*, 395 U.S. 444, 446 (1969).

Chapter 2

1. *Blyew v. United States*, 80 U.S. 581 (1871).

2. *Gong Lum v. Rice*, 275 U.S. 78 (1927).

3. A. Leon Higginbotham, *In the Matter of Color* (New York: Oxford University Press, 1978), 10.

4. Frederick Douglass, *Narrative of the Life of Frederick Douglass, an American Slave. Written by Himself* (Boston: The Anti-Slavery Office, 1845; reprinted: Chapel Hill: University of North Carolina, 1999), 33.

5. Higginbotham, *In the Matter of Color*, 258.

6. *Commonwealth v. Jennison*, Rec. 1783, fol. 85.

7. Prince Hall served in the Revolutionary Army and became a Methodist minister after the war. He is the founder of the Masonic Hall Order that bears his name, chartered in 1787. Hall started a school for Black children in his home in 1798.

8. Herbert Aptheker, ed., *A Documentary History of the Negro People in the United States: From Colonial Times through the Civil War* (New York: The Citadel Press, 1971), 19.

9. Ibid., 19.

10. *Roberts v. Boston*, 5 Cush. 198, 201 (1850).

11. Ibid.

12. Ibid.

13. Ibid.

14. Ibid., 206.

15. Ibid., 198, 209.

16. Aptheker, ed., *A Documentary History of the Negro People in the United States: From Colonial Times through the Civil War*, 297–299.

17. *The Liberator*, June 14, 1850.

18. John Hope Franklin and Alfred Moss, *From Slavery to Freedom: A History of African Americans*, 8th ed. (New York: Alfred A. Knopf, 2005), 181.

19. Ibid.

20. Am. 13, Sec. 1.

21. Am. 14, Sec. 1.

22. David Levering Lewis, *W. E. B. DuBois: Portrait of a Race, 1869–1919* (New York: Henry Holt, 1993), 112–114.

23. Franklin and Moss, *From Slavery to Freedom: A History of African Americans*, 8th ed., 257.

24. Ibid.

25. See also Paula Giddings, *When and Where I Enter: The Impact of Black Women on Race and Sex in America*, 95–97, and author's forthcoming article, "Statutory Rape Laws: Early Social Policies, Discrimination and the Moral Reform Movement."

26. Lewis, *W. E. B. DuBois: Portrait of a Race, 1869–1919*, 123. For example, Hampton Normal and Agricultural Institute, now Hampton University, was founded in 1868 by ex-Confederate General and railroad magnate Thomas Muldrop Logan; Howard University in Washington, D.C., was founded in 1867 by Otis Howard, Caucasian, a member of the Freedmen's Bureau.

27. Franklin and Moss, *From Slavery to Freedom: A History of African Americans*, 8th ed., 256–257.

28. E. Franklin Frazier, *Negro in the United States* (New York: Macmillan Company, 1957), 166.

29. Ibid., 141.

30. U.S. Statutes at Large, 38th Congress, Sess. II, chapter 90, 507–509.

31. *Georgia v. Stanton*, 73 U.S. 50 (1867).

32. DuBois, W. E. B., The Freedmen's Bureau, *Atlantic Monthly*, 87 (1901): 354–365.

33. Lewis, *W. E. B. DuBois: Portrait of a Race, 1869–1919*, 114.

34. Frazier, *Negro in the United States*, 141.

35. DuBois, 354–365.

36. Franklin and Moss, *From Slavery to Freedom: A History of African Americans*, 8th ed., 257.

37. Black Codes are laws with particular provisions applicable to Blacks. Civil laws restricted the freedoms of Blacks. Criminal laws carried a harsher punishment for Blacks.

38. *Plessy v. Ferguson*, 163 U.S. 537, 552 (1896).

39. See *King v. Gallagher*, 93 N.Y. 438 (1883).

40. Ibid., 457.

41. See *State ex rel. Garnes v. McCann*, 21 Ohio St. 198, 201.

42. *King v. Gallagher*, 93 N.Y. 438, 453 (1883).

43. *State ex rel. Garnes v. McCann*, 11 Ohio A146 (1919).

44. See *Plessy v. Ferguson*, 163 U.S. 537 (1896).

45. Ibid., 552.

46. Ibid., at 544.

47. Ibid., at 551.

48. Ibid., at 544.

49. Ibid.

50. Ibid.
51. *Plessy v. Ferguson*, 163 U.S. at 559.
52. *Cumming v. Richmond County Board of Education*, 175 U.S. 528 (1899).
53. Ga. Const. Art. 8 Sec. 1; *Cumming v. Richmond County Board of Education*, 175 U.S. at 543.
54. *Cumming v. Richmond County Board of Education*, 175 U.S. at 530.
55. Ibid., at 545.
56. *Berea College v. Kentucky*, 211 U.S. 45 (1908).
57. Kentucky, 1904, Chap. 85, 181.
58. Lewis, *W. E. B. DuBois: Portrait of a Race, 1869–1919*, 387.
59. Ibid.
60. Carl T. Rowan, *Dream Makers, Dream Breakers: The World of Justice Thurgood Marshall* (Boston: Little, Brown and Company, 1993), 27.
61. Lewis, *W. E. B. DuBois: Portrait of a Race, 1869–1919*, 1–3.
62. *Gong Lum v. Rice*, 275 U.S. 78, 87 (1927).
63. Ibid., 86.
64. Ibid., 87.
65. Ibid., 85.
66. *State of Missouri ex rel. Gaines v. Canada*, 305 U.S. 337, 342 (1938).
67. Ibid., 353
68. Ibid.
69. Ibid.
70. Constance Baker Motley, *Equal Justice Under Law* (New York: Farrar, Straus and Giroux, 1998), 99–101. Charles Hamilton Houston is known as the architect of the civil rights movement. He graduated from Amherst College and Harvard Law School. Houston was appointed dean of Howard University School of Law, where he developed strategies and fostered a level of intellectual growth needed to create the *Brown* victory. Thurgood Marshall attended Howard University Law School from 1933 to 1936.
71. Mark V. Tushnet, *Making Civil Rights Law* (New York: Oxford University Press, 1994), 6.
72. See *University of Maryland v. Murray*, 169 Md. 478 (1936); *State of Missouri ex rel Gaines v. Canada*, 305 U.S. 337 (1938).
73. Rowan, *Dream Makers, Dream Breakers: The World of Justice Thurgood Marshall*, 150.
74. See also *Sipuel v. Board of Regents*, 332 U.S. 631 (1948).
75. Ibid., 631, 632.
76. Ibid.
77. C. Vann Woodard, *The Strange Career of Jim Crow* (New York: Oxford University Press, 2002), 144.
78. *McLaurin v. Oklahoma*, 339 U.S. 637, 642 (1950).
79. *Sweatt v. Painter*, 339 U.S. 629 (1950).
80. *Brown v. Board of Education of Topeka*, 347 U.S. 483 (1954).

81. Ibid., 483, 486 (together with No. 2, *Briggs et al. v. Elliott et al.*, on appeal from the United States District Court for the Eastern District of South Carolina, argued December 9–10, 1952, reargued December 7–8, 1953; No. 4, *Davis et al. v. County School Board of Prince Edward County, Virginia et al.*, on appeal from the United States District Court for the Eastern District of Virginia, argued December 10, 1952, reargued December 7–8, 1953; and No. 10, *Gebhart et al. v. Belton et al.*, on certiorari to the Supreme Court of Delaware, argued December 11, 1952, reargued December 9, 1953).

82. *Brown v. Board of Education of Topeka*, 347 U.S. 483, 486 (1954).

83. Motley, *Equal Justice Under Law*, 102.

84. *Brown v. Board of Education*, at 494–495.

85. Motley, *Equal Justice under Law*, 240–241.

86. Lewis, David Levering, *W. E. B. DuBois: The Fight for Equality and the American Century, 1919–1963* (New York: Henry Holt, 2000), 521–523, 532–534 (W. E. B. DuBois drafts "An Appeal to the World: A Statement on the Denial of Human Rights to Minorities in the Case of Citizens of Negro Descent in the United States of America" and "An Appeal to the United Nations for Redress"); Motley, *Equal Justice Under Law*, 70.

87. Motley, *Equal Justice Under Law*, 5.

88. Ibid., 191.

89. Tushnet, *Making Civil Rights Law*, 204–205.

90. Motley, *Equal Justice Under Law*, 191.

91. Tushnet, *Making Civil Rights Law*, 206–207 (discussing the reargument of *Brown* and congressional questions of intent).

92. *Brown v. Board of Education*, at 494.

93. *Board of Education of the City of Ottawa et al. v. Tinnon, by his next friend, Elijah Tinnon*, 26 Kan. 1 (1881).

94. Ibid.

95. *Reynolds v. Board of Education of the City of Topeka*, 66 Kan. 672 (1903).

96. Ibid., 672, 684.

97. Ibid.

98. *Williams v. Board of Education of the City of Parsons*, 79 Kan. 202, 208 (1908).

99. *Thurman Watts v. Coffeyville*, 115 Kan. 328 (1924).

100. Ibid., 328, 333. See also *Kern v. City of Newton*, 147 Kan. 471 (1938).

101. *Brown v. Board of Education*, at 495.

102. See generally *Brown v. Board of Education II*, 349 U.S. 294 (1955).

103. Ibid., at 301.

104. Motley, *Equal Justice Under Law*, 110–111.

105. Tushnet, *Making Civil Rights Law*, 206–207 (discussing the reasons that led to local governments' control of *Brown*'s implementation).

106. *Brown v. Board of Education II*, 349 U.S. at 300. (The District Court is to consider administration, physical condition of the school plant, school transportation, personnel, attendance areas, and admissions). See also the *Green* factors with regard to faculty, staff, transportation, extracurricular activities, and facilities.

107. Motley, *Equal Justice Under Law*, 110–111.

108. Vann, 156.

109. Tushnet, *Making Civil Rights Law*, 240 (discussing the *Southern Manifesto*).

110. Ibid.

111. See *Cooper v. Aaron*, 358 U.S. 1 (1958).

112. Ibid.

113. Ibid. See generally the Court decision desegregating Central High School in Little Rock, Arkansas.

114. Garrow, David J., *Bearing the Cross: Martin Luther King, Jr. and the Southern Christian Leadership Conference* (New York: Quill Publishers, 1986), 98.

115. See Robert F. Burk, *The Eisenhower Administration and Black Civil Rights* (Knoxville: University of Tennessee Press, 1984).

116. Stephan Lesher, *George Wallace: American Populist* (New York: Addison–Wesley Publishing, 1994), 108–109. See Burk, *The Eisenhower Administration and Black Civil Rights*.

117. Lesher, *George Wallace: American Populist*, 108; Burk, *The Eisenhower Administration and Black Civil Rights*.

118. Garrow, *Bearing the Cross: Martin Luther King, Jr. and the Southern Christian Leadership Conference*, 106.

119. *Griffin v. County School Board of Prince Edward County*, 377 U.S. 218 (1964).

120. Ibid., 218, 224.

121. See *McDaniel v. Barresi*, 402 U.S. 39, 45–46.

122. *Florida Ex. Rel. Hawkins v. Board of Control of Florida; Muir v. Louisville Park Theatrical Association; Tureaud v. Board of Supervisors of Louisiana State University and Agricultural and Mechanical College*, 347 U.S. 971 (1954).

123. See *Commonwealth of Pennsylvania v. Board of Directors of City Trusts*, 353 U.S. 230 (1957).

124. *Wilmington v. Burton*, 157 A.2d 894, 898 (Del. 1960).

125. See *McDaniel v. Barresi*, 402 U.S. 39, 45–46 (1971).

126. Ibid.

127. *McDaniel v. Barresi*, 402 U.S. 39 (1971). A "neutral" desegregation plan that does not require integration is reversed as *per se* invalid.

128. See *Monroe v. Board of Commissioners*, 391 U.S. 450 (1968).

129. *McDaniel v. Barresi*, 402 U.S. 39, 45–46.

130. See *Green v. New Kent County School Board*, 391 U.S. 430 (1968). The Court sets forth once more the criteria established in *Brown II*.

131. Ibid., 430, 435.

132. Kevin Brown, *Law and Education in the Post-Desegregation Era: Four Perspectives on Desegregation and Resegregation* (Durham: N.C.: 2005), 176.

133. *Swann v. Charlotte–Mecklenburg*, 402 U.S. 1 (1971).

134. Ibid., at 15, citing *Green v. County School Board*, 391 U.S. at 439.

135. Tushnet, *Making Civil Rights Law*, 240–242 (discussing the litigation and countertactics used by school districts to avoid desegregation).

136. See Derrick Bell, *Race, Racism, and American Law* (New York: Aspen Law and Business, 2000), 179–180.

137. See Gary Orfield, *Must We Bus? Segregated Schools and National Policy* (Washington: Brookings Institution, 1978), 59–62.

138. *Runyon v. McCrary*, 427 U.S. 160 (1976).

139. *Jenkins v. Missouri*, 515 U.S. 70 (1995).

140. Ibid.

141. *Gomperts v. Chase*, 404 U.S. 1237 (1971).

142. See Margaret E. Montoya, *Affirmative Action in Higher Education: A Brief History of Chicana/o School Segregation: One Rationale for Affirmative Action*, 12 La Raza L. J. 159 (Fall 2001).

143. These provisions were eventually repealed (1947 Cal. Stats., c. 737, § 1); see also *Guey Heung Lee v. Johnson*, 404 U.S. 1215, 1215 (1971).

144. *Guey Heung Lee v. Johnson*, 404 U.S. 1215, 1216 (1971).

145. *Gomperts v. Chase*, 404 U.S. 1237, 1238 (1971).

146. Ibid., 1239.

147. Ibid.

148. Ibid., 1240.

149. *Guey Heung Lee v. Johnson*, 404 U.S. 1215 (1971)

150. Ibid.

151. For more information, see Paul E. Sracic, *San Antonio v. Rodriguez and the Pursuit of Equal Protection: The Debate Over Discrimination and School Funding* (Lawrence, KS: University Press of Kansas, 2006).

152. *San Antonio School District v. Rodriguez*, 411 U.S. 1 (1973).

153. San Antonio School District v. Rodriguez, 411 U.S. 1, 57–59 (1973).

154. *Crawford v. Board of Education of Los Angeles*, 458 U.S. 527 (1982).

155. Orfield, *Schools More Separate*; Janet Ward Schofield, Review of Research on School Desegregation's Impact on Elementary and Secondary School Students, in *Handbook of Research on Multicultural Education*, eds. James Banks and Cherry McGee Banks (New York: Simon & Schuster MacMillan, 1995), 597–617.

156. Derrick Bell, *Silent Covenants:* Brown v. Board of Education *and the Unfulfilled Hopes for Racial Reform* (New York: Oxford University Press, 2004), 109–110.

157. Ibid., 179–180.

158. Kenneth B. Clark and John Hope Franklin, *The Nineteen Eighties: Prologue and Prospect* (Washington, D.C.: Joint Center for Political Studies, 1970), 15.

159. Ibid.

160. Ibid.
161. *East Baton Rouge Parish School Board v. Knights of the Ku Klux Klan*, 454 U.S. 1075 (1981).
162. Ibid.
163. See *Missouri v. Jenkins*, 515 U.S. 70 (1995).
164. Bell, *Silent Covenants: Brown v. Board of Education and the Unfulfilled Hopes for Racial Reform*, 161–162.
165. Orfield, *Schools More Separate*; Schofield, in *Handbook of Research on Multicultural Education*, eds. James Banks and Cherry McGee Banks, 600–617.
166. Orfield, *Schools More Separate*; Schofield, in *Handbook of Research on Multicultural Education*, eds. James Banks and Cherry McGee Banks, 597–617; Gary Orfield, Susan Eaton, and the Harvard Project on School Desegregation, eds., *Dismantling Desegregation: The Quiet Reversal of Brown v. Board of Education* (New York: New Press, 1996).
167. The stated purpose of the legislation is to close the achievement gap of the disadvantaged (PL 107–110). Specifically, the purpose is "to ensure that all children have a fair, equal, and significant opportunity to obtain a high-quality education and reach, at a minimum, proficiency on challenging State academic achievement standards and state academic assessments" (Sec. 1001).
168. See *Campaign for Fiscal Equity, Inc. v. State of New York*, Supreme Court, Appellate Division, (NY Sup. Ct. June 25, 2002).
169. Ibid.
170. John Kenneth Galbraith, *The Affluent Society* (Boston: Mariner Books/Houghton/Mifflin, 1958), 237.
171. *Keyes v. School District, No. 1, Denver, CO., 413 U.S. 189 (1973); Milliken v. Bradley*, 433 U.S. 267 (1977); *Board of Ed. of Oklahoma City v. Dowell*, 498 U.S. 237 (1991); *Freeman v. Pitts*, 503 U.S. 467 (1992); United States v. Fordice, 505 U.S. 717 (1992); *Georgia State Conf. of Branches of NAACP v. Georgia*, 775 F.2d 1403 (11th Cir. 1985).
172. University of California Regents v. Bakke, 438 U.S. 265, 278 (1978).
173. Ibid., 265.
174. Ibid., at 297.
175. Ibid., 265, 366 note 42.
176. Ibid., at 297.
177. Ibid., at 289.
178. Ibid., 265, 356.
179. Ibid., at 297.
180. Bell, *Silent Covenants: Brown v. Board of Education and the Unfulfilled Hopes for Racial Reform*, 142.
181. *United Steelworkers of America v. Weber*, 443 U.S. 193 (1979).
182. *Fullilove v. Klutznick*, 448 U.S. 448 (1980).
183. *Firefighters Local Union No. 1784 v. Stotts*, 467 U.S. 561 (1984).
184. *Local 28 of the Sheet Metal Workers v. Equal Employment Opportunity Commission*, 478 U.S. 421 (1986).

185. *United States v. Paradise*, 480 U.S. 616 (1987).
186. *Wygant v. Jackson Board of Education*, 476 U.S. 267 (1986).
187. *City of Richmond v. Croson*, 488 U.S 469 (1989).
188. Ibid., 469, 511.
189. Ibid., 469, 511.
190. *Hopwood v. Texas*, 78 F 3d 932, 934–935 (1996).
191. Ibid., 932.
192. Ibid., at 994.
193. In *Sweatt v. Painter*, Herman Sweatt was initially denied admission to the University of Texas Law School based only on his race. An appeal to the U.S. Supreme Court was necessary to gain admission to the school.
194. *Cappaccione v. Charlotte–Mecklenburg* and *Belk v. Charlotte–Mecklenburg School District*, Nos. 99-2389(L); CA-97-482-3-P; CA-65-1974-3-P (September 19, 2001).
195. *Adarand Constructors, Inc. v. Pena*, 515 U.S. 200, 237-239 (1995).
196. *Wygant v. Jackson Board of Ed.*, 476 U.S. 267 (1986).
197. Ibid., 267, 273.
198. *Adarand Constructors, Inc. v. Pena*, 515 U.S. 200, 204.
199. Proposition 209. California Civil Rights Initiative. Title: Prohibition Against Discrimination or Preferential Treatment by State and Other Public Entities. Initiative Constitutional Amendment. Cal. Const. Art.1, Sec. 31 (a). n1.
200. See *Coalition for Econ. Equity v. Wilson*, 122 F.3d 692 (9th Cir. 1997).
201. See *Coalition for Econ. Equity v. Wilson*, 122 F.3d 692, 701 (9th Cir. 1997) cert. denied, 522 U.S. 963 (1997).
202. Joint Center for Political and Economic Studies, *Focus*, 25(4) (May 1997). "There has been a reported 80 percent drop in admissions of black students to UCLA's law school and a similarly sharp decline at UC Berkeley's law school. At the University of Texas at Austin, black and Hispanic undergraduate enrollments have declined 20 percent from last year. The university law school has also reported that the number of incoming black law students has plummeted from 65 last year to 10."
203. *Gratz v. Bollinger*, 539 U.S. 244 (2003); *Grutter v. Bollinger*, 539 U.S. 306 (2003).
204. *Gratz v. Bollinger*, 539 U.S. 244, 251 (2003).
205. Ibid., 253–254.
206. *Grutter v. Bollinger*, 539 U.S. 306, 317–318 (2003).
207. Ibid., 334–335.
208. Ibid., 342–343.
209. *University of California Regents v. Bakke*, 438 U.S. 265 (1978).
210. *Grutter v. Bollinger*, 539 U.S. 306, 315 (2003).
211. Ibid., 332.
212. Ibid.
213. See, Ira Katznelson, *When Affirmative Action Was White* (New York: W.W. Norton & Co., 2005).
214. Ibid., 171.

215. Ibid., 142–145.

216. *The Civil Rights Cases*, 109 U.S. 3, 61 (1883).

217. Orfield, *Schools More Separate*; Schofield, in *Handbook of Research on Multicultural Education*, eds. James Banks and Cherry McGee Banks, 597–617.

218. See *Meredith v. Jefferson Cty Bd. of Educ.*, 05-915 (2007); *Parents Involved in Community Schools v. Seattle School District, No. 1*, 05-908 (2007).

219. Exodus 5:16.

Chapter 3

1. Melvin L. Oliver and Thomas M. Shapiro, *Black Wealth/White Wealth: A New Perspective on Racial Inequality* (New York: Routledge, 1997).

2. Oliver and Shapiro, *Black Wealth/White Wealth: A New Perspective on Racial Inequality*.

3. Douglas S. Massey and Nancy A. Denton, *American Apartheid* (Cambridge, Mass.: Harvard University Press, 1994), 18.

4. *Yick Wo v. Hopkins*, 118 U.S. 356 (1886).

5. *Plessy v. Ferguson*, 163 U.S. 537 (1896).

6. *Bailey v. Alabama*, 211 U.S. 452, 456 (1908).

7. Ibid., 452, 455–456.

8. *Buchanan v. Warley*, 245 U.S. 60 (1917).

9. David Delaney, *Race, Place & the Law: 1836–1948* (Austin: University of Texas Press, 1998), 114–115.

10. *Buchanan v. Warley*, 245 U.S. 60 (1917).

11. Civil Rights Act of 1866, 14 Stat. 27-30 April 9, 1866; superseded by the Civil Rights Act of 1870, 16 Stat. 140.

12. Civil Rights Act of 1870, 16 Stat. 140.

13. Delaney, *Race, Place & the Law: 1836–1948*, 114–115.

14. Phyllis Vine, *One Man's Castle: Clarence Darrow in Defense of the American Dream* (New York: HarperCollins, 2004), 175; Kevin Boyle, *Arc of Justice: A Saga of Race, Civil Rights, and Murder in the Jazz Age* (New York: Henry Holt, 2004), 145, 201.

15. See Vine, *One Man's Castle: Clarence Darrow in Defense of the American Dream*; Boyle, *Arc of Justice: A Saga of Race, Civil Rights, and Murder in the Jazz Age*.

16. Boyle, *Arc of Justice: A Saga of Race, Civil Rights, and Murder in the Jazz Age*, 90–92, 99–100.

17. Vine, *One Man's Castle: Clarence Darrow in Defense of the American Dream*, 93–98.

18. Ibid., 175.

19. Vine, *One Man's Castle: Clarence Darrow in Defense of the American Dream*, 103–104, 109, 119; Boyle, *Arc of Justice: A Saga of Race, Civil Rights, and Murder in the Jazz Age*, 133–135.

20. Boyle, *Arc of Justice: A Saga of Race, Civil Rights, and Murder in the Jazz Age*, 151–156.
21. Vine, *One Man's Castle: Clarence Darrow in Defense of the American Dream*, 116–118.
22. See Vine, *One Man's Castle: Clarence Darrow in Defense of the American Dream*.
23. Boyle, *Arc of Justice: A Saga of Race, Civil Rights, and Murder in the Jazz Age*, 170.
24. Vine, *One Man's Castle: Clarence Darrow in Defense of the American Dream*, 118–119.
25. Boyle, *Arc of Justice: A Saga of Race, Civil Rights, and Murder in the Jazz Age*, 193. Judge Frank Murphy would serve as U.S. Attorney General and then Justice of the U.S. Supreme Court from 1940 to 1949.
26. Vine, *One Man's Castle: Clarence Darrow in Defense of the American Dream*, 181; Boyle, *Arc of Justice: A Saga of Race, Civil Rights, and Murder in the Jazz Age*, 193.
27. Clarence Darrow was a legendary defense attorney who successfully represented John Scopes, a high school biology teacher arrested for teaching evolution. Darrow also defended teen-aged murderers Nathan Leopold and Richard Loeb. For more information on the role of Clarence Darrow in the Sweet case, see Boyle, *Arc of Justice: A Saga of Race, Civil Rights, and Murder in the Jazz Age*, and Vine, *One Man's Castle: Clarence Darrow in Defense of the American Dream*.
28. Boyle, *Arc of Justice: A Saga of Race, Civil Rights, and Murder in the Jazz Age*, 299.
29. Boyle, *Arc of Justice: A Saga of Race, Civil Rights, and Murder in the Jazz Age*, 178.
30. Ibid., 244.
31. Boyle, *Arc of Justice: A Saga of Race, Civil Rights, and Murder in the Jazz Age*, 336; Vine, *One Man's Castle: Clarence Darrow in Defense of the American Dream*, 259–260.
32. *Hansberry v. Lee*, 311 U.S. 32 (1940).
33. The U.S. Supreme Court ruled on behalf of Hansberry on the narrow issue of whether the prior decision involving the former class of Black litigants would apply to the present litigants.
34. *Shelley v. Kraemer*, 334 U.S. 1 (1948).
35. Ibid., 1, 4–5.
36. *Sipes v. McGhee*, 316 Michigan 614, 25 N.W. 2d 638 (1947).
37. *Shelley v. Kraemer*, 334 U.S. 1, 19.
38. *Hurd v. Hodge*, 334 U.S. 24 (1948).
39. Cal. Gen. Laws (Supp 1945); Act 261 (Deering 1944).
40. See the concurring opinion of Justice Murphy with whom Justice Rutledge joined, *Oyama v. California*, 332 U.S. 633, 652.
41. See generally *Yick Wo v. Hopkins*, 118 U.S. 356 (1886); *Hirabayashi v. U.S.*, 320 U.S. 81 (1943); *Korematsu v. United States*, 321 U.S. 760 (1944).
42. 7 Fed. Reg. 1407.

44. See the dissent of Justice Roberts in *Korematsu v. United States*, 321 U.S. 760 (1944).

44. *Oyama v. California*, 332 U.S. 633 (1948).

45. Ibid., 633, 635.

46. Ibid., 633, 644.

47. Ibid., 633, 672.

48. Ibid., 633, 673.

49. *Brown v. Topeka Board of Education*, 347 U.S. 483 (1954).

50. *Berman v. Parker*, 348 U.S. 26 (1954).

51. "[N]or shall private property be taken for public use, without just compensation," Fifth Amend. U.S. Const.

52. *Kelo v. City of New London*, 125 S.t. 2655 (2005).

53. *Reitman v. Mulky*, 387 U.S. 369 (1967).

54. Ibid., 369, 371.

55. Akron Ordinance No. 873-1964, as amended by Akron Ordinance No. 926-1964. See *Hunter v. Erickson*, 393 U.S. 385, 386 (1969).

56. Akron City Charter 137; *Hunter v. Erickson*, 393 U.S. 385, 387 (1969).

57. *Hunter v. Erickson*, 393 U.S. 385 (1969).

58. Ibid., 385, 390 (1969).

59. Ibid.

60. Ibid.

61. *Arlington Heights v. Metropolitan Development Housing Corporation (MHDC)*, 429 U.S. 252 (1977).

62. *Memphis v. Greene*, 451 U.S. 100 (1981).

63. The Civil Rights Act of 1866 is subsumed into the Federal Civil Rights Statute 42 U.S.C., Section 1982.

64. *Memphis v. Greene*, 451 U.S. 100, 128 (1981).

65. Ibid., 100, 155 (1981).

66. Civil Rights Act of 1964, Pub. L. No. 88-352 (codified as amended at 42 U.S.C. 2000d [2004]). "[N]o person in the United States shall, on the ground of race, color, or national origin, be excluded from participation in, be denied the benefits of, or subjected to discrimination under any program or activity receiving financial assistance."

67. U.S. Commission on Civil Rights (1959); Leonard S. Rubinowitz and Ismail Alsheik, *A Missing Piece: Fair Housing and the 1964 Civil Rights Act*, 48 Howard L. J. 841 (Spring 2005).

68. 42 U.S.C. 3601 *et seq.*

69. See *Jones v. Alfred H. Mayer Company*, 392 U.S. 409 (1968).

70. Ibid., 409, 442–443.

71. Ibid., 409, 422.

72. *Sullivan v. Little Hunting Park, Inc.*, 396 U.S. 229 (1969).

73. *Tillman v. Wheaton-Haven Recreation Association*, 410 U.S. 431 (1973).

74. *Meyer v. Holley*, 537 U.S. 280 (2002).

75. The Attorney General's 2004 Annual Report to Congress Pursuant to the Equal Credit Opportunity Act, Amendments of 1976 (March 10, 2005).

76. The Attorney General's 2004 Annual Report to Congress Pursuant to the Equal Credit Opportunity Act, Amendments of 1976 (March 10, 2005).

77. U.S. Const. Art. I, Sec. 8.

78. *Civil Rights Cases*, 109 U.S. 1 (1883).

79. Ida B. Wells-Barnett, *Crusade for Justice: The Autobiography of Ida B. Wells*, ed. Alfreda M. Duster (Chicago: University of Chicago Press, 1970), 18–19.

80. Ibid.

81. *Chesapeake & Ohio & Southwestern Railroad Company v. Wells*, Tennessee Reports: Supreme Court of Tennessee for the Western Division, Jackson, April Term, 1887

82. Wells-Barnett, *Crusade for Justice: The Autobiography of Ida B. Wells*, 20.

83. Ibid.

84. *Mitchell v. United States*, 313 U.S. 80 (1941).

85. Arthur Wergs Mitchell (1883–1963) served in the U.S. House of Representatives from 1935 to 1943. For more information, see: Dennis S. Nordin, *The New Deal's Black Congressman: A Life of Arthur Wergs Mitchell* (Columbia: University of Missouri Press, 1997).

86. *Mitchell v. United States*, 313 U.S. 80, 89 (1941).

87. Ibid., 80, 90–91.

88. Ibid., 80, 94.

89. *Henderson v. United States*, 80 F. Su32, 39 (MD. 1948).

90. *Henderson v. United States*, 339 U.S. 816 (1950).

91. *Boynton v. Virginia*, 364 U.S. 454 (1960).

92. See Raymond Arsenault, *Freedom Riders: 1961 and the Struggle for Racial Justice* (New York: Oxford University Press, 2006); *Lewis v. Greyhound*, 199 F. Supp. 210 (M.D. AL. 1961). John Lewis was a U.S. representative.

93. See *Muir v. Louisville Park Theatrical Ass'n*, 347 U.S. 971 (1954).

94. *Sweeney et al. v. Louisville*, 120 F. Su525 (1951).

95. *Muir v. Louisville*, 202 F. 2d 275 (1953).

96. *Florida Ex. Rel. Hawkins v. Board of Control of Florida*; *Muir v. Louisville Park Theatrical Association*; and *Tureaud v. Board of Supervisors of Louisiana State University and Agricultural and Mechanical College*, 347 U.S. 971 (1954).

97. See *Wolfe v. North Carolina*, 364 U.S. 177 (1960).

98. *Burton v. Wilmington Parking Authority*, 365 U.S. 715 (1961).

99. *Bell v. Maryland*, 378 U.S. 226, 254 (1964).

100. See *Watson v. Memphis*, 373 U.S. 526 (1963); *Bell v. Maryland*, 378 U.S. 226, 252 (1964).

101. Civil Rights Act of 1964, Pub. L. No. 88-352, 78 Stat. 241 (July 2, 1964).

102. See *Georgia v. Rachel*, 384 U.S. 780 (1966).

103. *Brown v. Louisiana*, 383 U.S. 131 (1966).

104. Ibid., 131, 135–136.

105. Ibid., 131, 136.

106. Ibid.

107. Ibid., 131, 142.

108. *Palmer v. Thompson*, 403 U.S. 217 (1971).

109. Ibid., 217, 268.

110. Civil Rights Act of 1964 (78 Stat 241).

111. See *Heart of America Motel, Inc. v. United States and Robert F. Kennedy, Attorney General*, 231 F. Su393 (N.D. 1964).

112. Ibid., 379 U.S. 241, 245.

113. See *Katzenbach v. McClung*, 379 U.S. 294 (1964).

114. *McClung v. Katzenbach*, 233 F. Su815 (N.D. AL. 1964).

115. *Katzenbach v. McClung*, 379 U.S. 294, 296 (1964).

116. Ibid.

117. Ibid., 294, 297.

118. Ibid., 294, 298–299.

119. Ibid., 294, 304–305.

120. Civil Rights Act of 1964, Title II, 42 U.S.C. Sec. 2000a.

121. *McDonnell Douglas Corp. v. Green*, 411 U.S. 792 (1973).

122. Ibid., 792, 802.

123. Ibid.

124. Ibid.

125. See *NAACP v. Cracker Barrel Old Country Store Inc.*, No. 4:01-CV-325-HLM (N.D. Ga. April 11, 2002) (refused and insulted Blacks).

126. See *LaRoche v. Dennys, Inc.*, 62 F. Su2d 1375 (S.D. Fla. 1999) (interracial group refused service after being told by the manager "you don't look right"). See *Ridgeway v. Flagstar Corporation and Denny's, Inc., United States v. Flagstar Corporation and Denny's Inc.*, Case No. C 93-20202 JW, consolidated with C 93-20208 JW (N.D. Cal.. September 22, 1994) (class action brought by private plaintiffs and consolidated with action of U.S. Justice Department).

127. See *Slocum v. Waffle House*, 365 F. Su2d 1332 (N.D. GA. 2005). See *Wilson v. Waffle House*, No. Civ.A.97W647N, 1998 WL 1665880 (M.D. Ala. Apr. 28, 1998) (refused Black customers).

128. See *United States v. HBE Corporation d/b/a Adam's Mark Hotel*, C.A. No. 99-1604-CIV-ORL-22C (M.D. FL 2000) (refused and insulted Black customers).

129. Florence Wagman Roisman, *Keeping the Promise: Ending Racial Discrimination and Segregation in Federally Financed Housing*, 48 Howard L. J. 913 (Spring 2005).

130. Oliver and Shapiro, *Black Wealth/White Wealth: A New Perspective on Racial Inequality*, 18.

131. *Hills, Secretary of Housing and Urban Development v. Gautreaux et al.*, 425 U.S. 284 (1976).

132. *Department of Housing and Urban Development v. Rucker*, 535 U.S. 125 (2002).

133. 42 U.S.C. 1437d (1)(6).

134. *Cuyahoga Falls, Ohio, v. Buckeye Community of Hope Foundation*, 538 U.S. 188 (2003).

135. Ibid., 188, 192 (2003).
136. *Pigford v. Glickman*, 340 U.S. App.D.C. 420, 206 F. 3d 1215 (D.C. Cir. 2000).
137. See *Pigford v. Veneman*, 355 F. Su2d 148 (2005).
138. Ibid., 148, 151.
139. Ibid.
140. *Green v. Veneman*, 159 F. Su2d 360 (2001).
141. S. Law, *White Privilege and Affirmative Action*, 32 Akron L. Rev. 603, 615 (1999).
142. Ibid.
143. John Kenneth Galbraith, *The Affluent Society* (Boston: Mariner Books/ Houghton Mifflin Company, 1958), 237.
144. *Changing America: Indicators of Social and Economic Well-Being by Race and Hispanic Origin* (Washington, D.C.: Council of Economic Advisors for the President's Initiative on Race, September 1998), 60.
145. See Debbie Gruenstein Bocian, Keith S. Ernst, and Wei Li, Unfair Lending: The Effect of Race and Ethnicity on the Price of Subprime Mortgages (Center for Responsible Lending, May 31, 2006); www. centerforresponsiblelending.org/pdfs/rr011-unfair_lending-0506.pdf (last viewed on June 6, 2006).
146. The Fair Housing Act states seven criteria for discrimination: race, color, religion, national origin, sex, disability, and familial status.
147. In 2002: 2,513; in 2003: 2,745; in 2004: 2,817; and in 2005: 2,227. See FY 2005 Annual Report on Fair Housing. Bases in HUD Complaints (Table 3.1 FY 2002-FY 2005).
148. See FY 2005 Annual Report on Fair Housing. Bases in HUD Complaints (Table 3.1 FY 2002-FY 2005).
149. Ibid.
150. Ibid.
151. See Oliver and Shapiro, *Black Wealth/White Wealth: A New Perspective on Racial Inequality.*
152. U.S. Census Bureau, Census 2000: Housing and Household Economic Statistics Division (last revised June 27, 2005).
153. Ibid.
154. Changing America: Indicators of Social and Economic Well-Being by Race and Hispanic Origin September 1998; http://whitehouse.gov/ WH/EOP/CEA/html/publication.html.
155. U.S. Census Bureau, Census 2000 Redistricting Data (Public Law 94-171) Summary File, Table PL1.
156. U.S. Census Bureau, Census 2000. Housing Patterns. Chapter 5, Residential Segregation of Blacks or African Americans: 1980 to 2000. "The list includes 43 metropolitan areas with 3% or 20,000 or more Blacks or African Americans and 1,000,000 or more total population in 1980. The five most segregated metropolitan areas for Blacks in 2000 were, in order, Milwaukee–Waukesha, Detroit, Cleveland–Lorain–Elyria, St. Louis,

and Newark (Milwaukee–Waukesha and Detroit are less than one average rank apart). Cincinnati, Buffalo–Niagara Falls, and New York are roughly tied for number six, but each is more than one average rank behind Newark);" www.census.gov/hhs/www.housing/housing_patterns/ch5.html.

157. Ibid.

158. Ibid.

159. Ibid.

160. Changing America: Indicators of Social and Economic Well-Being by Race and Hispanic Origin, 60–61.

161. Levittown CDP, New York Statistics and Demographics (U.S. Census 2000).

162. www.Newsday.com (Levittown edition) (last viewed March 2006).

Chapter 4

1. *Bolling v. Sharp*, 347 U.S. 497, 499 (1954).

2. U.S. Const. 1st Amend.

3. *Bailey v. Poindexter*, 55 Va. 132 (1858).

4. Ibid.

5. Ibid. (as indicated, 45–46).

6. Ibid.

7. Statutes at Large of South Carolina, vol. 7, 353.

8. Va. Stat. 1682. Act III; Hening, Stat., Vol. 2, 18; A. Leon Higginbotham, *In the Matter of Color* (New York: Oxford University Press, 1978), 40.

9. See Peter M. Bergman, *The Chronological History of the Negro in America* (New York: Harper and Row, 1969).

10. For more information, see the Race and Slavery Petitions Project. Founded in 1991, this project was designed to locate, collect, organize, and publish virtually all surviving legislative petitions and a large selected group of county court petitions concerning slavery in the South. The project covers the period from the beginnings of statehood to the end of slavery (1770s to 1860s). Department of History, University of North Carolina-Greensboro, Greensboro, North Carolina. http://library.uncg.edu/slavery_petitions/about.asp (last viewed 7/1/06).

11. Herbert Aptheker, ed., *A Documentary History of the Negro People in the United States: From Colonial Times through the Civil War* (New York: Citadel Press, Inc., 1951), 20.

12. Ibid.

13. Ibid.

14. Manuscript in Slavery File No. 1, Free Persons of Colour, Historical Commission of South Carolina, Columbia.

15. *The Liberator*, June 28, 1844.

16. Aptheker, *A Documentary History of the Negro People in the United States: From Colonial Times through the Civil War*, 92.

17. Ibid.

18. Ibid., 93. The full title of Walker's appeal is Walker's Appeal, in Four Articles: Together with a Preamble, to the Coloured Citizens of the World, but in Particular, and very Expressly, to Those of the United States of America, Written in Boston, State of Massachusetts, September 28, 1829.

19. See *Prigg v. Pennsylvania*, 41 U.S. 539 (1842).

20. Ibid.

21. Aptheker, *A Documentary History of the Negro People in the United States: From Colonial Times through the Civil War*, 299.

22. Ibid., 305.

23. Statutes at Large of South Carolina, vol. 7, 357, 359–360; Higginbotham, *In the Matter of Color*, 177.

24. Statutes at Large of South Carolina, vol. 7, 360; Higginbotham, *In the Matter of Color*, 177.

25. Aptheker, *A Documentary History of the Negro People in the United States: From Colonial Times through the Civil War*, 194.

26. Ibid., 194–195.

27. Franklin E. Frazier, *The Negro in the United States* (New York: Macmillan Company, 1957), 88.

28. For more information on Toussaint L'Ouverture, see C. L. R. James, *The Black Jacobins: Toussaint L'Ouverture and the San Domingo Revolution* (New York: Vintage Books, 1963).

29. Frazier, *The Negro in the United States*, 88.

30. See John Killens, ed., *The Trial Record of Denmark Vesey* (Boston: Beacon Press, 1970); Herbert Aptheker, *American Slave Revolts* (New York: International Publishers, 1993).

31. Frazier, *The Negro in the United States*, 88.

32. See Killens, ed., *The Trial Record of Denmark Vesey*; Aptheker, *American Slave Revolts*.

33. Ibid.

34. Frazier, *The Negro in the United States*, 88.

35. See Killens, ed., *The Trial Record of Denmark Vesey*; Frazier, *The Negro in the United States*, 88. The number of co-conspirators has varied.

36. Frazier, *The Negro in the United States*, 88.

37. See Nat Turner, *Confessions of Nat Turner* (1831).

38. Ibid.

39. Ibid.

40. Ibid.

41. Ibid.

42. Ibid.

43. Ibid.

44. *N.Y. Evening Post*, November 19, 1831; Aptheker, *American Slave Revolts*, 302.

45. Turner, *Confessions of Nat Turner* (1831); Aptheker, *American Slave Revolts*, 302.

46. Aptheker, *American Slave Revolts*, 302.

47. General Assembly of the State of Maryland, Annapolis, 1832, chapters 281, 325; see also Aptheker, *American Slave Revolts*, 313.
48. Ibid.
49. Ibid.
50. Ibid.
51. Frazier, *The Negro in the United States*, 90–91.
52. Ibid.
53. See generally *United States v. the Libellants et al.*, 40 U.S. 518 (1841).
54. Ibid., 518, 588.
55. *Strader v. Graham*, 51 U.S. 82, 92–93 (1851).
56. Ibid., 82.
57. Ibid., 82, 93.
58. Ibid., 82, 94.
59. Ibid., 82, 96–97.
60. For more on A. Philip Randolph, see Jervis Anderson, *A. Philip Randolph: A Biographical Portrait* (Berkeley, Calif.: University of California Press, 1986); see Calvin Craig Miller, *A. Philip Randolph and the African American Labor Movement* (Greensboro, N.C.: Morgan Reynolds Publishing, 2005); see also A. Philip Randolph Institute: www.apri.org.
61. See Anderson, *A. Philip Randolph: A Biographical Portrait*.
62. Executive Order 8802 (see appendix).
63. See Anderson, *A. Philip Randolph: A Biographical Portrait*.
64. For more information on Mahatma Gandhi, see Mohandas K. Gandhi, *An Autobiography: My Experiments with Truth* (New York: Dover Publications, 1983).
65. Juan Williams, *Eyes on the Prize: America's Civil Rights Years, 1954–1965* (New York: Viking Penguin, Inc., 1987), 122–142.
66. For more information on Bayard Rustin, see John D'emilio, *Lost Prophet: The Life and Times of Bayard Rustin* (New York: Free Press, 2003).
67. For more information on Bayard Rustin, see David J. Garrow, *Bearing the Cross: Martin Luther King, Jr., and the Southern Christian Leadership Conference* (New York: William Morrow, 1986).
68. Ibid., 395-400.
69. See Arthur I. Waskow, *From Race Riot to Sit-In, 1919 to the 1960s: A Study in Connections between Conflict and Violence* (New York: Doubleday, 1966).
70. *Lombard v. Louisiana*, 373 U.S. 267 (1963).
71. Ibid., 267, 273.
72. Ibid., 267, 269.
73. Ibid.
74. Ibid.
75. Ibid., 267, 271.
76. Ibid., 267, 272.
77. Ibid.
78. *Edwards v. South Carolina*, 372 U.S. 229, 231 (1963).
79. Ibid., 229, 231.

80. Ibid.
81. Ibid., 229, 234.
82. Ibid., 229, 236.
83. Ibid., 229, 235.
84. Ibid., 229, 238.
85. *Cox v. Louisiana*, 379 U.S. 536 (1965).
86. Ibid., 536, 544.
87. Ibid., 536, 545, 549; La. Rev. Stat. Sec. 14:103.1 (Cum. Su1962).
88. *Cox v. Louisiana*, 379 U.S. 536, 549 (1965).
89. Ibid., 536, 552.
90. Ibid., 536, 551 (1965), quoting *Edwards v. South Carolina*, 372 U.S. 229, 236 (1963), and citing *Watson v. Memphis*, 373 U.S. 526, 535 (1966).
91. Ibid., 536, 552.
92. *Adderly v. Florida*, 385 U.S. 39 (1966).
93. Ibid., 39, 51.
94. Ibid., 39, 40.
95. Ibid., 39, 41.
96. Ibid., 39, 47–48.
97. Ibid., 39, 50.
98. Ibid., 39, 49.
99. Robert D. Schulzneger, *A Time for War: The United States and Vietnam 1941–1975* (New York: Oxford University Press, 1997).
100. See *Koon v. United States*, 518 U.S. 81 (1996).
101. On April 29, 1992, protests against the acquittal were immediate and spread across the country. Flames engulfed Los Angeles as homes and business were burned during six days of mass rioting. For further discussion of Rodney King, see Michael W. Markowitz and Delores Jones-Brown, eds., *The System in Black and White: Exploring Connections between Race, Crime, and Justice* (Westport, Conn.: Praeger, 2000), 86–91; *Koon v. United States*, 518 U.S. 81 (1996) (one count resulted in a hung jury).
102. *Koon v. United States*, 518 U.S. 81 (1996).
103. Rick DelVecchio and Suzanne Espinosa, "Bradley Ready to Lift Curfew. He Says L.A. is 'under control.'" *San Francisco Chronicle*, May 4, 1992, A1.
104. On August 4, 1992, a federal grand jury indicted the four officers under 18 U.S.C. § 242, charging them with violating King's constitutional rights under color of law. Powell, Briseno, and Wind were charged with willful use of unreasonable force in arresting King. Koon was charged with willfully permitting the other officers to use unreasonable force during the arrest.
105. See Report of the Independent Commission on the Los Angeles Police Department ("Christopher Commission report"), July 9, 1991; Delores D. Jones-Brown and Karen J. Terry, *Policing and Minority Communities: Bridging the Gap* (Upper Saddle River, N.J.: Pearson Education, 2004), 169.
106. *New York Times, Inc. v. Sullivan*, 376 U.S. 254, 256 (1964).
107. Ibid., 254, 257.

108. Ibid., 254, 257–258.
109. Ibid.
110. Ibid., 254, 260.
111. Ibid., 254, 259.
112. Ibid., 254, 262.
113. Ibid., 254, 256.
114. Ibid., 254, 263.
115. Ibid., 254, 264–265.
116. Ibid., 254, 283.
117. Ibid., 254, 282–283.
118. See Taylor Branch, *Parting the Waters: America in the King Years, 1954– 1963* (New York: Simon & Schuster, 1988).
119. See Lynne Olson, *Freedom's Daughters: The Unsung Heroines of the Civil Rights Movement from 1830 to 1970* (New York: Scribner, 2001).
120. See *Gayle v. Browder* and *Owen v. Browder*, 532 U.S. 903 (1956) (per curiam).
121. *NAACP v. Alabama ex rel. Patterson, Attorney General*, 357 U.S. 449 (1958).
122. Ibid., 449, 453.
123. Ibid., 449, 452.
124. Ibid.
125. Ibid., 449, 451.
126. Ibid., 449, 461.
127. Ibid., 449, 462.
128. Ibid., 449, 463.
129. Ibid., 449, 463–464.
130. See *Bryant v. Zimmerman*, 278 U.S. 63 (1928).
131. Ibid., 63, 76–77.
132. *Plessy v. Ferguson*, 163 U.S. 537, 559 (1896), quoting dissent of Justice Harlan: "[I]n view of the Constitution, in the eye of the law, there is in this country no superior, dominant, ruling class of citizens. There is no caste here. Our Constitution is color-blind, and neither knows nor tolerates classes among citizens. In respect of civil rights, all citizens are equal before the law. The humblest is the peer of the most powerful."
133. *NAACP v. Alabama ex rel. Patterson, Attorney General*, 357 U.S. 449, 465 (1958).
134. Ibid., 449, 465–466.
135. *NAACP v. Alabama*, 377 U.S. 288 (1964).
136. It was consolidated with a similar case, *Louisiana ex rel. Gremillion v. NAACP*, 366 U.S. 293 (1961).
137. *NAACP v. Alabama*, 377 U.S. 288, 292 (1964).
138. Ibid., 288, 292–293 (1964).
139. Ibid., 288, 302 (1964).
140. Ibid., 288, 304 (1964).
141. Ibid., 288, 307–308 (1964).

142. Ibid., 288, 304, 310–311 (1964), quoting *Bates v. City of Little Rock*, 361 U.S. 516, 523.

143. *Bates v. Little Rock,* 361 U.S. 516, 519 (1960).

144. Ibid., 516, 518.

145. *Bates v. City of Little Rock*, 229 Ark.819; 319 S.W.2d 37 (1958).

146. *Bates v. Little Rock,* 361 U.S. 516, 519 (1960).

147. Ibid.

148. Ibid., 516, 521.

149. Ibid., 516, 521–522.

150. Ordinance No. 10638. "An Ordinance Requiring Certain Organizations Functioning or Operating within the City of Little Rock, Arkansas to List Certain Information with the City Clerk: and For Other Purposes," October 14, 1957. The ordinance stated: "Whereas, it has been found and determined that certain organizations within the City of Little Rock, Arkansas, have been claiming immunity from…the payment of occupation licenses levied for the privilege of doing business within the city, upon the premise that such organizations are benevolent, charitable, mutual benefit, fraternal, or non-profit, and Whereas, many such organizations claiming the occupation license exemption are mere subterfuges for businesses being operated for profit which are subject to the occupation license ordinance…"

151. *Bates v. Little Rock,* 361 U.S. 516, 522 (1960).

152. Ibid., 516, 527.

153. Ibid., 516, 523–524.

154. Ibid., 516, 523.

155. *Louisiana v. NAACP*, 366 U.S. 293, 295-296 (1961); La. Rev. Stat., 1950, 14:385 (1958 Supp.).

156. La. Rev. Stat., 1950, 12:401–409; *Louisiana v. NAACP*, 366 U.S. 293, 295 (1961).

157. *Louisiana v. NAACP*, 366 U.S. 293, 295–296 (1961).

158. Ibid., 293, 296.

159. Ibid.

160. Ibid.

161. *NAACP v. Button*, 371 U.S. 415 (1963). For more information, see Geoffrey Stone, Louis Seidman, Sunstein Cass, and Mark Tushnet, *The First Amendment* (New York: Aspen Publishers, Inc., 1999), 393–395.

162. Chapters 31, 32, 33, 35, and 36 of the Virginia Acts of Assembly, 1956 Extra Session.

163. The NAACP headquarters was located on 20 West 40th Street in New York City. The organization moved to Baltimore, Maryland, in 1986.

164. *NAACP v. Button*, 371 U.S. 415, 418 (1963).

165. Ibid., 415, 428.

166. Ibid., 415, 428–429.

167. Ibid.

168. Massachusetts, chap. 6, 1705.

169. Ibid.

170. *Dred Scott v. Sandford*, 60 U.S. 393, 409 (1957).

171. *Pace v. Alabama*, 106 U.S. 583, 585 (1883).

172. Alabama Code of 1876, Section 4189.

173. Ibid., Section 4184.

174. *Pace and Cox v. Alabama*, 69 Ala. 231, 232 (1881).

175. Ibid.

176. *Pace v. Alabama*, 106 U.S. 583, 585 (1883).

177. Ibid.

178. *Hill, Warden v. U.S. ex. rel. Weiner*, 300 U.S. 105, 109 (1937).

179. *Plessy v. Ferguson*, 163 U.S. 537, 545 (1896).

180. Ibid.

181. Utah Code, 40-1-2, C.L. 17, Section 2967.

182. Ala. Const., Section 102 (1901).

183. *McLaughlin v. Florida*, 379 U.S. 184 (1964).

184. Fla. Stat., Section 798.05, F.S.A.

185. Ibid.

186. *McLaughlin v. Florida*, 379 U.S. 184, 187 (1964).

187. *McLaughlin v. Florida*, 153 So. 2d. 1 (1963).

188. *McLaughlin v. Florida*, 379 U.S. 184, 190 (1964).

189. Peter Wallenstein, *Tell the Court I Love My Wife: Race, Marriage, and Law—An American History* (New York: Palgrave Macmillan, 2004), 216.

190. Va. Code Ann. 20-58 (1960 Repl. Vol.).

191. Ibid.

192. *Loving v. Virginia*, 388 U.S. 1, 6 (1967).

193. Ibid., 1, 3.

194. Wallenstein, *Tell the Court I Love My Wife: Race, Marriage, and Law—An American History*, 217.

195. Ibid., 218.

196. *Loving v. Commonwealth of Virginia* (record no. 6163); *Loving v. Virginia*, 388 U.S. 1, 3 (1967).

197. *Loving v. Commonwealth of Virginia*, 206 Va. 924, 147 S.E. 2d 79 (1966).

198. *Loving v. Virginia*, 388 U.S. 1, 11 (1967).

199. Ibid.

200. Ibid., 1, 12.

201. *Bob Jones University v. United States*, 461 U.S. 574 (1983).

202. Ibid., 574, 580.

203. Ibid.

204. See *McCrary v. Runyon*, 515 F.2d 1082 (1975), aff'd, 427 U.S. 160 (1976).

205. *Bob Jones University v. United States*, 461 U.S. 574, 581 (1983).

206. Revenue Ruling 71-447, 1971-2 Cum. Bull. 230.

207. See *Bob Jones v. Simon*, 416 U.S. 725 (1974).

208. See *Bob Jones v. Simon*, 468 F. Su890, 907 (S. C.1978).

209. *Bob Jones University v. United States*, 461 U.S. 574, 583 (1983).

210. Ibid.

211. Derrick Bell, *Race, Racism and American Law*, 4th ed. (New York: Aspen Publishers, 2000), 345–348.

212. Ibid., 344.
213. *Bob Jones University v. United States*, 461 U.S. 574, 581–582 (1983), consolidated with *Goldsboro Christian School v. United States*, 644 F.2d 879 (4th Cir. 1981).
214. *Bob Jones University v. United States*, 461 U.S. 574, 605 (1983).
215. Ibid., 574, 612.
216. W. E. B. DuBois (1903) published in the second chapter of *The Negro Problem*, a collection of articles by African Americans. "These and others we may call the Revolutionary group of distinguished Negroes—they were persons of marked ability, leaders of a Talented Tenth, standing conspicuously among the best of their time" (writing of the responsibilities and obligations of the "talented tenth," a percentage of exceptional Black leaders, to the welfare and advancement of the Black race).
217. Bayard Ruston, *Time on Two Crosses: The Collected Writings of Bayard Ruston* (San Francisco: Cleis Press, 2003), 151.

Chapter 5

1. "Disfranchisement" is used to indicate persons who were never previously enfranchised and therefore could not be deemed disenfranchised.
2. Peter M. Bergman, *The Chronological History of The Negro in America* (New York: Harper and Row, 1969), 17.
3. Ibid., 24.
4. Herbert Aptheker, *American Negro Slave Revolts* (New York: International Publishers, 1963), 75.
5. *Cherokee Nation v. Georgia*, 30 U.S. 1 (1831); *Dred Scott v. Sandford*, 60 U.S. 393, 406 (1856).
6. 14 Stat. 27 (1866).
7. U.S. Const. Amend. XIV. (1964).
8. Ibid.
9. Ibid.
10. For further discussion of the debates leading to passage of the Fifteenth Amendment, see Daniel A. Farber and Suzanna Sherry, *A History of the American Constitution* (St. Paul, Minn.: Thomson/West, 2005), 455–487.
11. U.S. Const. Am. 15.
12. Ibid.
13. The Enforcement Act of May 31, 1870 (16 Stat. 140), later known as Section 5508 of the Revised Statute of 1873 (28 Stat. 36).
14. The Enforcement Act of 1870 (May 31, 1870). Section 5508 of the Revised Statute of the United States. Title: An Act to enforce the right of citizens of the United States to vote in the several States of this Union, and for other purposes. The Enforcement Act provided:

Sec. 5508. If two or more persons conspire to injure, oppress, threaten, or intimidate any citizen in the free exercise or enjoyment of any rights or privilege secured to him by the Constitution or laws of the United States, or because of his having so exercised the same, or if two or more persons go in disguise on the highway, or the premises of another, with intent to prevent or hinder his free exercise or enjoyment of any right or privilege so secured, they shall be fined not more than five thousand dollars and imprisoned not more than ten years; and shall, moreover, be thereafter ineligible to any office or place of honor, profit, or trust created by the Constitution or laws of the United States.

15. The Enforcement Act of 1870 (May 31, 1870). Section 5520 of the Revised Statute of the United States. Title: An Act to enforce the right of citizens of the United States to vote in the several States of this Union, and for other purposes. The statute provided:

Sec. 5520. If two or more persons in any State or Territory conspire to prevent by force, intimidation, or threat, any citizen who is lawfully entitled to vote, from giving his support or advocacy, in a legal manner, toward or in favor of the election of any lawfully qualified person as an elector for President or Vice President, or as a member of the Congress of the United States; or to injure any citizen in person or property on account of such support or advocacy; each of such persons shall be punished by a fine of not less than five hundred nor more than five thousand dollars, or by imprisonment, with or without hard labor, not less than six months nor more than six years, or by both such fine and imprisonment.

16. The Enforcement Act of 1870 (May 31, 1870) (16 Stat. 141). Section 5519 of the Revised Statute of the United States. Title: An Act to enforce the right of citizens of the United States to vote in the several States of this Union, and for other purposes.

17. Ku Klux Klan Act of April 20, 1871 (17 Stat. 13).

18. *United States v. Reese*, 92 U.S. 214, 224 (1876).

19. Ibid., 214, 215.

20. Ibid., 214, 217.

21. Ibid.

22. Ibid., 214, 219–221.

23. See *United States v. Cruikshank*, 92 U.S. 542 (1876).

24. Robert K. Carr, *Federal Protection of Civil Rights: Quest for a Sword* (Ithaca, N.Y.: Cornell University Press, 1947), 45.

25. See *United States v. Cruikshank*, 92 U.S. 542 (1876).

26. Ibid.

27. See James Haskins, *Pinckney Benton Stewart Pinchback* (New York: MacMillan Press, 1973).

28. Ibid.

29. Ibid.

30. For more information on the women's suffrage movement, see Eleanor Flexner, *Century of Struggle* (New York: Atheneum, 1970); Patricia A. Schechter, *Ida B. Wells-Barnett and American Reform, 1880–1930* (Chapel Hill: University of North Carolina Press, 2001).
31. See *Minor v. Happersett*, 88 U.S. 162 (1875).
32. Ibid., 162, 170–171.
33. Ibid., 162, 178.
34. The Nineteenth Amendment of the U.S. Constitution (ratified in 1920) granted women the right to vote.
35. See *United States v. Harris*, 106 U.S. 629 (1883).
36. Ibid., 629, 639, quoting *United States v. Cruikshank*, 92 U.S. 542 (1876).
37. See *Ex Parte Yarbrough*, 110 U.S. 651 (1884).
38. Ibid., 651, 655–657.
39. Ibid., 651, 652 (defendants Jasper Yarbrough, Dilmus Yarbrough, Jajes Yarbrough, Neal Yarbrough, Lovel Streetman, Bold Emory, State Lemmons, Jake Hayes, and E.H. Green).
40. Ibid., 651, 667.
41. Ibid., 651, 665.
42. Ibid.
43. *Plessy v. Ferguson*, 163 U.S. 537 (1896).
44. Ibid., 537, 545.
45. David Levering Lewis, *W. E. B. DuBois: Portrait of a Race, 1869–1919* (New York: Henry Holt, 1993), 260 (discussing the diminished Black vote in the South).
46. See *Giles v. Harris*, 189 U.S. 475 (1903).
47. Ibid., 475, 483.
48. Ibid., 475, 483–484.
49. *Giles v. Harris*, 189 U.S. 475, 483–484 (1903).
50. Ibid.
51. Ibid., 483.
52. Ibid., 483, 482.
53. Ibid.
54. Ibid., 475, 485.
55. That minimum damage amount was needed then for federal cases.
56. *Giles v. Harris*, 189 U.S. 475, 488 (1903).
57. Ibid., 483, 488.
58. David Josiah Brewer, an ultraconservative, was known for authoring *Holy Trinity Church v. United States*, 143 U.S. 471 (1892), in which the United States was declared a Christian nation. Justice Marshall Harlan wrote the famous dissent in *Plessy v. Ferguson*.
59. *Guinn and Beal v. United States*, 238 U.S. 347, 356 (1915).
60. See Section 5508, Rev. Stat. (now Section 19 of the Penal Code); (Rev. Stat. Sec. 2004).
61. See *Guinn and Beal v. United States*, 238 U.S. 347 (1915).
62. Ibid., 347, 364.
63. Moorfield Storey became president of the NAACP in 1910.

64. See *Lane v. Wilson*, 307 U.S. 268 (1939).

65. Ibid., 268, 270–271. See Sections 5652 , 5653 and 5654, Ok. St. Ann. Sections 72–74.

66. *Lane v. Wilson*, 307 U.S. 268, 270–271 (1939).

67. Ibid.

68. Ibid., 268, 273 (the Act of April 20, 1871, c. 22, 17 Stat. 13, which became Section 1979 of the Revised Statutes and is now 8 U.S.C. Section 43).

69. Ibid.

70. Ibid.

71. *Lane v. Wilson*, 98 F.2d 980 (1938).

72. *Lane v. Wilson*, 307 U.S. 268, 275 (1939).

73. *See Myers v. Anderson*, 238 U.S. 368, 377 (1915).

74. Ibid.; Laws of 1908, c. 525, 347.

75. Ibid., 368, 380.

76. See *Nixon v. Herndon*, 273 U.S. 536, 541 (1927). As the Fourteenth Amendment infringement was obvious, the Court chose not to consider the Fifteenth Amendment infringement issue.

77. Ibid., 536, 539.

78. Ibid.

79. Ibid.

80. Ibid.

81. Ibid.

82. Ibid., 536, 541.

83. See *Nixon v. Condon*, 286 U.S. 73 (1932).

84. Ibid., 73, 82.

85. Ibid.

86. Ibid., 73.

87. Ibid., 73, 89.

88. See *Grovey v. Townsend*, 295 U.S. 45, 55 (1935).

89. Ibid., 45, 47.

90. Ibid., 45, 48–49.

91. William Henry Hastie graduated first in his class from Amherst College in 1925 and attended Harvard Law School. Hastie was assistant solicitor, Department of the Interior, 1933–1937. He was a litigator with Charles Hamilton Houston, dean of Howard University School of Law, 1939–1946. Hastie was governor of the Virgin Islands, 1946–1949. Judge Hastie served in the Third Circuit Court of Appeals, 1949–1976.

92. *See Smith v. Allwright*, 321 U.S. 649, 663 (1944).

93. Ibid., 649, 666.

94. Ibid., 649, 670.

95. Executive Order 9981, signed July 26, 1948.

96. See *United States v. Raines*, 362 U.S. 17 (1960).

97. Ibid., 17, 27.

98. Ibid., 17, 24.

99. Ibid., 17, 25.

100. Fred Gray, Sr., was born in Montgomery, Alabama. At age twenty-four, Gray represented Mrs. Rosa Parks upon her arrest for failing to relinquish her seat on the public bus to a White male passenger. Gray was also the first civil rights lawyer for Dr. Martin Luther King, Jr. Gray was at the forefront of civil rights in Alabama, representing the men in the Tuskegee Syphilis Experiment and acting as lead counsel in cases involving racial discrimination in housing, education, jury service, and farm subsidies. Robert L. Carter graduated from Howard University School of Law in 1940 and earned his LL.M. from Columbia Law School in 1941. As counsel for the NAACP LDF, Carter successfully argued twenty-one civil rights cases before the U.S. Supreme Court. In 1972, he was appointed to the U.S. District Court for the Southern District of New York.

101. See *Colegrove v. Green*, 328 U.S. 549 (1946).

102. *Gomillion v. Lightfoot*, 364 U.S. 339, 341 (1960).

103. Ibid., 339, 342.

104. Ibid., 339, 347.

105. Ibid.

106. See *Reynolds v. Sims*, 377 U.S. 5334 (1964).

107. U.S. Const. Amend. XXIV. (1964).

108. See *Harper v. Virginia*, 240 F. Su270 (1964).

109. *Harper v. Virginia*, 383 U.S. 663, 668–669 (1966).

110. Ibid., 663, 669 (overruling *Breedlove v. Suttles*, 302 U.S. 377, 1937).

111. *Anderson v. Martin*, 375 U.S. 399, 403–404 (1964).

112. Ibid., 399, 402.

113. *Hamm v. Virginia State Board of Elections*, 379 U.S. 19 (1964), affirming *Hamm v. Virginia State Board of Elections*, 230 F. Su156 (1964).

114. Waskow, *From Race Riot to Sit-In, 1919 and the 1960s: A Study in the Connections between Conflict and Violence*, 265–266.

115. For more information on Medgar Evers, see Myrlie Evers-Williams and Manning Marable, *The Autobiography of Medgar Evers: A Hero's Life and Legacy Revealed through His Writings, Letters and Speeches* (New York: Basic Civitas Books, 2005).

116. See Federal Bureau of Investigation Web site on Medgar Evers at http://foia.fbi.gov/foiaindex/medgarevers.htm.

117. See Mayanne Vollers, *Ghosts of Mississippi: The Murder of Medgar Evers, the Trials of Byron De La Beckwith, and the Haunting of the New South* (New York: Little, Brown and Company, 1995).

118. See Federal Bureau of Investigation Web site on Medgar Evers at http://foia.fbi.gov/foiaindex/medgarevers.htm.

119. For more information on Viola Liuzzo, see Gary May, *The Informant: The FBI, the Ku Klux Klan and the Murder of Viola Liuzzo* (New Haven, Conn.: Yale University Press, 2005).

120. See Federal Bureau of Investigation Web site on Viola Liuzza at http://foia.fbi.gov/foiaindex/liuzzo.htm (last viewed June 22, 2006).

121. Ibid.

122. Ibid.
123. Waskow, *From Race Riot to Sit-Ins, 1919 and the 1960s: A Study in the Connections Between Conflict and Violence*, 263–268.
124. For more information on Fannie Lou Hamer (1917–1977), see Kay Mills, *This Little Light of Mine: The Life of Fannie Lou Hamer* (New York: Dutton Press, 1993); Chana Kai Lee, *For Freedom Sake: The Life of Fannie Lou Hamer* (Chicago: The Board of Trustee at the University of Illinois, 2000); Juan Williams, *Eyes on the Prize: America's Civil Rights Years 1954–1965* (New York: Viking Press, 1987).
125. Mills, *This Little Light of Mine: The Life of Fannie Lou Hamer*, 51.
126. Ibid., 59–60.
127. Testimony before the Credentials Committee, Democratic National Convention, Atlantic City, New Jersey, August 22, 1964.
128. Mills, *This Little Light of Mine: The Life of Fannie Lou Hamer*, 104.
129. Testimony before the Credentials Committee, Democratic National Convention, Atlantic City, New Jersey, August 22, 1964.
130. Ibid.
131. Jerry DeMuth, "Tired of Being Sick and Tired," *Nation*, 1 June 1964. Reprinted in *Reporting Civil Rights: Part II: American Journalism 1963–1973* (New York: Penguin, 2003), 99–106.
132. Fannie Lou Hamer, *To Praise Our Bridges: An Autobiography* (Jackson, Mich.: KIPCO,1967), quoted in *The Eyes on the Prize Civil Rights Reader: Documents, Speeches, and Firsthand Accounts from the Black Freedom Struggle, 1954–1990*, eds. Claiborne Carson et al. (New York: Penguin Books, 1991), 179.
133. Pub. L. 89-110, 79 Stat. 437.
134. Ibid.
135. Mills, *This Little Light of Mine: The Life of Fannie Lou Hamer*, 230.
136. See *Mobile v. Bolden*, 446 U.S. 55 (1980).
137. Ibid., 55, 66.
138. Ibid., 55, 58.
139. Derrick A. Bell, Jr., *Constitutional Conflicts, Part 1* (Cincinnati, Ohio: Anderson Publishing Co, 1997), 230.
140. *Mobile v. Bolden*, 446 U.S. 55, 72–75 (1980).
141. Ibid., 55, 80.
142. See *Shaw v. Reno*, 509 U.S. 630 (1993).
143. See *Holder v. Hall*, 512 U.S. 874 (1994); see *Miller v. Johnson*, 515 U.S. 900 (1995).
144. *Holder v. Hall*, 512 U.S. 874, 877–878 (1994).
145. Ibid., 874, 895
146. Ibid.
147. *Richardson v. Ramirez*, 418 U.S. 24, 27 (1974).
148. Ibid.
149. Ibid., 24, 28.
150. Ibid., 24, 31.
151. Ibid., 24, 30.

152. Ibid., 24, 56.
153. Ibid.
154. Ibid., 24, 48.
155. *Johnson v. Bush*, 353 F. 3d 1287, 1292 (11th Cir. 2003).
156. Ibid.
157. Fla. Const. art. VI, § 4 (1968).
158. *Johnson v. Bush*, 353 F. 3d 1287, 1292 (11th Cir. 2003).
159. Ibid.
160. *Johnson v. Bush*, 126 S. Ct. 650 (2005) (cert denied).
161. *Gore v. Harris*, 779 So. 2d 270 (2000).
162. See *Bush v. Gore*, 531 U.S. 98 (2000).
163. Ibid.
164. Ibid., 98, 122.
165. *NAACP v. Harris*, Case No. 01-CIV-120 (January 10, 2001).
166. See Jeff Manza and Christopher Uggen, *Locked Out: Felon Disenfranchisement and American Democracy* (New York: Oxford University Press, 2006).
167. Ibid.
168. Ibid.
169. Fannie Lou Hamer, Rosa Parks, and Coretta Scott King Voting Rights Act Reauthorization and Amendments Act of 2006.

Chapter 6

1. See Appendix D for a list of U.S. military conflicts.
2. Benjamin Quarles, *The Negro in the American Revolution* (Chapel Hill: University of North Carolina Press, 1961), 14.
3. A. Leon Higginbotham, *In the Matter of Color* (New York: Oxford University Press, 1980), 38.
4. Ibid., 108.
5. Act X, 1680; Higginbotham, *In the Matter of Color*, 39.
6. Allen D. Chandler, ed., *Colonial Records of Georgia (CROG)* (Atlanta, Ga.: Franklin Printing and Publishing Co., 1904), vol. 1, 25.; Higginbotham, *In the Matter of Color*, 259.
7. Pennypacker, 54–55; Higginbotham, *In the Matter of Color* (New York: Oxford University Press, 1980), 307.
8. Chandler, ed., *Colonial Records of Georgia (CROG)*, vol. 1, 40; Higginbotham, *In The Matter of Color*, 260.
9. For more information, see Simon Schama, *Rough Crossings: Britain, the Slaves and the American Revolution* (New York: HarperCollins, 2006).
10. Higginbotham, *In the Matter of Color*, 88.
11. Martin Binkin and Mark J. Eitelberg, *Blacks and the Military* (Washington, D.C.: Brookings, Institution, 1982), 12.
12. Higginbotham, *In the Matter of Color*, 88.
13. Schama, *Rough Crossings: Britain, the Slaves and the American*, 7–8; Higginbotham, *In the Matter of Color*, 137.

14. Ibid.
15. Ibid.
16. Robin Winks, *The Blacks in Canada: A History*, 2nd ed. (Montreal: McGill-Queen's University Press, 1997), 32.
17. William L. Katz, *Eyewitness: The Negro in American History* (New York: Pitman Publishing Corp., 1968), 46–48; Robert R. Greene, *Black Defenders of America, 1775–1973: A Reference and Pictorial History* (Chicago: Johnson Publishing Co., 1974), 3–5.
18. Katz, *Eyewitness: The Negro in American History*, 47.
19. Ibid.
20. First General Militia Act of 1785 (Massachusetts); Higginbotham, *In the Matter of Color*, 88.
21. Resolutions adopted by the Church Anti-Slavery Society on May 25, 1863, in Cheever Papers, James M. McPherson, *The Struggle for Equality, Abolitionists and the Negro in the Civil War and Reconstruction* (Princeton, N.J.: Princeton University Press, 1964), 193.
22. McPherson, *The Struggle for Equality, Abolitionists and the Negro in the Civil War and Reconstruction*, 196.
23. Frederick Douglass, "Men of Color, to Arms!" May 22, 1863.
24. McPherson, *The Struggle for Equality, Abolitionists and the Negro in the Civil War and Reconstruction*, 202, 205.
25 New York World, Dec. 13, 1863; McPherson, *The Struggle for Equality, Abolitionists and the Negro in the Civil War and Reconstruction*, 212.
26. U.S. Statutes at Large, XIII, 129–130; McPherson, *The Struggle for Equality, Abolitionists and the Negro in the Civil War and Reconstruction*, 217.
27. Binkin and Eitelberg, *Blacks and the Military*, 14.
28. Ibid., 15–16.
29. Ibid., 14–15.
30. Ibid., 14.
31. See James M. McPherson, *What They Fought For, 1861–1865* (New York: Anchor/Random House, 1995).
32. Gilbert Thomas Stephenson, *Race Distinctions in American Law* (New York: D. Appleton and Co., 1910), 145.
33. Ibid.
34. Ibid.
35. Although awarded the Congressional Medal of Honor during the Civil War, Sgt. Carney would not receive the medal until 1900.
36. Derrick Bell, *Race, Racism and American Law* (New York: Aspen Publishers, 2000), 55–56, quoting from Mary Frances Berry, *Toward Freedom and Civil Rights for the Freedmen: Military Policy Origins of the Thirteenth Amendment and the Civil Rights Act of 1866* (unpublished manuscript, Dept. of History, Howard University, 1975), note 2, 7–8.
37. Binkin and Eitelberg, *Blacks and the Military*, 15.
38. Gail Buckley, *American Patriots: The Story of Blacks in the Military from the Revolution to Desert Storm* (New York: Random House, 2001), 113.

39. Binkin and Eitelberg, *Blacks and the Military*, 15–16.
40. Ibid., 15.
41. Buckley, *American Patriots: The Story of Blacks in the Military from the Revolution to Desert Storm*, 153.
42. Ibid., 150.
43. Ibid., 160.
44. Ibid., 161.
45. Richard M. Dalfiume, *Desegregation of the U.S. Armed Forces—Fighting on Two Fronts 1939–1953* (Columbia: University of Missouri Press, 1969), 7.
46. For more information see Robert V. Haynes, *A Night of Violence: The Houston Riot of 1917* (Baton Rouge, LA: Louisiana State University Press, 1976).
47. Buckley, *American Patriots: The Story of Blacks in the Military from the Revolution to Desert Storm*, 163.
48. Ibid., 220–221.
49. See Buckley, *American Patriots: The Story of Blacks in the Military from the Revolution to Desert Storm*.
50. See Charles Hamilton Houston: A Gallery, sponsored by Cornell Law School. www.law.cornell.edu/houston/housbio.htm.
51. See Genna Rae McNeil, *Groundwork: Charles Hamilton Houston and the Struggle for Civil Rights* (Philadelphia: University of Pennsylvania Press, 1983).
52. Mario Azevedo, *Africana Studies: A Survey of Africa and the African Diaspora*, 3rd ed. (Durham, N.C.: Carolina Academic Press, 2005), 135.
53. Linda Wheeler, "Routing a Ragtag Army," *Washington Post*, April 12, 1999, A1; http://www.washingtonpost.com/wp-srv/local/2000/bonus0412.htm; "The Bonus Army: Eyewitness to History," www.eye.eyewitnesstohistory.com (2000).
54. Wheeler, "Routing a Ragtag Army."
55. David Levering Lewis, *W. E. B. DuBois 1868–1919: Biography of a Race* (New York: Henry Holt and Company, 1993), 578.
56. See Carl Sandburg, *The Chicago Race Riots, July 1919* (New York: Harcourt, Brace & Howe, 1919). For more information on the Chicago riots, see C. K. Doreski, "From News to History: Robert Abbott and Carl Sandburg Read the 1919 Chicago Riot," *African American Review*, 26, no. 4 (1992): 637–650.
57. See James Weldon Johnson, *Along This Way: The Autobiography of James Weldon Johnson* (New York: Penguin Press, 1933).
58. Ibid.
59. Dalfiume, *Desegregation of the U.S. Armed Forces—Fighting on Two Fronts 1939–1953*, 20.
60. Robert A. Gibson, The Negro Holocaust: Lynching and Race Riots in the United States, 1880–1950. www.yale.edu/ynhti/curriculum/units/1979/2/79.02.04.x.html.

61. Alan L. Gropman, *The Air Force Integrates: 1945–1964* (Washington, D.C.: Office of Air Force History, 1978), 5–6.

62. Buckley, *American Patriots: The Story of Blacks in the Military from the Revolution to Desert Storm*, 28.

63. Ibid., 39.

64. Ibid., 45.

65. Ibid., 40.

66. Ibid., 45.

67. Gropman, *The Air Force Integrates: 1945–1964* (Washington, D.C.: Office of Air Force History, 1978), 5–6.

68. Buckley, *American Patriots: The Story of Blacks in the Military from the Revolution to Desert Storm*, 84.

69. Gropman, *The Air Force Integrates: 1945–1964*, 1.

70. Buckley, *American Patriots: The Story of Blacks in the Military from the Revolution to Desert Storm*, 74.

71. See Stephen E. Ambrose, *D-Day June 6, 1944: The Climatic Battle of World War II* (New York: Simon and Schuster, 1994).

72. For more on A. Philip Randolph, see Jervis Anderson, *A. Philip Randolph: A Biographical Portrait* (Berkeley: University of California Press, 1986); Calvin Craig Miller, *A. Philip Randolph and the African American Labor Movement* (Greensboro, N.C.: Morgan Reynolds Publishing, 2005); A. Philip Randolph Institute: www.apri.org.

73. See Anderson, *A. Philip Randolph: A Biographical Portrait*.

74. Executive Order 8802.

75. See Anderson, *A. Philip Randolph: A Biographical Portrait*.

76. Congress failed to pass the Dyer Anti-Lynching bill of 1922 after years of debate in Congress. The Costigan–Wagner (Anti-Lynching) Bill of 1935 was debated in Congress for nearly twenty years and finally defeated by a contingent of Southern congressmen. The act would have held law enforcement responsible for failing to take action during a lynching.

77. See Robert J. Lilly and Michael J. Thomson, Executing U.S. Soldiers in England, WWII: The Power of Command Influence and Sexual Racism, 1995. http://sun.soci.niu.edu/~critcrim/dp/dppapers/lil.exec.us.gis.

78. Death Penalty Information Center. http://www.deathpenaltyinfo.org.

79. See Lilly and Thomson, Executing U.S. Soldiers in England, WWII: The Power of Command Influence and Sexual Racism, 1995. http://sun.soci.niu.edu/~critcrim/dp/dppapers/lil.exec.us.gis.

80. Ibid.

81. Ibid.

82. See William H. Johnson, Port Chicago Explosion and Mutiny, Moon over Harlem, www.webpawner.com/users/PortofChicago/.

83. Ibid.

84. Buckley, *American Patriots: The Story of Blacks in the Military from the Revolution to Desert Storm*, 310.

85. Ibid., 310; Johnson, Port Chicago Explosion and Mutiny, Moon over Harlem, www.webpawner.com/users/PortofChicago/.

86. Ibid.
87. Ibid.
88. Forty-Seventh Congress. Session I. 1882. Chapter 126. An act to execute certain treaty stipulations relating to Chinese.
89. *Ozawa v. United States*, 260 U.S. 178 (1922). See generally *Oyama v. California*, 332 U.S. 633 (1948).
90. 8 U.S.C. Section 703.
91. See *United States v. Wong Kim Ark*, 169 U.S. 649 (1898).
92. Ibid., 649, 705.
93. See *U.S. v. Bhagat Singh Thind*, 261 U.S. 204 (1923).
94. Ibid.
95. Frank Wu, *Yellow: Race in America beyond Black and White* (New York: Perseus, 2002), 13–16.
96. *Korematsu v. United States*, 323 U.S. 214, 226-7 (1944) (Roberts, J.) (dissent).
97. 7 Fed. Reg. 2601.
98. *Hirabayshi v. United States*, 320 U.S. 81, 95 (1943).
99. *Korematsu v. United States*, 214, 218–219.
100. *Ex Parte Mitsuye Endo*, 323 U.S. 283, 293 (1944).
101. *Korematsu v. United States*, at 214, 218–219.
102. For discussion of internment, see Frank Wu, *Yellow: Race in America beyond Black and White* (New York: Perseus, 2002), 95–103.
103. *Hirabayshi v. United States*, at 81, 96.
104. Ibid., at 96–97.
105. *Korematsu v. United States*, 214.
106. Ibid., at 220.
107. Ibid., at 223–224.
108. Ibid., at 225.
109. Ibid., at 243.
110. http://www.medalofhonor.com/AsianAmericanWorldWarII-Recipients.htm.
111. *Korematsu v. United States*, 584 F. Su1406 (N.D. Cal. 1984).
112. *Hirabayshi v. United States*, 828 F.2d 591 (9th Cir. 1987).
113. Ibid.
114. For more information, see Jeré Bishop Franco, *Crossing the Pond: The Native American Effort in World War II* (Denton, TX: University of Texas Press, 1999).
115. Snyder Act of November 2, 1921 (The Act of November 2, 1921, ch. 115, 42 Stat. 208; P.L. 94–482 (sec. 410) 90 Stat. 2233; 25 U.S.C. 13).
116. Carl Rowan, *Dream Makers, Dream Breakers: The World of Justice Thurgood Marshall* (Boston: Little, Brown and Company, 1993), 80.
117. Gropman, *The Air Force Integrates: 1945–1964*, 166–167.
118. Rowan, *Dream Makers, Dream Breakers: The World of Justice Thurgood Marshall*, 162.
119. Ibid., 167.

120. See Ira Katznelson, *When Affirmative Action Was White* (New York: W.W. Norton & Co., 2005).

121. Ibid., 13.

122. Ibid., 130–141, 170–171.

123. Robert D. Schulzneger, *A Time for War: The United States and Vietnam 1941–1975* (New York: Oxford University Press, 1997), 236–237.

124. Ibid.

125. *Bond v. Floyd*, 385 U.S. 116, 121 (1966).

126. Ibid.

127. Ibid., 116, 119.

128. Ibid.

129. Ibid., 116, 125.

130. Ibid.

131. Ibid., 116, 121.

132. Ibid., 116, 128.

133. Ibid.

134. Ibid.

135. Ibid., 116, 136.

136. The Vietnam War lasted from 1962 to 1973.

137. See Wallace Terry, *Bloods: An Oral History of the Vietnam War by Black Veterans* (New York: Ballantine Books, 1984).

138. Ibid., 137.

139. Ibid.

140. Schulzneger, *A Time for War: The United States and Vietnam 1941–1975*, 287.

141. *Clay, aka Ali, v. United States*, 403 U.S. 698 (1971).

142. For more on Muhammad Ali, see Muhammad Ali with Hana Yasmeen Ali, *Muhammad Ali, Soul of a Butterfly: Reflections on a Life's Journey* (New York: Simon & Schuster, 2004).

143. *Clay, aka Ali, v. United States*, 403 U.S. 698, 707 (1971).

144. Ibid., 698, 706–707.

145. Ibid., 698, 699.

146. Ibid., 698, 700.

147. Ibid., 698.

148. See Louis Stokes, Racism in the Military: A New System for Rewards and Punishment, Congressional Black Caucus Report, *Congressional Record*, 92nd Cong., 2d sess. (14 October 1972), 36582.

149. Black Panther Eldridge Cleaver wrote extensively on Vietnam. See Eldridge Cleaver, "The Black Man's Stake in Vietnam" in *Two Three... Many Vietnams: A Radical Reader on the Wars in Southeast Asia and the Conflicts at Home*, eds. Garrett Banning and Katherine Barkley (San Francisco: Canfield Press, 1971), 216–221; "Cleaver and Black Panther Group Attend Hanoi Observance," *New York Times*, August 19, 1970, 13.

150. James E. Westheider *Fighting on Two Fronts: African Americans and the Vietnam War* (New York: New York University Press, 1997), 137–139.

151. Ibid.

152. See CRS Report for Congress, American War and Military Operations Casualties: Lists and Statistics (Washington, D.C.: Library of Congress) (Updated July 13, 2005).

153. See Westheider, *Fighting on Two Fronts: African Americans and the Vietnam War.*

154. Ibid.; see Terry, *Bloods: An Oral History of the Vietnam War by Black Veterans.*

155. For more information, see Career Progression of Minority and Women Officers (Department of Defense: Office of the Under Secretary of Defense Personnel and Readiness, 1997).

156. Based on Bureau of Labor Statistics data. www.bls.gov (data extracted June 26, 2006).

157. Career Progression of Minority and Women Officers (Department of Defense: Office of the Under Secretary of Defense Personnel and Readiness, 1997).

158. United States Government Accountability Office, Military Personnel: Reporting Additional Servicemember Demographics Could Enhance Congressional Oversight, (GAO-04-952) September 2005, 9.

159. Ibid.

160. Ibid., 3; see *The Journal of Blacks in Higher Education*, Issue 49, Autumn 2005.

161. United States Government Accountability Office, Military Personnel: Reporting Additional Servicemember Demographics Could Enhance Congressional Oversight, (GAO-04-952) September 2005, 3.

162. Based on Bureau of Labor Statistics data. www.bls.gov (data extracted June 26, 2006); http://www.cbtu.org/2003website/takingastand/blackunemployment.html (last viewed June 26, 2006).

163. For more information, see Career Progression of Minority and Women Officers (Department of Defense: Office of the Under Secretary of Defense Personnel and Readiness, 1997).

164. United States Government Accountability Office, Military Personnel: Reporting Additional Servicemember Demographics Could Enhance Congressional Oversight, (GAO-04-952) September 2005, 34–36.

165. See *The Journal of Blacks in Higher Education*, Issue 49, Autumn 2005; United States Government Accountability Office, Military Personnel: Reporting Additional Servicemember Demographics Could Enhance Congressional Oversight, (GAO-04-952) September 2005, 34–36.

166. See *The Journal of Blacks in Higher Education*, Issue 49, Autumn 2005.

167. Dave Moniz and Tom Siquitieri, "Front-Line Troops Disproportionately White, Not Black," *USA Today*, January 21, 2003.

168. Congressional Research Service Report for Congress, American War and Military Operations Casualties: Lists and Statistics (Washington, D.C.: Library of Congress) (updated July 13, 2005), at CRS-6.

169. Ibid.

170. http://www.ojp.usdoj.gov/bjs/pub/pdf/vpj.pdf; see *Sourcebook of Criminal Justice* 2000. U.S. Department of Justice, Bureau of Justice Statistics (Washington, D.C.: USGPO, 2001).

171. Of 2,426 prisoners under military jurisdiction, 827 were Black. See U.S. Department of Justice, Office of Justice Programs. Bureau of Justice Statistics, Correctional Populations in the United States, 1998 (Table 8.5).

172. Bayard Ruston, *Time on Two Crosses: The Collected Writings of Bayard Ruston* (San Francisco: Cleis Press, 2003), 148.

173. Greene, *Black Defenders of America, 1775–1973: A Reference and Pictorial History*, 221–222.

Chapter 7

1. Delores Jones-Brown, *Race, Crime and Punishment* (Philadelphia: Chelsea House Publishers, 2000), 88.

2. Ibid.

3. See Zelma Weston Henriques and Norma Manatu-Rupert, "Living on the Outside: African American Women before, during, and after Imprisonment, *The Prison Journal*, 81(1), March 2001, 6–19.

4. Janice Joseph, Overrepresentation of Minority Youth in the Juvenile Justice System: Discrimination or Disproportionality of Delinquent Acts? In *The System in Black and White: Exploring the Connections between Race, Crime, and Justice*, Michael W. Markowitz and Delores Jones-Brown, eds. (Westport, Conn.: Praeger, 2000), 227.

5. A. Leon Higginbotham, *In the Matter of Color Race & The American Legal Process: The Colonial Period* (New York, Oxford University Press, 1978), 32, quoting William Goodell, *The American Slave Code in Theory and Practice* (1853); reprint. ed., New York: New American Library, 1969, 17.

6. Hening, Statutes, vol. 2, 270; Higginbotham, *In the Matter of Color: Race & the American Legal Process: The Colonial Period*, 36.

7. Ibid.

8. Statutes at Large of South Carolina, vol. 7, 360; Higginbotham, *In the Matter of Color: Race & The American Legal Process: The Colonial Period*, 177.

9. Robert B. Shaw, *A Legal History of Slavery in the United States* (Potsdam, N.Y.: Northern Press, 1972), 174.

10. Edward L. Ayers, *Vengeance & Justice: Crime and Punishment in the 19th Century American South* (New York: Oxford University Press, 1984), 61.

11. Melton McLaurin, *Celia, A Slave: A True Story* (Athens: University of Georgia Press, 1991), 135.

12. *State v. Celia, a Slave*, Celia File No. 4496.

13. McLaurin, *Celia, A Slave: A True Story*, 135.

14. Missouri Statutes, 1845, Art 2, Sec. 29, 180; see also McLaurin, *Celia, A Slave: A True Story*, 107.

15. Gloria J. Browne-Marshall, Denial of Innocence: Black Girls and the Statutory Rape Debate (conference presentation, March 2006).
16. McLaurin, *Celia, A Slave: A True Story*, 120.
17. Civil Rights Act, 14 Stat. at Large 27. (April 9, 1866).
18. Ibid.
19. Ibid.
20. *Blyew v. United*, 80 U.S. 581, 593 (1871).
21. See Herbert Aptheker, *American Negro Slave Revolts* (New York: International Publishers, 1943).
22. Frazier, E. Franklin, *The Negro in the United States* (New York: Macmillan Company, 1957), 91.
23. Fugitive Slave Act of 1850, Sec. 5 and Sec. 7.
24. Ibid.
25. *See Prigg v. Pennsylvania*, 41 U.S. 539 (1842).
26. Ibid., 626.
27. James Horton and Lois Horton, *A Federal Assault: African Americans and the Impact of the Fugitive Slave Law of 1850*, 68 Chicago-Kent L. Rev. 1179, 1187–1189 (2003).
28. Herbert Aptheker, ed., *A Documentary History of the Negro People in the United States: From Colonial Times through the Civil War* (New York: Citadel Press, Inc.), 299.
29. See *Abelman v. Booth*, 62 U.S. 506 (1859).
30. J. Horton and L. Horton, "A Federal Assault: African Americans and the Impact of the Fugitive Slave Law of 1850," 1179; *Norris v. Crocker*, 54 U.S. 429 (1852).
31. "And upon a full and careful consideration of the subject, the court is of opinion, that, upon the facts stated in the plea in abatement, Dred Scott was not a citizen of Missouri within the meaning of the Constitution of the United States, and not entitled as such to sue in its courts; and, consequently, that the Circuit Court had no jurisdiction of the case, and that the judgment on the plea in abatement is erroneous" *Scott v. Sandford*, 60 U.S. 393 at 427.
32. *Scott v. Sandford*, 60 U.S. at 413, 427, 454.
33. Sherrilyn A. Ifill, *Creating a Truth and Reconciliation Commission for Lynching*, 21 Law & Ineq. J. 263, 272 (Summer 2003) citing W. E. B. DuBois, *Black Reconstruction in America* 678 (Russell and Russell, 1962) (1935).
34. U.S. Const. Thirteenth Amend. (1865).
35. Ayers, *Vengeance & Justice: Crime and Punishment in the 19th Century American South*, 185–186.
36. *Blyew v. United*, 80 U.S. 581, 593 (1871).
37. Ibid.
38. Ifill, *Creating a Truth and Reconciliation Commission for Lynching*, 263, 272.
39. See Milfred C. Fierce, *Slavery Revisited: Blacks and the Southern Convict Lease System—1865 to 1933* (New York: Africana Studies Research Center, 1994).

40. Ayers, *Vengeance & Justice: Crime and Punishment in the 19th Century American South* (New York: Oxford University Press, 1984), 186.

41. Ibid., 214–216, 221.

42. *Time on Two Crosses: The Collected Writings of Bayard Rustin*, Devon W. Carbado and Donald Weise, eds. (New York: Cleis Press, 2003), 31–57.

43. See Anne Applebaum, *Gulag: A History* (New York: Doubleday, 2003).

44. Ifill, *Creating a Truth and Reconciliation Commission for Lynching*, 263, 272.

45. Fierce, *Slavery Revisited: Blacks and the Southern Convict Lease System—1865 to 1933*, 17.

46. Ifill, *Creating a Truth and Reconciliation Commission for Lynching*, 263, 272.

47. *Blyew v. United*, 80 U.S. 581, 593 (1871).

48. *Bailey v. Alabama*, 211 U.S. 452 (1908).

49. Ibid., 452, 456.

50. Ibid.

51. Ala. Gen. Acts 1907, 636, amending the Code of 1896, Sec. 4730.

52. *Bailey v. Alabama*, 211 U.S. 452, 453 (1908).

53. Ibid., 452, 454. "When coupled with the local rule that the party cannot testify to his actual intent, it is said practically to make a crime out of a mere departure from service, which it is said, and it seems to have been conceded by the Supreme Court of Alabama, could not be done."

54. Ida B. Wells-Barnett, *Crusade for Justice: The Autobiography of Ida B. Wells*, ed. Alfreda M. Duster. (Chicago: University of Chicago Press, 1970), 209; see *supra*, table 2.

55. Derrick Bell, *Race, Racism and American Law* (New York: Aspen Publishers, 2000), 59; Oliver Cox, "Lynching and the Status Quo," in *Race, Crime and Justice: A Reader*, S. Gabbidon and H. Greene, eds. (New York: Routledge, 2005), 28–30.

56. Stewart E. Tolnay and E. M. Beck, *A Festival of Violence: An Analysis of Southern Lynchings, 1882–1930* (Chicago: University of Illinois Press, 1995), 69–71.

57. Ibid.

58. Ibid., 19 (discussing lynching as a terroristic means of social control); Odem (discussing lynching as a mechanism to maintain White supremacy), 28–29.

59. *Slavery Revisited: Blacks and the Southern Convict Lease System, 1865–1933*, 6.

60. Lynching (to execute a person without due process of law) could include such torture as burning a person alive, castration, mutilation, amputation of limbs, and/or decapitation.

61. Ralph Ginzburg, *100 Years of Lynching* (Baltimore: Black Classic Press, 1962) ("Colored Woman Hanged," *Seattle Times*, March 31, 1914), 90.

62. Lynching of Blacks in 1892 by state:
Alabama   22
Arkansas   25

California	3	
Florida	11	
Georgia	17	
Idaho	8	
Illinois	1	
Kentucky	9	
Louisiana	29	
Maryland	1	
Mississippi	16	
Missouri	6	
Montana	4	
New York	1	
North Carolina		5
North Dakota		1
Ohio	3	
Oklahoma	2	
South Carolina		5
Tennessee	28	
Texas	15	
Virginia	7	
West Virginia		5
Wyoming	9	
Arizona Terr.		3

63. Ginzburg, *100 Years of Lynching*, 90.
64. Ralph Ginzburg, *100 Years of Lynching* (Baltimore: Black Classic Press, 1962) ("Was Powerless to Aid Sister Who Was Raped and Lynched," *New York Age*, April 30, 1914), 90.
65. Tolnay and Beck, *An Analysis of Southern Lynchings, 1882–1930*, 19; Odem, 28–29.
66. Fierce, *Slavery Revisited: Blacks and the Southern Convict Lease System, 1865–1933*, 6.
67. David J. Langum, *Crossing the Line: Legislating Morality and the Mann Act* (Chicago: The University of Chicago Press, 1994), 180.
68. For more information on Jack Johnson, see Geoffrey C. Ward, *Unforgivable Blackness: The Rise and Fall of Jack Johnson* (New York: Knopf, 2004); Jack Johnson, *Jack Johnson Is a Dandy: An Autobiography* (New York: Chelsea House, 1969).
69. The Mann Act, titled after Representative James Robert Mann, was also known as the White Slave-Traffic Act of 1910. The act criminalized the forced transportation of White women across state borders for prostitution. It was passed during a wave of hysteria over an alleged White slave trade. For more information on the Mann Act, see Langum, *Crossing the Line: Legislating Morality and the Mann Act*.
70. Langum, *Crossing the Line: Legislating Morality and the Mann Act*, 182–183.
71. Ibid., 180.

72. *Plessy v. Ferguson*, 163 U.S. at 544.

73. Phillip Dray, *At the Hands of Persons Unknown: The Lynching of Black America* (New York: Modern Library, 2000), 7–8.

74. Dray, *At the Hands of Persons Unknown: The Lynching of Black America*, 13–14; Deleso Alford Washington, Exploring the Black Wombman's Sphere and the Anti-Lynching Crusade of the Early Twentieth Century, 3 *Geo. J. Gender & L.* 895, 901–902 (Summer 2002).

75. *Plessy v. Ferguson*, 163 U.S. 537 (1896).

76. *U.S. v. Shipp*, 214 U.S. 386 (1909).

77. For more information on this case, see Mark Curriden and Leroy Phillips, Jr., *Contempt of Court: The Turn-of-the-Century Lynching That Launched a Hundred Years of Federalism* (New York: Random House, 1999).

78. *U.S. v. Shipp*, 214 U.S. 386, 406 (1909).

79. Dray, *At the Hands of Persons Unknown: The Lynching of Black America*, 151.

80. *U.S. v. Shipp*, 214 U.S. 386, 406 (1909).

81. Dray, *At the Hands of Persons Unknown: The Lynching of Black America*, 152.

82. *U.S. v. Shipp*, 214 U.S. 386, 406 (1909).

83. Ibid., 386, 407.

84. Ibid., 386, 407–408.

85. Dray, *At the Hands of Persons Unknown: The Lynching of Black America*, 153.

86. *U.S. v. Shipp*, 214 U.S. 386, 407–408 (1909).

87. Dray, *At the Hands of Persons Unknown: The Lynching of Black America*, 7, 153.

88. *U.S. v. Shipp*, 214 U.S. 386, 407–408 (1909).

89. Ibid., 386, 408–409.

90. Ibid., 386, 409.

91. Ibid., 386, 408–409.

92. Ibid., 386, 416; see Curriden and Phillips, Jr., *Contempt of Court: The Turn-of-the-Century Lynching That Launched a Hundred Years of Federalism*.

93. *U.S. v. Shipp*, 214 U.S. 386, 440 (1909). The petition was filed with the U.S. Circuit Court for the Northern Division of the Eastern District of Tennessee.

94. Ibid. The habeas petition states: "Petitioner had been denied a trial by a fair and impartial jury, and had been denied the aid of counsel in violation of the Fifth and Sixth Amendments to the Federal Constitution, and that said petitioner was also denied rights secured to him under the Fourteenth Amendment to the Federal Constitution."

95. *Chattanooga Times*, "Jury Technicality—The Lawyers Worked Every Point to Save Johnson: Condemned Negro Will Probably Be Brought Back from Nashville at Once as All Danger of Violence Has Disappeared," March 5, 1906.

96. Dray, *At the Hands of Persons Unknown: The Lynching of Black America,* 154.

97. Dray, *At the Hands of Persons Unknown: The Lynching of Black America.*

98. *U.S. v. Shipp,* 214 U.S. 386, (1909).

99. Ibid., 386, 411.

100. *U.S. v. Shipp,* 214 U.S. 386, 474 (1909). Dray, *At the Hands of Persons Unknown: The Lynching of Black America,* 157.

101. Dray, *At the Hands of Persons Unknown: The Lynching of Black America.*

102. *U.S. v. Shipp,* 214 U.S. 386, 413 (1909).

103. Ibid., 386, 412.

104. Dray, *At the Hands of Persons Unknown: The Lynching of Black America,* 157.

105. *U.S. v. Shipp,* 214 U.S. 386, 413 (1909).

106. Dray, *At the Hands of Persons Unknown: The Lynching of Black America,* 157.

107. *U.S. v. Shipp,* 214 U.S. 386, 414 (1909).

108. Dray, *At the Hands of Persons Unknown: The Lynching of Black America,* 157–156.

109. *Chattanooga Times,* "'God Bless You All—I Am Innocent' Ed Johnson's Last Words Before Being Shot to Death by a Mob like a Dog: Majesty of Law Outraged by Lynchers—Mandate of the Supreme Court of the United States Disregarded and Red Riot Rampant, March 20, 1906.

110. Ibid.

111. *U.S. v. Shipp,* 214 U.S. 386, 415 (1909). Charges were brought against Sheriff Shipp and Deputies Matthew Gallaway and Geremiah Gibson for aiding and abetting the crime. Nick Nolan, Luther Williams, Bart Justice, Henry Padgett, William Mayse, and Frank Ward were charged as participants in the murder.

112. *U.S. v. Shipp,* 214 U.S. 386, 419 (1909).

113. Dray, *At the Hands of Persons Unknown: The Lynching of Black America,* 159.

114. *U.S. v. Shipp,* 214 U.S. 386, 414 (1909).

115. Dray, *At the Hands of Persons Unknown: The Lynching of Black America,* 158.

116. Curriden and Phillips, Jr., *Contempt of Court: The Turn-of-the-Century Lynching That Launched a Hundred Years of Federalism.*

117. Dray, *At the Hands of Persons Unknown: The Lynching of Black America,* 158.

118. Gibson, The Negro Holocaust: Lynching and Race Riots in the United States, 1880–1950. www.yale.edu/ynhti/curriculum/units/1979/2/79.02.04.x.html.

119. David Levering Lewis, *W. E. B. DuBois: 1869–1919* (New York: Henry Holt, 1993) (reporting that seventy-eight Blacks were lynched in 1918 and commenting "in the boasts of white newspapers in the South about the bloody fate in store for any black man daring to come back from the war expecting to be treated like a white man"), 579.

120. W. E. B. DuBois, *The Souls of Black Folk* (New York: Signet Books, 1903). "The Negro of the South who would succeed cannot be frank and outspoken, honest and self-assertive, but rather he is daily tempted to be silent and wary, politic and sly; he must flatter and be pleasant, endure petty insults with a smile, shut his eyes to wrong...," 223.

121. See *Black Survival 1776–1976: The Urban League Perspective* (Philadelphia: The Philadelphia Urban League, 1977), 10–12.

122. According to *The American Heritage Dictionary*, 4th ed., lynching means to execute without due process of law. Lynching could include torture such as burning a person alive, castration, mutilation, amputation of limbs, and/or decapitation.

123. See *supra*, table 2 and table 3.

124. Ginzburg, *100 Years of Lynching*, ("Mob Lynches Negro Man, Flogs Three Negro Women," *Chicago Record-Herald*, July 2, 1903) ("Woman Pleading Innocence Lynched as Child Poisoner," *Chicago Record-Herald*, July 27, 1903).

125. Tolnay and Beck, *An Analysis of Southern Lynchings, 1882–1930*, 21; see Ginzburg, *100 Years of Lynching* ("Negro Mother and Child Killed," *Montgomery Advertiser*, March 13, 1913).

126. Ginzburg, *100 Years of Lynching* ("Negro and Wife Burned," *New York Press*, February 8, 1904, 62) ("Lynched Negro and Wife Were First Mutilated," *Vicksburg (Mississippi) Evening Post*, February 8, 1904, 63).

127. Tolnay and Beck, *An Analysis of Southern Lynchings, 1882–1930*, 19 (discussing far less serious "offenses" that resulted in death by lynching); Ginzburg, *100 Years of Lynching* ("Negro and Wife Hanged, Suspected of Barn-Burning," *St. Paul Pioneer Press*, November 26, 1914, 92).

128. Tolnay and Beck, *An Analysis of Southern Lynchings, 1882–1930*, 19–25.

129. Ginzburg, *100 Years of Lynching* ("Rape, Lynch Negro Mother," *Chicago Defender*, December 18, 1915, 96).

130. Fierce, *Slavery Revisited: Blacks and the Southern Convict Lease System, 1865–1933*, 34.

131. Lewis, *W. E. B. DuBois 1868–1919: Biography of a Race*, 536.

132. David Levering Lewis, *W. E. B. DuBois: The Fight for Equality and the American Century, 1919–1963* (New York: Henry Holt and Company, 2000), 7–8, 374.

133. See Carl Sandburg, *The Chicago Race Riots, July 1919* (New York: Harcourt, Brace & Howe, 1919). For more information on the Chicago riots, see C. K. Doreski, "From News to History: Robert Abbott and Carl Sandburg Read the 1919 Chicago Riot," *African American Review*, 26, no. 4 (1992): 637–650; see Alfred L. Brophy, *Reconstructing the Dreamland: The Tulsa Riot of 1921—Race, Reparations, and Reconciliation* (New York: Oxford University Press, 2002).

134. *Frank v. Mangum*, 237 U.S. 309, 324-325 (1915).

135. *Frank v. Mangum*, 141 Ga. 243 (Ala. 1913).

136. Crowds outside the courthouse shouted, "Hang the Jew." See www.ajhs.org/publications/chapters/chapter.cfm?documentID=284.

137. *Frank v. Mangum*, 141 Ga. 243, 253 (Ala. 1913).

138. *Frank v. Mangum*, 237 U.S. 309, 312 (1915).

139. Ibid.

140. *Frank v. Mangum*, 141 Ga. 243, 284 (Ala. 1913). Leo Frank requested a new trial twice, moved to set aside the verdict as a nullity, and appealed to the Georgia Supreme Court three times prior to a review of this case by the U.S. Supreme Court. See *Frank v. Mangum*, 237 U.S. 309, 344 (1915).

141. *Frank v. Mangum*, 237 U.S. 309, 345 (1915).

142. See http://www.ajhs.org/publications/chapters/chapter.cfm?documentID=284. The statement is equivocal because foreign nationals have been lynched in America, as well. See Wells-Barnett, *Crusade for Justice: The Autobiography of Ida B. Wells*, ed. Alfreda M. Duster, 209–212.

143. http://www.ajhs.org/publications/chapters/chapter.cfm?documentID=284.

144. *Ware v. State*, 146 Ark. 321, 327 (1920).

145. Ibid., 321, 350. The Committee of Seven consisted of members of the "Business Men's League of Helena, the sheriff, the county judge, the mayor of the city of Helena, and other prominent citizens."

146. *Ware v. State*, 146 Ark. 321, 324-325 (1920).

147. Ibid.

148. Ibid., 321, 325.

149. Scipio Africanus Jones was born into slavery in rural Arkansas in 1863. Around 1881, Jones moved to Little Rock, Arkansas, where he attended Philander Smith College and Shorter College, graduating with a bachelor's degree. He worked as a teacher while also studying law in a law office. Jones passed the bar examination in 1889 and proceeded to practice law in Little Rock for over fifty years. He was known as an excellent attorney, political insider, and champion of civil rights for Blacks. However, Jones is best remembered for representing the defendants convicted of murder in the Elaine Race Riot case. Jones became the lead attorney in the case after George Murphy, his White chief counsel, died suddenly. Jones wrote the briefs in the appeal to the U.S. Supreme Court. For more on the life and time of Scipio Jones, see Judith Kilpatrick, *(Extra) Ordinary Men: African-American Lawyers and Civil Rights in Arkansas before 1950*, 53 Ark. L. Rev. 299, 345–390 (2000).

150. *Ware v. State*, 146 Ark. 321, 324 (1920).

151. *Moore v. Dempsey*, 261 U.S. 86, 89 (1923).

152. Ibid. 86, 101. See *Banks v. State*, 143 Ark. 154 (1920) (new trials granted to Elaine defendants Alf Banks, Jr., and John Martin convicted of murder); *Ware v. State*, 146 Ark. 321 (1920) (Blacks excluded from jury. New trials granted to Elaine defendants Ed Ware, Will Wordlow, Albert Giles, Joe Fox, John Martin, and Alf Banks, Jr. The cases were consolidated for purposes of appeal.)

153. Dempsey was the warden of the Arkansas State Penitentiary.

154. *Moore v. Dempsey*, 261 U.S. 86, 87 (1923).

155. Ibid., 86, 89–90.

156. Kilpatrick, *(Extra) Ordinary Men: African-American Lawyers and Civil Rights in Arkansas before 1950*, 299, 368.

157. Kevin Boyle, *Arc of Justice: A Saga of Race, Civil Rights, and Murder in the Jazz Age* (New York: Henry Holt, 2004), 170.

158. Ibid., 178.

159. Ibid., 244.

160. Ibid., 336; Phyllis Vine, *One Man's Castle: Clarence Darrow in Defense of the American Dream* (New York: HarperCollins, 2004), 259.

161. *Boyle, Arc of Justice: A Saga of Race, Civil Rights, and Murder in the Jazz Age*, 336; Vine, *One Man's Castle: Clarence Darrow in Defense of the American Dream*, 259–260.

162. 56 Cong. Rec. 2, 151 (1900).

163. Senate Reports (7951), 67th Congress, 2nd session, 1921–1922, Vol. 2, 33–34.

164. Ibid.: Anti-lynching bill.

APRIL 20 (calendar day, JULY 28), 1922.—Ordered to be printed.

AN ACT To assure to persons within the jurisdiction of every State the equal protection of the laws, and to punish the crime of lynching.

Be it enacted by the Senate and House of Representatives of the United States of America in Congress assembled, That the phrase "mob or riotous assemblage," when used in this act, shall mean an assemblage composed of three or more persons acting in concert for the purpose of depriving any person of his life without authority of law as a punishment for or to prevent the commission of some actual or supposed public offense.

SEC. 2. That if any State or governmental subdivision thereof fails, neglects, or refuses to provide and maintain protection to the life of any person within its jurisdiction against a mob or riotous assemblage, such State shall by reason of such failure, neglect, or refusal be deemed to have denied to such person the equal protection of the laws of the State, and to the end that such protection as is guaranteed to the citizens of the United States by its Constitution may be secured it is provided:

SEC. 3. That any State or municipal officer charged with the duty or who possesses the power or authority as such officer to protect the life of any person that may be put to death by any mob or riotous assemblage, or who has any such person in his charge as a prisoner, who fails, neglects, or refuses to make all reasonable efforts to prevent such person from being so put to death, or any State or municipal officer charged with the duty of apprehending or prosecuting any person participating in such mob or riotous assemblage who fails, neglects, or refuses to make all reasonable efforts to perform his duty in apprehending or prosecuting to final judgment under the laws of such State all persons so participating except such, if any, as are to have been held to answer for such participation in any district court of the United States, as herein provided, shall be guilty of a felony, and upon conviction thereof shall be punished by imprisonment not exceeding five years or by a fine of not exceeding $5,000, or by both such fine and imprisonment.

Any State or municipal officer, acting as such officer under authority of State law, having in his custody or control a prisoner, who shall conspire, combine, or confederate with any person to put such prisoner to death without authority of law as a punishment for some alleged public offense, or who shall conspire, combine, or confederate with any person to suffer such prisoner to be taken or obtained from his custody or control for the purpose of being put to death without authority of law as a punishment for an alleged public offense, shall be guilty of a felony, and those who so conspire, combine, or confederate with such officer shall likewise be guilty of a felony. On conviction the parties participating therein shall be punished by imprisonment for life or not less than five years.

SEC. 4. That the district court of the judicial district wherein a person is put to death by a mob or riotous assemblage shall have jurisdiction to try and punish, in accordance with the laws of the State where the homicide is committed, those who participate therein: *Provided*, That it shall be charged in the indictment that by reason of the failure, neglect, or refusal of the officers of the State charged with the duty of prosecuting such offense under the laws of the State to proceed with due diligence to apprehend and prosecute such participants the State has denied to its citizens the equal protection of the laws. It shall not be necessary that the jurisdictional allegations herein required shall be proven beyond a reasonable doubt, and it shall be sufficient if such allegations are sustained by a preponderance of the evidence.

SEC. 5. That any county in which a person is put to death by a mob or riotous assemblage shall, if it is alleged and proven that the officers of the State charged with the duty of prosecuting criminally such offense under the laws of the State have failed, neglected, or refused to proceed with due diligence to apprehend and prosecute the participants in the mob or riotous assemblage, forfeit $10,000, which sum may be recovered by an action therefor in the name of the United States against any such county for the use of the family, if any, of the person so put to death; if he had no family, then to his dependent parents, if any; otherwise for the use of the United States. Such action shall be brought and prosecuted by the district attorney of the United States of the district in which such county is situated in any court of the United States having jurisdiction therein. If such forfeiture is not paid upon recovery of a judgment therefor, such court shall have jurisdiction to enforce payment thereof by levy of execution upon any property of the county, or may compel the levy and collection of a tax, therefor, or may otherwise compel payment thereof by mandamus or other appropriate process; and any officer of such county or other person who disobeys or fails to comply with any lawful order of the court in the premises shall be liable to punishment as for contempt and to any other penalty provided by law therefor.

SEC. 6. That in the event that any person so put to death shall have been transported by such mob or riotous assemblage from one county to another county during the time intervening between his capture and putting to death, the county in which he is seized and the county in which he is put to death shall be jointly and severally liable to pay the forfeiture herein provided.

SEC. 7. That any act committed in any State or Territory of the United States in violation of the rights of a citizen or subject of a foreign country secured to such citizen or subject by treaty between the United States and such foreign country, which act constitutes a crime under the laws of such State or Territory, shall constitute a like crime against the peace and dignity of the United States, punishable in like manner as in the courts of said State or Territory, and within the period limited by the laws of such State or Territory, and may be prosecuted in the courts of the United States, and upon conviction the sentence executed in like manner as sentences upon convictions for crimes under the laws of the United States.

SEC. 8. That in construing and applying this act the District of Columbia shall be deemed a county, as shall also each of the parishes of the State of Louisiana.

That if any section or provision of this act shall be held by any court to be invalid, the balance of the act shall not for that reason be held invalid.

165. In 2005, the Senate passed a resolution presenting a formal apology for failing to pass antilynching legislation.

166. Lewis, *W. E. B. DuBois 1868–1919: Biography of a Race*, 509–511.

167. J. McPherson, *The Struggle for Equality: Abolitionists and The Negro in the Civil War and Reconstruction* (Princeton, N.J.: Princeton University Press, 1964, 230.

168. Costigan–Wagner Bill, 73rd Congress, 2nd Session (3rd January, 1935): A bill to assure to persons within the jurisdiction of every State the equal protection of the laws, and punish the crime of lynching.

Be it enacted by the Senate and House of Representatives of the United States of America in Congress assembled, That, for the purposes of this Act, the phrase "mob or riotous assemblage," when used in this Act, shall mean an assemblage composed of three or more persons acting in concert, without authority of law [for the purpose of depriving any person of his life, or doing him physical injury], to kill or injure any person in the custody of any peace officer, with the purpose or consequence of depriving such person of due process of law or the equal protection of the laws.

Sec. 2. If any state or governmental, subdivision thereof fails, neglects, or refuses to provide and maintain protection to the life or person of any individual within its jurisdiction against a mob or riotous assemblage, whether by way of preventing or punishing the acts thereof, such State shall by reason of such failure, neglect, or refusal be deemed to have denied to such person due process of law and the equal protection of the laws of the State, and to the end that the protection guaranteed to persons within the jurisdiction of the United States, may be secured, the provisions of this Act are enacted.

Sec. 3. (a) Any officer or employee of any State or governmental subdivision thereof who is charged with the duty or who possesses the power or authority as such officer or employee to protect the life or person of any individual injured or put to death by any mob or riotous assemblage or any officer or employee of any State or governmental subdivision thereof having any such individual in his [change as a prisoner] custody, who fails, neglects, or refuses to make all diligent efforts to protect such individual from being so injured or being put to death, or any officer or employee of any State or governmental subdivision thereof charged with the duty of apprehending, keeping in custody, or prosecuting any person participating in such mob or riotous assemblage who fails, neglects, or refuses to make all diligent efforts to perform his duty in apprehending, keeping in custody, or prosecuting to final judgment under the laws of such State all persons so participating, shall be guilty of a felony, and upon conviction thereof shall be punished by a fine not exceeding $5,000 or by imprisonment not exceeding five years, or by both such fine and imprisonment.

(b) Any officer or employee of any state or governmental subdivision thereof, acting as such officer or employee under authority of State law, having in his custody or control a prisoner, who shall conspire, combine, or confederate with any person who is a member of a mob or riotous assemblage to injure or put such prisoner to death without authority of law, or who shall conspire, combine, or confederate with any person to suffer such prisoner to be taken or obtained from his custody or control [for the purpose of being] to be injured or put to death [without authority of law] by a mob or riotous assemblage shall be guilty of a felony, and those who so conspire, combine, or confederate with such officer or employee shall likewise be guilty of a felony. On conviction the parties participating therein shall be punished by imprisonment of not less than five years or [for life] not more than twenty-five years.

Sec. 4. The District Court of the United States judicial district wherein the person is injured or put to death by a mob or riotous assemblage shall have jurisdiction to try and to punish, in accordance with the laws of the State where the injury is inflicted or the homicide is committed, any and all persons who participate therein: Provided, That it is first made to appear to such court (1) that the officers of the State charged with the duty of apprehending, prosecuting, and punishing such offenders under the laws of the State shall have failed, neglected, or refused to apprehend, prosecute, or punish such offenders; or (2) that the jurors obtainable for service in the State court having jurisdiction of the offense are so strongly opposed to such punishment that there is [no] probability that those guilty of the offense [can be] will not be punished in such State court. A failure for more than thirty days after the commission of such an offense to apprehend or to indict the persons guilty thereof, or a failure diligently to prosecute such persons, shall be sufficient to constitute prima facie evidence of the failure, neglect, or refusal described in the above proviso.

Sec. 5. Any county in which a person is seriously injured or put to death by a mob or riotous assemblage shall [forfeit $10,000, which sum may be recovered by suit therefor in the name of the United States against such county for the use of the family, if any, of the person so put to death; if he had no family then of his dependent parents, if any; otherwise for the use of the United States] be liable to the injured person or the legal representatives of such person for a sum of not less than $2,000 nor more than $10,000 as liquidated damages, which sum may be recovered in a civil action against such county in the United States District Court of the judicial district wherein such person is put to the injury or death. Such action shall be brought and prosecuted by the United States district attorney [of the United States] of the district in the United States District Court for such district. If such [forfeiture] amount awarded be not paid upon recovery of a judgment thereof, such court shall have jurisdiction to enforce payment thereof by levy of execution upon any property of the county, or may otherwise compel payment thereof by mandamus or other appropriate process; and any officer of such county or other person who disobeys or fails to comply with any lawful order of the court in the premises shall be liable to punishment as for contempt and to any other penalty provided by law therefor. The amount recovered shall be exempt from all claims by creditors of the deceased. The amount recovered upon such judgment shall be paid to the injured person, or where death resulted, distributed in accordance with the laws governing the distribution of an intestate decedent's assets then in effect in the State wherein such death occurred.

Sec. 6. In the event that any person so put to death shall have been transported by such mob or riotous assemblage from one county to another county during the time intervening between his seizure and putting to death, the county in which he is seized and the county in which he is put to death shall be jointly and severally liable to pay the forfeiture herein provided. Any district judge of the United States

District Court of the judicial district wherein any suit or prosecution is instituted under the provisions of this Act, may by order district that such suit or prosecution be tried in any place in such district as he may designate in such order.

Sec. 7. Any act committed in any State or Territory of the United States in violation of the rights of a citizen or subject of a foreign country secured to such citizen or subject by treaty between the United States and such foreign country, which act constitute a like crime against the peace and dignity of the United States, punishable in a like manner in its courts as in the courts of said State or Territory, and able in a like manner in its courts as in the courts of said State or Territory, and may be prosecuted in the courts of the United States, and upon conviction the sentence executed in like manner as sentences upon convictions for crimes under the laws of the United States.

Sec. 8. If any provision of this Act or the application thereof to any person or circumstances is held invalid, the remainder of the Act, and the application of such provision to other persons or circumstances, shall not be affected thereby.

169. Ibid.
170. In 2005, the Senate passed a resolution presenting a formal apology for failing to pass antilynching legislation.
171. See Hilton Als, Jon Lewis, Leon F. Litwack, and James Allen, *Without Sanctuary: Lynching Photography in America* (Santa Fe, N.M.: Twin Palms Publisher, 2000); See J. Madison, *A Lynching in the Heartland: Race and Memory in America* (New York: Palgrave–MacMillan, 2001).
172. Bell, *Race, Racism and American Law*, 59; Cox, in *Race, Crime and Justice: A Reader*, S. Gabbidon and H. Greene, eds., 28–30.
173. Carol Anderson, *Eyes off the Prize: The United Nations and the African American Struggle for Human Rights, 1944–1955* (Cambridge, U.K.: Cambridge University Press, 2003), 58.
174. Gibson, The Negro Holocaust: Lynching and Race Riots in the United States, 1880–1950. www.yale.edu/ynhti/curriculum/units/1979/2/79.02.04.x.html.
175. See James Weldon Johnson, *Along This Way: The Autobiography of James Weldon Johnson* (New York: Penguin Press, 1933).
176. See Roy L. Brooks, ed., *When Sorry Isn't Enough: The Controversy over Apologies and Reparations for Human Injustice* (New York: New York University Press, 1999).
177. See Michael D'Orso, *Like Judgment Day: The Ruin and Redemption of a Town Called Rosewood* (New York: G.P. Putnam's Sons, 1996).
178. "Last Negro Homes Razed in Rosewood," *New York Times*, Jan. 8, 1923.
179. See Michael D'Orso, *Like Judgment Day: The Ruin and Redemption of a Town Called Rosewood*.
180. Ibid.

181. Florida House Bill 591 was introduced by Representatives De Grandy and Lawson. *The Claim of Arnett Goins, Minnie Lee Langley et al. v. State of Florida* includes a finding of fact and claim seeking $7.2 million for damages resulting from the 1923 destruction of Rosewood, Florida.

182. See Florida House Bill HR 591, 1994 Compensation for Victims of Rosewood Massacre and Florida Senate Bill SB 1774, 1994 Compensation for the Victims of Rosewood Massacre.

183. See Brophy, *Reconstructing the Dreamland: The Tulsa Riot of 1921—Race, Reparations and Reconciliation.*

184. Sue Ann Pressley, "Three Held in Black Man's Dragging Death," *The Times Picayune*, v. 162 n. 138, June 10, 1998.

185. Ashley Craddock, The Jaspar Myth, Salon.com, October 25, 1999.

186. Whites have received the death penalty for serial murders that include Black victims. But, this is the only case of White defendants receiving the death penalty for the murder of one Black person.

187. Steve Barnes, "Grave Desecrated a Second Time," *New York Times*, May 8, 2004.

188. Title: Apologizing to the victims of lynching and the descendants of those victims for the failure of the Senate to enact anti-lynching legislation" Cong. 109, 1st Sess., S. Res. 39, June 13, 2005.

189. James Allen, Hilton Als, et al., *Without Sanctuary: Lynching Photography in America* (Twin Palms Publishers, 2000).

190. Cong. 109, 1st Sess., S. Res. 39, June 13, 2005.

191. Ibid.

192. See Dray, *At the Hands of Persons Unknown: The Lynching of Black America.*

193. See Sandra Gunning, *Race, Rape, and Lynching: The Red Record of American Literature, 1890–1912* (New York: Oxford University Press, 1996); see also Browne-Marshall, *Denial of Innocence: Black Girls and the Statutory Rape Debate.*

194. See James Elbert Cutler, *Lynch Law: An Investigation into the History of Lynching in the United States* (New York: Negro Universities Press, 1969).

195. Wells-Barnett, 16 Lynch Law in Georgia, Daniel P. Murray Pamphlets 12 (1899); see also Washington, *Exploring the Black Wombman's Sphere and the Anti-Lynching Crusade of the Early Twentieth Century*, 902.

196. Gibson, The Negro Holocaust: Lynching and Race Riots in the United States, 1880–1950. www.yale.edu/ynhti/curriculum/units/1979/2/79.02.04.x.html.

197. Arthur F. Raper, *The Tragedy of Lynching* (Montclair, N.J.: Patterson Smith, 1969), 1.

198. Nancy F. Cott, ed., *History of Women in the United States: Social and Moral Reform* (New Providence: K. G. Saur, 1994), 527. Ida B. Wells exposed the economic motivation behind the lynching of three Black businessmen in Memphis.

199. Tolnay and Beck, *An Analysis of Southern Lynchings, 1882–1930*, 43.

200. See, generally, Raper, *The Tragedy of Lynching*, 1.

201. See Richard Rubin, "The Ghosts of Emmett Till," *New York Times Magazine*, July 31, 2005.
202. *New York Times*, September 23, 1955, "Mississippi Jury Acquits Two in Youth's Killing," 38.
203. The jury's position was that Emmett Till was so disfigured to be unidentifiable. The Tallahatchie River had been used in a number of murders of Black men in Mississippi. The body could have been that of another Black person.
204. Rubin, "The Ghosts of Emmett Till," 55–56.
205. See John Patterson, ed., *We Claim Genocide* (New York: Civil Rights Congress, 1951), 58–66.
206. See *Without Sanctuary* (discussing the lynching of Rubin Stacey); Leon F. Litwack, *Trouble in Mind: Black Southerners in the Age of Jim Crow* (First Vintage Books, 1998); Morton Sosna, *In Search of the Silent South: Southern Liberals and the Race Issue* (New York: Columbia University Press: 1977).
207. *Screws v. U.S.*, 325 U.S. 91, 92 (1945).
208. *Screws v. U.S.*, Ibid., 91, 92–93.
209. Criminal Code, 18 U.S.C. 52, Sec. 20.
210. Criminal Code, 18 U.S.C. 88, Sec. 20.
211. *Screws v. U.S.*, 325 U.S. 91, 138 (1945) (quoting from the dissent of Justice Murphy).
212. See Cong. Globe, 41st Cong., 2d Sess., 3807, 3808, 3881. Flack, *The Adoption of the Fourteenth Amendment* (1908) 19-54, 219, 223, 227.
213. Since they were tried under a federal statute, the case was tried in federal district court.
214. Criminal Code, 18 U.S.C. 52, Sec. 20.
215. *Screws v. U.S.*, 325 U.S. 91, 112-113 (1945).
216. *Screws v. United States*, 140 F.2d 662 (5th Cir. 1944).
217. See *Screws v. U.S.*, 325 U.S. 91 (1945).
218. Ibid., 91, 110–113.
219. Ibid., 91, 113.
220. Bell, *Race, Racism and American Law*, 464–471, 475–479.
221. Ibid., 477–481; Liyah Kaprice Brown, *Colloquium: Relearning Brown: Applying the Lessons of Brown to the Challenges of the Twenty-First Century: Officer or Overseer? Why Police Desegregation Fails as an Adequate Solution to Racist, Oppressive, and Violent Policing in Black Communities*, 29 N.Y.U. Rev. L. & Soc. Change 757 (2005); Jones-Brown, *Race, Crime and Punishment*.
222. *Mapp v. Ohio*, 367 U.S. 643 (1961).
223. *Mapp v. Ohio*, 367 U.S. 643, 645.
224. Section 2905.34, Ohio Revised Code.
225. *Mapp v. Ohio*, 170 Ohio St. 427, 429 (1960).
226. Ibid., 427, 429.
227. *Weeks v. United States*, 232 U.S. 383 (1914).
228. *Wolf v. Colorado*, 338 U.S. 25, 28 (1949).

229. *Mapp v. Ohio*, 170 Ohio St. 427, 430 (1960).

230. Ibid., 434.

231. See *Wolf v. Colorado*, 338 U.S. 25 (1949).

232. *Mapp v. Ohio*, 367 U.S. 643, 655 (1961).

233. Ibid., 643, 660.

234. For further information on police brutality, see, generally, Delores D. Jones-Brown and Karen J. Terry, *Policing and Minority Communities: Bridging the Gap* (Upper Saddle River, N.J.: Pearson Education, 2004).

235. See *Koon v. United States*, 518 U.S. 81 (1996).

236. Ibid., 87.

237. Ibid., 81, 87.

238. On April 29, 1992, protests against the acquittal were immediate and spread across the country. Flames engulfed Los Angeles as homes and business were burned down during six days of mass rioting. For further discussion of Rodney King, see *The System in Black and White: Exploring Connections between Race, Crime, and Justice*, Michael W. Markowitz and Delores Jones-Brown, eds., 86–91; *Koon v. United States*, 518 U.S. 81 (1996) (one count resulted in a hung jury).

239. *Koon v. United States*, 518 U.S. 81 (1996).

240. Rick DelVecchio and Suzanne Espinosa, "Bradley Ready to Lift Curfew. He Says L.A. Is 'Under Control,'" *San Francisco Chronicle*, May 4, 1992, A1.

241. On August 4, 1992, a federal grand jury indicted the four officers under 18 U.S.C. § 242, charging them with violating King's constitutional rights under color of law. Powell, Briseno, and Wind were charged with willful use of unreasonable force in arresting King. Koon was charged with willfully permitting the other officers to use unreasonable force during the arrest.

242. King received $3.8 million in a settlement with the city of Los Angeles.

243. See Report of the Independent Commission on the Los Angeles Police Department (Christopher Commission Report), July 9, 1991; Jones-Brown and Terry, *Policing and Minority Communities: Bridging the Gap*, 169.

244. Jones-Brown and Terry, *Policing and Minority Communities: Bridging the Gap*, 169.

245. Under the sentencing guidelines, Koon and Powell could have been sentenced to seventy to eighty-seven months of imprisonment. However, "the District Court (1) granted the officers a downward departure under the Guidelines of five offense levels on the basis of a finding that the suspect's misconduct—which included driving while intoxicated, fleeing from the police, refusing to obey the officers' commands, and attempting to escape from police custody—had provoked the officers' offensive behavior; and (2) granted an additional three level downward departure on the basis of the combination of the officers' (a) unusual susceptibility to abuse in prison, (b) job loss and preclusion from law enforcement

employment, (c) burdens of successive state and federal prosecutions, and (d) low risk of recidivism; and (3) having thus reduced the sentencing range to 30–37 months, sentenced each officer to 30 months in prison" *Koon v. United States*, 518 U.S. 81, 89–90 (1996).

246. See *Koon v. United States*, 518 U.S. 81 (1996).

247. Ibid, 81, 89.

248. Jones-Brown and Terry, *Policing and Minority Communities: Bridging the Gap*, 183.

249. *Hudson v. McMillian*, 929 F.2d 1014 (5th Cir. 1990); *Hudson v. McMillan*, 503 U.S. 1 (1992).

250. *Hudson v. McMillian*, 503 U.S. 1, 4 (1992).

251. Ibid.

252. Ibid., 1, 12.

253. Ibid., 1, 4–5.

254. Ibid., 1, 4.

255. Ibid., 1, 5.

256. See *Estelle v. Gamble*, 429 U.S. 97 (1976).

257. See Kadiatou Diallo, *My Heart Will Cross This Ocean: My Story, My Son, Amadou* (New York: One World/Ballantine, 2004).

258. Bronx, New York. Grand Jury #: 40894/99 (dated March 25, 1999).

259. Civil complaint filed December 17, 1999. A civil action was brought against the individual police officers as well as the city of New York. The civil lawsuit alleged that the individual officers acted in a reckless, wanton, and grossly negligent manner and in complete disregard for the rights and safety of Diallo in approaching him without reasonable suspicion that he had committed a crime and without any lawful justification, and in firing forty-one bullets at him without any justification and in otherwise acting in a reckless, wanton, and grossly negligent manner. The lawsuit accused the city of New York and the individual defendants of racial profiling. The suit alleged that New York was negligent in the training and supervision of the defendants and in assigning them to the Street Crimes Unit without adequate training and supervision.

260. *New York Post*, "NYPD to Scuttle Diallo Cop Unit," April 10, 2002, 7.

261. *New York Post*, "Diallo Cop Ruling Draws Hostile Fire," April 29, 2001, 16.

262. *New York Post*, "NYPD Clears Diallo Cops—with Retraining," April 26, 2001, 6.

263. *Jet Magazine*, "Riverside, CA, Officers Who Shot Tyisha Miller Fired from Force," July 5, 1999.

264. Manuscript in Slavery File No. 1, Free Persons of Colour, Historical Commission of South Carolina, Columbia.

265. See *Blyew v. United States*, 80 U.S. 581 (1871).

266. *Strauder v. West Virginia*, 100 U.S. 303, 305 (1880).

267. *Carter v. Texas*, 177 U.S. 442, 447 (1900).

268. *Swain v. Alabama*, 275 Ala. 508, 509 (1963).

269. *Swain v. Alabama*, 380 U.S. 202, 209–210 (1965).

270. Ibid., 202, 222–224.

271. Ibid. Additionally, the Court held that Swain was not constitutionally entitled to a proportionate number of his race on the jury that tried him.

272. *Swain v. Alabama*, 380 U.S. 202, 214–220 (1965).

273. Ibid., 202, 221–222.

274. *Norris v. Alabama*, 294 U.S. 587, 591, 592 (1935).

275. Ibid., 587, 591–594.

276. Ibid., 587, 591.

277. Ibid., 587, 596.

278. *Batson v. Kentucky*, 476 U.S. 79 (1986).

279. See, for example, *Strauder v. West Virginia*, 100 U.S. 303 (1880); *Ex Parte Virginia*, 100 U.S. 339 (1880); *Neal v. Delaware*, 103 U.S. 370 (1881); *Gibson v. Mississippi*, 162 U.S. 565 (1896); *Franklin v. South Carolina*, 218 U.S. 161 (1910); *Moore v. Dempsey*, 261 U.S. 86 (1923); *Norris v. Alabama*, 294 U.S. 587 (1935); *Hollins v. Oklahoma*, 295 U.S. 394 (1935) (*per curiam*); *Hale v. Kentucky*, 303 U.S. 613 (1938); *Pierre v. Louisiana*, 306 U.S. 354 (1939); *Patton v. Mississippi*, 332 U.S. 463 (1947); *Avery v. Georgia*, 345 U.S. 559 (1953); *Hernandez v. Texas*, 347 U.S. 475 (1954); *Whitus v. Georgia*, 385 U.S. 545 (1967); *Jones v. Georgia*, 389 U.S. 24 (1967) (*per curiam*); *Carter v. Jury Comm'n of Greene County*, 396 U.S. 320 (1970); *Castaneda v. Partida*, 430 U.S. 482 (1977); *Rose v. Mitchell*, 443 U.S. 545 (1979); *Vasquez v. Hillery*, 474 U.S. 254 (1986).

280. *Batson v. Kentucky*, 476 U.S. 79 (1986).

281. The Kentucky Rules of Criminal Procedure authorize the trial court to permit counsel to conduct *voir dire* examination or to conduct the examination itself (Ky. Rule Crim. Proc. 9.38). After jurors have been excused for cause, the parties exercise their peremptory challenges simultaneously by striking names from a list of qualified jurors equal to the number to be seated plus the number of allowable peremptory challenges (Rule 9.36). Since the offense charged in this case was a felony and an alternate juror was called, the prosecutor was entitled to six peremptory challenges and defense counsel to nine (Rule 9.40). See *Batson v. Kentucky*, 476 U.S. 79, 82 (1986).

282. *Batson v. Kentucky*, 476 U.S. 79, 83 (1986).

283. Ibid., 79, 100. To the extent that anything in *Swain v. Alabama*, 380 U.S. 202 (1965), is contrary to the principles we articulate today, that decision is overruled.

284. *Batson v. Kentucky*, 476 U.S. 79 (1986).

285. Ibid., 79, 84–89.

286. *Miller-El v. Dretke*, 125 U.S.2317 (2005).

287. *Blyew v. U.S.*, 80 U.S. 581, 584 (1871).

288. Ibid., 581, 583.

289. Ibid., 581, 584.

290. Ibid., 581, 584–585.

291. Ibid., 581, 586.

292. Ibid., 581, 585.

293. Revised Statutes of Kentucky, section 1, chapter 107, vol. 2, 470 (1860).
294. *Blyew v. U. S.*, 80 U.S. 581, 592 (1871).
295. Civil Rights Act, 14 Stat. at Large 27 (April 9, 1866).
296. *Blyew v. U.S.*, 80 U.S. 581, 595 (1871).
297. "[Mary Hamilton] had been the only female Field Secretary (organizer) for the Congress of Racial Equality (CORE). She was only the third woman to have the job: Genevieve Hughes was the first, Frederika Teer the second, but they had not been allowed to work in the South. Mary Hamilton was the first female CORE organizer allowed to work in the South." From archive of Sheila Michaels, civil rights activist: CORE 1961–1963 SNCC 1962–1964. www.crmvet.org/nars/sheila.htm.
298. *Ex parte Mary Hamilton*, 275 Ala. 574 (1963) reversed by *Hamilton v. Alabama*, 376 U.S. 650 (1964). Incident of abuse of witness based on race is cited by Court as a vestige of slavery in the sit-in case of *Bell v. Maryland*, 378 U.S. 226, 248 (1964).
299. Alabama Code, Tit. 13, Sec. 2.
300. *Johnson v. Virginia*, 373 U.S. 61 (1963).
301. Ibid., 61, 61–62.
302. Ibid.
303. Randall Kennedy, *Race, Crime and the Law* (New York: Pantheon Books, 1997), 128.
304. See Ayers, *Vengeance and Justice: Crime and Punishment in the 19th Century American South.*
305. *Brown v. Board of Education*, 347 U.S. 483 (1964); see James Jacobs, *New Perspectives on Prisons and Imprisonment* (Ithaca, N.Y.: Cornell University Press, 1983) (discussing limits of racial desegregation's application to prisons), 80–81.
306. *Lee, Commissioner of Corrections of Alabama v. Washington*, 390 U.S. 333 (1968).
307. *Lee v. Washington*, 263 F. Supp. 327 (MD. AL. 1966).
308. The Alabama statutes requiring segregation of the races in the prisons and jails of Alabama are §§ 4, 52, 121, 122, 123, 172, and 183 of Title 45, Code of Alabama, recompiled 1958.
309. *Lee, Commissioner of Corrections of Alabama v. Washington*, 390 U.S. 333, 334 (1968).
310. Ibid., 333. The Supreme Court upheld the ruling of a three-judge federal court.
311. *Lee v. Washington*, 263 F. Supp. 327, 332 (MD. AL. 1966).
312. *U.S. v. Wyandotte*, 480 F.2d 969 (10th Cir. 1973).
313. Ibid., 969, 970.
314. Ibid., 969, 970–971.
315. Ibid., 969, 970 (citing *Lee v. Washington*, 390 U.S. 333, 1968).
316. *United States v. Wyandotte County, Kansas*, 480 F.2d 969 (10th Cir. 1973) *cert. denied* 414 U.S. 1068 (1973).
317. *Johnson v. California*, 543 U.S. 499, 503 (2005) (Fourth Amended Complaint 3, Record, Doc. No. 78).

318. Ibid., 499, 503–504.

319. Ibid., 499, 504–505.

320. Ibid., 499, 503 (Fourth Amended Complaint 3, Record, Doc. No. 78).

321. The Court of Appeals for the Ninth Circuit affirmed the trial court's grant of summary judgment in favor of the California Department of Corrections (*Johnson v. U.S.*, 21 F.3d 791, 9th Cir. 2003).

322. Ibid.

323. See *Johnson v. California*, 543 U.S. 499 (2005).

324. Ibid., 499, 509.

325. *Turner v Safley*, 482 U.S. 78 (1987).

326. *Johnson v. California*, 543 U.S. 499, 509 (2005). For more on strict scrutiny, see chapter 2, affirmative action section, in this book. See also Bell, *Race, Racism and American Law.*

327. *Johnson v. California*, 543 U.S. 499, 512 (2005). For a discussion of California's common sense argument, see James E. Robertson, "Foreword: 'Separate but Equal' in Prison: John v. California and Common Sense Racism, *Journal of Criminal Law and Criminology* 96, no. 3 (Spring 2006).

328. *Johnson v. California*, 543 U.S. 499, 509 (2005).

329. Ibid., 499, 515.

330. *Terry v. Ohio*, 392 U.S. 1, 5 (1968).

331. Ibid., 1, 5–6.

332. Ibid., 1, 6.

333. Ibid., 1, 5.

334. Ibid.

335. Ibid., 1, 6.

336. Ibid.

337. Ibid., 1, 7–8.

338. Ibid., 1, 7.

339. Ibid., 1, 5.

340. Ibid., 1, 7.

341. Ohio Rev. Code Sec. 2923.01 (1953) provides in part that "no person shall carry a pistol, bowie knife, dirk, or other dangerous weapon concealed on or about his person."

342. *Terry v. Ohio*, 392 U.S. 1, 5 (1968).

343. Ibid., 1, 7.

344. Chilton died during the appeal process (*Terry v. Ohio*, 392 U.S. 1, 5 note 2, 1968).

345. U.S. Const. 4th Amend.

346. *Terry v. Ohio*, 392 U.S. 1, 10 (1968).

347. Ibid.

348. Ibid., 1, 10–11.

349. *Terry v. Ohio*, 392 U.S. 1, 10 (1968). Although McFadden had decades of police experience to support his "reasonable suspicion" of criminal activity, the Court failed to require any particular level of experience or training to support a police officer's suspicion.

350. See *Terry v. Ohio*, 392 U.S. 1, 15–16 (1968), quoting L. Tiffany, D. McIntyre, and D. Rotenberg, *Detection of Crime: Stopping and Questioning, Search and Seizure, Encouragement and Entrapment*, (1967), 47–48 ("[I]t cannot help but be a severely exacerbating factor in police–community tensions. This is particularly true in situations where the 'stop and frisk' of youths or minority group members is 'motivated by the officers' perceived need to maintain the power image of the beat officer, an aim sometimes accomplished by humiliating anyone who attempts to undermine police control of the streets.'")

351. *Terry v. Ohio*, 392 U.S. 1, 14–15 (1968).

352. See *Weeks v. United States*, 232 U.S. 383 (1914) and *Mapp v. Ohio*, 367 U.S. 643 (1961).

353. See Adina Schwartz, *"Just Take Away Their Guns":The Hidden Racism of Terry v. Ohio*, 23 Fordham Urb. L. J. 2 (1996).

354. *Terry v. Ohio*, 392 U.S. 1, 15 (1968).

355. Ibid., 1, 5.

356. Ibid., 1, 7.

357. See *Hiibel v. Nevada*, 542 U.S. 177 (2004) and *Brown v. Texas*, 443 U.S. 47 (1979).

358. See *Illinois v. William aka Sam Wardlow*, 528 U.S. 119 (1999).

359. See *Whren v. United States*, 517 U.S. 806 (1996).

360. See *City of Chicago v. Jose Morales et al.*, 177 Ill. 2d 440 (1997) (consolidated cases); *Chicago v. Morales*, 527 U.S. 41 (1999).

361. *Chicago v. Morales*, 527 U.S. 41, 47 (1999).

362. Chicago Municipal Code Sec. 8-4-015 (added June 17, 1992), reprinted in App. To Pet. For Cer. 61a–63a; *Chicago v. Morales*, 527 U.S. 41, 47 (1999).

363. Chicago Municipal Code Sec. 8-4-015 (added June 17, 1992), reprinted in App. To Pet. For Cer. 61a–63a.

364. *Chicago v. Morales*, 527 U.S. 41, 49 (1999).

365. Ibid., 41, 63–64.

366. Ibid., 41, 53 (1999). The freedom to loiter for innocent purposes is part of the liberty protected by the due-process clause of the Fourteenth Amendment.

367. *Chicago v. Morales*, 527 U.S. 41, 64 (1999).

368. Ibid.

369. Ibid., 41, 63–64.

370. See *United States v. Armstrong*, 517 U.S. 456 (1996).

371. Ibid., 456, 459–460.

372. Ibid., 456, 458–460.

373. Ibid., 456, 460–461.

374. *Oyler v. Boles*, 368 U.S. 448 (1962).

375. *United States v. Armstrong*, 517 U.S. 456, 459 (1996).

376. Ibid., 456, 459–460.

377. Ibid., 456, 461.

378. Ibid., 456, 460.

379. *United States v. Armstrong*, 48 F.3d 1508, 1516 (1995).

380. *United States v. Armstrong*, 517 U.S. 456, 470–471 (1996).

381. Patterson, *We Charge Genocide*, 150.

382. *Powell v. Alabama*, 287 U.S. 45 (1932).

383. The crime of rape remained a capital offense—punishable by death—in America until 1977. See *Coker v. Georgia*, 433 U.S. 584 (1977).

384. Kwando Kinshasa, *The Man from Scottsboro—Clarence Norris in His Own Words,* Jefferson (North Carolina: McFarland & Co., 1997), 197.

385. *Powell v. Alabama*, 287 U.S. 45, 49 (1932).

386. Ibid. "But no counsel had been employed, and aside from a statement made by the trial judge several days later during a colloquy immediately preceding the trial, the record does not disclose when, or under what circumstances, an appointment of counsel was made, or who was appointed."

387. *Powell v. Alabama*, 287 U.S. 45, 49 (1932).

388. *Ozie Powell, Willie Roberson, Andy Wright, and Olen Montgomery v. Alabama; Haywood Patterson v. Alabama; Charley Weems and Clarence Norris v. Alabama*, 287 U.S. 45 (1932).

389. *Powell v. Alabama*, 287 U.S. 45, 49–50 (1932).

390. Chief Justice Anderson believed the defendants had not been accorded a fair trial and strongly dissented (*Powell v. Alabama*, 224 Ala. 524; *id.* 531; *id.* 540; 141 So. 215, 195, 201).

391. *Powell v. Alabama*, 287 U.S. 45, 72 (1932).

392. http://www.law.umkc.edu/faculty/projects/FTrials/scottsboro/SB_BBates.html.

393. See *Norris v. Alabama*, 294 U.S. 587 (1935).

394. Ibid., 587, 597.

395. Ibid., 587, 592–593.

396. Ibid., 587, 599.

397. See *Chambers v. Florida*, 309 U.S. 227 (1940).

398. Ibid., 227, 229.

399. Ibid., 227, 229–230.

400. *Chambers v. Florida*, 136 Fla. 568, 570–572 (1939).

401. Ibid., 568, 569.

402. Ibid., 568, 572.

403. *Chambers v. Florida*, 309 U.S. 227, 241.

404. Ibid., 227, 240 (note 15).

405. *Georgia v. Furman*, 408 U.S. 238 (1972).

406. U.S. Const. Amend. XIII.

407. *Georgia v. Furman*, 408 U.S. 238, 255 (1972).

408. Ibid., 238, 310.

409. *Gregg v. Georgia*, 428 U.S. 153, 180-182 (1976).

410. Ibid., 153.

411. Source: Bureau of Justice Statistics, Capital Punishment, 1996; Death Penalty Information Center: http://www.deathpenaltyinfo.org/article.php?scid=8&did=245.

412. http://www.abanet.org/moratorium/.

413. The study was conducted by Professors David C. Baldus, Charles Pulaski, and George Woodworth. The Baldus study is based on more than 2,000 murder cases in Georgia from 1973 to 1978 and involves data relating to the victim's race and the defendant's race. See David C. Baldus et al., *Monitoring and Evaluating Temporary Death Sentencing Systems: Lessons From Georgia*, 18 U.C. Davis L. Rev. 1375 (1985); David C. Baldus et al., *Comparative Review of Death Sentences: An Empirical Study of the Georgia Experience*, 74 J. Crim. L. & Criminology 661 (1983).

414. *McClesky v. Kemp*, 481 U.S. 279, 312–313 (1987).

415. U.S. General Accounting Office, Death Penalty Sentencing: Research Indicates Pattern of Racial Disparities (1990), 5.

416. See *Atkins v. Virginia*, 536 U.S. 304 (2002).

417. See *Roper v. Simmons*, 543 U.S. 551 (2005).

418. Ellis Cose, *The Envy of the World: On Being a Black Man in America* (New York: Washington Square Press Publication, 2002), 100–118.

419. Jones-Brown, *Race, Crime and Punishment*, 88.

420. Bureau of Justice Statistics Correctional Surveys (The National Probation Data Survey, National Prisoner Statistics, Survey of Jails, Census of Jail Inmates, and The National Parole Data Survey) as presented in Correctional Populations in the United States, 1997, and Prison and Jail Inmates at Midyear, 2005.

421. U.S. General Accounting Office, Death Penalty Sentencing, February 1990; see Richard C. Deiter, *The Death Penalty in Black and White: Who Lives, Who Dies, Who Decides* (Washington, D.C.: Death Penalty Information Center, June 1998).

422. http://www.deathpenaltyinfo.org/article.php?scid=5&did=184 (last viewed June 7, 2006).

423. See Henriques and Manatu-Rupert, *The Prison Journal*, 81, no. 1, March 2001, 6–19; Bureau of Justice Statistics, Prison and Jail Inmates at Midyear 2001, 5 (2002).

424. Bureau of Justice Statistics, Prison and Jail Inmates at Midyear 2001, 5, 12 (2002); Gloria J. Browne-Marshall, "To Be Female, Black, Incarcerated, and Infected with HIV/AIDS: A Socio-Legal Analysis," *Criminal Law Bulletin*, 41, no. 1 (2005), 48.

425. Joseph, in *The System in Black and White: Exploring the Connections between Race, Crime, and Justice*, Michael W. Markowitz and Delores Jones-Brown, eds., 227.

426. John A. Davis, "Blacks, Crime, and American Culture," *Crime and Justice in America, 1776–1976*, 423 (The Annals of The American Academy of Political and Social Science), 91.

427. See Wackenhut Corrections Corporation: (New York Stock Exchange ticker: WHC). "Wackenhut Corrections Corporation. The Group's principal activity is to offer correctional and related institutional services to federal, state, local and overseas government agencies. Correctional services include the management of a broad spectrum of facilities, including male and female adult facilities, juvenile facilities, community corrections,

work programs, prison industries, substance abuse treatment facilities and mental health, geriatric and other special needs institutions." http://www.business.com/directory/government_and_trade/by_country/united_states/correctional_facilities/wackenhut_corrections_corporation/profile/   (last viewed June 10, 2006).

428. See official Web site of The GEO Group, Inc., a division of Wackenhut Corrections Corporation. The GEO Group, Inc. (New York Stock Exchange ticker: GGI); Press release of The GEO Group, Inc., "Launches Offering of 3.0 Million Shares of Common Stock," dated May 25, 2006. /PRNewswire-FirstCall/ ("GEO announced today that it plans to offer 3,000,000 shares of its common stock in an underwritten public offering pursuant to a shelf registration statement previously filed with the Securities and Exchange Commission. GEO also plans to grant the underwriters a 30-day option to purchase up to an aggregate of 450,000 additional shares of common stock. http://www.wcc-corrections.com/whatwedo.asp (last viewed June 10, 2006).

429. Jill Nelson, ed., *Police Brutality* (New York: W. W. Norton, 2000), 96.

430. Jones-Brown, *Race, Crime and Punishment*, 87–91.

431. Nelson, ed., *Police Brutality*, 92.

Chapter 8

1. William Patterson, *We Charge Genocide* (New York: Civil Rights Congress, 1951), 193.

2. History has demonstrated the successful contribution of Blacks within the Department of State. Ebenezer D. Bassett, the first African-American ambassador, led a U.S. delegation to Haiti in 1869. Nobel Peace Prize Laureate Ralph Bunche is celebrated for his role in the Middle East. Gen. Colin Powell and Condoleeza Rice have served as secretaries of state.

3. Paul Sieghart, *The International Law of Human Rights* (New York: Oxford University Press, 1983), 11.

4. See Frank Newman and David Weissbrodt, *International Human Rights: Law, Policy, and Process* (Cincinnati: Anderson, 1996), 2–4; Sieghart, *The International Law of Human Rights*, 11–12.

5. Harold Ball, *Prosecuting War Crimes and Genocide: The Twentieth-Century Experience* (Lawrence: University of Kansas Press, 1999), 12.

6. A. Leon Higginbotham, *In the Matter of Color* (New York: Oxford University Press, 1978), 334.

7. See Steven M. Wise, *Though the Heavens May Fall: The Landmark Trial That Led to the End of Human Slavery* (Cambridge, Mass.: Da Capo Press, 2005).

8. See Mark S. Weiner, *Black Trials: Citizenship from the Beginnings of Slavery to the End of Caste* (New York: Alfred A. Knopf, 2004), 73–77.

9. For more information, see generally Wise, *Though the Heavens May Fall: The Landmark Trial That Led to the End of Human Slavery*.

10. *Somerset's Case*, Howell, state trials, 802.

11. Ibid., 802–803.

12. Higginbotham, *In the Matter of Color*, 353.

13. See Wise, *Though the Heavens May Fall: The Landmark Trial That Led to the End of Human Slavery*.

14. United States Constitution, Art. I, Sec. 9.

15. *Prigg v. Pennsylvania*, 41 U.S. 539, 626 (1842).

16. In Congress, July 4, 1776, Declaration of the Independence of the Thirteen United States of America.

17. Robin Winks, *The Blacks in Canada: A History*, 2nd ed. (Montreal: McGill-Queen's University Press, 1997), 32.

18. See Simon Schama, *Rough Crossings: Britain, the Slaves and the American Revolution* (New York: HarperCollins, 2006).

19. Winks, *The Blacks in Canada: A History*, 2nd ed., 32.

20. Ibid.

21. Ibid., 33.

22. Ibid., 39–40.

23. Ibid, 38.

24. Ibid.

25. Ibid, 156.

26. Ibid.

27. See generally Robin Winks, *The Blacks in Canada: A History*, 2nd ed.

28. Ibid., 168.

29. Ibid.

30. Peter Bergman, *The Chronological History of the Negro in America* (New York: Harper & Row, 1969), 140–141.

31. For more information on Harriet Tubman, see Catherine Clinton, *Harriet Tubman: The Road to Freedom* (New York: Little Brown & Company, 2004).

32. Sarah H. Bradford, *Harriet Tubman: The Moses of Her People* (Bedford, Mass.: Applewood Books, 1886).

33. Winks, *The Blacks in Canada: A History*, 2nd ed., 240.

34. See Martin R. Delany and R. Campbell, *Search for a Place: Black Separatism and Africa: 1860* (Ann Arbor: University of Michigan Press, 1969); Hanes Walton and Robert Smith, *American Politics and the African American Quest for Universal Freedom*, 3rd ed. (New York: Pearson/Longman, 2006), 267.

35. General Assembly of the state of Maryland, Annapolis, 1832, chapters 124, 325; see also, Herbert Aptheker, *American Slave Revolts* (New York: International Publishers, 1993), 313–314.

36. Martin R. Delany, Official Report of the Niger Valley Exploring Party, 1861; see Delany and Campbell, *Search for a Place: Black Separatism and Africa: 1860*, 47, 77–79.

37. There are questions as to whether the treaty is binding. Individuals are prohibited from entering into treaty agreements. However, a contract for land use or a business agreement would not fall within this prohibition.

38. Delany and Campbell, *Search for a Place: Black Separatism and Africa: 1860*, 43.

39. Ibid., 64–66.

40. Hanes, 190–191.

41. J. Horton and L. Horton, A Federal Assault: African Americans and the Impact of the Fugitive Slave Law of 1850, 68 *Chi.-Kent. L. Rev.* 1179, 1187–1189 (1993).

42. Speech by Frederick Douglass before the American Social Science Association, September 12, 1879, and published in the *Journal of Social Science* (Boston, May 1880), XI, 1–35; "Frederick Douglass and Richard T. Greener on the Negro Exodus, 1879," in *A Documentary History of the Negro People in the United States*, ed. Herbert Aptheker (New York: Citadel Press, 1951), 724.

43. Walton, 121.

44. smithsonianeducation.org/migrations/legacy/almleg.html; L. Gomez, Off-White in an Age of White Supremacy: Mexican Elites and the Rights of Indians and Blacks in Nineteenth-Century New Mexico, *Chicano-Latino L. Rev.* 9, 17–18.

45. Gomez, Off-White in an Age of White Supremacy: Mexican Elites and the Rights of Indians and Blacks in Nineteenth-Century New Mexico, 9, 42–43.

46. R. Anderson, *Redressing Colonial Genocide under International Law: The Heroes' Cause of Action against Germany*, 93 Calif. L. Rev. 1155, 1168 (2005).

47. Leon Litwack, *North of Slavery: The Negro in the Free States (1790–1860)* (Chicago: The University of Chicago Press, 1961), 42.

48. Ibid.

49. See Frederick Douglass, *Narrative of the Life of Frederick Douglass: An American Slave* (Boston; reprinted New York: Bonanza Books, 1962).

50. See William Wells Brown, *My Three Years in Europe; or, Places I Have Seen and People I Have Met* (Boston, 1852). Brown, credited with publishing the first novel by an African in America, wrote *Clotel, or, the President's Daughter: A Narrative of Slave Life in the United States*. Written in 1853, *Clotel* recounts the relationship between President Thomas Jefferson and Sally Hemings, his slave, and their children. Wells also wrote *The Escape; or a Leap for Freedom*, considered the first stage play by an African in America.

51. See Brown, *My Three Years in Europe; or, Places I Have Seen and People I Have Met*; C. Peter Ripley et al., eds., *The Black Abolitionist Papers: Vol. II: Canada, 1830–1865* (Chapel Hill: University of North Carolina Press, 1987), 1992.

52. *Dred Scott v. Sandford*, 60 U.S. 393, 436 (1856).

53. Leon Litwack, *Been in the Storm So Long: The Aftermath of Slavery* (New York: Random House, 1979), 276–277.

54. Ida B. Wells-Barnett, *Crusade for Justice: The Autobiography of Ida B. Wells*, ed. Alfreda M. Duster (Chicago: University of Chicago Press, 1970), p 189.

55. Ibid, 187–188.

56. The term "White slavery" referred to kidnapping White women from America for sexual bondage in other countries (allegedly in Asia).

57. Wells-Barnett, *Crusade for Justice: The Autobiography of Ida B. Wells*, ed. Alfreda M. Duster, 209.

58. Arthur F. Raper, *The Tragedy of Lynching* (Montclair, N.J.: Patterson Smith, 1969), 1.

59. Derrick Bell, *Race, Racism and American Law* (New York: Aspen Publishers, 2000), 59; Oliver Cox, "Lynching and the Status Quo," in *Race, Crime and Justice: A Reader*, S. Gabbidon and H. Greene, eds. (New York: Routledge, 2005), 28–30.

60. Wells-Barnett, *Crusade for Justice: The Autobiography of Ida B. Wells*, ed. Alfreda M. Duster. See table 2.

61. *Plessy v. Ferguson*, 163 U.S. 537 (1896).

62. According to *The American Heritage Dictionary*, 4th ed., lynching is to execute without due process of law; lynching could include torture such as burning a person alive, castration, mutilation, amputation of limbs, and/or decapitation.

63. David Levering Lewis, *W. E. B. DuBois 1868–1919: Biography of a Race* (New York: Henry Holt and Company, 1993), 249.

64. Ibid., 247–250.

65. Ibid., 4.

66. Ibid., 316.

67. The legal committee of the NAACP would eventually evolve into the NAACP Legal Defense and Educational Fund, Inc.

68. Marcus Garvey (1887–1940). Chapters of the Universal Negro Improvement Association and African Communities League remain in existence today.

69. For more information on Marcus Garvey, see Thomas Crawford, ed., *Selected Writings and Speeches of Marcus Garvey* (Mineola, N.Y.: Dover Publications, Inc., 2004); John Henrik Clarke, *Marcus Garvey and the Vision of Africa* (New York: Vintage Books, 1974); Amy Jacques-Garvey, ed., *Philosophy and Opinions of Marcus Garvey of Africa for the Africans* (London: Frank Cass & Co. Ltd, 1967); Robert A. Hill, ed., *Marcus Garvey and Universal Negro Improvement Association Paper* (Berkeley: University of California Press, 1983).

70. Lewis, *W. E. B. DuBois 1868–1919: Biography of a Race*, 67–81.

71. *Garvey v. United States*, 4 F. 2d 974 (2nd Cir. 1925).

72. *Garvey v. United States*, 267 U.S. 604 (1925) (cert. denied).

73. Geoffrey Best, *War and Law: Since 1945* (New York: Oxford University Press, 2002), 55.

74. See the covenant of the League of Nations. The covenant stated: "In order to promote international co-operation and to achieve international peace and security by the acceptance of obligations not to resort to war, by the prescription of open, just and honourable relations between nations, by the firm establishment of the understandings of international law as the actual rule of conduct among Governments, and by the maintenance of justice and a scrupulous respect for all treaty obligations in the dealings of organised peoples with one another."

75. Kriansak Kittichaisaree, *International Criminal Law* (New York: Oxford University Press, 2001), 5.

76. Gloria J. Browne-Marshall, "Introduction to International Criminal Justice," in *The Development of International Criminal Law* (New York: McGraw–Hill), 101–102.

77. See Jordan J. Paust, M. Bassiouni, M. Scharf, J. Gurule, L. Sadat, B. Zagaris, and S. Williams, *International Criminal Law* (Durham: Carolina Academic Press, 2000).

78. See Hill, ed., *Marcus Garvey and Universal Negro Improvement Association Papers*; Jacques-Garvey, ed., *Philosophy and Opinions of Marcus Garvey of Africa for the Africans*.

79. Browne-Marshall, in *The Development of International Criminal Law*, 101; see Paust et al., *International Criminal Law*.

80. See, for example, Geneva Convention for the Amelioration of the Condition of the Wounded and Sick and Armed Forces in the Field, Aug. 12, 1949, art. 49, 6 U.S.T. 3114, 75 U.N.T.S. 31; Geneva Convention for the Amelioration of the Condition of Wounded, Sick and Shipwrecked Members of Armed Forces at Sea, Aug. 12, 1949, art. 50, 6 U.S.T. 3217, 75 U.N.T.S. 85; Geneva Convention Relative to the Treatment of Prisoners of War, Aug. 12, 1949, art. 129, 6 U.S.T. 3316, 75 U.N.T.S. 135; Geneva Convention Relative to the Protection of Civilian Persons in Time of War, Aug. 12, 1949, art. 146, 6 U.S.T. 3516, 75 U.N.T.S. 287.

81. Henry Dumant wrote of the horrendous treatment of wounded soldiers at the Battle of Solferino in 1859, describing wounded men crushed under horses and soldiers in battle. In 1864, the first humanitarian treaty—the Convention for the Amelioration of the Condition of the Wounded in Armies in the Field of 1865—was created. In 1882, the United States became a signatory to what is referred to as the Geneva Convention.

82. Best, *War and Law: Since 1945*, 58.

83. Phillippe Sands, ed., *From Nuremberg to the Hague: The Future of International Criminal Justice* (New York: Cambridge University Press, 2003), 6.

84. Frank Newman and David Weissbrodt, *International Human Rights: Law, Policy, and Process* (Cincinnati: Anderson Press, 1996), 44; Browne-Marshall, in *The Development of International Criminal Law*, 102–103.

85. Browne-Marshall, in *The Development of International Criminal Law*, 126; Paust et al., *International Criminal Law*, 29–30.

86. Kittichaisaree, *International Criminal Law*, 43.

87. Paust et al., *International Criminal Law*, 625.

88. Yves Beigbeder, *Judging War Criminals: The Politics of International Justice* (New York: St. Martin's Press, 1999), 52.

89. Browne-Marshall, in *The Development of International Criminal Law*, 126; Beigbeder, *Judging War Criminals: The Politics of International Justice*, 53.

90. Paust et al., *International Criminal Law*, 29; Browne-Marshall, in *Introduction to International Criminal Tribunals*, 126.

91. The Preamble of the Charter of the United Nations, 1946.

92. www.un.org.

93. http://www.ohchr.org/english/about/index.htm.

94. Carol Anderson, *Eyes Off the Prize: The United Nations and the African American Struggle for Human Rights, 1944–1955* (Cambridge, U.K.: Cambridge University Press, 2003), 58.

95. Ibid., 81; National Negro Congress, *A Petition to the United Nations on Behalf of 13 Million Oppressed Negro Citizens of the United States of America* (New York: National Negro Congress, 1946), 2–3.

96. Ibid., 90–91.

97. Ibid., 92.

98. Ibid., 92.

99. Ibid., 96.

100. Gloria J. Browne-Marshall, Eleanor Roosevelt: Her Civil Rights/Human Rights Dilemma, presented at the conference on Eleanor Roosevelt, Hofstra University, 1999; Anderson, *Eyes Off the Prize: The United Nations and the African American Struggle for Human Rights, 1944–1955*, 130.

101. Convention on the Prevention and Punishment of the Crime of Genocide, 78 U.N.T.S. 277.

102. Phillippe Sands, ed., *From Nuremberg to The Hague: The Future of International Criminal Justice* (Cambridge: University of Cambridge Press, 2003), 147.

103. U.S. Const. Art. VI.

104. The United States signed the Genocide Convention in 1987.

105. Universal Declaration of Human Rights, G.A. Res. 217 A (III), adopted by the U.N. Doc. A/810 (Dec. 10, 1948).

106. Anderson, *Eyes Off the Prize: The United Nations and the African American Struggle for Human Rights, 1944–1955*, 131.

107. Universal Declaration of Human Rights, G.A. Res. 217 A (III), adopted by the U.N. Doc. A/810 (Dec.10, 1948).

108. See Newman and Weissbrodt, *International Human Rights: Law, Policy, and Process*.

109. Mary Dudziak, *Cold War/Civil Rights: Race and the Image of American Democracy* (Princeton, N.J.: Princeton University Press, 2000), 79.

110. Anderson, *Eyes Off the Prize: The United Nations and the African American Struggle for Human Rights, 1944–1955*, 107.

111. Dudziak, *Cold War/Civil Rights: Race and the Image of American Democracy*, 66, 70–72, 80–82.

112. Ibid., 72–76; Anderson, *Eyes Off the Prize: The United Nations and the African American Struggle for Human Rights, 1944–1955*, 262.

113. Paul Robeson, *Here I Stand* (Boston: Beacon Press, 1971), 63–64; Dudziak, *Cold War/Civil Rights: Race and the Image of American Democracy*, 71.

114. *Kent v. Dulles*, 357 U.S. 116 (1957).

115. Anderson, *Eyes Off the Prize: The United Nations and the African American Struggle for Human Rights, 1944–1955*, 203–206; Dudziak, *Cold War/Civil Rights: Race and the Image of American Democracy*, 105.

116. *Kent v. Dulles*, 357 U.S. 116 (1957).

117. Ibid.

118. 22 CFR § 51.135; *Kent v. Dulles*, 357 U.S. 116, 118 (1957).

119. Ibid.

120. *Korematu v. United States*, 319 U.S. 432 (1944).

121. *Kent v. Dulles*, 357 U.S. 116, 125 (1957).

122. Ibid., 116, 130.

123. Lewis, *W. E. B. DuBois: The Fight for Equality and the American Century, 1919–1963*, 555.

124. Eleanor Roosevelt and Thurgood Marshall were cochairs of the legal committee of the NAACP, which would become the NAACP Legal Defense and Educational Fund, Inc.

125. Lewis, *W. E. B. DuBois: The Fight for Equality and the American Century, 1919–1963*, 534; Anderson, *Eyes Off the Prize: The United Nations and the African American Struggle for Human Rights, 1944–1955*, 144–145. The employment contract between the NAACP and W. E. B. DuBois was not renewed.

126. Anderson, *Eyes Off the Prize: The United Nations and the African American Struggle for Human Rights, 1944–1955*, 145–146.

127. See William Patterson, ed., *We Charge Genocide: The Historic Petition to the United Nations for Relief from a Crime of the United States Government against the Negro People* (New York: Civil Rights Congress, 1951).

128. Ibid., 4, 57–192.

129. Ibid., 44.

130. Anderson, *Eyes Off the Prize: The United Nations and the African American Struggle for Human Rights, 1944–1955*, 180.

131. Ibid.

132. Dudziak, *Cold War/Civil Rights: Race and the Image of American Democracy*, 58–60.

133. *Brown v. Topeka Board of Education*, 347 U.S. 483 (1954); Anderson, *Eyes Off the Prize: The United Nations and the African American Struggle for Human Rights, 1944–1955*, 150–151.

134. *Brown v. Topeka Board of Education*, 347 U.S. 483, 495 (1954).

135. See Dudziak, *Cold War/Civil Rights: Race and the Image of American Democracy*, and Anderson, *Eyes Off the Prize: The United Nations and the African American Struggle for Human Rights, 1944–1955*, 223.

136. www.un.org.

137. See International Convention on the Elimination of All Forms of Racial Discrimination, G.A. res. 2106 (XX), Annex, 20 U.N. GAOR Su(No. 14), U.N. Doc. A/6014 (1966), 660 U.N.T.S. 195 entered into force Jan. 4, 1969.

138. Five other committees with comparable constitutions and functions have been created: the Human Rights Committee (which has responsibilities under the International Covenant on Civil and Political Rights), the Committee on the Elimination of Discrimination against Women, the Committee against Torture, the Committee on Economic, Social and Cultural Rights, and the Committee on the Rights of the Child. See http://www.unhchr.ch/html/menu6/2/fs12.htm#n_2_.

139. See International Convention on the Elimination of All Forms of Racial Discrimination, G.A. res. 2106 (XX), Annex, 20 U.N. GAOR Su(No. 14), U.N. Doc. A/6014 (1966), 660 U.N.T.S. 195 entered into force Jan. 4, 1969, entered into force in the U.S. Nov. 20, 1994.

140. Ibid.

141. *Grutter v. Bolinger*, 539 U.S. 306, 344 (2003).

142. Ibid., 306.

143. See International Covenant on Civil and Political Rights, G.A. res. 2200A, (XXI), December 16, 1966, 21 U.N. GAOR Su(No. 16). U.N. Doc. A/6316 (1966), 999 U.N.T.S. 171, entered into force March 23, 1976, entered into force in the U.S. September 8, 1992.

144. See International Covenant on Economic, Social and Cultural Rights, G.A. res. 2200A(XXI), 21 U.N. GAOR Su(No. 16), U.N. Doc. A/6316 (1966), 993 U.N.T.S. 3, entered into force Jan. 3, 1976.

145. See Convention on the Elimination of All Forms of Discrimination against Women, G.A. Res. 34/180, U.N. GAOR, 34th Sess., U.N. Doc. A/34/46 (1980), entered into force Sept. 8, 1981.

146. See Convention against Torture and Other Cruel, Inhuman or Degrading Treatment or Punishment, G.A. Res. 39/46, Annex, 39 U.N. GAOR Su(No. 51), U.N. Doc. A/39/51 (1984), entered into force June 26, 1987, entered into force in U.S. November 20, 1994.

147. See Convention on the Rights of the Child, 166, U.N. Doc. G.A. Res. Res. 44/49, entered into force Sept. 2, 1990.

148. See U.N. Charter, 59 Stat. 1031, T.S. 993, 3 Bevans 1153, entered into force Oct. 24, 1945.

149. www.un.org.

150. See Statute of the International Criminal Tribunal for Rwanda, S.C. Res. 955, U.N. SCOR, 49th Sess., 3453 mtg., preamble, 1994; Sands, *From Nuremberg to The Hague: The Future of International Criminal Justice*, 45.

151. Beigbeder, *Judging War Criminals: The Politics of International Justice*, 174.

152. Sands, ed., *From Nuremberg to The Hague: The Future of International Criminal Justice*, 44; Browne-Marshall, *International Criminal Tribunals*, 127–128.

153. Sands, ed., *From Nuremberg to The Hague: The Future of International Criminal Justice*, 6; Browne-Marshall, *International Criminal Tribunals*, 129.

154. See Statute of the Special Court for Sierra Leone, pmbl. (explaining the agreement pursuant to Security Council Resolution 1315 established the Special Court for Sierra Leone), available at http://www.sierra-leone. org/specialcourtstatute.html; Sands, *From Nuremberg to The Hague: The Future of International Criminal Justice*, 6; Browne-Marshall, G., *International Criminal Tribunals*, 129.

155. Ball, *Prosecuting War Crimes and Genocide: The Twentieth-Century Experience*, 94; Browne-Marshall, *International Criminal Tribunals*, 130.

156. Ball, *Prosecuting War Crimes and Genocide: The Twentieth-Century Experience*, 95–96.

157. Browne-Marshall, *International Criminal Tribunals*, 130; See Cesare P. R. Romano, A. Nollkaemper, and J. Kleffner, *Internationalized Criminal Courts and Tribunals* (New York: Oxford University Press, 2004).

158. See Rome Statute of the International Criminal Court, July 17, 1998, pmbl., 2187 U.N.T.S. 90, U.N. Doc. A/CONF.183/9 (1998).

159. Ibid.

160. Sands, ed., *From Nuremberg to The Hague: The Future of International Criminal Justice*, 107.

161. Browne-Marshall, "The Development of International Criminal Law," in *Introduction to International Criminal Justice*, ed. M. Natarajan (Boston: McGraw–Hill Company, 2005).

162. Speech by Vicente Fox delivered on May 13, 2005, in Puerto Vallarta, Mexico.

163. Sambo is a caricature of Black children, with grotesquely large lips and eyes. Al Jolson was a White vaudeville entertainer who wore black make-up.

164. See Randall Robinson, *Quitting America: The Departure of a Black Man from His Native Land* (New York, Plume/Penguin Group, 2004).

Afterword

1. Fannie Lou Hamer, *To Praise Our Bridges: An Autobiography* (Jackson, Miss.: KIPCO, 1967), quoted in *The Eyes on the Prize Civil Rights Reader: Documents, Speeches, and Firsthand Accounts from the Black Freedom Struggle, 1954–1990*, Claiborne Carson et al., eds. (New York: Penguin Books, 1991), 179.

2. The Elders, Oraibi, Arizona, Hopi Nation.

Bibliography

Books

Acker, J. R., and D. C. Brody. *Criminal Procedure: A Contemporary Perspective*, 2nd ed. Boston: Jones & Bartlett, 2004.

Ali, M., and H. Y. Ali. *The Soul of a Butterfly: Reflections on Life's Journey*. New York: Simon & Schuster, 2004.

Alpheus, D., and S. Grier, Jr. *American Constitutional Law Introductory Essays and Selected Cases*, 14th ed. Upper Saddle River, N.J.: Pearson/Prentice Hall, 2005.

Als, H., J. Lewis, L. F. Litwack, and J. Allen. *Without Sanctuary: Lynching Photography in America*. Hong Kong: Twin Palms, 2000.

Anderson, C. *Eyes Off the Prize: The United Nations and The African American Struggle for Human Rights, 1944–1955*. Cambridge, U.K.: Cambridge University Press, 2003.

Appiah, K. A., and A. Gutmann. *Color Conscious: The Political Morality of Race*, Princeton, N.J.: Princeton University Press, 1996.

Aptheker, H. *A Documentary History of the Negro People in the United States*, vol. 1. New York: Citadel Press, 1971.

———. *American Negro Slave Riots*, 50th anniversary ed. New York: International Press, 1993.

Arsenault, R. *Freedom Riders: 1961 and the Struggle for Racial Justice*. New York: Oxford University Press, 2006.

Atkinson, P. *An African American's View*, Brown vs. Topeka: *Desegregation and Miseducation*. Chicago: Independent, 1993.

Ayers, E. L. *Vengeance and Justice: Crime and Punishment in the 19th Century American South*. New York: Oxford University Press, 1984.

Ayittey, G. B. N. *Africa in Chaos*. New York: St. Martin's Griffin, 1999.

Azevedo, M. *Africa Studies: A Survey of Africa and the African Diaspora*, 3rd ed. Durham, N.C.: Carolina Academic Press, 2005.

Baker, R. S. *Following the Color Line: American Negro Citizenship in the Progressive Era*. New York: Harper & Row, 1964.

Barrett, P. M. *The Good Black: A True Story of Race in America*. New York: Penguin, 1999.

Bell, D. *Civil Rights: Leading Cases*. Boston: Little, Brown & Co., 1980.

———. *And We Are not Saved*. New York: Basic Books, 1987.

———. *Confronting Authority: Reflections of an Ardent Protester*. Boston: Beacon, 1994.

———. *Constitutional Conflicts Part I*. Cincinnati, Ohio: Anderson, 1997.

———. *Race, Racism and American Law*, 4th ed. New York: Aspen, 2000.

————. *Silent Covenants*: Brown v. Board of Education *and the Unfulfilled Hopes for Racial Reform*. New York: Oxford University Press, 2004.

Bergman, P. M. *The Chronological History of the Negro in America*. New York: Harper & Row, 1969.

Best, G. *War & Law since 1945*. New York: Oxford University Press, 2002.

Bond, H. M. *Black American Scholars: A Study of Their Beginnings*. Detroit, Mich.: Balamp, 1972.

Bowen, W. G. *The Shape of the River: Long-Term Consequences of Considering Race in College and University Admissions*. Princeton, N.J.: Princeton University Press, 1998.

Boyle, K. *Arc of Justice: A Saga of Race, Civil Rights and Murder in the Jazz Age*. New York: Owl Books, 2004.

Branch, T. *Parting the Waters: America in the King Years 1954–63*. New York: Simon & Schuster, 1988.

Brest, P., S. Levinson, J. M. Balkan, and A. R. Amar. *Process of Constitutional Decision Making Cases and Materials*, 4th ed. New York: Aspen, 2000.

Brophy, A. L. *Reconstructing the Dreamland: The Tulsa Riot of 1921: Race, Reparations and Reconciliation*. New York: Oxford University Press, 2002.

Browne-Marshall, G. *The Constitution: Critical Cases and Controversies*. Boston: Pearson Publishing, 2006.

Brown, K. *Race, Law, and Education in the Post-Desegregation Era: Four Perspectives on Desegregation and Resegregation*. Durham, N.C.: Carolina Academic Press, 2005.

Buckley, G. *American Patriots: The Story of Blacks in The Military from the Revolution to Desert Storm*. New York: Random House, 2001.

Bushwell, J. O., III. *Slavery, Segregation, and Scripture*. Grand Rapids, Mich.: Eerdmans Publishing, 1964.

Carnes, M. C., and J. A. Garraty. *American Destiny: Narrative of a Nation Vol. II—since 1865*. New York: Longman, 2003.

Carr, R. K. *Federal Protection of Civil Rights: Quest for a Sword*. Ithaca, N.Y.: Cornell University Press, 1947.

Carson, C., D. J. Gill, V. Harding, and D. C. Hine. *The Eyes on the Prize: Civil Rights Reader—Documents, Speeches, and Firsthand Accounts from The Black Freedom Struggle 1954–1990*. New York: Penguin Books, 1991.

Catterall, H. T. *Judicial Cases Concerning American Slavery and the Negro*. New York: Octagon Books, 1968.

Chapman, F. *Race, Identity and Myth in the Spanish Speaking Caribbean: Essays on Biculturalism as a Contested Terrain of Difference*. New York: Chapman & Associates Inc., 2002.

Chemerinsky, E. *Constitutional Law*. New York: Aspen, 2001.

The Civil Rights Congress. *We Charge Genocide*. New York: Civil Rights Congress, 1951.

Clark, K. B., and J. H. Franklin. *The Nineteen Eighties: Prologue and Prospect*. Washington, D.C.: Center for Political Studies, 1981.

Clarke, J. H. *Christopher Columbus and the Afrikan Holocaust: Slavery and the Rise of European Capitalism*. New York: A&B Publishers Group, 1998.

Cole, F. G., and C. E. Smith. *The American System of Criminal Justice*, 10th ed. California: Wadsworth, 2004.

Corlett, J. A. *Race, Racism and Reparations*. Ithaca, N.Y.: Cornell University Press, 2005.

Cose, E. *The Envy of the World: On Being a Black Man in America*. New York: Washington Square Press, 2002.

Coulter, M. E. *The South during Reconstruction 1865–1877*. Baton Rouge, La.: Louisiana State University Press, 1947.

Dalfiume, R. M. *Desegregation of the U.S. Armed Forces: Fighting on Two Fronts 1939–1953*. Columbia: Missouri University Press, 1969.

Davis, J., and G. A. Martinez. *A Reader on Race, Civil Rights and American Law—A Multicultural Approach*. Durham, N.C.: Carolina Academic Press, 2001.

Davis, D. B. *The Problem of Slavery in Western Culture*. New York: Oxford University Press, 1966.

——— *Inhuman Bondage: The Rise and Fall of Slavery in the New World*. New York: Oxford University Press, 2006.

Delgado, R., and J. Stefanic. *Critical Race Theory: An Introduction*. New York: New York University Press, 2001.

Delany, M. R., and R. Campbell. *Search for a Place: Black Separatism and Africa 1860*. East Lansing, Mich.: Michigan University Press, 1969.

Dorf, M. C. *Constitutional Law Stories*. New York: Foundation, 2004.

Douglass, F. *Narrative of the Life of Frederick Douglass*. New York: Dover, 1995.

Dray, P. *At the Hands of Persons Unknown: The Lynching of Black America*. New York: Modern Library Paperbacks, 2002.

Du Bois, W. E. B. *The World and Africa: An Inquiry into the Part Which Africa Has Played in World History*. New York: International Publishers, 2003.

Dudziak, M. L. *Cold War, Civil Rights, Race and the Image of American Democracy*. Princeton, N.J.: Princeton University Press, 2000.

Duster, A. M. *Crusade for Justice: The Autobiography of Ida B. Wells*. Chicago: Chicago University Press, 1970.

Encyclopedia Britannica Educational Corporation. *The Negro in American History III. Slaves and Masters 1567–1854*. Arizona: Benton, 1969.

Epstein, L., and Thomas G. Walker. *Constitutional Law for a Changing America: A Short Course*. Washington, D.C.: Congressional Quarterly Inc., 1996.

Evers-Williams, M., and M. Marable. *The Autobiography of Medgar Evers: A Hero's Life and Legacy Revealed through His Writings, Letters and Speeches*. New York: Basic Civitas Books, 2005.

Fallon, Richard H., Jr. *The Dynamic Constitution: An Introduction to the Constitutional Law*. London: Cambridge University Press, 2004.

Farber, D. A., and S. Sherry. *A History of the American Constitution*, 2nd ed. St. Paul, Minn.: Thomson/West, 2005.

Feelings, T. *The Middle Passage: White Ships Black Cargo*. New York: Dial Books, 1995.

Fierce, M. C. *Slavery Revisited—Blacks and the Southern Convict Lease System 1865–1933*. New York: Africana Studies Research Center, 1994.

Finkelman, P. *Slavery in the Courtroom*. Washington, D.C.: Library of Congress, 1985.

Fisher, L. *American Constitutional Law*, 2nd ed. New York: McGraw–Hill, 1995.

Flexner, E. *Century of Struggle*. New York: Atheneum, 1970.

Fogel, W. R., and S. L. Engerman. *Time on the Cross: The Economics of American Negro Slavery*. New York: W. W. Norton & Co., 1989.

Fogel, W. R. *The Rise and Fall of American Slavery without Consent or Contract*. New York: W. W. Norton & Co., 1989.

Foner, P. S. *W. E. B. Dubois Speaks. Speeches and Addresses (1920–63)*. New York: Path Finder, 1970.

Foster, J. C., and S. M. Leeson. *Constitutional Law: Cases in Context Vol. II. Civil Rights and Liberties Part A*. Upper Saddle River, N.J.: Prentice Hall, 1998.

———. *Constitutional Law: Cases in Context Vol. II. Civil Rights and Liberties Part B*. Upper Saddle River, N.J.: Prentice Hall, 1998.

Franklyn, H., J. Moss, and A. Alfred, Jr. *From Slavery to Freedom: A History of African Americans*, 8th ed. New York: Alfred A. Knopf, 2005.

Frazier, F. E. *Negro in the United States*. New York: Macmillan Co., 1971.

Furnas, J. C. *The Americans—A Social History of the United States 1587–1914*. New York: G. P. Putnam, 1969.

Galbraith, J. K. *The Affluent Society: 40th Anniversary Edition*. New York: Houghton Mifflin Company/Mainer Books, 1998.

Gandhi, M. *An Autobiography: My Experiments with Truth*, New York: Doer Publications, 1983.

Garrow, D. J. *Bearing the Cross: Martin Luther King and the Southern Christian Leadership Conference*. New York: First Quill Edition, 1999.

Garvey, M. *Philosophy and Opinions of Marcus Garvey*. London: Frank Cass & Co. Ltd., 1967.

———. *Selected Writings and Speeches of Marcus Garvey*. New York: Dover Publishing Inc., 2004.

Gordon-Reed, A. *Race on Trial: Law and Justice in American History*. New York: Oxford University Press, 2002.

Graglia, L. A. *Disaster by Decree: The Supreme Court Decisions on Race and the Schools*. Ithaca, N.Y.: Cornell University Press, 1976.

Grant, J. M. *The Maroons in Nova Scotia*. Halifax, N.S.: Formac, 2002.

Gray, F. *Bus Ride to Justice*. Montgomery, Ala.: New South Books, 1995.

——— *The Tuskegee Syphilis Study*. Montgomery, Ala.: Black Belt Press, 1998.

Greene, G. S. L. *Race, Crime, Justice: A Reader. New* York: Routledge, 2005.

Greene, R. E. *Black Defenders of America 1775–1973*. Chicago: Johnson Publishing Co., 1974.

Gropman, A. L. *The Air Force Integrates 1945–1964*, Washington, D.C.: U.S. Gov. Printing Office, 1978.

Gunther, G., and K. M. Sullivan. *Constitutional Law*, 13th ed. New York: Foundation Press, 1997.

Haines, H. H. *Black Radicals and the Civil Rights Mainstream 1954–1970*, Knoxville, Tenn.: Tennessee University Press, 1989.

Harr, J. S., and K. M. Hess. *Constitutional Law and the Criminal Justice System*, 3rd ed. Belmont, Cal.: Wadsworth, 2005.

Harrison, M., and S. Gilbert. *Death Penalty Decisions of the United States Supreme Court*. Carlsbad, Cal.: Excellent Books, 2003.

Haskins, J. *Pinckney Benton Stewart Pinchback*. New York: MacMillan Press, 1973.

Haynes, R. V. *A Night of Violence: The Houston Riot of 1917*. Baton Rouge, La.: Louisiana State University Press, 1976.

Higginbotham, L. A., Jr. *In the Matter of Color, Race and the American Legal Process: The Colonial Period*. New York: Oxford University Press, 1978.

———. *Shades of Freedom*. New York: Oxford University Press, 1996.

———. *Race Law Cases, Commentary and Questions*, 2nd ed. Durham, N.C.: Carolina Academic Press, 2005.

Higginbotham, M. F. *Race Law Cases, Commentary and Questions*, 2nd ed. Teacher's manual. Durham, N.C.: Carolina Academic Press, 2005.

Hill, H., and J. E. Jones. *Race in America: The Struggle for Equality*. Madison, Wisc.: The University of Wisconsin Press, 1993.

Hill, R. A. *The Marcus Garvey and Universal Negro Improvement Association Papers Vol. I 1826–August 1919*. Los Angeles: University of California Press, 1983.

Hodges, G. R. *Root and Branch African Americans in New York and East Jersey 1613–1863*. Chapel Hill, N.C.: University of North Carolina Press, 1999.

Horn, J. P. *A Land as God Made It: Jamestown and the Birth of America*. New York: Basic/Perseus Books, 2005.

Ides, A., and C. N. May. *Constitutional Law: Individual Rights Examples & Explanations*, 2nd ed. New York: Aspen Law and Business, 2001.

Ivers, G., *American Constitutional Law Power and Politics Vol. II Civil Rights and Liberties*. Boston: Houghton Mifflin Co., 2002.

Jacobs, J. B. *New Perspectives on Prisons and Imprisonment*. Ithaca, N.Y.: Cornell University Press, 1983.

James, C. L. R. *The Black Jacobins Toussaint L'Ouverture and the San Domingo Revolution*. New York: Random House Inc., 1963.

Johnson, J. W. *Along the Way: Autobiography of James Weldon Johnson*. Cambridge, Mass.: Da Capo Press, 2000.

Jones-Browne, D. D. *Race, Crime, and Punishment*. Philadelphia: Chelsea House, 2000.

Joseph, J., and D. Taylor. *With Justice for All: Minorities and Women in Criminal Justice*. Upper Saddle River, N.J.: Prentice Hall, 2003.

Katz, W. L. *Eyewitness: The Negro in American History*, text ed. New York: Pitman Publishing Co., 1967.

Katznelson, I. *When Affirmative Action Was White*. New York: W. W. Norton & Co., 2005.

Kennedy, R. *Race, Crime, and the Law*, New York: Pantheon Books, 1997.

Killens, J. O. *The Trial of Denmark Vessey*. Boston: Beacon Press, 1970.

Kinshasa, K. M. *The Man from Scottsboro: Clarence Norris in His Own Words.* Jefferson, N.C.: McFarland & Co. Publishers, 1997.

————. *Black Resistance to the Ku Klux Klan in the Wake of the Civil War.* Jefferson, N.C.: McFarland & Co., 2006.

Kolchin, P. *American Slavery: 1619–1877.* New York: Hill & Wang, Farrar, Straus and Giroux, 1993.

Langum, D. J. *Crossing over the Line: Legislating Morality and the Mann Act.* Chicago: The University of Chicago Press, 1994.

Lemann, N. *Redemption: The Last Battle of the Civil War.* New York: Farrar, Straus and Giroux, 2006.

Lewis, D. L. *W. E. B. Dubois. Biography of a Race 1868–1919.* New York: Henry Holt & Co., 1994.

————. *W. E. B. Dubois—The Fight for Equality and the American Century, 1919–1963.* New York: Henry Holt & Co., 2000.

Lipman, P. *High Stakes Education: Inequality, Globalization, and Urban School Reform (Critical Social Thought).* New York: Routledge, 2004.

Litwack, L. F. *North of Slavery.* Chicago: Chicago University Press, 1961.

Lively, D. E. *The Constitution and Race.* New York: Praeger Publishers, 1992.

Lively, D. E., P. A. Haddon, D. E. Roberts, R. L. Weaver, and W. D. Araiza. *Constitutional Law Cases, History and Dialogues,* 2nd ed. Cincinnati, Ohio: Anderson Publishing Co., 2000.

Lopez, I. F. *White By Law: The Legal Construction of Race.* New York: New York University Press, 1996.

Madison, J. H. *A Lynching in the Heartland, Race and Memory in America.* New York: Palgrave/Macmillan, 2001.

Markowitz, M. W., and D. D. Jones-Brown. *The System in Black and White: Exploring the Connections between Race, Crime and Justice.* Westport, Conn.: Praeger Publishers, 2001.

Massey, D. S., and N. A. Danton. *American Apartheid Segregation and the Making of the Underclass.* London: Harvard University Press, 1993.

Massey, C. *American Constitutional Law. Powers and Liberties.* New York: Aspen, 2001.

Mason, A. T., and D. G. Stephenson, Jr. *American Constitutional Law: Introductory Essays and Selected Cases,* 11th ed. Upper Saddle River, N.J.: Prentice Hall Inc., 1996.

May, G. *The Informant: The FBI, the Ku Klux Klan, and Murder of Viola Luizzo.* New Haven, Conn.: Yale University Press, 2005.

Mayer, H. *All on Fire: William Lloyd Garrison and the Abolition of Slavery,* New York: St. Martin's Press, 1998.

McCaul, R. L. *The Black Struggle for Public Schooling in Nineteenth-Century Illinois.* Chicago: Southern Illinois University Press, 1987.

McConnell M. W., J. H. Garvey, and T. C. Berg. *Religion and the Constitution.* New York: Aspen, 2002.

McLaurin, M. A. *Celia, a Slave. A True Story.* New York: Avon Books, 1993.

McPherson, J. P. *The Struggle for Equality.* Princeton, N.J.: Princeton University Press, 1964.

Meltzer, M. *In Their Own Words. A History of the American Negro 1865–1916.* New York: Thomas, 1965.

Mills, K. *This Little Light of Mine: The Life of Fannie Lou Hamer.* New York: Dutton Book, 1993.

Morgan, E. S. *American Slavery, American Freedom: The Ordeal of Colonial Virginia.* New York: W. W. Norton, 1995.

Munford, C. J. *Race and Reparations: A Black Perspective for the Twenty-First Century.* Trenton, N.J.: Africa World Press, 1996.

Natarajan, M. *Introduction to International Criminal Justice.* New York: McGraw–Hill, 2005.

National Urban League. *The State of Black America 2005. The Equality Index: Black Health, Voting Rights, Education.* New York: National Urban League, 2005.

Nieman, D. G. *Promises to Keep.* New York: Oxford University Press, 1991.

Nelson, J. *Police Brutality: An Anthology.* New York: W. W. Norton & Co., 2001.

Nordin, D. S. *The New Deal's Black Congressman: A Tale of Arthur Wergs Mitchell.* Columbia, Mo.: The University of Missouri Press, 1997.

Norment, N., Jr. *The African American Studies Reader.* Durham, N.C.: Carolina Academic Press, 2001.

O'Brien, D. M. *Constitutional Law and Politics Vol. I Struggle for Power and Governmental Accountability,* 2nd ed. New York: W. W. Norton & Co., 1995.

———. *Constitutional Law and Politics Vol. II Civil Rights and Liberties,* 3rd ed. New York: W. W. Norton, 1997.

Oliver, M. L., and T. M. Shapero. *Black Wealth/White Wealth.* New York: Routledge, 1997.

Olson, L. *Freedom's Daughters: The Unsung Heroines of the Civil Rights Movement from 1830 to 1970.* New York: Scribner, 2001.

Orfield, G., and E. Miller. *Chilling Admissions: The Affirmative Action Crisis and the Search for Alternatives.* Cambridge, Mass.: Harvard Educational Publishing Group, 1998.

Orfield, G. *Dropouts in America: Confronting the Graduation Rate Crisis.* Cambridge, Mass.: Harvard Educational Publishing Group, 2004.

Pagan, E. D. *Murder at the Sleepy Lagoon: Zoot, Race, and Riot in Wartime L.A.* Chapel Hill, N.C.: University of North Carolina Press, 2003.

Painter, N. I. *Creating Black Americans: African-American History and Its Meanings, 1619 to the Present.* New York: Oxford University Press, 2006.

Perry, J. B. *A Hubert Harrison Reader.* Middletown, Conn.: Wesleyan University Press, 2001.

Powell, C. L., and J. E. Persico. *My American Journey.* New York: Ballantine Books, 1996.

Quarles, B. *The Negro in the Making of America.* New York: Collier Books, 1987.

Randall, R. S. *American Constitutional Development: The Power of Government Vol. I.* New York: Addison Wesley Longman Inc., 2002.

Randall, V. R. *Dying While Black.* Dayton, Ohio: Seven Principles Press, 2006.

Redlich, N., B. Schwartz, and J. Attanasio. *Understanding Constitutional Law.* New York: Matthew Bender & Co. Inc., 1998.

Robeson, P. *Here I Stand.* Boston: Beacon Press, 1958.

Robinson, R. *Quitting America: The Departure of a Black Man from His Native Land.* New York: Penguin, 2004.

Ross, M. H. *Justice of Shattered Dreams: Samuel Freeman Miller and the Supreme Court during the Civil War Era.* Baton Rouge, La.: Louisiana State University Press, 2003.

Rowan, C. T. *Dream Makers, Dream Breakers: The World of Justice Thurgood Marshall.* Boston: Little Brown & Co., 1993.

Samuels, S. *Law, Politics and Slavery.* Boston: Houghton Mifflin, 2006.

Santos, M. G. *About Prison.* Belmont, Cal.: Thomson Wadsworth, 2004.

Sarat, A., and C. J. Ogletree. *From Lynch Mobs to the Killing State: Race and the Death Penalty in America.* New York: New York University Press, 2006.

Saunders, D. E. *The Kennedy Years and the Negro.* Chicago: Johnson Publishing Co., 1964.

Schama, S. *Rough Crossings: Britain, the Slaves and the American Revolution.* New York: Ecco/Harper Collins, 2005.

Scheb, J. M., and J. M. Scheb, II. *Criminal Law,* 4th ed. Belmont, Cal.: Thomson Wadsworth, 2005.

Schechter, P. A. *Ida B. Wells-Barnett and American Reform, 1880–1930.* Chapel Hill, N.C.: University of North Carolina Press, 2001.

Schmalleger, F. *Criminal Law Today: An Introduction with Capstone Cases,* 3rd ed. Upper Saddle River, N.J.: Pearson Prentice Hall, 2006.

Schulzneger, R. D. *A Time for War: The United States and Vietnam 1941–1975.* New York: Oxford University Press, 1997.

Shaw, R. B. *A Legal History of Slavery in the United States.* New York: Northern Press, 1991.

Snyder, B. *A Well-Paid Slave: Curt Flood's Fight for Free Agency in Professional Sports.* New York: Viking, 2006.

Stannard, David E. *Honor Killing: Race, Rape, and Clarence Darrow's Spectacular Case.* New York: Penguin Press, 2005.

Stephenson, G. T. *Race Distinctions in the American Law.* New York: D. Appleton & Co., 1910.

Stewart, J. C. *1001 Things Everyone Should Know about African American History.* New York: Mainstream Books, 1996.

Stone, G., L. M. Seidman, C. R. Sunstein, and M. V. Tushnet. *The First Amendment.* New York: Aspen Law & Business, 1999.

———. *Constitutional Law,* 4th ed. New York: Aspen Publishers Inc., 2001.

Suggs, J. C. *Whispered Consolations: Law and Narrative in African American Life.* Ann Arbor, Mich.: The University of Michigan Press, 2000.

Sullivan, H. J. *Civil Rights and Liberties: Provocative Questions and Evolving Answers,* 2nd ed. Upper Saddle River, N.J.: Pearson Prentice Hall, 2005.

Sullivan, K. M., and G. Gunther. *Constitutional Law,* 15th ed. New York: Foundation Press, 2004.

Terry, W. *Bloods: An Oral History of the Vietnam War by Black Veterans.* New York: Ballantine Books, 1985.

The Constitutional Project. *Mandatory Justice: Eighteen Reforms to the Death Penalty.* Washington, D.C.: The Constitutional Project, 2001.

Thomas, H. *The Slave Trade: The Story of the Atlantic Slave Trade 1440–1870,* New York: Simon & Schuster, 1997.

Thurgood Marshall Scholarship Fund. *Brown vs. Board of Education: Its Impact on Public Education 1954–2004.* New York: Word for Word Publishing Co., 2005.

Tushnet, M. V. *Making Civil Rights Law.* New York: Oxford University Press, 1994.

United States Department of State. *Civil and Political Rights in the United States.* Washington, D.C.: U.S. Department of State, 1994.

Vine, P. *One Man's Castle: Clarence Darrow in Defense of the American Dream.* New York: Harper Collins Publishers, 2005.

Wallenstein, P. *Tell the Court I Love My Wife: Race, Marriage and Law—An American History.* New York: Oxford University Press, 2002.

Walton, H., Jr., and R. C. Smith. *American Politics and the African Quest for Universal Freedom,* 3rd ed. New York: Pearson Education Inc., 2006.

Ward, G. C. *Unforgivable Blackness: The Rise and Fall of Jack Johnson.* New York: Knopf, 2004.

Wasby, S. L., and A. A. D'Amato. *Desegregation from* Brown *to* Alexander: *An Exploitation of Supreme Court Strategies.* Chicago: Southern Illinois University Press, 1977.

Washington, B. T. *Up from Slavery: An Autobiography of Booker T. Washington.* New York: Doubleday, Page Co., 1901.

———. *Up From Slavery.* New York: The Heritage Press, 1970.

Washington, J. R. *Puritan Race Virtue, Vice and Values, 1620–1820: Original Calvinist True Believers' Enduring Faith and Ethics Race Claims in Emerging Congregationalist Presbyterian and Baptist Power Denominations.* New York: Peter Lang, 1987.

Weiner, M. S. *Black Trials: Citizenship from the Beginnings of Slavery to the End of Caste.* New York: Knopf, 2004.

West, C. *Race Matters.* Boston: Beacon Press, 1993.

Westheider, J. E. *African Americans and the Vietnam War: Fighting on Two Fronts.* New York: New York University Press, 1997.

Williamson, J. *The Crucible of Race: Black–White Relations in the American South since Emancipation.* New York: Oxford University Press, 1984.

Williams, J. A., and C. F. Harris. *Amistad 1. Writing on Black History and Culture.* New York: Random House, 1970.

Williams, J. *Eyes on the Prize: America's Civil Rights Years 1954–1965.* New York: Viking, 1987.

Wiley, B. I. *Southern Negroes 1861–1865.* New Haven, Conn.: Yale University Press, 1938.

Winbush, R. *Should America Pay?: Slavery and the Raging Debate on Reparations.* New York: Harper/Collins-Amistad, 2003.

Winks, R. W. *The Blacks in Canada: A History,* 2nd ed. London: McGill–Queens University Press, 1997.

Wise, S. M. *Though the Heavens May Fall: The Landmark Trial That Led to the End of Human Slavery.* Cambridge, Mass.: Da Capo Press, 2005.

Withrow, B. L. *Racial Profiling from Rhetoric to Reason.* Upper Saddle River, N.J.: Pearson Prentice Hall, 2006.

Woodward, V. C. *The Strange Career of Jim Crow. A Commemorative Edition.* New York: Oxford University Press, 2002.

Wright, B. *Black Robes, White Justice: Why Our Legal System Doesn't Work for Blacks.* New York: Carol Publishing Group, 1987.

Wright, T. *Rape in Paradise.* Honolulu: Mutual Publishing, 1966.

Wu, F. H. *Yellow Race in America. Beyond Black and White.* New York: Basic Books, 2002.

Articles, Book Chapters, and
Other Publications

The Black Collegian 1st Semester Super Issue, 36(1), October (2005).

Bocian, D. G., K. S. Ernst, and W. Li. *Unfair Lending: The Effect of Race and Ethnicity on the Price of Subprime Mortgages.* Center for Responsible Lending, 2006.

Bracey, C. A. *Louis Brandeis and the Race Question*, 52 Alabama L. Rev. 859 (2001).

Council of Economic Advisors for the President's Initiative on Race. *Changing America Indicators of Social and Economic Well-Being by Race and Hispanic Origin*, 2004.

Criminology and Criminal Justice, journal published by Sage Publications, California, 2005.

CRS Report for Congress: *American War and Military Operations Casualties: List and Statistics.* Hannah Fischer Information Research Specialist Knowledge Services Group, 2005.

Dieter, R. C. *The Death Penalty in Black and White: Who Lives, Who Dies, Who Decides.* Washington, D.C.: Death Penalty Information Center, 1998.

Horton, J. O., and L. E. Horton. *A Federal Assault: African Americans and the Impact of the Fugitive Slave Law of 1850*, 68 Chicago–Kent L. Rev. 1179 (1993).

Kilpatrick, J. *(Extra) Ordinary Men: African-American Lawyers and Civil Rights in Arkansas before 1950*, 53 Arkansas L. Rev. 299 (2000).

Law, S. A., *White Privilege and Affirmative Action*, 32 Akron L. Rev. 603 (1999).

Mickelson, R. A. *Essay: Achieving Equality Quality Of Educational Opportunity in the Wake of Judicial Retreat from Race Sensitive Remedies: Lessons from North Carolina*, 52 Am. U. L. Rev. 1477 August (2003).

Newman, G. R. "Crime and Justice in America 1776–1996," *The Annals of the American Academy of Political and Social Science.* Philadelphia, 1976.

Panel Discussion: Brown v. Board of Education: An Exercise in Advocacy, 52 Mercer L. Rev. 581 (2001).

Roisman, F. W. *Keeping the Promise: Ending Racial Discrimination and Segregation in Federally Financed Housing*, 48 Howard L. J. 913 (2005).

Rubinowitz, L. S. *A Missing Piece: Fair Housing and the 1964 Civil Rights Act*, 48 Howard L. J. 841 (2005).

Spann, G. A. *Symposium: Race Jurisprudence and the Supreme Court. Where Do We Go from Here? Neutralizing* Grutter, 7 Univ. Penn. J. Const. L. 633 (2005).

Urofsky, M. I. *Civil Rights: Looking Back–Looking Forward: The Supreme Court and Civil Rights since 1940: Opportunities and Limitations*, 4 Barry L. Rev. 39 (2003).

U.S. Department of Labor, The Negro Family: The Case for National Action, Office of Policy Planning & Research, March, 1965.

Statute

Massachusetts Body of Liberties (1641).

Index